STEAM
LOCOMOTIVES
OF THE
BURLINGTON
ROUTE

The original oil painting by ALVIN F. STAUFFER.

STEAM
LOCOMOTIVES
OF THE
BURLINGTON
ROUTE

By *Bernard Corbin*
William Kerka

BONANZA BOOKS · NEW YORK

Dedicated
to our wives for being so patient and cooperative
in this endeavor.

This edition is published by Bonanza Books,
a division of Crown Publishers, Inc.,
by arrangement with Corbin-Kerka.
   b c d e f g h
Manufactured in the United States of America.
BONANZA 1978 PRINTING

Library of Congress Cataloging in Publication Data
Corbin, Bernard G.
    Steam locomotives of the Burlington route.
    Bibliography: p.
    1. Locomotives—History.   2. Chicago, Burlington and
Quincy Railroad.   I. Kerka, William, joint author.
II.   Title.
TJ603.3.C47C67   1978   385′.36′10977   78-10929
ISBN 0-517-26195-2

Foreword

At one time or another most everyone gets the urge to write a book. It may be that one has some personal experience or conviction to relate, or perhaps to expand the knowledge of some past or present historical event.

In the case of Messrs. Corbin and Kerka, the motivating force fell in neither category. For years both have been data collectors. A person falling victim to this pastime usually finds himself with a vast amount of information which he feels can only maintain its value by exposing it to others. With this in mind, the authors have endeavored to assemble this information in an orderly sequence. The resulting book is the culmination of their efforts.

While no claim to literary perfection has been made in this work, it is felt that the following photographs, plans, and data on the locomotives of the Burlington Route will add to the enjoyment and knowledge of those who wish to study an era in railroading now past. Although Messrs. Corbin and Kerka have called themselves "authors", the true authors are those unnamed persons who have been responsible for the forging of a great railroad together with its motive power. To those persons from whom information has so generously been drawn, a word of gratitude is extended.

To make a well-rounded story, a section on the development of the Burlington System has also been included. Because it is interesting to study the complex structure of this railroad, the numerous lines from which the System has been formed are included for those who wish to trace out its progressive development on the maps of Illinois, Iowa, Nebraska, Missouri, and Colorado.

The book should be of particular interest to scale-model locomotive builders. The locomotive plans included are representative of Burlington motive power. It would have been a measure of thoroughness to have included detailed drawings for every class of engine used on the Burlington, but time and cost have prevented this. For those discriminate persons who wish to build accurately detailed models, the assignment sheets list the accessories (feedwater heater system, stoker type, etc.) used on each locomotive. The many photographs will be helpful in adding piping and other details.

Bernard G. Corbin
Red Oak, Iowa

William F. Kerka
Parma, Ohio

Acknowledgments

1. To the Chicago, Burlington & Quincy Railroad for their fine cooperation in furnishing valuable information about the road and its motive power.

2. To Charles E. Fisher and The Railway & Locomotive Historical Society, Inc. for their permission to reproduce the CB&Q rosters appearing in their past bulletins.

3. To "Railway Age", Simmons-Boardman Corp., New York City, for their permission to reproduce locomotive plans appearing in past issues of the "Railroad Gazette", "Railway Age", and the "Railway and Engineering Review".

4. To the Baldwin-Lima-Hamilton Corporation for their permission to reproduce material in past publications of the Baldwin Locomotive Works.

5. To E. L. DeGolyer, Jr. and Jim Ehernberger for their work in compiling the Colorado & Southern motive-power roster.

6. To L. E. Griffith for his assistance in locating many old-time photographs.

7. To Al Holck for the use of his photographs.

8. To Lou Schmitz for the Class K-2 drawing made especially for this book.

Table of Contents

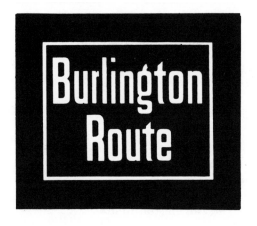

SIGNS THAT DISTINGUISH A GREAT RAILROAD

Section 1

THE DEVELOPMENT OF THE BURLINGTON SYSTEM—A STORY OF CONSOLIDATION

The "consolidation of forces" has always been the by-word of American railroads. For reasons of economy, and for the continuance of progress this practice has flourished in the past; and there is every reason to believe that will continue in the future. Of all the great railroads that have resulted from the merging of smaller lines, the Burlington system is perhaps the most vivid example. Unlike the Union Pacific and Northern Pacific Railroads, which were each built from large parent roads consolidated with a number of shorter lines, the Chicago, Burlington and Quincy is an amalgamation of some 204 separate companies.

THE ORIGINAL LINES

The birth of the present system occurred in 1849. But even before this time, a small link that was to play a part in the road's future had been created. In 1835, Governor Duncan of Illinois brought to the attention of the State Legislature the need for improving transportation facilities within the Commonwealth. As a result, action taken by the Legislature authorized the construction of State railroads totaling 1,300 miles; and bonds were issued to cover their cost. This was indeed a bold venture for that day and age—so bold that the effort nearly proved a complete failure, as only one road, the Northern Cross, was actually built. The road was opened on November 8, 1838 and extended eastward from Meredosia for a distance of eight miles. For the next ten years, the Northern Cross was the only railroad operating in the state of Illinois. In 1847 the road was sold at auction for $21,000, a small sum considering that $1,000,000 worth of bonds had been issued to cover its construction.

The original Burlington system was derived from the consolidation of three railroads. The first road, the Aurora Branch, was organized when the citizens of Aurora, Illinois obtained a charter on February 12, 1849 to build a road 12 miles long, and extending from Aurora to Turner Junction (now West Chicago). At this point it connected with the Galena & Chicago Union Railroad (later to be-

The borrowed engine "Pioneer," with which the CB&Q started operations.

—Lad Arend.

come part of the Chicago & North Western system). Construction of the Aurora Branch was begun in December, 1849; and on September 2, 1850 the first locomotive moved cautiously over its wooden and strap iron rails. The locomotive (the now-famous C&NW "Pioneer") had been leased along with a single coach from the Galena & Chicago Union for the inaugural run, since at that time the Aurora Branch owned no rolling stock of its own. A month later regular service between Aurora and Chicago was begun. The second road, the Peoria & Oquawka, was also organized in 1849, when the town of Peoria succeeded in raising enough money to build 14 miles of railroad from Peoria west to Edwards Siding. This section was completed in 1851.[1] Not to be out-done, the citizens of Galesburg, Illinois, desiring their own railroad, secured a charter in 1851 for a road called the "Central Military Tract". The charter authorized the construction of a line from Galesburg, northeasterly, and to a point connecting with any other railroad leading into Chicago.

During 1851 the three original roads were plagued with financial difficulties. At this time the Central Military Tract was still a "paper railroad" as not one foot of track had been laid. In the spring of 1852 Elisha Wadsworth, president of the Aurora Branch, James W. Grimes, then director of the Peoria and Oquawka (and later governor of Iowa), and Chauncey Colton of the Central Military Tract met in Boston, Massachusetts and succeeded in interesting John Murray Forbes, a New England financier, in their ventures. Mr. Forbes had invested in the state-built Michigan Central Railroad, and was looking to the west for an outlet for the potential lake trade. The three original lines were to be consolidated and serve as a connecting link between Chicago and the Mississippi River, with Mr. Forbes supplying the necessary funds.

In June, 1852 the charter of the Aurora Branch was amended to provide for an extension of the line to Mendota, Illinois. During the same year the name of the road was changed to the Chicago & Aurora. The line to Mendota was completed before the end of 1853. In 1852 the Central Military Tract, with Forbes' backing, finally started construction; and in December, 1854 a link between Galesburg and Mendota was completed. Simultaneously the Peoria & Oquawka, with the same financial support, began building its line from Galesburg west toward the Mississippi River. This line was completed in March, 1855 and terminated across from Burlington, Iowa. In the same year the name of the Chicago & Aurora was changed to the Chicago, Burlington and Quincy; and in July, 1856 the Central Military Tract merged with the company. Since that time, the name of the parent railroad has remained unchanged. While the line from Peoria to Burlington via Galesburg had been constructed under the name "Peoria & Oquawka", the company fell into financial straits, and was later reorganized as the "Peoria & Burlington". The road was consolidated with the Chicago, Burlington and Quincy in June, 1864.

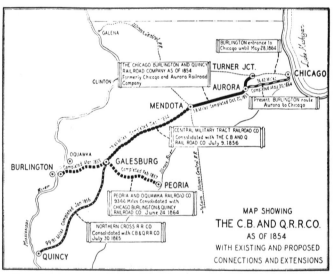

By 1856, the title Chicago, Burlington and Quincy exactly described the rapidly developing railroad system.

GROWTH DURING THE CIVIL WAR PERIOD

During the Civil War, little railroad construction was carried on in Illinois. In 1864, however, the Burlington completed a line 36½ miles long directly from Aurora into Chicago via Naperville. Previous to this time, trains had entered Chicago over the Galena and Chicago Union Railroad. The "Northern Cross" railroad, the last of the original consolidations of the Burlington in Illinois, had been completed from Quincy to Galesburg in January, 1856, with financial backing from Mr. Forbes. In June, 1864 the Burlington purchased the road at sheriff's sale; and at the end of the year, the system was composed of 460 miles of line, all in the state of Illinois.

---

[1] One reference indicates that the Peoria & Oquawka "existed on paper only" prior to financial backing it received in 1852.

Engine No. 59 was taken at Batavia, Ill. in 1864. She was built at the Aurora Co. shops in 1861, and was retired prior to 1879.

—O. H. Means.

RAPID GROWTH FOLLOWING CIVIL WAR

After the War between the States had come to an end, expansion in the Burlington system was rapid, as it was in other railroads throughout the country. It absorbed the American Central Railroad, a line which it had promoted in 1868. The road had been built between Galva, Illinois and New Boston. Through similar promotions, two other companies were purchased in 1869. They were the Dixon & Quincy, from Arpee to Keithsburg; and the Dixon, Peoria & Hannibal, extending from Buda to Elmwood, Illinois, a total distance of 44 miles. In the same year, the Carthage & Burlington, extending from East Burlington to Carthage, 30 miles, was completed and purchased along with the Keokuk & St. Paul, which ran from Burlington, Iowa to Keokuk via Fort Madison. In August, 1870 the Ottawa, Oswego & Fox River Valley, which had built lines from Montgomery, Illinois to Streator and from Aurora to Geneva, was completed and acquired by the system. The year 1870 also saw two other roads come under the control of the parent company. They were the Illinois Grand Trunk, which owned a line from Mendota to Prophetstown, and the Quincy & Warsaw, which extended from Quincy, Illinois to Carthage, a distance of 40 miles. By the end of the decade the Chicago, Burlington & Quincy had become a system with 810 miles of track.

No. 27, an inboard-coupled engine, was typical of early 4-4-0 wheel arrangements used on the Burlington system.

Built by Amoskeag in 1855 and named the "Grey Hound."

—O. H. Means

GROWTH OF THE SYSTEM FROM 1870 TO 1880

The growth of the Burlington during the 1870 to 1880 decade was largely made in the state of Iowa, although some important mileage was acquired in Illinois. An independent company, the St. Louis, Rock Island & Chicago had completed a line, after years of delay, between Sterling and East Alton via Rock Island. The road had originally been chartered in February, 1865 as the Rockford,

Rock Island and St. Louis Railroad. Its name was changed, however, after the company was reorganized in 1875. The road, along with two small branch lines, was purchased by the Burlington in February, 1877. The acquisition gave the system an additional 275 miles of trackage, and most important of all, an entrance into the St. Louis area. Another step in the growth of the system in Illinois took place when the Quincy, Alton and St. Louis, a line 43 miles long and running from Quincy to Pike, was completed in 1876 and purchased.

The Burlington's large-scale expansion into the state of Iowa officially made its mark on December 31, 1872 when it secured the "Burlington & Missouri River", extending from Burlington, Iowa westward to the Missouri River, with a branch line from Red Oak to Hamburg. The Burlington & Missouri River Railroad Company had been formed in 1852 and the line was completed to East Plattsmouth on January 1, 1870. In August, 1868, a bridge had been completed across the Mississippi River at Burlington, Iowa, thus providing a link with the CB&Q and a through line to Chicago. In 1872, the Creston branch of the B&MR, from Creston, Iowa to Hopkins, Mo., 42 miles, and the Chariton branch, from Chariton, Iowa to Leon, 36 miles, were also secured. During this period the

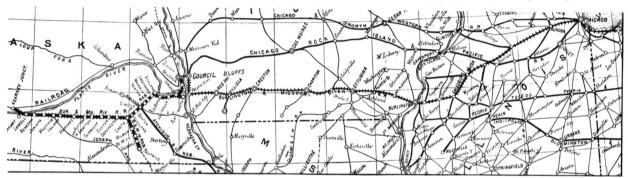

The Burlington Route West in 1873,—The CB&Q and the B&MR in Iowa and Nebraska.

physical condition of the road was being improved. Double-tracking was in progress between Chicago and Aurora, and iron rails which had formerly been used were being replaced by steel (weighing 56 lb. and 60 lb. per yard) as soon as the latter could be obtained.

The remainder of the decade saw many roads in Iowa, Missouri, and some in Nebraska being absorbed by the parent system (the more important lines are listed in the Appendix of this section). At the conclusion of the 1870's, the CB&Q was operating 2,100 miles of line mainly in Illinois, Iowa, and Missouri.

WIDESPREAD GROWTH FROM 1880 TO 1890

In the 1880's the growth of the Burlington was widespread over the Middle West. New lines in northern Illinois, lines in Missouri, and further extensions of the western lines in Iowa and Nebraska were completed. The growth of the system in northern Illinois was very extensive. Among the roads acquired during this period were the Chicago & Iowa, 101 miles long and extending from Aurora west to Forreston and Rockford; the Chicago & Rock River, a line from Shabbona to Rock Falls, a distance of 47 miles; the Illinois Valley & Northern, from Walnut to Streator, a distance of 60 miles; the Joliet, Rockford & Northern, a line extending from Sheridan Junction to Paw Paw, 20 miles; and the Galesburg and Rio, running from Galesburg to Rio Station, a distance of 12 miles.

No. 134, with its passenger consist, is loading up at Burlington, Iowa in 1885. Note the long pencil bar link and air hose to reach across the extended pilot. Engine is an ex American Central, built by Manchester in 1869.

—O. H. Means

During this decade the Burlington system also entered the state of Missouri on a large scale. Having lines west of the Missouri River in Nebraska, and connecting across Iowa and Illinois to Chicago, it became important to obtain direct connections to the south through Kansas City, St. Joseph and St. Louis, Mo. Not only would access to the trade markets of these cities be advantageous, but they could also serve as outlets for the Burlington's business to the southern states. The plan was accomplished through the acquisition of the Hannibal and St. Joseph Railroad in 1880. This important link had been forged back in February, 1847 when the Missouri Legislature granted a charter for 206 miles of railroad between Hannibal and St. Joseph. Construction did not begin until 1852 when Congress offered the company substantial land grants in return for reduced rates on the transportation of government troops, property, and mail. Inspired by this act, John M. Forbes and his associates supplied the necessary capital to move ahead with the project. Construction was started on each end of the line, and on February 13, 1859 the two gangs of workmen met between Chillicothe and Cream Ridge. On the next day a train made a through-run from Hannibal to St. Joseph for the inauguration of rail service between the Mississippi and Missouri Rivers. On April 1, 1860 a line was completed between Palmyra, Mo. and West Quincy, providing a connection by ferry, with the Chicago, Burlington and Quincy.

From the outset, the Hannibal and St. Joseph had shown its importance. Transcontinental mail had been traveling west by steamer and stage coach; but on April 3, 1860, a special train, pulled by a wood-burning 4-4-0 type locomotive, carried the mail from Hannibal to St. Joseph in a little over four hours. The post was then given to a Pony Express rider for its inaugural run to the Far West. Two years later the first railroad car with facilities for sorting out mail in transit was in-

A replica of the first mail car with facilities for sorting out mail in transit has been preserved by the CB&Q. Photo taken at Red Oak, Iowa in 1953.

troduced for service between Quincy and the Missouri River. In November, 1868, the H & St. J. was linked with the Chicago, Burlington and Quincy by the completion of a bridge across the Mississippi at Quincy, Ill. In 1869 a branch was completed from Cameron Junction and a bridge built across the Missouri River into Kansas City. In obtaining the Hannibal and St. Joseph Railroad, the Burlington system was increased by a total of 272 miles of line.

During the same decade, an entrance into Council Bluffs, Iowa was gained via Pacific Junction on the tracks of the Kansas City, St. Joseph & Council Bluffs. As the name implied, the road extended from Kansas City north to the bluffs of the Missouri River at Omaha, Nebraska. Branch lines also extended to Hopkins, Burlington Junction, and Northboro giving a total of 314 miles of trackage. The official consolidation of the road with the Burlington system did not take place until 1900.

Other noteworthy acquisitions during the 1880 to 1890 decade were the St. Louis, Keokuk & Northwestern, extending from Mt. Pleasant, Iowa through Keokuk to St. Louis, Mo.; the Chicago, Burlington & Kansas City, with a 221-mile line from Vielle, Iowa to Carrollton, Mo.; the St. Joseph & Des Moines, extending from St. Joseph, Mo. to Albany, and the St. Joseph & Nebraska, a line running from Napier, Mo. to the east bank of the Missouri River opposite Rulo, Nebr. This now gave the Burlington system about 1,100 miles of road in the state of Missouri.

The Burlington's most important expansion in this decade, however, was in its lines west of the Missouri River. In 1864, Congress had granted the B & MR permission to build in Nebraska, and

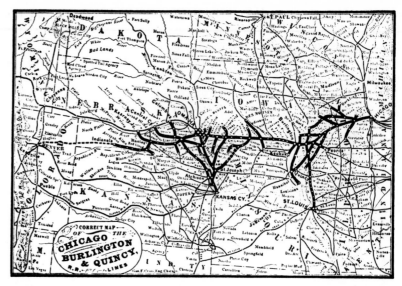

Map of CB&Q about 1880, showing projected line to Denver. The Twin Cities Line had not been built and the H&St.J was not yet included in the system.

as an inducement, a land grant of more than two million acres was given. In July, 1869, work was started at Plattsmouth, and during the next summer the rails reached Lincoln, Nebr. Despite construction difficulties and the threat of attacks from hostile Indians, the road was completed to Kearney Junction on September 18, 1872, with a mainline of 194 miles. To create a direct connection between its Iowa and Nebraska lines, the Burlington constructed a bridge across the Missouri River at Plattsmouth, and opened it to traffic on September 12, 1880. The Burlington and Missouri River Railroad in Nebraska was purchased outright by the parent road in July, 1880. In 1871, control of the Omaha & Southwestern had been obtained, thus gaining an entrance into South Omaha from Oreapolis, along with a line from Crete to Beatrice, Nebr. Consolidation with this road also took place in 1880. When the rails of the Burlington reached Denver, Col., on May 29, 1882, the road was the first to provide through service from Chicago under a single management.

In 1886, the purchase of the Grand Island & Wyoming Central, running from Grand Island, Nebr. via Alliance to the Wyoming-South Dakota border, with branches from Edgemont to Deadwood and Spearfish, paved the way for the present Burlington line running from Kansas City to Billings. Montana. Numerous other roads throughout Nebraska and Colorado, consolidated with the parent system during the 1880's (a tabulation of the more notable ones is given in the Appendix). By the end of 1889, the Burlington system had grown to over 5,600 miles of line.

SLOWER DEVELOPMENT BETWEEN 1890 AND 1900

Although the pace of merging with smaller lines was not so rapid during the 1890-1900 decade, an important link was made to the region northwest from Chicago. The cities of St. Paul and Minneapolis, Minn. had become important market and transfer points since the Great Northern and Northern Pacific Railroads had terminated there. As their trade with Chicago and St. Louis was steadily increasing, it was evident that it would grow even more if a direct means of transporting the lumber and wheat from Wisconsin and Minnesota southward, and the coal from Illinois northward, could be achieved. With this in mind, the Burlington had promoted the building of the Chicago, Burlington and Northern in the nature of an extension to the Twin Cities. The road was begun in 1885 and first ran from Oregon, Ill. via Savanna and East Dubuque to the Wisconsin-Illinois state line, a total of 85 miles. A branch also extended from Savanna to Fulton, Ill. The consolidation divisions of the CB&N in Wisconsin and Minnesota completed the line from north of East Dubuque along the east bank of the Mississippi to St. Paul, a distance of 245 miles. On October 24, 1886 the first train ran from St. Paul to Chicago in eleven hours and 10 minutes. Merging of the road with the parent system took place in 1899, and this northern extension of the CB & Q has remained virtually unchanged to this day.

Other roads purchased during this period were the Grant City & Southern, a small line extending from Grant City, Mo. to Albany Junction, the Keokuk & Western (1898), and the Big Horn Southern. The Big Horn Southern was absorbed in 1894, and extended from the northern terminus of the Grand Island & Northern Wyoming to Huntley, Mont. near Billings where a connection with the Northern Pacific Railroad was made. The addition of the lines (672 miles in all) during this decade gave the Burlington a system of nearly 6,300 miles of trackage.

A reproduction of an early day timetable cover,
listing the controlled roads at that time.

EXPANSION OF THE BURLINGTON AFTER 1900

In the far west, the company added to its property by leasing and purchasing a number of new roads. Among these were the Nebraska, Wyoming & Western, extending from Alliance, Nebr. to Guernsey, Wyo.; the Denver & Montana, which ran from a connection with the N.W. &W. on the northern boundary of the State of Colorado to Sterling; the Denver, Utah and Pacific, extending from Denver to Lyons, Colo.; and the Big Horn Railroad, which had lines from Warren, Mont. to Fromberg and from Frannie, Wyo. to Orin Junction, giving a total of 350 miles. The Burlington also added to its trackage by constructing a line from Toluca, Mont. to Cody, Wyo., 130 miles; and another line from Guernsey, Wyo. to Wendover, 9 miles. With the acquisition of these roads, the extension of the Chicago, Burlington & Quincy into the far West was virtually completed.

An extension of the system to the coal fields south of Centralia, Illinois was accomplished through a subsidiary road, the Northern & Southern Illinois. The line extended from Centralia to Herrin and was acquired by lease in 1906. The last important acquisition of the Burlington was made in 1914, when the Herrin & Southern, extending from Herrin Junction, Ill. to Nielson and from West Vienna to Metropolis merged with the system. In the same year, the 10-mile Chalco-Yutan cut-off in Nebraska was constructed. Other important roads absorbed during the early 1900's are listed in the Appendix.

On April 17, 1901 the New York papers ran headlines announcing that the extensive property of the Burlington system had come under control of James J. Hill and J. P. Morgan. The reasons for this momentous event had outgrown from many factors, some being similar to those that had

Engines No. 80 and 77, snowbound near Sharpsburg, Iowa in 1907.

motivated the Burlington to expand into the Twin City area several years before. After Hill had forged his Great Northern Railroad to the Pacific coast in 1893, he had acquired interests in the Northern Pacific. The principal products carried by these two northern lines were ore, livestock, and lumber. Much of this eastbound traffic, especially lumber, was destined for the treeless plain states served by the Burlington. It was also advantageous to have direct lines to Omaha, Kansas City, and Chicago where the packing houses and markets for the livestock of the northwestern ranges were located. Furthermore, connections to the coal fields and manufacturing centers in Illinois were desirable. In the other direction, raw and manufactured cotton coming from the southern states through St. Louis and Kansas City would have more direct routes for their ultimate shipment over the northern roads to the Orient. The new alliance gave the Burlington permanent connections to Puget Sound along with valuable traffic interchanges, making it unnecessary for the system to build its own lines to the Pacific Northwest. Control by the Great Northern and Northern Pacific was instrumented by each acquiring 48.6 percent of the Burlington's stock.

On December 21, 1908 another major extension of the CB&Q took place when control of the Colorado & Southern and its subsidiary, the Fort Worth and Denver City, was secured. Presently the Colorado and Southern operates 718 miles of track extending primarily from Wendover, Wyo. through Denver, Colo. to Texline on the New Mexico-Texas state line, a distance of 589 miles. The Fort Worth & Denver operates 1,362 miles of track in the state of Texas. Its mainline is a continuation of the C&S from Texline to Galveston, a distance of 792 miles. The FW & D, in turn, controls the Class II, Wichita Valley Railroad. In June 1950, the Fort Worth and Denver along with the Rock Island leased the property of the Burlington-Rock Island Railroad over which their respective trains now operate south of Fort Worth, Texas. One of the major line constructions undertaken by American railroads in recent years was the Burlington's Centennial cut-off completed in October, 1952. The rail distance between Chicago and Kansas City was reduced by 22¼ miles, and heavy grades and sharp curves were by-passed. The Burlington system is presently composed of nearly 11,000 miles of line. Of this, the CB&Q comprises 8,806 miles, with the C&S, FW&D and subsidiaries making up the remainder.

In all, the Burlington system was formed from 47 different companies in Illinois and Wisconsin, 97 in Iowa and Missouri, and 61 different companies west of the Missouri River. While many of these roads were created by the Burlington for the purpose of constructing new lines, and then taken over by the parent organization, considerably more than half of those now included in the present system were local companies built and operated as independent properties prior to their consolidation. However, some of the independent companies organized by local communities had "existed on paper only" because of the lack of funds.

OTHER FACTS ABOUT THE BURLINGTON SYSTEM

As early as 1856 the Central Military Tract division of the system studied the use of coal as locomotive fuel. The experiment proved so successful that by 1857 all new engines placed on the

The CB&Q back shop at Galesburg in Oct. 1900. The first engine is Galesburg & Great Eastern No. 2, which the Q was giving a general repair, at the time.

—L. E. Griffith.

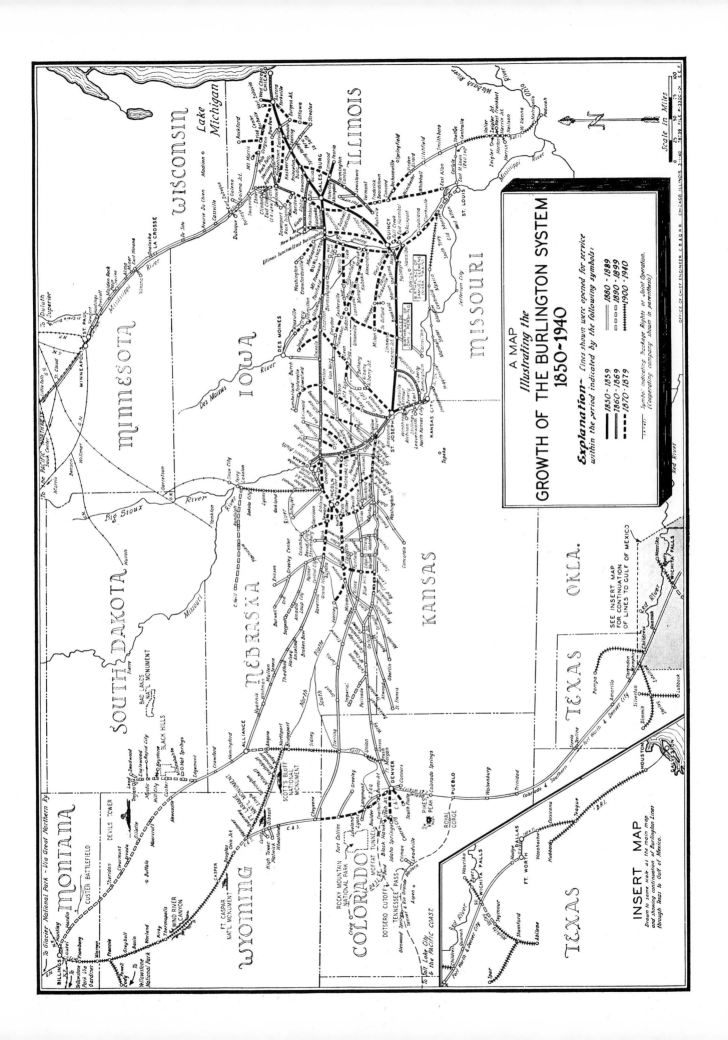

A MAP
Illustrating the
GROWTH OF THE BURLINGTON SYSTEM
1850-1940

Explanation - Lines shown were opened for service
within the period indicated by the following symbols:

INSERT MAP

Drawn to same scale as the main map
and showing continuation of Burlington Lines
through Texas to Gulf of Mexico.

road were constructed for burning coal. Earlier wood-burning locomotives were converted as soon as they required major overhauling. In 1876 the CB&Q established a testing laboratory in Aurora, Ill. to study and determine which materials were most suited for the construction of locomotives, cars, bridges, and track. A dynamometer car was built in 1884 to obtain information for improving the efficiency of steam locomotives and for determining their proper tonnage rating. At the West Burlington shops in 1886 and 1887, extensive tests were made on power brakes; and it was there that George Westinghouse invented the triple valve which brought the air brakes into universal use. Since its establishment, the company's laboratory has studied every phase of railroad operation. For example, the successful treatment of boiler water to eliminate "scaling", had been an important factor in improving steam locomotive performance. The Burlington's pioneering ventures with the diesel-powered "Zephyrs" is, by now, a well-known story. The Burlington has built many of its own steam locomotives in its shops at Aurora and West Burlington. The B&MR also built engines in the shops at Havelock, Nebraska. The installation at Havelock is now the system's main car shops.

In 1884 the CB&Q was chosen by the Postmaster-General of the United States as a special route for handling fast mail between Chicago and Omaha. The first trains covered the 500-mile distance in 16½ hours for an average speed of 30.3 miles per hour. This service has now passed its 75th anniversary; and today the schedule for fast mail has been reduced to one-half the time.

The fast mail at Burlington, Iowa, shortly after the service was inaugurated between Chicago and Council Bluffs-Omaha in 1884. Powered by the company—built No. 78, resplendent in polished brass and black iron, pulling its then gleaming white mail cars at a break-neck speed of 31 mph average.   —Burlington Route.

NOTABLE "FIRSTS" ON THE BURLINGTON ROUTE

1. First to bridge the Missouri River at Kansas City.
2. First to provide Chicago-Denver service under one name.
3. First to set up printing telegraph.
4. First to operate a diesel-powered streamliner.
5. First to run a train for a thousand miles non-stop.
6. First to use search-light signals.
7. First to install a modern dome car.
8. First to use the slumber coach.

APPENDIX TO SECTION I

ADDITIONAL ROADS ACQUIRED FROM 1870 TO 1880

1. Brownsville & Nodaway Valley—Clarinda Junction, Iowa to Burlington Junction, Mo.—35 miles—acquired in 1872.
2. Albia, Knoxville & Des Moines—Albia, Iowa to Knoxville—32 miles.
3. Des Moines & Knoxville—Knoxville, Iowa to Des Moines—35 miles.
4. Chariton, Des Moines & Southern—Chariton, Iowa to Indianola—33 miles.
5. Clarinda, College Springs & Southwestern—Clarinda, Iowa to Northboro—16 miles.
6. Nebraska City, Sidney & Northeastern—Hastings, Iowa to Sidney—21 miles.
7. Leon, Mount Ayr & Southwestern—Leon, Iowa to Grant City, Mo., and from Bethany Junction, Mo. to Albany—a total of 103 miles.
8. Creston & Northern—Creston, Iowa to Fontanelle—27 miles.
9. Hastings & Avoca—Hastings, Iowa to Carson—16 miles.
10. Red Oak & Atlantic—Red Oak, Iowa to Griswold—18 miles.
11. Humeston & Shenandoah—Van Wert, Iowa to Shenandoah—95 miles.
12. Western Iowa—Fontanelle, Iowa to Cumberland—20 miles.

ADDITIONAL ROADS ACQUIRED FROM 1880 TO 1890

1. Nebraska Railway—Nemaha via Nebraska City to York, Nebr.—acquired in 1880.
2. Atchison & Nebraska—Atchison, Kans., via Rulo, Nebr. to Lincoln—acquired in 1880.
3. Lincoln & North Western—Lincoln, Nebr. to Columbus—acquired in 1880. Valley Railroad at the Colorado state line to Denver—acquired in 1881.
4. Burlington & Colorado—extending from a connection with the Republican Valley Railroad at the Colorado state line to Denver—acquired in 1881.
5. Republican Valley—a line in southern Nebraska extending from Salem west to the Nebr.-Colo. state line, and another from Lester north to Central City—purchased by the Burlington in 1882.
6. Nebraska & Colorado—crossing Nebraska from east to west with several north and south branches. The main line extended from DeWitt in east to the Colorado state line at Venango —acquired October 1, 1883.
7. Omaha & North Platte—short line from South Omaha to Ashland in eastern Nebraska—acquired in 1886.
8. Colorado & Wyoming—from Nebraska state line to Sterling, Colo.—purchased in 1887.
9. Cheyenne & Burlington—connection with the Colorado & Wyoming RR to Cheyenne, Wyo.—acquired in 1887.
10. Lincoln & Black Hills—Central City, Nebr. to Ericson—acquired 1887-88.
11. Oxford & Kansas—Orleans, Nebr. to Marion—1887-88.
12. Beaver Valley—Line from connection with the Oxford & Kansas westerly to St. Francis—1887-88.
13. Republican Valley, Kansas & Southwestern—Republican, Nebr. southwest through Nebraska and Kansas to Oberlin, Kan.—1887-88.
14. Chicago, Nebraska & Kansas—line from a connection with the Republican Valley RR west of Odell, Nebr. to a connection on the Nebr.-Kansas state line with the Chicago, Iowa & Kansas RR—1887-88.
15. Grand Island & Northern Wyoming—line extending from connection with the Grand Island & Wyoming Central at the Wyo.-South Dak. state line northwest to the Wyo.-Mont. state line. This was the last line acquired in this decade, 1889.

ADDITIONAL ROADS ACQUIRED AFTER 1900

1. Chicago, Ft. Madison & Des Moines—Ft. Madison, Iowa to Ottumwa.

2. Murray & Creston—Murray, Iowa to Creston.

3. Chillicothe & Chariton—Frederic, Iowa to Albia.

4. Fairfield & Ottumwa—Fairfield, Iowa to Batavia.

5. Burlington & Western—a narrow gauge line from Winfield, Iowa to Tracy. The Burlington & Northwestern was also a part of this road. Converted to standard gauge by the CB&Q in 1902.

6. Kansas City & Omaha—Stromsburg to Fairbury, Nebr. and from McCool Junction via Fairfield to Alma, a total of 192 miles. Purchased in 1902.

7. Jacksonville & St. Louis—Concord, Ill. via Jacksonville to Centralia, 121 miles. Purchased in 1904.

8. Sioux City & Western—Sioux City, Iowa to Ashland, Nebr. with branch to O'Neill, 127 miles. Acquired in 1907.

9. Adair County Railroad—Youngstown, Mo. to a point 5 miles west. Acquired in 1911.

10. Iowa & St. Louis RR—Chartered on May 1, 1901—St. Louis, Mo. to Sioux City, Iowa. Line completed from Elmer, Mo. to Sedan, Iowa when purchased by the CB&Q in 1903.

11. Davenport, Rock Island & Northwestern—Clinton, Iowa to Twin Cities. Leased jointly by CB&Q and Milwaukee Road in 1902.

12. Fulton County Narrow Gauge Railroad—Havana, Ill. to Fairfield, 29.7 miles plus branches. Converted to standard gauge by CB&Q in 1905 and 1906.

13. Deadwood Central—Black Hills & Fort Pierre—Two 3 ft. gauge lines acquired by the B&MR in 1901.

OTHER LINES ACQUIRED BY BURLINGTON SYSTEM DURING ITS PERIOD OF GROWTH

1. Quincy, Omaha & Kansas City.

2. Missouri, Iowa & Nebraska Railway Co.

3. Chicago, Dubuque & Minnesota Railroad.

4. Leavenworth, Lawrence & Gibson Railroad.

BIBLIOGRAPHY—SECTION I

Most of the information in Section I was obtained from the following two publications:

1. "The First Ninety Years", An Historical Sketch of the Burlington Railroad, 1850-1940, by R. C. Overton, Chicago, Illinois, 1940.

2. "How Large Systems Are Formed", an article from Railway Age, Vol. 78, No. 30, June 27, 1925 pp. 1653-1656. (This is a condensation of material from book written by W. W. Baldwin, past vice president of the CB&Q).

OTHER INTERESTING REFERENCES

1. "Burlington West" by R. C. Overton, Published 1941.

2. "Granger Country" by L. Lewis and S. Pargellis. (A Pictorial and Social History of the Burlington RR), published 1949.

3. "Handbook of American Railroads", by Robert G. Lewis. Simmons-Boardman Corp., New York second edition, published 1956, pp. 48-52.

STEPHEN F. GALE
AURORA BRANCH R.R.
FEB. 22, 1849 - FEB. 21, 1851
FEB. 20, 1852 - FEB. 21, 1853

ELISHA S. WADSWORTH
AURORA & CHICAGO R.R.
FEB. 21, 1851 - FEB. 20, 1852

CHARLES MASON
B. & M. R.R. CO. IN IOWA
1852 - 1853

JOHN W. BROOKS
B. & M. R.R. IN IOWA
1853 - 1855 - 1864-1865

ALVIN W. SAUNDERS
B. & M. R.R. IN IOWA
1855

JONATHAN C. HALL
B. & M. R.R. IN IOWA
1855 - 1856

WILLIAM F. COOLBAUGH
B. & M. R.R. IN IOWA
1856 - 1857

F. L. BAKER
B. & M. R.R. IN IOWA
1857 - 1864

JAMES F. JOY
B. & M. R.R. IN IOWA
FEB. 21, 1853-JUNE 12, 1857
C. B. & Q. R.R.
JULY 12, 1865 - JULY 12, 1871

GEORGE TYSON
B. & M. R.R. IN NEBRASKA
1863 - 1865

JOHN VAN NORTHWICK
C. B. & Q. R.R.
JUNE 12, 1857 - JULY 12, 1865

JAMES M. WALKER
C. B. & Q. R.R.
JULY 12, 1871 - MAR. 2, 1876

ROBERT HARRIS
C. B. & Q. R.R.
MAR. 2, 1876 - MAY 25, 1878

JOHN MURRAY FORBES
C. B. & Q. R.R.
MAY 25, 1878 - SEPT. 29, 1881

CHARLES E. PERKINS
C. B. & Q. R.R.
SEPT. 29, 1881 - MAR. 1, 1901

GEORGE B. HARRIS
C. B. & Q. R.R.
MAR. 1, 1901 - JAN. 31, 1910

DARIUS MILLER
C. B. & Q. R.R.
JAN. 10, 1910 - AUG. 23, 1914

HALE HOLDEN
C. B. & Q. R.R.
AUG. 27, 1914 - JULY 18, 1918
FEB. 15, 1920 - JAN. 1, 1929

CHARLES E. PERKINS JR.
C. B. & Q. R.R.
JULY 18, 1918 - FEB. 15, 1920

FREDERICK E. WILLIAMSON
C. B. & Q. R.R.
JAN. 1, 1929 - DEC. 31, 1931

RALPH BUDD
C. B. & Q. R.R.
JAN. 1, 1932 - AUG. 31, 1949

HARRY C. MURPHY
C. B. & Q. R.R.
SEPT. 1, 1949

PRESIDENTS

OF

CHICAGO, BURLINGTON & QUINCY RAILROAD COMPANY

AND CONSOLIDATED COMPANIES

Section 2

HISTORY OF BURLINGTON MOTIVE POWER.

THE EARLY MOTIVE POWER

The little "Pioneer", the first locomotive to run on the Aurora Branch, was according to records the thirty-seventh locomotive built by the Baldwin Locomotive Works. It originally carried the number 7 when it was completed for the Utica & Schenectady Railroad in 1836. It was later sold to the Michigan Central Railroad and named "Alert", and in 1848 the Galena & Chicago Union R.R. purchased the engine. Renaming the little engine, "Pioneer", was very appropriate as it was the first locomotive to enter Chicago, an event which occurred on October 10, 1848. The 4-2-0 wheel arrangement of the "Pioneer" was the basic type built by Baldwin prior to 1842. Burlington records indicate that the engine had 11" x 16" cylinders and 50" driving wheels. The illustration on page 9 shows the locomotive as it was later rebuilt with new cab, valve gear, and other fittings.

Inside - coupled No. 14 was named the "Starlight". She was built by New Jersey in 1857 and weighed 32 tons.

—O. H. Means

The No. 14 after a rebuilding at Galesburg has received a sand dome and the bell has been moved forward.

—O. H. Means

The "Rocket", a 4-4-0 type, was the first locomotive purchased by the Chicago & Aurora Railroad. Originally it had been built for the Boston & Worcester R.R., but in 1846 was sold to the Michigan Central. Before being shipped west it was probably rebuilt to a 4-4-0 type at the Hinkley Locomotive Works. The Michigan Central sold the "Rocket" to the Chicago & Aurora in July, 1852, and as of that date the latter road owned a total of three locomotives. The other two engines, the "Whittlesey" and the "Pigeon", had been inherited from the Aurora Branch. The 12-ton four-drivered "Whittlesey", purchased from the Buffalo and Niagara Falls Railway in 1850, was traded to the Galena & Chicago Union R.R. in 1853 for the "Winnebago." This latter engine was subsequently changed to "No. One." When the Chicago & Aurora was changed in name to the Chicago, Burlington and Quincy on February 21, 1855, a total of 15 locomotives were on its roster. The Central Military Tract had 19 locomotives, acquired between 1853 and 1855, when it consolidated with the C.B.&Q. on July 9, 1856. During this period the parent company had also added motive power, and on May 1, 1858 a total of 58 engines were listed. The "Rocket" was in service until April, 1859.

Early locomotives of the Burlington System were primarily of the 4-4-0 type. Records of the Manchester Locomotive Works show that locomotives with shop numbers 1 through 6 were completed in the spring of 1855 for the Central Military Tract, the C.B.&Q., and the Chicago & Aurora. The engines were outside connected except for one, and had driving wheels of either 60" or 66" diameter and cylinders of 15" bore and 20" or 22" stroke. The total weight of each engine was 48,000 lbs. The eight-wheeled tender had a capacity of 1,400 gal. of water. In the early fall of 1855, the Manchester Locomotive Works completed five inside-connected engines for the Burlington that were somewhat larger than those previously built. They were wood burning and had fireboxes that were 50" x 39". The boilers, 46" in diameter, contained 154 tubes 2" in diameter and 10'6" long. The 16" x 20" cylinders transmitted power to the 66" driving wheels. Larger tenders carried 1,800 gal. of water. The locomotives were built for passenger service and were given the poetic names of "North Wind", "West Wind", "South Wind", "Golden Eagle", and "Grey Eagle."

Engine No. 94 was probably a marvel of efficiency in its day, an early 4-4-0T light weight locomotive built by Rogers in 1863. Almost more ornate than useful was the elaborately painted oil headlight.

—O. H. Means

With the abundance of bituminous coal along the right-of-way of the System, and as a result of the successful experiments conducted by the Central Military Tract in adapting coal to locomotive use, it was announced that four new locomotives were to be designed and built especially for burning coal. This announcement, made in June, 1856 by James F. Joy, President of the Central Military Tract Railroad, contained some rather interesting remarks. One statement in particular indicated that the locomotives were to be constructed so as to burn the smoke of the coal, thus reducing the problem of air pollution and avoiding any serious objection that had formerly been aimed against coal-burning locomotives. It would appear that Mr. Joy was referring to the problem of maintaining good combustion efficiency through the use of proper grate and firebox design with adequate air-fuel ratios. In June of 1857, Mr. Joy, then President of the Chicago, Burlington & Quincy Railroad Company, reported that a coal-burning locomotive had been in service for over a year, and so successful was its operation that all new engines which had been placed on the road were constructed for burning coal.

Engine No. 50 was built by Manchester in 1857. The original engine cab had been replaced, when this photograph was taken at Galesburg, Ill. in 1876. Shown sitting on a turntable with a full revolving cover.

—O. H. Means

Engine No. 56 was built by Manchester in 1856. The rounded cab windows were popular on early Burlington engines.

—O. H. Means

The "new engines" referred to in this report were probably those built by the Manchester Locomotive Works in 1856 and 1857. There were ten of these in number, and all were of the 4-4-0 type. Four of the engines had 15" x 24" cylinders, and the other six had 16" x 24" cylinders. Builder's records indicate that the total weight of each engine was 60,000 lb. The early motive-power rosters of the Burlington show that a number of 4-6-0, and a few 0-4-0 types were also included along with the mainstay of 4-4-0 American-type engines. The Baldwin-built 4-2-0, "Pigeon", a rare-wheel arrangement on the Burlington, was probably similar to the Galena & Chicago Union "Pioneer." The "Pigeon" had originally been built for the Michigan Central RR, but it was later purchased by the Aurora Branch. Engine No. 9, an inside connected 4-4-0 type, is sometimes referred to as the "Lonsdale", and was supposedly constructed in the Burlington's shops at Aurora, Illinois. However, there is some mystery regarding the exact identity of this locomotive,

No. 9, an inboard-coupled 4-4-0 type, sometimes referred to as the "Lonsdale". The engine had an unusual tender, coupled by knuckle joints. The original builder is not known, although Taunton built a machine of that name for Providence & Worcester, which it reclaimed in 1856. Characteristics of the New England builder were apparent, even after rebuilding at Aurora shops in 1864-5.

—Burlington Route

as the boiler may have come from another engine. No. 9 differed somewhat from most of the other 4-4-0 types in that the small tender was supported on a single 4-wheel truck. The frame of the tender was attached to the main locomotive frame by knuckle joints. This arrangement provided for vertical motion between tender and engine, whereas the design of the tender truck allowed for the necessary lateral motion when rounding curves. No. 9 could run equally well in either direction.

When the American Central Railroad merged with the Burlington System in 1869, the highest locomotive number appearing on the parent road's roster was 133.[1] Two engines were acquired from American Central (and were numbered 134 and 135) along with three others from the Keokuk and St. Paul when this latter road was purchased on February 10, 1869 (although only one of the K. & St.P. engines, assigned No. 141, was apparently placed on the roster). Engines No. 142 through 233 were mostly of the 4-4-0 type and were constructed by such locomotive works as Danforth Cooke, Manchester, Grant, and Rogers. Twelve engines, including Baldwin-built No. 176 and 177, were of the 0-4-0 wheel arrangement. On December 31, 1872 when the C.B. & Q. took perpetual lease of the Burlington & Missouri River Railroad, the latter road owned 68 locomotives. These were assigned to the Burlington System as No. 234 through 302. Engines No. 234 through 243 were of the 4-4-0 type and built primarily by Mason, Manchester, and the B.&M.R. shops at West Burlington. Of the remaining original B.&M.R. engines, No. 244 was the only 0-4-0 type; the rest were of the 4-4-0 wheel arrangement and built by the Manchester Locomotive Works between 1867 and 1872.

Crosshead pumps fed the H & St. J No. 76, built by Manchester in 1870. The bearded crew were evidently proud of their ward. The location is St. Joseph, Mo. in the 1870's.

Collection.
—B. G. Corbin

---

[1] Many of the early engine numbers were later vacated, and new engines of the same number were assigned in their place. The numbers referred to here are those of the first engines carrying this number. Most of the replacement engines are included in the 1904-1959 roster.

No. 170, an elegantly painted early 4-4-0 type, was built by the Manchester Locomotive Works in 1871. The use of brass trim on the domes, cylinders and boiler bands was the practice of the day.

—B. G. Corbin Collection

In the October 28, 1871 issue of the "Railroad Gazette", a description of the C.B.&Q. locomotive shops at Aurora, Ill. was published. Included in the article was an account of two new fast passenger engines that were being constructed under the supervision of the Superintendent of Machinery, Mr. F. C. Jauriet. The locomotives each weighed 64,000 lbs. and had 16" x 24" cylinders which furnished power for their 68" driving wheels. The boilers were of the wagon-top type and were 48" in diameter. The fireboxes were made of copper except for the crownsheet. A water space extending back and upward over the fire (patented by Mr. Jauriet) consisted of a 4" wide water leg. Its position was similar to that of the brick arch extensively used on later locomotive designs. The success of this water space was open to question, however. The engine's steam-admission system contained rather long steam ports and large slide valves, which were of the Robinson balanced type. These were apparently easier to operate than the unbalanced type valves then in general use.

The locomotive frames were forged solid at the rear, but the front sections were made of 1¾" x 5¼" bar stock. The trucks under the engine and tender were designed with lateral swing motion and were patented by Mr. Jauriet. The tender tank was of the generally used 1,800 gal. capacity. An interesting feature of these locomotives was their steam-operated bell ringers. The two Aurora-built engines were assigned to the road as No. 139 and 140.

The Baldwin Locomotive Works built two 0-4-0 type locomotives, No. 176 and 177, for the C B. & Q in 1871.

—Baldwin Loco. Wks.

The first locomotives purchased directly by the Burlington System from the Baldwin Locomotive Works were the two 0-4-0 types completed in April, 1871 and numbered 176 and 177. The boilers had copper fireboxes and iron tubes, and were of the wagon-top type. The water-injection system consisted of two crosshead-driven pumps and one steam-fed injector.   Stephenson valve-gear motion was used.   The tenders were of the typical eight-wheeled type with straight tank tops and a capacity for 1,600 gal. of water.   In appearance the locomotives were very similar to engine No. 202, (illustrated on p 43) an 0-4-0 type built at the C.B.&Q. shops in 1877.   The early Baldwins, however, were elaborately painted and finished with brass cylinder casings, steam chests, and dome. Polished brass jacket bands also encircled the boiler.   Engines No. 176 and 177 had 16" x 22" cylinders, drivers of 49" diameter, and each had a total engine weight of 56,000 lbs.

By the year 1880, the highest engine number on the Burlington's roster was 350.   Following the acquisition of the B.&M.R. motive power in 1873, engines No. 303 through 324 were added to the System, and were mainly of the 4-4-0 type built primarily by Manchester, Hinkley, Baldwin, and the C.B.&Q. shops.   Engines No. 325 and 326 were the first Burlington locomotives of the 2-8-0 wheel arrangement and were constructed by Baldwin in 1879.   The two Consolidation types were eventually classed as D-1 in 1898.   Seven engines, Nos. 327-333, were also of the 4-4-0 type and were built by Manchester in 1879.   Of the remaining 17 engines, No. 334-336 were 0-6-0 types, No. 337-341 were Baldwin-built 4-4-0 engines, and No. 342-344 were company-built 0-4-0 switchers.   Engines Nos. 345-350 were 2-8-0 Consolidations built by Baldwin in 1880.   In February, 1877 when the St. Louis, Rock Island & Chicago Railroad was purchased, this road owned 30 locomotives.   These were assigned to the Burlington System in 1880 as No. 351-380.

B&MR No. 18 is met by a surrey with the fringe on top, at Arcadia, Nebr. in 1900.   —Jim Ehernberger Collection

Chicago & Iowa No. 17 is shown here on a caboose hop at Forreston, Ill. in June of 1884.   A fine example of an American standard locomotive.   —B. G. Corbin Collection.

2 This replaced an earlier engine of the same number when the earlier one (the No. 20, 4-6-0 "Tiger") was vacated from the roster and retired.

THE CLASS A, AMERICAN-TYPE ENGINES

During the summer and early fall of 1879, the Burlington received 13 locomotives of the 4-4-0 type. These engines were built by Baldwin in accordance with drawings and specifications furnished by the railroad company, and were assigned road numbers 317-324 and 337-341 as previously noted. The principal dimensions as given in the builder's records were as follows:

Cylinders	17"x24"	Heating surface, firebox	113 sq. ft.
Driving-wheels, diam.	63"	Heating surface, tubes	1,164 sq. ft.
Boiler, diam.	51"	Heating surface, total	1,277 sq ft.
Firebox, length and width	65-7/8"x35-1/4"	Wheel base, driving	8' 0"
Tubes, number	195	Wheel base, total engine	22' 0-1/4"
Tubes, diam.	2"	Weight on drivers	46,300 lbs.
Tubes, length	11' 5-1/4"	Weight, total engine	72,500 lbs.
Grate area	16 sq. ft.	Tank capacity	2,750 gal.

The engines operated on a boiler pressure of 130 psi, which was customary for that time. A 12,200 lb. tractive effort and a weight-on-drivers of 46,300 lbs. gave them a ratio of adhesion of 3.8. The boiler was of the wagon-top type, formed from steel plate, and the steam dome, 28" in diameter, was placed over the firebox. The boiler accessories included rocking grates, two brass feed pumps, and one injector. The stack was of the "diamond" type with a minimum internal diameter of 16". A tender tank capacity of 2,750 gal. was rather large for an engine of this size, and indicated that these locomotives were to be used for long runs and heavy service.

B&MR engine No. 35 was used on the System's lines in Neb. Built at Plattsmouth in 1881.

—J. L .Heaney

No. 72 was built at Aurora in 1878. She became Class A-2 No. 1072 in 1898 and No. 213 in 1904.

—Lou Schmitz Collection

Engine No. 286 was built by Manchester in 1885 for the C. B. & Q. and leased to the Humeston & Shenandoah. She became No. 1286 in 1898 and was classed as A-2. Scrapped in June 1903.

—B. G. Corbin Collection

Cylinder cocks open, the ballon-stacked No. 70 and the crew seem ready to go at Galesburg in 1878.

—B. G. Corbin Collection

The engine crew was getting the No. 7 oiled up at St. Joseph, Mo. on April 14, 1886, for its run to Villisca, Iowa.

—Harry Draper

—29—

A 4-4-0 type, fitted for weed-burning, was death to weeds as well as the fireman's back. By pulling a damper, which blocked off the stack, a shower of live coals, soot, steam and sparks was directed at the offending weeds, ties and all. Shown in the siding, waiting for the mail to pass at Plano, Ill. in 1888.

—Bert LaCure

No. 230 was built by Manchester in 1874. The crew was at ease when this photo was taken at Maitland, Mo. in 1894 on the Villisca branch.

—Harry Boggs

No. 35 was originally built at Aurora for the H&St. J as No. 66 in 1892. Renumbered H&St.J 666 in 1898 and became CB&Q 359 in 1904. Rebuilt at Denver in June, 1932 for exhibition at the Century of Progress and lettered B&MR 35. She was on display at the county centennial in 1953 at Red Oak, Ia.

—B. G. Corbin

No. 1040 with a high wagon-top boiler was built at the Galesburg shops. Pausing at Buda, Ill. in 1900 with a passenger consist.

—Harry Boggs

The No. 249, with its capped, stove-pipe stack, was working at Mendota, Ill. in the 1880's. Became No. 1249, Class A-2 in 1898.

—O. H. Means

"Big 16," the crew members called her. The conductor checks his watch at Red Oak, Iowa. in 1900. No.1016 was a Class A-2.

—B. G. Corbin Collection

Everyone around seems to be concerned about the Hinkley-built No. 331. Taken at Galesburg in about 1905. —B. G. Corbin Collection

CB&Q No. 1607 was taken at Galesburg in 1900. Built by Pittsburg in 1882 for the Humeston & Shenandoah R. R. and acquired by the CB&Q in 1896. From the small size of the drivers, the 1607 was probably built for freight service.

—Harry Boggs

No. 77 & 45 wait for stock being loaded at New Market, Iowa, in 1907. The No. 77 was originally CB&N 55, and the No. 45 was H&St.J No. 22.

—B. G. Corbin Collection

The No. 288, Class A-2, had the honor of pulling the campaign special for Wm. Jennings Bryan back in 1908. Bryan, wearing the white hat, poses with the crew at Red Oak, Iowa.

—B. G. Corbin Collection

Class A-1, No. 1153, on train No. 19 at Princeton, Ill. In 1900.

—Harry Boggs

Class A-3, No. 419, taken at Burlington, Ia., Oct. 31, 1914.

—O. H. Means

Most of these Baldwin-built engines were classed as A-2 in 1898. During this period all of the other 4-4-0 types still in service on the road were given "A" classifications, and included those built in the Burlington shops as well as those purchased from the numerous locomotive builders of the day. In 1893 the Rogers Locomotive Company built a 4-4-0 engine with a straight boiler and a Belpaire-type firebox. This engine, No. 550, was originally a Class M, but in 1898 was classed as an A-6. One of the last engines of the 4-4-0 type to be acquired by the System was the D.R.I. & N. W., No. 2, built by Baldwin in 1901. This engine was classed as an A-6 but differed in design from No. 550 in that it had a wagon-top boiler.

The No. 550, Class A-6, built by Rogers, in 1893, was proudly displayed at the Columbian Exposition.

—Burlington Route

The No. 550 was regularly assigned to pull the mail, and is shown stepping if off south of Council Bluffs, Iowa on Sept. 6, 1897.
—B. G. Corbin Collection.

Class A-2, No. 462, was rebuilt from A-1, No. 71, in 1917. Shown here at Eola, Ill., on Sept. 7, 1930.

—O. H. Means

No. 200, Class A-6, was ex-DRI&NW No. 2. Davenport, Iowa in 1917.

—O. H. Means

Class A-6, No. 477, was resting her rods at Galesburg, Ill. on Aug. 8, 1914.

—O. H. Means

During the period from 1915 to 1918 the Burlington rebuilt a number of the Class A-1 and A-2 engines. When rebuilt they were all classed as A-2, and were equipped with new boilers, cabs, and in some cases with new cylinders. Some of the 4-4-0 locomotives were rebuilt into inspection engines, and had a superstructure of wood attached to the pilot and extended back to a point just beyond the stack. At least one engine had a superstructure running the full length of the boiler and connected to the cab. This arrangement gave the officials a more convenient view of the road-bed, bridges, and right-of-way. The 4-4-0 types made ideal branch-line engines, but with the decline of this type of operation, they were gradually retired and scrapped.

The No. 1370 was the first inspection engine on the System. She was rebuilt at Aurora, in 1899. The full-length cab gave it a look of distinction.

—B. G. Corbin
Collection

CB&Q Class A-2 No. 360 was rebuilt as an inspection engine and is shown here in that official capacity. She was originally built at Hannibal, Mo. for the St. LK&NW.

—B. G. Corbin
Collection

THE CLASS D, CONSOLIDATIONS

The first Consolidation-type locomotives used on the Burlington, No. 325 and 326, represented the heaviest type of power for road service at the time they were built. On these engines the straight boiler shell was built from iron plate, and it had a centrally located steam dome. The shell of the firebox was of steel, stayed with crown bars, and it was located between the third and fourth driving wheels. A short combustion chamber extended forward into the boiler barrel. The water-injection system consisted of a crosshead-driven pump on the left side and an injector on the right side. The smokebox was short and was fitted with a diamond stack. Power was transmitted to the second pair of drivers, which necessitated short main rods and short eccentric rods on the Stephenson valve motion. Plain tires were used on the first and third pairs of driving wheels, and greasers were employed on the front flanged tires (second pair). Although the driving wheel base was 14' 9", the absence of the flanges gave a rigid wheel base of only 9'. As was the practice of the day, the boiler extended through the cab. A roof over the fuel space of the tender protected the firemen from inclement weather. The eight-wheel tender was of the typical flat-deck design and had a capacity for 2,750 gal. of water.

No. 325 became a Class D-1 in 1898. Rebuilt to G-4A, No. 1601.   —J. L. Heaney

In the summer of 1880 six duplicate engines, No. 345-350, were built by the Baldwin Locomotive Works. In 1881 and 1882 Baldwin furnished the road with 18 additional 2-8-0 types, No. 389-396 and 414-423, of the same dimensions and general appearance. The boilers of these engines, however, were constructed from Otis steel plate, 7/16" thick. Rigid specifications were placed on the metallurgical properties of the steel regarding its tensile strength, toughness, and other properties. On each engine the boiler was fed by two injectors, and the water pump that had been used on earlier types was abandoned.

Baldwin also built for the Burlington two Consolidation types, No. 397 and 398, with wide fireboxes of the Wootten type. This firebox design had proved successful in burning low-grade anthracite coal on the eastern roads, and was to be adapted to the bituminous slack found in the Middle West. The fireboxes on engines No. 397 and 398 were 9' 6" long x 8' wide, with a combustion chamber 25" long. The firetubes had a length of only 9' 5 1/4". Whereas anthracite-burning Wootten engines were equipped with water-tube grates and straight-open stacks, the Burlington locomotives had rocking grates and diamond stacks. The cab was located on top of the firebox instead of straddling the boiler in the middle.

In the summer of 1884 the Baldwin Locomotive Works completed ten 2-8-0 types, No. 449-458, similar to their earlier models, but built in accordance with plans and specifications furnished by the railroad company. The boiler on this design was 56" in diameter and of the straight-top type. Steel plate was used throughout, including the firebox which was radially stayed. The earlier Consolidations had short main rods connected to the second pair of drivers, but these latest en-

No. 422 poses for her photo in about 1890 at Villisca, Iowa. The engine was used for years on the hill run between Red Oak and Villisca. Rebuilt to G-4A, No. 1619.

—B. G. Corbin Collection

gines had longer rods coupled to the third pair. Because the firebox was also built between the third and fourth pair of driving wheels, it was necessary to locate the eccentrics on the second axle. The main frames were forged steel with welded braces. The connecting rods and crank pins were also of forged steel. Westinghouse brake equipment was applied on driving and tender wheels. The tender tank capacity was 3,000 gal., and the feedwater system employed two injectors. The cylinder dimensions were the same as the earlier types, but the driving-wheel diameter was increased to 52".

No. 97, a B&MR engine, was built by Baldwin in 1882. Syracuse, Nebr. in 1897.

—B. G. Corbin Collection

Class D-1, No. 1420, was ex No. 420. In switching service at Galesburg in Oct., 1900.

—Harry Boggs

In 1886 the Rhode Island Locomotive Works completed 12 additional 2-8-0 types, No. 434-445, each having a total weight of 111,300 lbs. These engines along with the earlier 2-8-0 locomotives were classed as D-1 in 1898. The D-1 Class had been originally used on the heavy grade service of the Iowa divisions, but the appearance of the Class H locomotives caused them to be removed and assigned to switching service. In 1900 the road began converting the D-1 Class to 0-6-0 switchers of the G-4 Class. This rebuilding was completed by 1903. The following tabulation shows the order in which the D-1 Consolidations were placed in service:

Numbers	Builder	Cyls.	Date	Drs.	Wt., Drs.	Total
325 and 326	Baldwin	20" x 24"	1879	50"	78,920 lbs.	89,200 lbs.
345 to 350	Baldwin	20" x 24"	1880	50"	88,000 lbs.	100,000 lbs.
389 to 396	Baldwin	20" x 24"	1881	50"	88,000 lbs.	100,000 lbs.
397 and 398	Baldwin	20" x 24"	1882	50"	88,000 lbs.	100,000 lbs.
414 to 423	Baldwin	20" x 24"	1882	50"	88,000 lbs.	100,000 lbs.
449 to 458	Baldwin	20" x 24"	1884	52"	91,880 lbs.	106,290 lbs.
434 to 445	Rhode Island	20" x 24"	1886	52"	•	111,300 lbs.
Five engines	Co. Shops		1888			

In 1887 a new 2-8-0 design was placed in service on the Burlington and Missouri River Railroad[3]. Its firebox was of the Belpaire type, and the straight boiler shell was 60" in diameter at the smallest ring. The firebox was located over the frame between the third and fourth driving wheels. The working steam pressure of these engines was increased to 150 psi compared to 130 psi for the D-1 Class. The main rods were coupled to the third pair of drivers, and the eccentrics were located on the second axle. The second and third driving wheels had plain tires. Robertson's balanced slide valves controlled the steam distribution, and a combined vacuum and safety valve was fitted to the front end of each steam chest.

Twenty-five of these engines were built by the Baldwin Locomotive Works during 1887 and 1888. They were assigned to the B&MR as No. 173-197. Their tank capacity was 2,900 gal., although the last five built had tender tank capacities of 3,480 gal. Except for the Belpaire-type firebox, the locomotives were similar in weight and general dimensions to the earlier Consolidations. In 1898 the engines were classed as D-2 (along with several built in the Burlington's shops), but like the D-1 types they were later rebuilt into 0-6-0 switchers.

In 1898 the Pittsburgh Locomotive Works built four 2-8-0 types for the B.&M.R., No. 333-336, and these were classed as D-3. Like the D-2 Consolidations the D-3 engines had Belpaire-type fireboxes. Their driving wheel diameter was 52" and their driving wheel base was 15' 0". The diameter of the boiler at the smallest ring was 74", and the working steam pressure was 180 psi. Westinghouse-American air brakes were employed. The tender had a tank capacity of 5,000 gal. and fuel space for 10 tons. These engines spent their final days in switching service, and by the end of 1928 all were retired.

The diamond stack on No. 3146 indicates that it was built as a lignite burner. The extended piston rod guides were later removed.
Sheridan, Wyo., 1908.
—Joe Shambo

[3] From this point hence, reference to the B.&M.R. will imply the B.&M.R.R.R. in Nebraska since this road had separate engine numbers until 1904 when the re-numbering of all motive power on the Burlington System took place.

Class D-4A, No. 3124, had an extended smokebox and a cinder bonnet when this photo was taken at Denver in May, 1932. This smokebox arrangement could better house the netting and spark arrestor, hence the diamond stacks that had been used for lignite fuel were abandoned.

—B. G. Corbin Collection

Retired in Oct. 1933, engine No. 3116 is at the Eola, Ill. scrap dock, waiting to be dismantled. Built by Schenectady in 1903.

—B. G. Corbin Collection

D-4A, No. 3103, at Galesburg in May, 1925. The coping on the tender was inset for better vision in switching service.

—B. G. Corbin Collection

While the Prairie type was being developed for fast freight service, a new Consolidation design, Class D-4, was introduced for heavy slow-speed freight hauls. Twenty-five of these engines were built by the Baldwin Locomotive Works in 1903. Fifteen of them were assigned to the B.&M.R. as No. 3310-3316 and 3326-3333, and the remaining ten went to the H. & St. J. as No. 693-700 and 860-861. Seventy-five similar 2-8-0 types were built by the Schenectady Works of the American Locomotive Co. in 1903, and these were also assigned to the H.&St.J. and B.&M.R. as well as to the parent C.B.&Q. System.

The D-4 engine had a straight-top boiler with a wide radially stayed firebox located above the last pair of driving wheels. Piston valves of 12" diameter were employed for steam distribution, and were operated by Stephenson link motion. Some of the engines were equipped for burning bituminous coal, and others had front-end arrangements for lignite burning. The lignite burners had somewhat larger exhaust nozzles in order to reduce the draft and thus lessen the chance of lifting the lignite fires bodily from the grates. A diamond stack was also employed for this type of fuel. The engines operated on a working steam pressure of 210 psi, and the cylinder dimensions were 22" x 28". With 57" drivers and a total engine weight of about 200,000 lbs., a tractive force of 42,400 lbs. was developed. The tenders were of wood underframe except for the center sill which was of steel. The tank capacities were either of 6,000 gal. or 7,000 gal. depending upon the type of fuel employed.

No. 3119 in switching service at Omaha, Nebr.

—Robert Graham

The fireman in the cab of No. 3119 pauses for his photo at Sioux City, Iowa on Aug. 22, This D-4A was the last 2-8-0 to work on the system.

—G. M. Best

The Baldwin-built, 2-8-0 types were classed as D-4B and the Schenectady engines were classed as D-4A. In the Baldwin engines many of the detail parts were interchangeable with the R-3, Prairie-type locomotives (described later). Most of the D-4 engines saw service until the late 1920's and the early 1930's when they were finally retired.

No. 3182 was getting a drink of water at Beardstown, Ill. on July 21, 1925. The D-4B was built by Baldwin in 1903.

—O. H. Means

Engine No. 3188, Class D-4B, at Sandwich, Ill. in Oct., 1940.

—B. G. Corbin Collection

No. 3191, a D-4B, was ex B&MR No. 3316. Photo taken at Denver. Colo. about 1925.

—O. H. Means

Although in 1904 numbers were reserved for future D-5 and D-6 engines, these classes were never used. The last of the 2-8-0 types were inherited from the Iowa and St. Louis Railroad when this road was purchased in 1903. The two Baldwin-built locomotives were classed as D-7, and were assigned to the B.&M.R. as Nos. 3450 and 3451. In general appearance the engines differed from the other standard 2-8-0 types used on the Burlington System.

No. 3031 was one of two Class D-7 engines. She was built by Baldwin in 1903, for the I&St.L as No. 8. Shown at Denver in 1910.

—O. H. Means

CB&Q No. 537 was built for the Narrow-Gauge Deadwood Central in 1896. Was later used on the C&S between Como and Leadville. Notice the outside engine frame. The spark arrestor was standard on narrow gauge power.

—Lad Arend

THE CLASS E-1, 0-4-0 TYPES

The two 0-4-0 engines built by Baldwin in 1871 were retired before the final classification system went into effect in 1898. Many of the earlier 0-4-0 types had oil headlights, ornamental check-valve covers, and other bric-a-brac. In the days before air brakes, the engines were stopped by throwing over the Johnson bar or by putting it in a reverse position, and then giving the cylinders a little burst of steam. This was the customary way of braking trains before the introduction of the Westinghouse system.

Ballon-stacked No. 20 at Mendota, Ill. in 1880.

—O. H. Means

The oldest engine of the 0-4-0 type to find its way on the 1904 roster was No. 351, built by McKay & Aldus in 1869. This engine had been acquired from the St. Louis, Rock Island and Chicago Railroad in 1880, and was a tank type with a cab coal box. It was used for many years as a roundhouse goat. Many of the 0-4-0, Class E-1 engines were built at the C.B.&Q. shops at Aurora. Others were built at the Plattsmouth shops, and those acquired from the C.B.&N. were built by the Rhode Island Locomotive Works in 1886. Some of the E-1 engines had boilers with straight tops and others were of the wagon-top type. On the wagon-type boilers the dry pipe in the steam dome was well above the water line. In the other type, however, where the steam takeoff was near the water line; it was not uncommon for the cylinder heads to blow off from slugs of water getting into the steam supply system. In 1904 all of the engines were renumbered from 550 through 577. The E-1 engines had 52" drivers and a total weight of about 60,000 lb. With a boiler pressure of 145 psi, their tractive force was 13,300 lb.

Roundhouse goat No. 1351 stands on the turntable at Galesburg in about 1900.

—B. G. Corbin Collection

Most of the crew got in the act when this photo of No. 315 was taken in the 1880's.

—B. G. Corbin Collection

No. 4 gets an oiling at Red Oak, Ia. in 1898. The paneled wood cab was standard equipment on the early 0-4-0.

—Harry Draper

The solemn gentleman with a handlebar moustache poses with No. 562. The photo was taken about 1905.

—B. G. Corbin Collection

Class E-1, No. 1018, was in service on grade-reduction work at Princeton, Ill. in 1899.

—Harry Boggs

CB&Q No. 573 was sold to a gravel company in 1928. It is shown here working at N. Aurora, Ill. in Aug., 1935.

—B. G. Corbin Collection

THE CLASS G, 0-6-0 SWITCHERS

The earliest 0-6-0 type engines used by the Burlington were built in the company shops in 1879. They were numbered 334-336 and were known as Class F. The six-coupled switchers came into general use about 1885. Many of the Class G-1 types were built by the company shops at Aurora, Plattsmouth, Havelock and West Burlington. During the period from 1888 to 1892, the Baldwin Locomotive Works built 30 switchers of the 0-6-0 type in accordance with drawings and specifications furnished by the railroad. They each weighed 83,200 lb. in working order and developed a tractive force of 18,500 lb. Their eight-wheeled tenders each had a tank capacity of 2,300 gal. The G-1 switchers saw service on all parts of the System and were assigned to such roads as the H.&St.J., the B.&M.R., the K.C.St.J.&C.B., and the C.B.&N., as well as the parent C.B.&Q. The last of the G-1 engines were built at Havelock in 1898. The tenders were carried on two four-wheeled trucks and had a capacity of 3,000 gal. of water and 3 tons of coal. Some of the G-1 switchers were converted to tank engines and spent their last days as yard goats. A few of the engines were sold to independent roads, and by the early 1930's all of this class were retired.

G-1 switchers lined up for their early morning assignments at Galesburg, Ill. in 1898. No. 461 became No. 1461, then No. 1308, and was sold in 1914.

—O. H. Means

G-1, No. 1369 in switching service at Denver on Sept. 22, 1906.

—Lou Schmitz Collection

The crew relaxes at Red Oak, Ia. in 1893 with No. 460, later the double bad-luck number 1313. These were the days of oil headlights, wooden cabs, and link and pin couplers. —B. G. Corbin Collection.

The tall-stacked No. 1322, with its saddle water tank, served as a roundhouse goat at Galesburg in 1914.

—O. H. Means

CB&Q No. 1315 was sold to the Yorktown, Hoopole & Tampico R. R. in 1915. It served that road four decades. Galesburg, Ill., June 24, 1934.

—B. G. Corbin Collection

Baldwin - built in 1892, the No. 1363 was modernized with electric lights, generator, and steel cab. Galesburg, Ill., April 18, 1926.

—O. H. Means

Only two of the G-2 Class, 0-6-0 switchers, were built. Both were constructed by the Burlington in 1899. One was assigned to the C.B.&Q. as No. 1476 and the other went to the C.B.&K.C. as No. 801. After a number of years of switching service, both were sold to the D.R.I. & N.W. in 1926. The tractive effort of the G-2 engines was 25,500 lb., the boiler pressure was 180 psi, and the drivers were 52" in diameter. Slide valves were employed and were coupled to Stephenson link motion. Except for the valve arrangement, the G-2 engines were similar in appearance to the G-3 switchers.

One hundred and thirty of the G-3 switchers were built at the company's Aurora, West Burlington, and Havelock shops between 1900 and 1913. The G-3 engines were equipped with piston valves actuated by Stephenson link motion. Some of the switchers used small tenders holding 6 tons of coal and 3,900 gal. of water. Others were equipped with larger tenders having capacities of 8 tons and 6,000 gal. The tractive effort of the G-3 Class was 28,200 lb. Like the G-1 engines, some of the G-3 switchers were converted to tank engines for roundhouse service where their

No. 308, on the turntable with exhibition engine No. 637, at Galesburg, Ill.   —R. R. Wallin.

short wheel base was needed for pulling dead engines on to the turntables. A number of variations were incorporated into the size and shape of the saddle tanks, cab coal bunkers, and other accessor-

G-3, No. 1429, at Rockford, Ill. in April, 1937.

—L. E. Griffith

Converted to a shop switcher in March, 1931, the 1500 was later renumbered 310.

—L. E. Griffith

—49—

Wearing a cinder bonnet to catch those stray sparks, the No. 1465 sits at Galesburg, Ill. in 1938.

—B. G. Corbin Collection

No. 1553 was the last engine of the G-3 class used in service. Taken at Sterling, Colo. in Nov., 1953.

—Lou Schmitz Collection.

No. 1414 at Galesburg, Ill. on May 23, 1925.

—O. H. Means

Shop switcher No. 1351 was formerly a conventional G-1 engine. Photo taken at Hannibal, Mo. on June 9, 1928.

—O. H. Means

These interesting G-3 switchers were used with diamond stacks around warehouse areas as late as 1925, to reduce the hazard of fire.

All photos were taken at Denver, Colo. in 1923. The box on the left running board housed a fire hose— just in case.

—H. E. High

The closed-off portion of the fireman's side of the cab housed a coal bunker. Most shop switchers were one-man operated. Lincoln, Nebr., April 14, 1952.

—Al Holck

No. 300 at W. Eola, Ill. in 1937.

—L. E. Griffith

No. 311 at Alliance, Nebr. in Oct., 1953.

—Art Stensvad

No. 302 at W. Eola, Ill. in 1939.

—B. G. Corbin

No. 304 at Denver, Colo. in Nov., 1937.

—B. G. Corbin

While the D-1 Consolidations were first rebuilt to 0-6-0 switchers and classed as G-4, the D-2 engines were later converted into switchers of the same type. As a result, the original G-4 engines were re-classed as G-4A and the latter became G-4B. Converting to 0-6-0 switchers was done by simply removing the rear set of driving wheels and the front pony truck. In some instances a plate was placed over the opening in the frame where the fourth drive-wheel box had been removed. Most of the engines had their bells relocated so that another sand dome could be added between the steam dome and the cab. Eventually some of the class had their wooden-paneled cabs replaced with ones made from steel. Some of their tenders were converted to the slope-back type. The G-4B engines still employed their original Belpaire-type fireboxes. Like the G-4A switchers their boilers had not been rebuilt. Class G-4B engines No. 1668 and 1601-1603 were eventually changed to G-4C. Engine No. 1650, a G-4A, also became a Class G-4C in later years.

G-4A, No. 1415, at Galesburg, Ill. in 1900. Notice cover on rear driving box.

—Harry Boggs

Time out for refreshments, the No. 1632 gets her tank filled at Keokuk, Iowa on July 19, 1925.

—B. G. Corbin Collection.

The No. 1650 was kept in service after all her class had been retired. She was used at Moline, Ill. where a bridge would not support a heavier engine. Taken at Rock Island, Ill. on April 29, 1934.

—O. H. Means

The original rimmed sand domes on No. 1652 had been replaced with modern ones when this photo was taken at Council Bluffs, Ia. in 1917.

—O. H. Means

The No. 1654 wears a cinder bonnet to hold down sparks while switching in warehouse districts. Taken at Galesburg, Ill. on July 11, 1926.

—O. H. Means

The G-5 switchers were built in accordance with the United States Railroad Administration standards. Ten of these six-coupled engines were first delivered to the Burlington in 1919, and were constructed by the Cooke Works of the American Locomotive Company. In 1920 Baldwin built fifteen similar engines and these were classed as G-5A. The main difference between the two classes was the omission of the steam superheater on the G-5A engines. Very little was done throughout the years in charging the appearance of these switchers, except for an occasional change in the tenders. Baker valve gear and cross-compound air compressors were standard on the engines. The U.S.R.A. switchers were very successful and turned in many years of faithful service.

No. 500 was the first of the U.S.R.A., 0-6-0 switchers. She carried a Sunbeam headlight. Photo taken at Eola, Ill.

—Al Holck

No. 506 rests at Streater, Ill. on Oct. 14, 1945. Like most of the other G-5 engines, it had a CB&Q type headlight.

—B. G. Corbin

G-5, No. 509, was at W. Eola, Ill. on Sept. 3, 1950 when this shot was taken.

—B. G. Corbin Collection

G-5A, No. 510, was taken at Galesburg, Ill. on May 22, 1938. She had just come from the shops with a new paint job.

—B. G. Corbin

A photo showing the tender detail on engine No. 510.

—Lou Schmitz

With generator exhausting steam, No. 512 stands at Galesburg on May 22, 1938.

—Al Holck

An 0-6-0 switcher was inherited from the Keokuk and Western in 1898 and it was originally classed as G-5. The engine was probably retired shortly after 1904, and hence should not be confused with the later U.S.R.A. switchers of the same class.

The G-6 switchers were similar in appearance to the G-3 engines. All twenty-two were built in the company shops over the years from 1905 through 1910. The twenty that were built during 1905 and 1906 were initially numbered 1500 through 1519, but in 1910 when the G-3 Class began extending into the 1500 series, they were renumbered 1680 through 1699. The two G-6 switchers built in 1910 were numbered 1678 and 1679. The operating boiler pressure of the G-6 engines was 180 psi. With a total weight of 147,700 lb. and with 21" x 26" cylinders, they exerted a tractive effort of 33,700 lb. Many were still in service in the early 1930's.

No. 1686 stands at Denver in Oct., 1937. It sports a straight stack and the sides of the tender have been recessed for better visibility.

—B. G. Corbin

Engine No. 1686, a Class G-6, had a diamond stack when this photo was taken in Denver, Colo. in the mid 1920's.

—O. H. Means

No. 1681 was at Denver, Colo. in Oct., 1937. The painted yellow square on the tender indicates that she was a lignite burner.

—B. G. Corbin

No. 1695 at Burlington, Ia. on Oct. 31, 1914.

—O. H. Means

G-6, No. 1696, was in ex CB&N territory when this shot was taken at LaCross, Wis. on Sept. 5, 1937.

—B. G. Corbin Collection

The G-7, G-8, G-9, G-9A, and G-10 engines were the result of the Burlington's effort to rebuild some of the out-dated Prairie types into more useful motive power. The two G-7 switchers were rebuilt from R-1 engines by removing the front and rear trucks, reducing the wheel base, and by shortening the boiler barrels. The Belpaire-type fireboxes were still used on the rebuilt engines. Like most of the other 0-6-0 switchers, drivers of 52" diameter were used on the G-7 Class. With an engine weight of 137,800 lb. and a boiler pressure of 190 psi, the engines produced a tractive effort of 26,900 lb. Both saw yard service until the early 1930's when they were retired.

G-7, No. 1702 was rebuilt from an R-1 engine of the same number. Taken at Eola, Ill. on Aug. 2, 1928.

—O. H. Means

No. 1703 was missing her main rods when this photo was made at Eola, Ill. in 1931. —O. H. Means

Switchers of the G-8 Class were rebuilt from the R-2, 2-6-2 type engines. This was done at the company shops during the years from 1918 through 1925, although records indicate that No. 1741 was rebuilt in 1929. The R-2 engines originally had Belpaire fireboxes, but when rebuilt, fireboxes of the conventional radial-stay design were used. Some of the other major changes included removing the leading and trailing trucks and rebuilding the engine frame at the front and rear, shortening the boiler tubes and replacing the front tube sheet, altering the spring rigging, replacing the driver brake rigging, adding another sand dome, replacing the drivers with ones of 52" diameter, adding a cast-steel front pilot beam, and rebuilding the cab deck. The driving wheel base was not changed, but the tenders were altered for switching service.

The crew waits patiently as No. 1721 was photographed at E. St. Louis, Ill. on April 7, 1947.

—Al Holck

No. 1714 at Galesburg in Aug., 1938.

—Wm. Bissinger

Class G-8, No. 1725 had a diamond stack at Denver, Colo. in May, 1923.　　　—H. E. High

The low tenders on many of the 0-6-0 engines afforded good visibility when switching. No. 1725 at Omaha, Nebr. in Nov., 1938.

—B. G. Corbin

It was a windy day when No. 1740 was standing at Denver, Colo. on April 18, 1939.

—B. G. Corbin

No. 1751 had her main rods removed for towing when this photo was taken at Omaha, Nebr. on June 2, 1940.

—B. G. Corbin

No. 1755 at E. St. Louis on Oct. 15, 1938.   —B. G. Corbin Collection

The G-9 and G-9A, six-coupled engines were rebuilt from the R-3 Prairies. The G-9 switchers were rebuilt with radially stayed fireboxes, but the G-9A Class retained the original Belpaire type. About the same changes were made in rebuilding these engines as noted for the G-8 Class.

No. 1827 at Burlington, Ia. in July, 1949. The G-9 engines had rebuilt fireboxes.

—B. G. Corbin

No. 1828, Class G-9, at Galesburg, Ill. on Oct. 6, 1946.   —Al Holck

No. 1808 at Peoria,

Ill. on April 26, 1936.

B. G. Corbin

Collection

Belpaire-type fireboxes were a distinctive feature on the G-9A engines. No. 1806 at Eola, Ill. on Aug. 27, 1938.
   —Al Holck

G-9A, No. 1839 stands ready for service at Galesburg, Ill. on May 22, 1938.   —B. G. Corbin

The last of the 0-6-0 switchers, Class G-10, were rebuilt from R-4 engines. In general appearance they resembled the G-8 and G-9 engines except that inboard piston valves were used in the cylinder arrangement. These cylinders were also used on the R-4 Prairies. Although the G-7, G-8, and G-9 switchers retained their same engine numbers when converted from 2-6-2 types, the G-10 switchers were numbered 560 through 594. Some of the G-10 engines were still performing switching duties until the early 1950's.

The G-10 switchers were the only ones on the Burlington with inboard piston valves. No. 568, an oil burner, stands at Greybull, Wyo. in Aug., 1947. —Al Holck

No. 573, at Galesburg in Aug., 1949. —Al Holck

No. 580 waits for an assignment at Omaha on warm July day in 1939.

—B. G. Corbin

—63—

The low-slung, G-10, 0-6-0 engines were a trademark of the Burlington in many of the towns served by the System. No. 578 was shuffling around the yards at Denver in Dec., 1938.
—B. G. Corbin

THE CLASS F, 0-8-0 SWITCHERS

Ten locomotives of the 0-8-0 wheel arrangement, and designated Class F-1, were built by the Brooks Works of the American Locomotive Company in 1919, and followed the design set forth by the United States Railroad Administration. With a tractive force of 50,060 lb., these engines were the work horses of the yards. They were found performing heavy switching duties in such locations as Chicago, the Galesburg hump yards, and in Beardstown hustling coal.

No. 542 was shifting cars at Clyde, Ill. in Sept., 1937.
—B. G. Corbin

No. 544 was stored at Centralia, Ill. in Sept., 1952.

—Al Holck

Class F-1, No. 545 trails a little smoke at W. Quincy station, Mo. in Aug., 1950.   **—Al Holck**

With her front coupler missing, F-1, No. 548 stands at Centralia, Ill. in Oct., 1937 waiting for repairs.

—B. G. Corbin

The F-2, 0-8-0 switchers were rebuilt from the T-1 articulateds when the latter engines became inefficient to operate and too costly to maintain. Most of the rebuilding was done at the company's shops in 1927. Although as much of the original engine as possible was retained, rebuilding to 0-8-0 engines required new engine frames, new cylinders with piston valves, shortened boilers with new tubes and tube sheets, rebuilt Walschaert Valve gear, new main and side rods, new throttle rigging, new steam and dry pipes, new driving box wedges, and new stack and front end arrangement, among other changes. The same 56" driving wheels were retained. With a boiler pressure of 200 psi, the F-2 switchers exerted a commendable 60,700 lb. tractive force.

The chunky F-2 engines were rebuilt from 2-6-6-2 Mallets. No. 551 is shown at Galesburg on Oct. 14, 1934.

—Robert Graham

No. 554 was taking on water at Galesburg, Ill. on Aug. 8, 1937.　　　—L. E. Griffith

No. 555 at Galesburg in Oct., 1939.

—Al Holck

A Class F-3 engine was created when one of the O-1 Mikados, No. 5020, had its front and rear trailing trucks removed. Evidently this experiment was not too successful as none of the other 2-8-2 engines were converted.

Class F-3, No. 5020, an orphan, was the Burlington's attempt to convert a Mikado into an 0-8-0 switcher. Taken at Centralia, Ill. in Nov. 1936.

—Robert Graham

THE CLASS L-1, 0-10-0 TYPE

In 1891 the Rogers Locomotive Company built three ten-coupled engines for the B.&M.R. Railroad. The engines were used in heavy pushing and transfer service between Pacific Junction, Iowa and Plattsmouth, Nebraska, a distance of five miles. The Class L-1 locomotives had straight-top boilers and Belpaire fireboxes. The engines were equipped with air brakes on all drivers, and pilots and headlights were located at each end. In spite of the multitude of driving wheels, only one sand dome was used. Pressed steel was employed on such parts as cylinder-head covers and smoke-stack base. The 0-10-0 type had an engine weight of 150,300 lb., an operating boiler pressure of 160 psi, and exerted a tractive force of 36,800 lb. All three L-1 locomotives were retired in October, 1916.

An article describing these engines, and appearing in the July 24, 1891 issue of "Railroad Gazette," mentioned that their design had taken special note of the ratio of cylinder volume to weight on drivers. To avoid slipping, energy from the steam was to be derived from its expansion over the last portion of the stroke, thus resulting in fuel economy compared to steam admission over the full stroke. The article was, of course, referring to the use of "limited cutoff", a method so extensively used in later-day steam power.

No 275 was one of three Class L-1 loco-motives built by Rogers in 1891.

—Rogers

THE CLASS H, MOGULS

The 2-6-0 type designated as Class H was first introduced on the System in 1888, and was intended for general road service. The engines were used extensively for freight service, but also proved highly successful for fast passenger service. The Class H-1 engines were first built with 19" x 24" cylinders and 62" drivers for freight hauling, and 68" drivers for passenger work. The boiler on these Moguls had a straight top with a Belpaire-type firebox placed above the frame. Because the Burlington was located on fairly level country, and the curvature of its line was generally light, the two-wheeled leading truck proved satisfactory on high-speed runs.

Class H-1, No. 1138 was decked in flags, when it hauled the J. I. Case Steam Thresher Co. special through Princeton, Ill. in 1900. Engine later became CB&Q No. 1088.

—Harry Boggs

CB&Q No. 125 became No. 1004 in 1904. The photo was taken prior to 1898.

—O. H. Means

No. 1011, at Burlington in Oct., 1914.

—O. H. Means

Class H-1, No. 1054 waits for an assignment at Galesburg in May, 1925.

—O. H. Means

The original Class H design was modified from time to time, and a number of the engines were fitted with Richmond cross-compound cylinders. The high and low-pressure cylinder diameters were 20" and 29" respectively. The compounds were eventually converted to single-expansion engines. Both the Class H-1 and H-2 engines were built with slide valves, but some were later rebuilt with cylinders employing piston valves.

In 1892 a series of interesting tests were run between Chicago and Galesburg in order to determine the relative efficiencies of different types of locomotives used in heavy, fast passenger service. The locomotives taking part in the study were two single-expansion Class H Moguls (one having 62" drivers and the other 68" drivers); a cross-compound Class H engine with 62" drivers; an American, 4-4-0 type, known as Class M (later to become Class A-6); and an experimental 4-6-0 type with Vauclain compound cylinders, built and owned by the Baldwin Locomotive Works. The tests were conducted on trains No. 1 and 6. Train No. 1 was originally handled by Class A engines covering the 162.5 mile distance in 4 hrs. and 45 min. This run was later "stepped up" and the running time for the Class A types was reduced to 4 hrs. and 2 min., representing an average speed of 40 mph with a load of 12 cars and a weight of about 400 tons behind the tender.

The tests made on the several types of motive power, using a dynamometer car, clearly indicated that for this particular service, the single-expansion Mogul engines were superior to any of the others. On trains of ten cars or less the 2-6-0 engine with 68" drivers was more economical to operate, but with trains of more than ten cars the Mogul with 62" drivers proved the least costly to operate. The 68" drivered Mogul showed an average consumption per dynamometer horsepower of 5.76 lb. of coal and 32.9 lb. of water.

No. 1157, Class H-2, in work train service at Sugar Grove, Ill. in 1913.　　—J. L. Heany

The afternoon sun casts shadows on No. 1521 standing at Princeton, Ill. in 1898.

—B. G. Corbin Collection

The Class H-3 engines were built in the West Burlington and the Aurora shops in 1898 and 1899. They were a somewhat modified design over the preceding classes, and had a greater engine weight and an increased tractive force. Piston valves were used rather than slide-type; however, the same boiler and firebox design was used. The standard Stephenson valve-link motion actuated the steam-admission system.

No. 1217 was ready to be scrapped at Eola, Ill. when this photo was taken in 1930.   —Al Holck

The crew of engine No. 1541, Class H-3, was waiting for the highball at Princeton, Ill. in 1900. The tender gate was used to keep the fireman from getting pitched out at high speed.

—Harry Boggs

No. 1200
at
Creston, Iowa
in 1917.

—O. H. Means

Except for the location of the sand dome and bell, the H-4 Moguls were of the same general appearance as the H-3 engines. The H-4 engines had tapered boilers, but the same firebox design was employed. Although most of them were built with 64" drivers, some were equipped with 72" driving wheels for fast passenger service. The first fifteen engines of the H-4 Class were built by Baldwin in 1899, and the rest were constructed by Rogers and in the Burlington shops. Compared to the H-1 engines built in 1890, the H-4, 2-6-0 types showed an increase in tractive effort of 32 percent with an increase in engine weight of only 15 percent. Eventually all of the Class H Moguls were furnished with 64" drivers.

For over ten years after the Class H engines made their appearance, they were used on mainline passenger and freight service. During this time they made some rather remarkable runs on mail trains. In April, 1895 engine No. 512, a Rogers-built Mogul running on a westbound trip with the fast mail, made the 162.5 mile run from Chicago to Galesburg in 165 minutes while hauling six cars. The running time included two stops of six minutes each to transfer mail, one crossing stop and three slow downs. On November 10, 1895 the same engine with four cars ran from Galesburg to Galva, 22½ miles, in 21 minutes, and from Kawanee to Buda, 15 miles, in 13 minutes, while making up time between Galesburg and Aurora. In April, 1900 engine No. 1510, an H-2 Mogul with 69" drivers, ran eastbound with four cars on train No. 8 from Burlington to Chicago, 206 miles, in 209 minutes on one occasion and 203 minutes on another. Considering that this time included stops, the running speeds were high, especially between Mendota and Aurora where the distance was covered in 37 minutes for a speed of 73.6 mph. Although today these speeds may not sound outstanding, in the 1890's they were considered extraordinary.

As the Atlantic and Prairie types began to come more into general use, the Class H engines were gradually assigned to branch line and local service. Some of the H-4 locomotives were rebuilt to K-10, 4-6-0 types.

A cinder bonnet was used on No. 1228 when this photo was taken at McCook, Nebr. in Aug., 1937.

—B. G. Corbin

The compact-looking No. 1261, Class H-4, was getting ready to move out of E. St. Louis, Ill. in Oct., 1939.
—B. G. Corbin Collection

A builder's photo of B&MR No. 56. This H-4 engine was numbered 1238 in 1904. —Harry Draper

No. 1255 waits at Red Oak, Ia. in Aug., 1940 while it s crew is having lunch.

—B. G. Corbin

A number of 2-6-0 type engines were inherited from the Kansas City & Omaha, and one was obtained from the Iowa and St. Louis. These were classed as H-5, but none were of the standard Burlington design. The H-5 engines had small drivers and low-slung boilers. All of the K.C.&O. engines were retired before 1917. The one I.& St. L. engine was rebuilt to G-1, No. 1382.

B&MR No. 428, Class H-5, was brought into Havelock shops for an overhaul in 1902. Note the extreme forward position of the feedwater check valve. She became No. 1271 in 1904. 　　　　　　　　　　　　　　　　　　　　　　　　 —Harry Draper.

THE CLASS I-1, SUBURBAN TANK ENGINE

With the commuter service becoming a noticeable segment of the passenger travel around Chicago in the late 1880's, the Burlington built five engines especially suited to suburban runs. The engines, Class I-1, were of the tank type and had an 0-6-2 wheel arrangement. They were equipped to operate in either direction, and in many details followed the design of the Class H Moguls. The frames were extended to the rear to carry the water tank and coal bunker, and this weight was supported by the two-wheel trailing truck fitted with a swing holster and radius bar.

The well-groomed No. 500, Class I-1, poses in Downers Grove, Ill. in 1901. 　　　　　 —L. E. Griffith

The driving wheels, 56" in diameter, were separately equalized on each side and were independent of the trailing truck. The straight boiler was fitted with a Belpaire-type firebox as on the Class H engines. The sandbox on the I-1 engines was actually a saddle-shaped tank fitted over the boiler in front of the cab. The brakes were of the clasp design, with two shoes to one driving wheel. Two cylinders were used to actuate the brake system, one vertically mounted in front of the cylinder saddle, and the other horizontally located under the tank. The Class I-1 engines each weighed 113,000 lb., operated on a boiler pressure of 160 psi, and produced a tractive force of 15,500 lb. By the year 1911, all of the 0-6-2 tank engines were retired.

THE CLASS K. TEN WHEELERS

The first locomotives of the 4-6-0 wheel arrangement that were used on the Burlington were constructed in the mid 1850's by such builders as Amoskeag, Schenectady, and the New Jersey Locomotive Works. Unfortunately no known photographs of these early locomotives are available, hence their appearance and details of construction may forever be lost in the annals of time.

The first 4-6-0 engines of the K-1 Class were built by Baldwin in 1891 and were assigned to the B.&M.R. as Nos. 253-260. The locomotives were used for both fast freight and heavy passenger service, and in many details were similar to the Class H Moguls. The rest of the K-1 engines were constructed by the Rogers Locomotive Company in 1892 and were also placed in service on the B.& M.R. The Baldwin engines had 58" drivers, whereas those built by Rogers had drivers of 62" diameter. Unflanged tires were used on the center pair of wheels. Straight-top boilers with Belpaire fireboxes were a design feature of the K-1 Class. The boiler pressure of the Baldwin-built K-1 engine was 155 psi, their total engine weight was 118,600 lb., and they exerted a tractive force of 19,700 lb. The Rogers-built Ten Wheelers operated on 180 psi and had a 21,400 lb. tractive force.

Diamond stacked No. 603, with No. 3112 and No. 800, heads up a stockmen's convention special train at Alliance, Nebr. in 1911.   —Bostwick Studio.

Low-drivered No. 605 was built by Baldwin in 1891. This K-1 engine is shown at Eola, Ill. where it was retired in 1931.

—O. H. Means

No. 625 was making up a train for a branch-line local out of Ashland, Nebr. in Dec., 1938.

—B. G. Corbin

No. 627 on switching duty at Red Oak, Iowa in Dec., 1943. —B. G. Corbin

The K-2 engines were similar in appearance to the K-1 Class except that they were somewhat heavier and exerted a greater tractive force. Twenty-five of the K-2 locomotives were built by Rogers in 1892 and 1893, and were equipped with 64" driving wheels. Of the remaining fifteen engines, three were constructed by Grant and the rest were built in the company's shops. Some of the company-built locomotives had 58" drivers. All of the K-2 engines were originally assigned to the B.&M.R. Later some of them, along with a number of K-1 Ten Wheelers, were placed in suburban service at Chicago where they remained for a number of years before being replaced by Class K-10 engines. When in suburban service, the sand dome was sometimes moved forward to allow room for a king-size generator that supplied power to the commuter cars. Many of the engines had the sand dome in this position when they were scrapped.

CB&Q suburban trains lined up at Downers Grove, Ill. for the early morning commuter rush hour. The photo of these K-2 class engines was taken about 1910. —L. E. Griffith

Class K-2, No. 630, at Chicago, Ill. on July 4, 1937.   **—L. E. Griffith**

633 was caught at Red Oak, Iowa in Feb., 1938 as she was being turned.   **—B. G. Corbin**

No. 637 on the Red Oak turntable in Aug. 1936. The engine was refitted with a diamond stack and used in the Railroad Fair Pageant at Chicago in 1949. She has been retained for exhibition purposes.

—B. G. Corbin

Used for stand-by service, the No. 656 pulls the broken-down No. 9852 Gas-Electric car at Red Oak in Jan., 1941.

—B. G. Corbin

No. 660 was getting turned at Red Oak, Iowa in June, 1937. —B. G. Corbin

The K-3 locomotives were inherited from the Chicago, Burlington & Northern when this road was absorbed in 1899. All fifteen of these engines were built by Hinkley in 1887 and were known as Class B when on the C.B.&N. roster. In appearance they differed from the K-1 and K-2 Ten-Wheelers. Their boilers were of the wagon-top type with radially stayed fireboxes. Some of the K-3 engines had 69" drivers and some had 64". Steam admission to the 19" x 24" cylinders was controlled by slide valves. With a total engine weight of 117,200 lb. and a boiler pressure of 160 psi, the K-3 locomotives exerted a tractive force of 17,100 lb. or 18,400 lb. depending on the driving wheel diameter.

With cylinder cocks open, K-3, No. 677, was standing at Rock Island, Ill. in 1913.

—O. H. Means

Class K-3, No. 677 waits for head-end revenue to be loaded at Galesburg, Ill. in 1906.
Built by Hinkley in 1887, retired in 1916.   —O. H. Means

No. 680 on the turntable at Rock Island, Ill. in July, 1914.

—O. H. Means

While pounding the iron over the Nebraska prairies, No. 690 stopped long enough to have it s photo taken, in about 1915.

—Art Stensvad

All of the Ten Wheelers of the K-4 Class were constructed at the B.&M.R. shops at Havelock from 1900 to 1904.   They were built for high-speed passenger service and had 72" drivers, 19" x 26" cylinders, and a total engine weight of 156,600 lb.   Some of the first engines were lettered K-3. but were soon changed to K-4.   Evidently it was planned to place these engines in the K-3 Class, but with the acquisition of the C.B.&N. 4-6-0 types they were classed as K-4 instead.

On March 24, 1902 B.&M.R. locomotive No. 41, a K-4, made a notable eastbound run on train No. 6 with nine cars from Eckley to Wray, Colorado. The distance of 14.8 miles on a slightly descending grade was covered in 9 minutes flat for an average speed of 98.6 mph. The time was independently recorded by several observers and was declared officially correct.

It is interesting to note that the K-4 engines were assembled at Havelock by piece work. For example, a workman received $17.00 for assembling the pilot truck. In later years the engines were equipped with 64" drivers and were down-graded to local and branch-line service. Some were converted to oil burners. A few of the K-4 engines were still in service in the early 1950's.

The boiler of a K-4 engine at the B&MR erecting shops at Havelock, Nebr. in 1902. The engine frame is in the immediate foreground.

—Harry Draper

Fresh out of the shops, B&MR engine No. 27 stands on her high drivers at Havelock, Nebr. in 1902.

—Harry Draper

K-4, No. 706, at Rushville, Ill. on July 26, 1936.

—B. G. Corbin

Engine No. 718 in passenger service at Brookfield, Mo. in June, 1928.

—O. H. Means

K-4, No. 919, an oil burner, was formerly No. 719. She was the last Ten-Wheeler in service on the Burlington.

—Jim Ehernberger

No. 722 in branch-
line service at Clar-
inda, Iowa in April,
1939.

—B. G. Corbin

The K-5 locomotives were developed from the K-4 engines and were intended for passenger service. The eight K-5 engines were built at the Havelock shops in 1904 and 1906, and had tapered boilers with wide Belpaire-type fireboxes placed over the last pair of 69" driving wheels. Some were equipped with piston valves and some had the slide-type valves. The engines that were modified for burning lignite fuel had an extension added to the smokebox. This gave them a decided over-thrust appearance. By 1930 all of the K-5 Ten Wheelers were retired from service.

No. 803, at Denver,
Colo., date unknown.
She was fitted with
piston valves and
burned oil as fuel.

—O. H. Means

No. 807, a Class K-5 engine, had been a lignite burner. Shown at Eola, Ill. in Sept.,
1930, ready for scrapping.
—O. H. Means.

Left side view of K-5, No. 806 showing the location of the air pump. Omaha in 1909.

—Bostwick Studio

Little data are available on the K-6, K-7, and K-9 engines. The three K-6 and the three K-7 Ten Wheelers were acquired from the Keokuk & Western. All were built by Rogers, the former in 1897 and the latter in 1896. The two K-9 engines came from the Jacksonville and St. Louis and were constructed by the Rhode Island Locomotive Works in 1890. The K-6 Ten Wheelers had 16" x 24" cylinders and 54" drivers, the K-7 engines had 17" x 24" cylinders and 56" drivers, and the K-9 Class had 18" x 24" cylinders and 56" drivers. None of these engines were built to Burlington standards. All were retired prior to 1917. There is no evidence that a K-8 engine class ever existed on the System.

Engine No. 940, Class K-9, was originally Jacksonville & St. Louis No. 7. Built by the Rhode Island Loco. Wks., in 1890, and acquired by the CB&Q about 1903.

—Burlington Route

The last of the Ten Wheelers, Class K-10, were rebuilt from Class H-4 Moguls. This revamping was done at the Aurora and Havelock shops from 1908 to 1914. Nineteen 2-6-0 engines were modified by extending the boiler barrel and by adding a four-wheel lead truck. The K-10 locomotives were assigned to the road as No. 950-968. Some were used in suburban commuter service at Chicago as late as 1930. The K-10 engines, like most of the other Ten-Wheeler types, spent their last days in local and branch-line service.

No. 950
at
Clarinda, Iowa
in
July, 1939.

—B. G. Corbin.

Piston valves and Stephenson valve gear were standard on the K-10 Ten Wheelers.
No. 953 on Mainline local service at Naperville, Ill. in Aug., 1933.   —L. E. Griffith

No. 955 had a sunbeam headlight and a short stack. Photo taken at Wymore, Nebr.

—Dick Rumbolz

—83—

THE CLASS N-1, COLUMBIA TYPE

One of the truly "high steppers" used on the Burlington was the Class N-1, 2-4-2 type, built by Baldwin in 1895 and assigned to the road as No. 590. This engine was an experimental design, and was to handle a train of six cars from Chicago to Galesburg in three hours, for an average speed of over 54 mph. It was one of the first engines designed for burning bituminous coal with a wide firebox placed to the rear of the driving wheels and over the trailing truck. The boiler was of the straight-top type with a combustion chamber extending forward from the firebox. Unfortunately this combination did not prove entirely satisfactory, and the engine was rebuilt in 1897 with a new firebox, the combustion chamber being omitted. The 2-4-2 type had 84 ¼" drivers with cast steel centers. The first pair of drivers was equalized w i t h t h e leading truck, and underhung springs were used under all wheels. The cylinders were 19" x 26" and inboard piston valves of 10" diameter were located above the front frame extension. The valve-link motion was placed entirely between the driving wheels.

The tender appears to have been influenced by European design, since it was of a six-wheel type with all three axles held in place by a rigid frame. The springs on the second and third axles were connected by equalizing bars. Although the N-1 engine was never duplicated, its design features were adopted on the 4-4-2 type locomotives that were to follow. In 1905 the Columbia type was rebuilt to a 4-4-2 wheel arrangement and reclassed as P-4.

No. 590 had just arrived from the builders when this photo was taken at

Galesburg, Ill. in 1895.   **—O. H. Means**

N-1, No. 1590,
ex No. 590,
was in passenger
service at
Princeton, Ill.
in 1900.

—Harry Boggs

THE CLASS P, ATLANTICS

The first of the Atlantic 4-4-2 types to appear on the System were Baldwin-built Vauclain compounds. Two were constructed in 1899, and three others of similar design followed in 1900. They were assigned to the road as No. 1591-1595 and classed as P-1-C. As was typical of Vauclain compounds, the high-pressure cylinders, 13 ½" x 26", were located above the larger lower-pressure cylinders, 23" x 26", on each side. Stephenson valve gear·actuated the 13" inboard-piston valves. Their boilers were similar to the 2-4-2 type, but the firebox was narrower and was located in part between the second set of drivers and the trailing wheels. Underhung and equalized spring rigging was used under the drivers and trailing wheels. The tenders of the P-1-C engines were similar to the one used on the Columbia type, although tenders having two four-wheeled trucks were later employed.

Engines No. 1591 and 1592 were first assigned to run between Chicago and Burlington where they performed exceedingly well. Engine No. 1591 was first placed in service on April 7, 1899, and was not shopped for general repairs until July 30, 1900. During this time she had chalked up 160,-806 miles of service. Engine No. 1592 also turned in a fine record of mileage and speed. On December 5, 1899, with a train of 4 cars weighing about 200 tons, No. 1592 hauled the eastbound fast mail from Mendota to Chicago, 83 miles, in 77 minutes. Including two stops, the average speed was 64.6 mph.

No. 2500, ex No.
1591, waits at the
station platform at
Denver, Colo. in
1910.

—O. H. Means

No. 1592, on train
No. 1, rounds a curve
near Princeton, Ill.
in 1899.

—Harry Boggs

No. 1592, a Class P-
1-C, rolls along near

Chicago in 1902.

—Burlington Route

No. 1594 at a station
stop in the early
1900's.

—O. H. Means

From 1913 to 1915 the P-1-C engines were rebuilt to simple types with cylinders of 19" x 26" and reclassed as P-1. All were retired in January, 1933.

P-1, No. 2502, at W. Burlington in Oct., 1914. She was retired in 1933.

—O. H. Means

Class P-1, No. 2504, was rebuilt from a compound. The location is Hannibal, Mo. in June, 1928.

—O. H. Means

Locomotives of the P-2-C Class were also Baldwin-built Vauclain compounds. Six were constructed in 1902 and were numbered 1584-1589. The P-2-C Atlantics were heavier and had larger cylinder diameters than the P-1-C engines. The firebox was also wider and was located behind the second pair of drivers and over the trailing truck, the latter being supported by an outside frame and journals. A wagon-top boiler was used on these locomotives. With a total engine weight of 183,100 lb. and a boiler pressure of 210 psi, the P-2-C Class exerted a tractive force of 19,850 lb.

During 1902 and 1903 the Rogers Locomotive Company constructed twenty-five similar engines, except that they were fitted with single-expansion cylinders having dimensions of 20" x 26". Steam distribution was controlled by inboard piston valves and Stephenson link motion. The engines were classed as P-2 and were assigned to various roads on the System including the B.&M.R., the H.&St.J., the St. L.K.&N.W. and the parent C.B.&Q. The P-2 Class had a total engine weight of 174,000 lb., an operating steam pressure of 210 psi, and exerted a tractive force of 22,000 lb.

No. 2541 was heading a passenger local at Savanna, Ill. in Aug., 1930.

—O. H. Means

No. 2513, a Class P-2-C, was a Vauclain compound.   —B. G. Corbin Collection.

P-2, No. 2526

at the Rock Island

Roundhouse in 1925.

—O. H. Means

The crew pose with
No. 2539, at Rochelle,
Ill. in 1910.

—B. G. Corbin

Collection.

The P-3-C engines were of the balanced-compound type. Twenty of these were built by Baldwin in 1904 and 1905, and were assigned to the road as No. 2700-2719. The first ten had 78" drivers while the rest were fitted with 74" drivers. The locomotives had all four of their cylinders in the same horizontal plane. The high-pressure cylinders were placed between the frame and drove the first pair of drivers through a cranked axle. The outside low-pressure cylinders were coupled to the second pair in the usual manner. Stephenson link motion controlled the steam distribution through piston valves. The inside and outside cranks on the same side were positioned 180 degrees apart so as to neutralize the disturbing forces. The first engine of this class had a one-piece, forged-steel crank axle. The rest had axles built up from nine separate pieces, this type proving more satisfactory. In general appearance, the P-3-C engines were similar to the P-2-C Atlantics except that the cylinders were located further forward to accommodate the inside driving rods to the first axle. This also resulted in a somewhat longer boiler and tube length, 19' for the P-3-C compared to 16' 9" for the P-2-C.

Trial runs with the first P-3-C engine, No. 2700, were made in July, 1904 between McCook, Nebr. and Akron, Colo., a distance of 143 miles. Compared to three single-expansion locomotives, a 2-6-2 type and two P-2 Atlantics, engine No. 2700 developed a greater capacity and consumed less fuel and water per horsepower hour than the others. She hauled a twelve-car train, weighing about 580 tons, over the distance in 32 minutes, for an average speed of 42.26 mph. During the same month, engine No. 2700 made a continuous run from Creston to Chicago in 9 hrs. The average speed for the 393-mile distance was 43.67 mph. At that time this was regarded as an unusual performance.

P-3-C, No. 2700 was taken at Denver, Colo. in 1910.

—O. H. Means

No. 2718 was double-heading on the Colorado Ltd. when this photo was taken in 1910.

—B. G. Corbin Collection

No. 2702 in passenger service at Denver, Colo. in 1910.　　—O. H. Means

P-4, No. 2599, the rebuilt N-1, was similar in appeaarnce to the other Atlantic types. Taken at Rock Island, Ill. in 1926.

—O. H. Means

No. 2599 at Galesburg, Ill. on April 18, 1926.　　—O. H. Means

The Class P-5 Atlantics were created by rebuilding the six P-2-C engines and fourteen of the P-3-C locomotives. This was accomplished by adding new cylinders; new front engine frame; Schmidt-type superheater; new tube sheets, tubes and tube arrangement; and by applying Walschaerts valve gear among other changes. The P-5 engines rebuilt from the P-2-C Class were fitted with 78" driving wheels, whereas the others were equipped with 74". The 8' long engine cabs were eventually replaced with shorter ones.

No. 2564 on a local passenger run at Lincoln, Nebr. in Aug., 1949.

—Al Holck

No. 2565, Class P-5, at the Galesburg engine terminal in Aug., 1937.   —Lou Schmitz collection.

No. 2565 at St. Louis, Mo., on Dec. 22, 1940.

—Al Holck

—91—

P-6, No. 2574 was getting coal at Hannibal, Mo. in Aug., 1936.

—B. G. Corbin

The P-6 engines were rebuilt from six of the P-3-C balanced compounds, and the P-6A locomotives were rebuilt from eight of the P-2 simple Atlantics. The changes made in rebuilding these engines were similar to those previously noted for the P-5 Class. Drivers of 69" diameter were used on the P-6 and P-6A Class 4-4-2 types. A few of these engines were in service until the end of 1949.

P-6, No. 2580 has just brought in the mainline local from Creston, Ia. and is standing at Red Oak in June, 1944.

—B. G. Corbin

No. 2585 at Red Oak, Ia., Nov., 1939.

—B. G. Corbin

P-6A, No. 2595, was on a local passenger run at E. St. Louis, Ill. in April, 1939.

—B. G. Corbin Collection

No. 2592 also at E. St. Louis in April, 1939.

—B. G. Corbin Collection

THE CLASS R, PRAIRIES

An important step in the development of Burlington motive power was made in 1899 when the first of the 2-6-2 type engines was designed by Mr. F. A. Delano, Superintendent of Motive Power. Four of these locomotives, classed as R-1, were built in the Burlington shops in 1900. Although the wheel arrangement of the engines was not new, it was the first time on this type that a wide firebox was placed behind the drivers and over the rear trailing truck. The trailing axle was supported by outside journals and frame, an arrangement also used on the 4-4-2 type and later on the 4-6-2 type engines. The R-1 Prairies were designed to haul fast freight over relatively level country, where train load was mainly a function of the engine steaming capacity. Although the engines were of moderate size, they did stir a great deal of interest in the locomotive industry because of their new design features.

Class R-1, No. 1701, was photographed soon after she came from the W. Burlington Shops in 1900.

—Ry. & Loco. Eng.

The boilers of the R-1 Class were tapered at the first ring behind the smokebox, and were fitted with a Belpaire-type firebox with a grate 6' wide and 7' long. The lead truck was equalized with the first pair of driving wheels as in the Consolidation or Mogul types. The trailing truck was equalized with the last pair of drivers through transverse steel bars linked to the journal support frames. The journals were allowed a small amount of lateral motion by rollers placed above the boxes. The R-1 Prairies had 19" x 24" cylinders, a total engine weight of 151,220 lb., and developed a tractive force of 21,900 lb. With about 68 percent of the engine weight carried on the drivers, their ratio of adhesion was equal to 4.38. The steaming capacity of the R-1 engines was liberal compared to the Mogul and Ten-Wheeler types, and sub-bituminous coal (lignite), which was thought to be unsuited for locomotive fuel, was used quite successfully.

No. 1702 was double heading at Galesburg in Oct., 1900.

—J. L. Heaney

With the satisfying operation of the Class R-1 Prairies, it was only natural that a larger engine of the same type, to handle heavier train loads, should be developed. The Class R-2 locomotive was the result. Fifty engines of this class were built by Baldwin in 1901, and an additional ten were completed in the West Burlington shops during the same year. Six of the Baldwin-built locomotives were Vauclain compounds having cylinders of 16" and 27" x 24". The remaining R-2 engines were single-expansion types, and had cylinder dimensions of 20" x 24". As on the R-1 Class, piston valves placed above the cylinders and actuated by Stephenson link motion controlled steam flow. Straight boilers with Belpaire fireboxes were used on both the compounds and the single-expansion engines. A longer tube length and a greater number of tubes increased the heating surface to 2888 sq. ft., compared to 2076 sq. ft. for the R-1 engines. The design of the main frame, running gear, spring rigging, trailing truck suspension, and driving wheel diameter, 64", was the same as the Class R-1 engines. With a total engine weight of 170,000 lb. and a boiler pressure of 200 psi, the R-2 types developed a tractive force of 25,500 lb.

R-2, No. 1713 stands with a local freight at Council Bluffs, Ia. in 1917.

—O. H. Means

No. 1711 was at
Savanna, Ill. in 1914.

—O. H. Means

The Class R-3 was a further development of the Prairie type. Fifty engines of this class were built by Baldwin in 1902, and were assigned to the road as No. 1721-1770. The boilers and fire-boxes were similar to the R-2 engines, except that the tube length was increased by 14". The cylinder dimensions were also increased to 21" x 26", and driving wheels of 69" diameter were used. The size of the drivers thus made the R-3 Class suitable for heavy passenger service as well as fast-freight service. The total engine weight of the R-3 type was 181,920 lb., and they developed a tractive force of 28,200 lb.

No. 1801 at Gales-
burg, Ill. in May,
1926.

—O. H. Means

No. 1831 hides be-
hind a pole at Bar-
stow, Ill. in May,
1923 but this didn't
discourage the rail-
fan photographer.

—Harry Draper
Collection

No. 1803 at Rock Island, Ill. in Feb., 1925.　　　　　—O. H. Means

No. 1805, an R-3
Prairie type, was
photographed at
Savanna, Ill. in 1925.

—O. H. Means

In 1904 the R-4 Prairies made their appearance on the road. During that year forty engines were built by Baldwin, and were assigned engine No. 1900-1939. In 1905 the Brooks Works of the American Locomotive Company completed fifty similar engines, No. 1940-1989, and during the following year, Baldwin constructed fifty additional locomotives of this class, No. 2000-2049. The boilers, cylinders, and engine weight were enlarged over those of the R-3 engines. The total engine weight of the R-4 Prairies was 208,550 lb., their operating steam pressure was 210 psi, and they exerted a tractive force of 35,000 lb.

No. 1907, an oil
burner, was at Los
Angeles in March,
1942. Note the black-
out shield on the
headlight.

—B. G. Corbin
Collection

The boilers were of the straight-top design, but in place of the Belpaire-type firebox used on preceding classes, ones of radial-stay construction were used. The 12" piston-type valves were of the inboard type and were actuated by Stephenson link motion. The cylinder arrangement was similar to the P-2 Atlantics. Although the piston rods were extended forward of the cylinders (for additional bearing support) on the first Baldwin-built Class R-4 engines, this was later modified and the extended portion was removed. Some of the R-4 locomotives had 22" x 28" cylinders, and others were equipped with cylinders of 25" bore. The operating steam pressure was reduced to compensate for the increase in cylinder diameter.

By the end of 1925, fourteen of the R-4 Prairies were rebuilt with new cylinders of 25" x 28" and Walschaerts valve gear was applied to them. These engines were reclassed as R-4A. A number of the R-4 locomotives were rebuilt to G-10 switchers. The rest retained their original construction features. During World War II when the Southern Pacific Railroad became short of motive power, several of the R-4 engines were leased by that road and sent to the West Coast where they performed yard and branch-line duties.

Far away from home, Burlington engines No. 1955 and 1907, Class R-4, and No. 2974,
a Class S-3 Pacific, triple head through Alhambra, Calif. in Feb., 1942 on the S. P.   —G. M. Best

R-4, No. 1928, in
switching service at
Columbus, Nebr. in
Oct., 1939.

—Robert Graham

The R-5 Class, 2-6-2 type, was basically an R-4 engine with a redesigned boiler. Fifty locomotives, No. 2050-2099, were built by Baldwin in 1906, and fifty similar engines, No. 2100-2149, were built by the Brooks Works of the American Locomotive Company in the same year. The following year, seventy-five additional engines, No. 2150-2224, were constructed by the latter company. The R-5 Prairie had a boiler with a sloping course at the forward end of the barrel. The boiler shell diameter was thus tapered from 70" at the front to 79" at the firebox throat. Two of the Baldwin engines were fitted with fire-tube steam superheaters of the Emerson type. The successful performance of the superheaters (which increased the available energy from the steam for conversion to useful work) eventually led to their installation on the other R-5 and R-4 locomotives.

Although the total engine weight of the R-5 Prairies was somewhat greater than that of the R-4 Class, they developed about the same tractive force. Their cylinder dimensions, operating boiler pressure, and driving wheel diameter were also the same. By the mid 1920's fifteen of the R-5 engines had been rebuilt with new cylinders and valve gear of the Walschaerts type. The engines were reclassed as R-5A.

Like much of the moderately sized motive power used on the Burlington System, the R-4 and R-5 Prairies were eventually assigned to local and branch-line service as the demand for heavier mainline traffic increased. Originally both of the classes had been used for fast freight and passenger service. Their performance was always highly regarded by the engine men who operated them.

The following table shows the comparative performance and dimensions of the Class R engines:

Class	Cylinders	Drivers, Diameter	Steam Pressure, Pounds	Grate Area		Heating Surface		Weight on Drivers		Weight, Total Engine		Tractive Force	
				Square Feet	Per Cent Increase	Square Feet	Per Cent Increase	Pounds	Per Cent Increase	Pounds	Per Cent Increase	Pounds	Per Cent Increase
R-1	19" x 24"	64"	190	42	......	2076	......	96,000	......	140,000	......	21,900	......
R-2	20" x 24"	64"	200	42	......	2888	39	130,000	35	170,000	21	25,500	16
R-3	21" x 26"	69"	200	42	......	3055	47	134,550	40	181,920	30	28,200	29
R-4	22" x 28"	69"	210	55	31	3560	71	151,070	57	208,550	49	35,000	60
R-5	22" x 28"	69"	210	55	31	3560	71	159,540	66	216,000	54	35,000	60

Figures in columns headed "Per Cent Increase" show growth in dimensions and weights of Classes R-2 to R-5 as compared with Class R-1.

Although it was September in Red Oak, Iowa when No. 2179 was passing through, she was already prepared for winter. An open-end combination car and non-operating motor car No. 9852 are coupled to her tender. The year — 1942.

—B. G. Corbin

No. 2062 was at Downer Grove, Ill. in Feb., 1949.

—Al Holck

No. 2062, a Class R-5A, had been rebuilt with outside valves and Walschaerts valve gear. Photo taken at Red Oak in Dec., 1937. —B. G. Corbin.

Oil-burning No. 2222, the four deuces, is shown at Galveston, Texas in August, 1935 while working on the FW&D. —B. G. Corbin Collection.

THE CLASS S, PACIFIC TYPES

The Class S-1 Baldwin-built Pacifics were a direct development of the R-5 Prairies. Thirty S-1 engines, No. 2800-2829, made their appearance on the road in 1906, followed by fifteen Schenectady-built engines, No. 2830-2844, in 1907. The boilers of the S-1 types were similar to the R-5 Prairies, except that their tube length was increased by 24". Although the driving wheel diameter was increased to 74" on the S-1 engines, the cylinders as well as the driving and trailing axle journals were of the same dimensions as the R-5. This permitted the interchangeability of parts in the machinery and running gear of the Pacific and Prairie-type engines.

In 1909 the Baldwin Locomotive Works completed twenty-five modified S-1 engines, No. 2845-2869. The principal changes were the substitution of Walschaerts valve gear for the Stephenson type, an increase in the diameter of the driving axle journals, and an increase in the width of the water spaces around the firebox. These changes gave the modified Class S-1 Pacifics a total engine weight of 235,300 lb. compared to 230,940 lb. for the preceding engines.

Class S-1, No. 2828 pulling the Denver Limited in 1910.　　—B. G. Corbin Collection

No. 2829 was waiting for the highball in Denver in 1910.　　—B. G. Corbin Collection.

No. 2848 was a later
S-1 engine equipped
with Walschaerts valve
gear. Photo taken at
Denver in 1910.

—B. G. Corbin
Collection

Engine No. 2801, an
S-1, had a rebuilt cab,
and was used on com-
muter trains in the
Chicago area. W. Eo-
Ia, Ill. in Sept., 1935.

—L. E. Griffith

Slim - boilered No. 2833, Class S-1A, was equipped with a Delta-B trailing truck. Galesburg, Ill., May 3, 1939.

—Al Holck

No. 2867 was fitted with a Worthington feedwater heater. Photo taken at Omaha Nebr. in June, 1940.
—B. G. Corbin.

Smoke deflectors were a rarity on the Burlington. Engine No. 2838 is shown with a crude type of deflector as it waited at the Aurora station in June, 1937.

—B. G. Corbin Collection

In 1910 fifty Baldwin-built, 4-6-2 types were assigned to the road as No. 2900-2949, and were classed as S-2. Their design and appearance were similar to the S-1 engines constructed in 1909, but with a few modifications. A fire-tube superheater of the Emerson type was applied, and the working steam pressure was reduced to 160 psi to compensate for the larger cylinder bore of 25" compared to 22" on the S-1 engines. For better performance on heavy grades, the Class S-2, 4-6-2 types were fitted with driving wheels of 69" diameter (although some were later fitted with 74"). With these modified features, the engines developed a tractive force of 34,500 lb. compared to 31,000 lb. for the S-1 Pacifics built in 1909.

With her nose thrust forward, S-2 engine No. 2919 stands at Savanna, Ill. in Aug., 1925.

—L. E. Griffith

During the mid 1920's, the great majority of the S-1 and S-2 locomotives were rebuilt and re-classed as S-1A and S-2A respectively. Among the changes made during this rebuilding period were the application of new cylinders and accessories, new main frames and frame crossties, application of Schmidt-type superheater, new tube sheets and tubes to suit superheater, new Walschaerts valve gear, new steam pipes, new front deck plate, application of cross-compound air pumps, new main axles and main driving boxes, and the application of either Worthington or Elesco feedwater-heating systems. Some of the rebuilt engines were fitted with Delta-B trailing trucks having Franklin boosters. Most of the tenders on the S-1A and S-2A engines were also rebuilt, and 4-wheel Commonwealth trucks were substituted for the pedestal type. Some of the Pacifics spent their last days in suburban service around the Chicago area. By the end of 1950 just about all had been retired.

Engine No. 2912 was in commuter service at Downer's Grove, Ill. in 1933. It remained an S-2 Class until its retirement in June, 1935.

—B. G. Corbin Collection

With an Elesco heater and plenty of piping piled on her front end, engine No. 2913 pauses at the St. Louis station in May, 1947.
—Al Holck.

No. 2914 was running extra at Red Oak when this photo was taken in March, 1938.

—B. G. Corbin

Although rebuilt to an S-2A Class, No. 29-33 still retained its outside-frame trailing truck. Downers Grove in Oct., 1949.

—Al Holck

A new 4-6-2 design, heavier than the preceding Pacifics, was assigned to the road in 1915. Fifteen of these engines, No. 2950-2964, were built by Baldwin and classed as S-3. In 1918 ten additional locomotives, No. 2965-2974, were completed for the road. Shorter engine cabs were fitted to these latter Pacifics. The S-3 engines developed a tractive force of 42,400 lb. and had a total engine weight of 269,200 lb. Their boilers were of a tapered design, and the fireboxes were radially stayed, each having a combustion chamber 30" long. A brick arch was supported on angle irons studded to the side sheets of the firebox. To reduce the dynamic augment when running at high speeds, the driving mechanism on the S-3 locomotives was made as light as possible. The piston rods, crosshead pins, crank pins, and driving axles were made from heat-treated alloy steel, and were hollow bored. The pistons and the Laird-type crossheads were cast from 0.40 percent carbon steel and were carefully annealed.

Walschaerts valve gear, controlled by a Ragonnet power reverse mechanism, was applied to the S-3 engines, and for the first time on the Burlington, a trailing truck of the Rushton type was employed. The S-1 and S-2 Pacifics had used the outside-frame type adopted from the Class R Prairies. The Rushton trailing truck also embodied an outside frame and journal. Lateral motion was accomplished by swing bars connecting the journal box to the frame. Equalizing bars coupled the trailing-truck springs to the main springs on the last pair of drivers. Eventually the Class S-3 engines were equipped with Elesco or Worthington feedwater-heating systems, and several were fitted with Delta-B trailing trucks.

In 1922 two locomotives of the S-3 design were built for the Fort Worth and Denver City Railroad, and three for the Colorado and Southern Railway. The F.W.&D. engines were equipped to burn oil as a fuel, and the C.&S. engines were built as coal burners. The three Pacifics for the latter road had driving wheels of only 69" diameter compared to 74" used on the standard S-3 Class. The smaller drivers were better for heavy grade conditions, and they increased the tractive force of the engines to 44,000 lb.

Ready to move to
the lower yards at
Red Oak, Ia.
No. 2950
poses for a photo in
August, 1939.

—B. G. Corbin

Class S-3, No. 2964 is in the Gibson yards at Omaha, being used in passenger train
protection and freight service in 1948.　　　　　　　　—B. G. Corbin

Lignite burner, No.
2971, in the yards at
Denver in May, 1938.

—H. E. High

No. 2974, an oil
burner, was at the
Denver roundhouse in
May, 1939.

—B. G. Corbin

THE CLASS S-4, HUDSONS

Some of the most beautiful and well proportioned locomotives to polish the rails of the Burlington System were the S-4 and S-4A Hudsons. Twelve 4-6-4 type engines of the S-4 Class, No. 3000-3011, were first built by the Baldwin Locomotive Works in 1930, and were followed by No. 3012, constructed at the West Burlington shops in 1935, with its boiler furnished by Baldwin. The S-4 Hudsons were placed in service to handle such crack trains as the "Black Hawk", the "Aristocrat" and the "Ak-Sar-Ben". They replaced the Mountain-type engines which had performed this duty, and they were able to handle long runs which had previously required two locomotives operating in relay fashion.

Home-made engine No. 3012, an S-4, waits with mail train No. 7 at Red Oak in Oct. 1937.

—B. G. Corbin

With the increased operation of the streamlined diesel - powered Zephyrs, the Burlington found it necessary to convert one of its Hudson-type engines to serve as standby power. The engine was to look as much like the Zephyrs as possible. With this idea in mind, the "Aeolus" was created. Engine No. 3002 was recalled to the West Burlington shops, and in 1937 she emerged with a streamlined shroud, light-weight, roller-bearing side rods, and box-pok main drivers. She was renumbered 4000 and given a new classification of S-4A. The engine was properly named, since in Greek mythology, "Aeolus" meant "Keeper of the Wind." She was also affectionately called, "Big Alice the Goon", by railroad men, a nickname which stuck with her even after her streamlined shroud had been removed.

In 1938 the West Burlington shops built another streamlined "Aeolus" and numbered it 4001. It was the only Hudson on the System with a vestibule cab. Like its running mate, however, the streamlined shroud was later removed, thus producing a conventional-looking, Class S-4A engine. Also in 1938, S-4 engines No. 3008, 3009, and 3011 were rebuilt with light-weight, roller-bearing rods and renumbered 4002, 4003, and 4004 respectively. These locomotives were also reclassed as S-4A but were not given streamlined shrouds.

Engine No. 3002, a Class S-4, pulling train No. 2 at Red Oak in Oct., 1935.

—B. G. Corbin

The streamlined "Aeolus" at Red Oak, Ia. in Sept., 1938. She was rebuilt from No. 3002 and renumbered 4000.

—B. G. Corbin

"Big Alice", as she looked at Red Oak in Sept., 1945 after the streamlined hood had been removed.

—B. G. Corbin

The second "Aeolus" was numbered No. 4001. Photo taken at Red Oak in August, 1939.

—B. G. Corbin

The Hudson-type engines were equipped with Elesco-type feedwater heaters, except No. 4001 which carried the Worthington type-S system. They operated on a boiler pressure of 250 psi, and had cylinder dimensions of 25" x 28". Their tractive force was 47,700 lb., and with the trailing-truck booster it was increased to 59,400 lb. Their 78" drivers gave them an adequate margin of speed. On August 12, 1938, one of the Hudsons, No. 3002, while making up time with a late train, No. 22, between Cochrane and LaCrosse, Wisconsin, maintained a speed of 112 mph with a train of 10 standard passenger cars. The 4-6-4 types were perhaps some of the most successful locomotives used on the Chicago Burlington & Quincy. No. 3001 was still in steam in 1958 when it served as motive power for a rail fan trip.

No. 4001, Class S-4A with shroud removed, was the only Burlington Hudson with a vestibule cab. Red Oak, Iowa in June, 1945.　　　　—B. G. Corbin.

THE CLASS B, MOUNTAINS

In 1922, in order to meet the urgent need for additional passenger power, the Burlington received eight locomotives of the 4-8-2 wheel arrangement from the Lima Locomotive Works. The engines were numbered 7000-7007 and classed as B-1. They were designed to handle the heaviest trains on the line without doubleheading. To meet this requirement, the B-1 engines were equipped with automatic stokers of the Duplex type. Their total engine weight of 350,000 lb., with 235,500 lb. of this carried on the drivers, gave them a tractive force of 52,750 lb. The Lima-built Mountain types were designed to burn lignite (some were later altered to burn bituminous coal). Although the engines were delivered without feedwater heaters, they were later equipped with Worthington-type systems. The weight of the firebox, which was of the radially stayed design, was supported by a Rushton-type trailing truck. Four-wheel trucks of the pedestal design were used on the tenders.

The first Mountain-type engines proved so successful that thirteen similar engines, No. 7008-7020, were ordered from the Baldwin Locomotive Works in 1925 and classed as B-1A. They were nearly 1800 lb. heavier than the B-1 engines, but developed the same tractive force. Seven were designed to burn lignite fuel and six to burn bituminous coal. The running gear of the B-1A engines followed the design of the S-3 Pacifics in that heat-treated alloy steel was used for the piston rods, cross-head pins, crank pins, driving axles, main and side rods, and side-rod knuckle pins. The cylinders had 14" diameter piston valves operated by Walschaerts link motion. Feedwater heaters of the Worthington type were used, although engine No. 7011 was furnished with an Elesco system. Delta-B trailing trucks were fitted on the B-1A, 4-8-2 types, and six-wheel trucks of the Commonwealth type were used on the tenders.

Class B-1, No. 7001 waits with a freight haul on a siding at Red Oak in July, 1945.

—B. G. Corbin

No. 7001 was at Galesburg in May, 1939.

—Al Holck

Locomotive No. 7017 was later fitted with roller bearings on the valve linkage, and engine No. 7014, 7018, and 7020 were equipped with roller bearings on the main drivers. Twelve of the Mountain-type engines were also equipped with box-pok wheel centers on the main drivers, and three of B-1A engines were converted to oil burners. A few engines of this class were still in service in the early 1950's.

B-1A, No. 7014 heads the "Aristocrat" through Red Oak in Aug., 1939.

—B. G. Corbin

No. 7009 was pulling train No. 7 at Red Oak in March, 1939.

—B. G. Corbin

Engine 7011, a B-1A, carried an Elesco heater on her smokebox. Denver, Colo. in Aug., 1939.

—Joe Schick.

The Rushton trailing truck used on the B-1 Mountains. This type was also used on the S-3 Pacifics.

—B. G. Corbin

THE CLASS O, MIKADOS

The Burlington System was among the first great railroads to adopt the Mikado-type locomotive on a large scale. With heavier freight hauls occurring on mainline traffic after the turn of the century, the 2-6-2 Prairie types were unable to meet the increasing demands of this service. It was only natural, therefore, that the 2-8-2 type should rally to this need. In 1910 fifty locomotives, No. 5000-5049, of the Mikado type were built by Baldwin and assigned to the road as Class O-1. They were "all round" engines, suited to either heavy drags or to fast-freight service, and were the first of a general type that was subsequently built in large numbers for the Burlington System.

The O-1 engines, when first built, operated with a boiler pressure of 170 psi, and developed a tractive force of 49,500 lb. The boiler was tapered at the first ring behind the smokebox, and a fire-tube superheater of the Emerson type was employed. The weight of the wide radially stayed firebox was supported by a Hodges-type trailing truck equalized with the drivers through a transverse bar. Lateral motion of the truck journal was derived through the action of swing links. The firebox measured 7' deep at the front and 6' 1" at the rear, and had neither a brick arch nor a combustion chamber. In the cylinder arrangement, piston valves were of the inside-admission type and were actuated by Walschaerts link motion. Although the engines were first equipped with hand reverses, power-reverse mechanisms were applied in later years. In 1911 Baldwin furnished the road with ten additional Class O-1 locomotives, No. 5050-5059.

No. 5083 passed through Red Oak in Dec., 1940 on the mainline local.

—B. G. Corbin

No. 5032 at Red Oak in Oct., 1939.

—B. G. Corbin

Most of the O-1 Mikados were rebuilt with shorter engine cabs, and cross-compound air compressors replaced the older types. Engine 5055 at Edgemont, S. D. in July, 1948.

—Al Holck

0-1, No. 5049 was at Herrin, Ill. in July, 1949. —Al Holck.

Beginning in 1917, a number of Baldwin-built engines that were modifications of the Class O-1 engines were assigned to the System as No. 5060-5074 and classed as O-1A. One hundred and thirty-three additional engines of this class were also constructed by Baldwin between 1917 and 1923. The O-1A Mikados built in 1923 were numbered 4940-4999, since those engines completed in 1922 had numbers that were beginning to approach the 5200's assigned to the Class O-2, 2-8-2 types.

The O-1A types, like the O-3 engines, were fitted with outside admission piston valves and light-weight reciprocating and revolving parts. Laird type crossheads were also employed. The boilers were tapered at the first ring, and the radially stayed firebox was fitted with a combustion chamber. Schmid-type superheaters were also used. Like the O-3 engines, the Hodges trailing trucks on the O-1A Mikados were somewhat modified compared to the earlier types. Whereas on the O-1 and O-2 engines, the swing links on the rear truck coupled the springs to transverse support bars, the Hodges truck on the later 2-8-2 types had the front swing links coupled directly to the equalizing bars, and the rear ones were coupled to castings that were bolted to the rear engine frame. The O-1A engines that were completed in the early 1920's were fitted with feedwater heaters, and in later years most of the other O-1A Mikados were equipped with ones of either the Worthington or Elesco type.

Engine No. 5136, a Class 0-1A. Date and place unknown.

—Al Holck

No. 4940, an 0-1A, carried a Worthington feedwater heater on her left side. Centralia, Ill.

—B. G. Corbin Collection

—112—

Engine No. 4966 rests her rods at Centralia in the summer of 1953.

—Al Holck

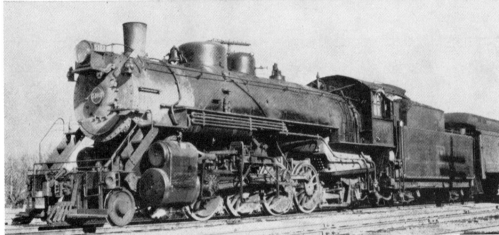

No. 5103 was doing mainline local chores at Red Oak in the fall of 1941.

—B. G. Corbin

No. 4972, a Class 0-1A, at Centralia, Ill. in May, 1939.   —Al Holck

The Hodges trailing-truck arrangement as used on the Class 0-1A Mikados.

—B. G. Corbin

In 1912 a heavier Mikado-type engine made its appearance on the Burlington System. Eighty-eight of these engines were completed by the Baldwin Locomotive Works during that year, and were followed by twelve additional engines in 1913. The new engines were classed as O-2 and were numbered 5200-5299. In general appearance, the running gear of the O-2 Mikados was similar to that of the O-1 engines. Their boilers, however, were larger in bore and were of the straight-top type fitted with an Emerson-type superheater. The Class O-2 engines were designed for a maximum load of 60,000 lb. per pair of driving wheels. With an operating steam pressure of 180 psi, and cylinders of 28" x 32", they developed a tractive force of 60,000 lb. Like the O-1 Mikados, the firebox on the O-2 locomotive did not have a combustion chamber or a firebrick arch. Power-reverse mechanisms of the Ragonnet type were used on the O-2 engines.

When No. 5207 was converted for burning oil, it was re-classed as an O-2B. Alliance, Nebr. in July 1950.

—Al Holck

No. 5234, an O-2A, was taking on coal at St. Louis, Mo. in May, 1940.

—B. G. Corbin Collection

No. 5248 at St. Louis, Mo. in Oct., 1938.　　　　—B. G. Corbin

Beginning in the mid 1920's, the railroad began rebuilding many of the Class O-2 types into more efficient motive power. The major changes made in reconstruction included new engine frames, new cylinders and accessories, new engine cabs, a new firebox with combustion chamber, the installation of new Schmidt-type superheaters, new Walschaerts valve gear, and the application of Worthington or Elesco feedwater-heating systems. The rebuilt Mikados were classed as O-2A. Those engines assigned to the western divisions were usually given an extended smokebox for burning either lignite or bituminous coal. For twenty-odd years the O-2A Mikados performed a variety of road services. By the early 1950's only a few remained on the active roster.

A line-up of 0-2 engines at West Burlington in about 1920.　　—B. G. Corbin Collection.

No. 5284 in the South Omaha yards in April, 1939.

—B. G. Corbin

Class 0-2, No. 5283 was performing switching duties at Chicago, Ill. in April, 1934.

—B. G. Corbin Collection.

—115—

The O-3, 2-8-2 types were a modification of the O-2 engines. Sixty engines of the O-3 Class were built by Baldwin over the period extending from 1915 to 1919. They were assigned to the road as No. 5300-5359. Although the first fifteen O-3 engines, built in 1915, were equipped with alligator-type crossheads, the subsequent O-3 Mikados were all fitted with those of the Laird type. Accessories on the Class O-3 locomotives, when first built, included a combustion chamber, a brick arch in the firebox, a Schmidt-type superheater, and a Street automatic stoker.

No. 5302, an early O-3 engine, had alligator-type crossheads. Photo taken at St. Louis, June, 1940.

—B. G. Corbin

O-3, No. 5328 was equipped with an exhaust - steam injector. Red Oak, Ia. in Oct., 1939.

—B. G. Corbin

No. 5334 at Red Oak in June, 1936. The O-3 engines were satisfactory locomotives except when speed was required on tonnage trains. Their limited steaming capacity prevented them from measuring up to this strenuous service.

—B. G. Corbin

In later years the O-3 engines were modified with shorter engine cabs, the single-stage air compressors were replaced with cross-compound types, and feedwater-heating systems of either the Worthington or Elesco types were applied on many. Some of the locomotives were fitted with exhaust-steam injectors, and a few others had Coffin feedwater heaters mounted on the front of their smokeboxes. As on the O-2A Mikados, the O-3 engines were eventually furnished with automatic stokers of either the Duplex or Standard MB types. The Coffin feedwater heaters used on the locomotives of other roads were usually recessed in the smokebox, and hence were not so conspicious as the forward-mounted position used on the Burlington. The Coffin system was a closed type; that is, the feedwater was pumped through piping in the heater and gained energy from the exhaust steam flowing and condensing around the piping. No direct mixing of the two fluids occurred. The heated feedwater was then fed to the boiler through a check valve, and the condensate from the heat exchanger drained to the tender. The closed type was also incorporated in the Elesco system, the heat exchanger being located on top of the smokebox ahead of the stack, and the feedwater pump mounted on the left side of the boiler. The Elesco heater was equipped with a live-steam valve, for the purpose of heating the feedwater with live steam when exhaust steam was not available during stand-still periods.

The Worthington-BL system was of the open type. The heater and the feedwater pump were mounted as one unit, and the exhaust steam was directly mixed with the feedwater in the heater section. When necessary, the oil (picked up in the cylinders) had to be separated from the exhaust steam before the latter was mixed with the feedwater. If the oil had carried over to the boiler, it could have seriously reduced the transmission of heat and caused the overheating of metal parts subjected to high temperatures. The exhaust-steam injector was also an open-type system, and its use gave a water saving of 10 to 15 percent by utilizing the otherwise-wasted exhaust steam. During stand-stills when low-pressure exhaust steam was not available, the injector automatically changed over to live steam to maintain the delivery of warm water to the boiler.

Beetle-browed No. 5320 was built by Baldwin in 1917. The Coffin feedwater heaters were applied to four of the 0-3 engines, but were later removed. —B. G. Corbin.

Long-boilered No. 5335 stood at Lincoln, Nebr. in Aug., 1949.

—Al Holck

Crossheads of the Laird type were used on the later O-3 engines. No. 5332 stands at
Omaha, Nebr. in Sept., 1950.   —Al Holck.

Locomotives of the O-4 Class were of the U.S.R.A. heavy-Mikado type. These Baldwin-built
2-8-2 types were assigned to the road in 1919 as No. 5500-5514. The general appearance of the O-4
engines was altered little throughout their years of service, except that feedwater-heating systems
were applied and the fireboxes and tenders were modified for burning oil. At least one engine, No.
5508, had its Cole-type trailing truck replaced with a Delta-B type. The U.S.R.A. Mikados were
assigned to the western divisions of the System and some were leased to the Fort Worth and Denver from time to time.

No. 5508 sported a
Delta-B trailing truck
at Fort Worth, Texas
in Aug., 1956.

—B. G. Corbin
Collection.

No. 5512, an O-4, was
fresh from the shops
when this photo was
taken at Casper, Wyo.
in Sept., 1937.

—B. G. Corbin
Collection.

No. 5506 was an 0-4 oil burner. Built by Baldwin in 1919.

No. 5509 was taking on oil at Lincoln, Nebr. in Sept., 1937.

—B. G. Corbin Collection.

The 5505 blasts over the ridge in South Omaha, after a steady upward climb from its starting point across the Missouri River in Council Bluffs.   —J. L. O'Donnell.

THE CLASS O-5, NORTHERNS

Designed to meet the ever-increasing need for moving tonnage at near breakneck speeds, the Burlington's O-5 Class commanded the respect of the System in carrying out this challenge. Their ability to hold down passenger schedules as demanding as those of the Zephyrs is also not to be overlooked.

The first eight 4-8-4 types were built by the Baldwin Locomotive Works and were assigned to the road in 1930 as No. 5600-5607. So successful was their performance that thirteen more engines of this wheel arrangement, No. 5608-5620, were constructed under the trussed roof of the West Burlington erecting shops in 1937. The eight Baldwin-built, O-5 engines were equipped with Elesco-type, feedwater-heating systems; and in general resembled the lines of S-4 Hudsons except that the boiler was lengthened to accommodate the additional pair of driving wheels. The O-5 Northerns built at the West Burlington shops (their boilers were furnished by Baldwin) were fitted with the Worthington-Type SA feedwater heaters, with the hot-water pump located under the smokebox and behind a shield, and the cold-water pump located below the cab on the engineer's side.

Class O-5, No. 5600 was brand new when she was photographed in Omaha in Sept. 1930. The engine was on exhibit.   —Bostwick Studio.

No. 5604 at Galesburg in Oct., 1939.   —Al Holck

—120—

No. 5621 at the Burlington System's main erecting and repair shop at
West Burlington, Iowa.

—Burlington Route.

An 0-5A locomotive
being built at the
West Burlington
shops.

—B. G. Corbin
Collection.

The trim-looking No. 5618 served as head-end power for a fan trip in July, 1958. Taken along the Mississippi near E. Winona, Wis.　　　　—Max Zimmerlein.

O-5, No. 5604 at Red Oak, Ia. in Oct., 1939.

—B. G. Corbin

No. 5610 stands at E.
St. Louis, Ill. in the
fall of 1938.

—B. G. Corbin
Collection.

The shield in front of
the hot-water pump is
evident on engine
5619, an 0-5A. Red
Oak, Ia. in July, 1941.

—B. G. Corbin

The zenith in the design of the Burlington's 4-8-4 types was reached when, in 1938 and 1940 engines No. 5621-5635 were built at West Burlington and placed in service on the System. These last Northern types were fitted with cast-steel solid pilots, box-pok drivers, light-weight rods, roller bearings, and vestibule cabs. They were classed as 0-5A. All of the Burlington's 4-8-4 types were equipped with soot blowers, and they operated on a boiler pressure of 250 psi. With 74" drivers and cylinders of 28" x 30", the engines bit into the rails with a tractive force of 67,500 lb. The 0-5 Northerns were always straining at their draw bars, and as one fireman put it, "they steamed best under a wide-open throttle, and on a light train one had to keep the reverse down in the corner."

To coax more power and speed out of the older 4-8-4 engines, some were equipped with light-weight rods, roller bearings, and box-pok drivers. The engines receiving these and other improvements were reclassed as 0-5A. Like other roads, the Burlington experimented with the Franklin steam-distribution system employing poppet valves. These were applied to engine No. 5625 in 1942 with noteworthy but unsuccessful results. The poppet valves operated well enough when they were carefully maintained, but their ruggedness could not stand up to the abundance of power that was packed into the 0-5 Northerns. After a trial life of a few years on the System, No. 5625 was retired and eventually scrapped, rather than invest money in converting it back to its original status. This decision was no doubt influenced by the fact that diesel engines were then coming into more general use.

On October 17, 1944 a Class 0-5 locomotive handled a record-breaking, 82-car mail train loaded with mail and packages for servicemen overseas. Without a doubt, the performance of the Burlington's Northern types was not often surpassed. In late years most of the remaining engines in this class were equipped with mars lights, and some were converted for burning oil. Engine No. 5632 was still pounding the rails in 1958 and 1959 when it was serving as head-end power for rail fan trips.

No. 5625, Class 0-5A, as she was originally built. Pulling train No. 6, at Red Oak, Iowa on Sept. 17, 1939.

—B. G. Corbin.

The application of poppet valves on No. 5625 made it necessary to remount the hot-water pump on the left side of the boiler.

—Burlington Route.

The cast-steel pilot on No. 5632 gave her an impressive front-end appearance. An 0-5A engine on train No. 7 at Red Oak in Nov., 1940.

—B. G. Corbin

THE CLASS M, SANTA FE TYPES

The Class M engines were the Burlington's answer to moving long, heavy freight drags. The M-1, 2-10-2 types, No. 6000-6004, were constructed by Baldwin in 1912, and at that time were the heaviest non-articulated locomotives ever built. They were intended for service in the Illinois coal fields where train loadings were becoming increasingly heavy. The M-1 engines exerted a tractive force of 71,500 lb. with a weight-on-drivers of 301,800 lb. This gave them a ratio of adhesion of 4.22.

The boiler of the M-1 was straight on top, but in order to provide adequate water space under the combustion chamber, which was 27" long, the last boiler ring sloped downward on the bottom, thus increasing the boiler diameter from 88½" at the first ring to 96½" at the throat. The radially stayed firebox contained no arch, but a 9"-wide brick wall was fitted across the throat of the combustion chamber. The first 2-10-2 types were equipped with stokers of the Barnum under-feed type, which forced coal by screw conveyors through four horizontal troughs in the bottom of the firebox. These stokers did not perform too successfully, and were eventually replaced with over-feed types. Fire-tube superheaters of the Emerson design were used on the M-1 engines.

The steam distribution to the cylinders was controlled by 15" piston valves of the inside-admission type, and these were actuated by Walschaerts valve gear. The Ragonnet power-reverse mechanism was employed, since the tremendous size of the engine would have made hand reversing difficult. Although their rigid wheel base was 20' 9", the M-1 locomotives could negotiate a 21-degree curve, as considerable lateral motion was allowed in the first and fifth driving axles. To provide for this, the knuckle pins were fitted into spherical bushings of case-hardened steel in the side-rod stubs on the second and fourth pair of drivers. The engine frame construction and transverse bracing was made exceptionally strong.

No. 6000, an M-1, had the headlight mounted in an unusual position. Galesburg—
July, 1931.
—O. H. Means.

An unusual feature on the M-1 locomotives was the use of additional counterweights on the main driving axle. This consisted of two cast-steel "bobs" placed between the frames and keyed to the axle. The mass of the reciprocating and revolving parts, and the small size of the driving wheels, would have made it impossible to balance the engines properly without these additional counterweights. The tenders used on the M-1 Class were considered large at the time they were built. Their capacity was 10,000 gal. of water and 15 tons of coal. The tender trucks were of the four-wheel, arch-bar type.

No. 6000 at Galesburg

in May, 1930.

—O. H. Means

Class M-1, No. 6001 was equipped with an Elesco feedwater system. Galesburg—
August, 1931.   —O. H. Means.

The successful operation of the first five 2-10-2 types prompted the Burlington to order additional engines of this wheel arrangement from the Baldwin Locomotive Works. Engines No. 6104-6125 were delivered in 1914 and were classed as M-2. No. 6110 was exhibited at the Panama Pacific International Exposition held in San Francisco during that year. The M-2 Class incorporated a number of modifications compared with those engines built in 1912. For example, a superheater of the Schmidt type was employed, a brick arch (supported on water-tubes) was placed in the firebox, and an automatic Street stoker fired the boiler. A number of other detail changes were incorporated, but basically the M-1 and M-2 engines were closely similar in principal dimensions, weights, and hauling capacity.

To reduce the dynamically unbalanced forces on the rails, two of the M-2 locomotives, No. 6108 and 6109, were experimentally fitted with light-weight reciprocating parts made from heat-treated alloy steels. As was done on the Class S-3 Pacifics, the piston rods and crank pins were bored hollow, and to further reduce weight, the Laird-type crossheads were adopted. By reducing the aggregate weight of the reciprocating parts by 379 lb. (or 16 percent) compared to the earlier 2-10-2 types, the additional counterweights that had been keyed to the main axles of the M-1 engines were no longer needed. Engines No. 6108 and 6109 were then classed as M-2A.

M-2, No. 6100 looked bare on its left side with the absence of a feedwater heating system. Centralia, Ill. —March, 1937.

—B. G. Corbin

No. 6119 had an Elesco heater perched on top of its extended smokebox. The place is Sheridan, Wyo. in August, 1948. —Al Holck.

No. 6110 was at E. St. Louis, Ill. on Sept. 7, 1939. —B. G. Corbin.

M-2, No. 6102 was caught at Beardstown, Ill. in 1939.

—Al Holck

To show to what extent the light-weight reciprocating parts reduced the stresses on tracks and bridges, a series of bridge deflection tests were conducted with four locomotives. This included two engines with light-weight reciprocating parts, an S-3 Pacific and one of the M-2A types, and two engines with standard parts, an S-2 Pacific and an M-1 type. The S-2 and S-3 Pacifics carried 153,000 lb. and 170,000 lb. on their drivers respectively. Both of the 2-10-2 engines weighed about 300,000 lb. on drivers. The test results showed that the S-3 locomotive produced stresses that were no greater than those generated by the S-2 engine, even though the axle loading of the former was greater. The Class M-2 and M-2A locomotives showed about the same results up to a speed of 5 mph, but above that speed the superiority of the M-2A engine, in reducing stresses due to rotational unbalance, was evident. At a speed of 40 mph, the impact in excess to the static load was 60 percent greater for the M-1 engine with standard parts, than for the M-2A type with light-weight parts. So outstanding were the results of this test, that all of the other Class M-2A, 2-10-2 types, built by Baldwin between 1915 and 1921 (Engines No. 6126-6170), were equipped with light-weight running gear. Most of the M-1, M-2, and M-2A locomotives were later fitted with feedwater-heating systems, and the M-2A engines were equipped with disc centers on the main drivers for faster operation.

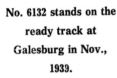

No. 6132 stands on the ready track at Galesburg in Nov., 1939.

—B. G. Corbin Collection.

No. 6132 at Denver in the fall of 1946.

—Al Holck

Class M-2A, No. 6133 was running extra at Brookfield, Mo. in Sept., 1936.

—B. G. Corbin

No. 6139, an M-2A, at Chillicothe, Mo. in Oct., 1936.

—B. G. Corbin

No. 6146 was parked outside of the roundhouse at Denver in May, 1940.

—Al Holck

M-2A, No. 6134 stands at Centralia, Ill. in Dec., 1951. Notice the disc center on the main driver.

—Al Holck.

The Elesco heater on No. 6150 was mounted on the forward section of the extended smokebox. Denver, Colo., April, 1930.

—H. E. High.

Looking like a plumber's dream, No. 6160 releases some steam from the cylinder cocks at Denver in May, 1939.

—B. G. Corbin.

The Class M-3, 2-10-2 types were built by the Brooks Works in 1919, and followed the U.S.R. A. standards for locomotive design. Their general appearance and construction details were similar to the 0-4 Mikados, except that Southern valve gear was employed. The M-3 engines were assigned to the road as No. 6300-6309. They operated on a boiler pressure of 190 psi, weighed in at 293,000 lb. on drivers, and exerted a tractive force of 73,800 lb. Their cylinder dimensions were identical to the Class M-2 and M-2A engines. The M-3 locomotives saw most of their service on Colorado and Southern tracks, as they were leased to this subsidiary by the parent Burlington. All of the engines were equipped with Worthington feedwater heaters except No. 6303 and 6308, which were fitted with Elesco systems. The U.S.R.A. Santa Fe types performed notably during their 30 years of service on the road.

The U.S.R.A. engines were delivered to the road with the large letters on the tender.
Built by Brooks in 1919, No. 6306 was classed as an M-3.   —Brooks Loco. Wks.

No. 6301 at Denver in May, 1941. Notice the added tender panels to increase the coal-carrying capacity.

—R. R. Wallin Collection.

No. 6300 was getting serviced at Denver in Oct., 1938.

—B. G. Corbin

No. 6308 at the
Denver roundhouse
in August, 1940.

—B. G. Corbin

THE CLASS M-4, TEXAS TYPES

The M-4, 2-10-4 type engines were the undisputed champions of the Burlington in hauling long, heavy freight drags. Twelve of these locomotives, No. 6310-6321, were built by Baldwin in 1927, and were followed by six additional engines, No. 6322-6327, in 1929. The M-4 Class were used principally in hauling coal on the Beardstown division. When built, their 31" x 32" cylinders, 64" drivers, and their weight-on-drivers of over 353,000 lb. gave them a tractive force of 90,000 lb.

The boilers of the M-4 engines were straight on top, but the second ring sloped downward on the bottom to give a boiler diameter of 92" at the first ring and 104" at the throat. The weight of the mammoth radially stayed firebox was supported by a four-wheel, cast-steel truck of the Commonwealth type. Steam distribution was controlled by 15" piston valves actuated by Baker valve gear. Duplex stokers, Schmidt type-E superheaters, Barco power-reverse mechanisms, soot blowers, and feedwater-heating systems were standard equipment on the Class M-4 locomotives.

Because of the large
boilers, the stacks on
the M-4A engines
were short in order
to maintain
clearances. No. 6322.
Date and place
unknown.

—Al Holck

M-4A, No. 6320, at
Centralia, Ill. in Feb.,
1950.

—Al Holck

Next to the 0-5 Northerns and the S-4 Hudsons, the 2-10-4 types were perhaps the most handsome and photogenic motive power used on the System. During the late 1930's the M-4 engines were upgraded for high-speed mainline service. This was accomplished by fitting them with disc-centered main drivers, roller bearings, light-weight main rods and reciprocating parts, and by reducing the cylinder bore from 31" to 28". The engines receiving these modifications were classed as M-4A. Although their operating speed was increased, their tractive force was reduced to 83,300 lb. Without a doubt, the M-4 types were some of the most efficient motive power used on the Burlington System.

M-4, No. 6313 had a new paint job when snapped at Galesburg in August, 1937.

No. 6323 was on display for a railfans' excursion at Galesburg in July, 1956.

—Lou Schmitz Collection.

The M-4A brutes were capable of pulling 150 carloads of coal from the Southern Illinois coal fields without assistance. No. 6311 at Centralia, Ill.— July, 1955.

—R. R. Wallin Collection.

Getting up a head of steam, No. 6324 waits at Pacific Junction, Iowa in April, 1945.

—B. G. Corbin

THE CLASS T, MALLETS

The articulated compound never met with any great success on the Burlington. During the years, 1908-1911, all nineteen of the Mallets that operated on the System were built by the Baldwin Locomotive Works. The first of the articulated engines, Class T-1, 2-6-6-2 types, were delivered in 1908 as No. 4000-4002. The locomotives had originally been built for the Great Northern as No. 1905-1907. In 1909 five similar engines, No. 4003-4007, of the 2-6-6-2 wheel arrangement were acquired by the System and classed as T-1A. Engines No. 4000-4002 were later classed as T-1A and No. 4003-4007 became T-1B.

The straight boilers were equipped with wide fireboxes of the Belpaire type, and the steam dome was centrally located on the barrel. External pipes carried the steam from the dome throttle to the high-pressure cylinders. The high-pressure exhaust passed forward through a flexible pipe to the low-pressure cylinders. Balanced slide valves were fitted to all cylinders, and were actuated by Walschaerts-type valve gear. The four valve motions were simultaneously controlled by a Ragonnet power-reverse mechanism. Although the total wheel base of the Class T-1 engines was 44' 10", the rigid wheel base was only 10'; this gave them a great deal of flexibility on sharp curves. The T-1 Mallets were used for several years in hump yard service at Galesburg, Ill. All but No. 4001 were rebuilt to Class F-2, 0-8-0 switchers, in 1926 and 1927. No. 4001 was retired in June, 1927.

A builder's photo of No. 4004, Class T-1A. The Burlington added another sand dome after delivery.   —Baldwin.

No. 4000 gets a little attention at Galesburg in 1923.   —O. H. Means

T-1, No. 4002, at Galesburg in 1923.   —O. H. Means

No. 4007 was rebuilt to an F-2 switcher, No. 554, in 1927.   —O. H. Means.

Ten additional Mallet engines, No. 4100-4109, were delivered in 1910 and were also of 2-6-6-2 wheel arrangement, but differed considerably in dimensions and details compared to the T-1 types. The most novel feature on these Class T-2 engines was the boiler: it was composed of two sections bolted together to form one rigid structure. The joint was located forward of the high-pressure cylinders. The rear section of the boiler was built along conventional lines and contained a smokebox and a superheater of the Emerson type. The forward boiler section consisted of a smokebox containing the exhaust nozzle, netting, and deflection plates; and a feedwater - heater compartment, which was closed by front and rear tube sheets connected by 406 smoke tubes, 2¼" in diameter, and one large flue 17" in diameter and 8' 11" long.

The injectors, located under the cab, forced water into the front pre-heater section through right and left-side check valves. The heated feedwater left the front section through an outlet on the top centerline, and entered the evaporating section through right and left-side check valves located near the forward part of the rear boiler section. With this arrangement, the pre-heater section was always full of water at operating boiler pressure. The exhaust steam from the high-pressure cylinders first passed through a nest of 19 tubes, each 2" in diameter and located within the 17" flue, before entering the low-pressure cylinders. This arrangement reheated the steam, by taking some of the energy from the hot furnace gases that passed around the tubes and through the large flue.

The firebox on the T-2 articulateds was of the radially stayed type, and its weight was supported by a Hodges trailing truck. The engines were designed to operate on 1.6 grades and 20 degree curves. Although they were initially built to burn lignite fuel, the T-2 Mallets were later converted to oil burners. The water-injection system was also altered, and Elesco feedwater systems were later applied to some of the engines. In general, the Class T-2 engines were difficult to maintain. They were primarily used in the Black Hills on the Edgemont-Deadwood line, but occasionally served as helpers in the Bridgeport, Nebr. area. By the end of 1949, all of the T-2 Class had been retired.

Deep in the heart of the Black Hills, T-2, No. 4100 was shifting cars at Mysic, S. D. in May, 1939.
— B. G. Corbin.

All of the T-2 Mallets were converted to oil burners. No. 4101 stands idle at Denver in Nov., 1948.

—R. H. Kindig

The Elesco heater on this T-2 compound was mounted on a bracket above the smoke-box. No. 4107 at Hill City, S. D.—July, 1941. —B. G. Corbin.

No. 4108 had just come from the Denver shops when this photo was taken at Tampa, Colo., on June 6, 1939. —Joe Schick.

Engine No. 4105, Class T-2 wheels a two-car passenger train, No. 141, near Nahant, So. Dakota on Nov. 21, 1945. —W. R. McGee.

Only one engine of the 2-8-8-2 wheel arrangement was ever used on the Burlington. This locomotive was classed as T-3 and was placed in service in 1911 as No. 4200. When built, the T-3 Mallet weighed 448,000 lb., with 406,000 lb. on the drivers. Its boiler was in two sections as on the T-2 engines. With cylinders of 26" and 40" x 32", and a boiler pressure of 200 psi, the 2-8-8-2 type developed a notable tractive force of 93,000 lb.

The original water-injection system on the T-3 was later modified, and the engine was eventually converted to burn oil. It was first placed in service around the Galesburg area, but this orphan Mallet spent its last days in the western divisions around Alliance, Nebraska.

The T-3 Mallet as it appeared when it was first delivered by Baldwin. —B. G. Corbin Collection.

No. 4200 at work at Browning Hill, St. Louis Division, in Aug., 1912. —B. G. Corbin Collection.

The second version of the 4200 after rebuilding at W. Burlington in 1920. —B. G. Corbin Collection.

No. 4200 as she looked after being converted to oil. Alliance, Nebr.—1932.　　–B. G. Corbin Collection.

TENDERS AND DETAILS

Tender on No. 4978.

The coal bunker on the tender of this G-5A switcher had been extended for greater capacity.

The type of tender used on many Class R, Class S-1 and Class H engines. Now in work train service.

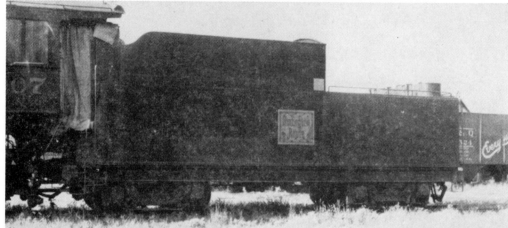

Tender for a B-1 Lima Mountain.

The mammoth tender used on the M-4 Class.

A 13,000 gal. tender used on the 0-3 engines.

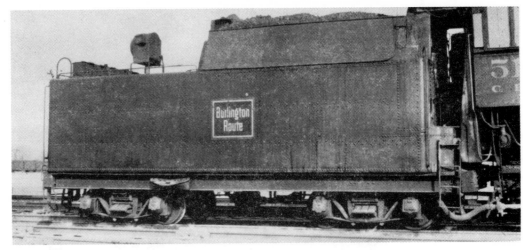

The coping on the tender of this 0-1A engine has been sloped for better visibility in switching service.

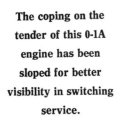

Tender used on the Class 0-5B oil burners.

The standard tender used on the S-4A engines.

A tender from a Class S-2 engine fitted for use with a wrecking crane at Lincoln, Nebr.

—Lou Schmitz

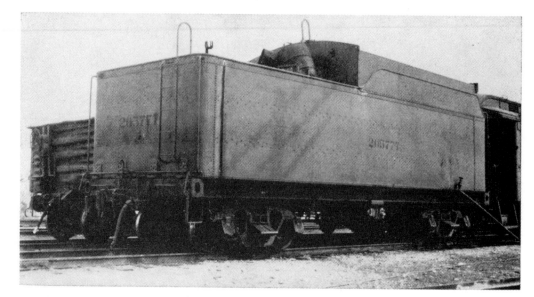

An ex U.S.R.A.
tender from a Class
M-3 engine.

Tender on Hudson
No. 4001.

Tender on a K-4
engine fitted for oil.

Builder's plate on the O-5A Class.

—Lou Schmitz.

Rear-end view
of the tender on No. 4001.

The Hodges trailing

truck used on the

T-2 engines.

The Worthington

feedwater pump on

an O-1A.

The front of exhibition engine No. 35.
—L. L. Fiehert.

Class R-5 front-end arrangement.

Front-end view of the 0-3 Mikado.

No. 6324, a big locomotive from any angle.
—R. C. Jack.

The front-end arrangement on the O-5A
Northerns gave them a formidable appearance.

No. 3007 was pulling the Aristocrat at Denver in
April, 1934. —H.E. High.

The running gear on No. 5346, a Class O-3.
—Lou Schmitz.

Front-end detail on No. 5617.

The large firebox of the 0-5A was supported on a four-wheeled Commonwealth trailing truck. This truck was also used on M-4 and S-4 engines.

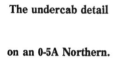

The undercab detail

on an 0-5A Northern.

Turret detail on No.

4001.

Cab view of the
fireman's side of
Mikado No. 5318.

The Baker valve-
gear arrangement
on an M-4 engine.

The running gear
and power reverse
of an M-4A.

The cylinders of a standard BK stoker engine.

This early type Elesco feedwater pump was mounted on an 0-1A Mikado.

Cab interior of an 0-5A engine.

Engineer's side of No. 2196, a 2-6-2.
—Don Andrews.

The Elesco pump

used on many of the

Burlington engines.

STEAM OPERATION ON THE BURLINGTON ROUTE

The high point in the operation of the steam power on the Burlington was reached during the mid 1920's. During these golden years of railroading, many early-type engines were still in operation, and with the introduction of new and more modern motive power during this period, the era was indeed one of fascination. The number of steam engines used on the System during the mid 1920's reached an all-time high. The accompanying table shows the distribution of steam power as of December 31, 1925:

TYPE	NUMBER OF LOCOMOTIVES	TRACTIVE FORCE	
		Total	Average per Locomotive
American (4–4–0)	124	1,817,050	14,653
Mountain (4–8–2)	21	1,107,750	52,750
Consolidation (2–8–0)	106	4,258,900	40,178
Switching (0–4–0)	3	33,600	11,200
Switching (0–8–0)	10	500,600	50,060
Switching (0–6–0)	362	10,268,265	28,365
Mogul (2–6–0)	179	3,711,500	20,735
Ten-wheeled (4–6–0)	117	2,506,880	21,426
Santa Fe (2–10–2)	86	6,717,310	78,108
Mikado (2–8–2)	383	22,140,580	57,808
Atlantic (4–4–2)	57	1,355,285	23,777
Prairie (2–6–2)	368	12,183,980	33,109
Pacific (4–6–2)	142	5,227,100	36,810
Mallet Articulated	19	1,362,000	71,684
Totals	1977	73,190,800	37,021

Between the 1890's and 1925, the weight and power of the engines placed in service became greater as the demands for heavier train loadings increased. The accompanying table indicates the average tractive force for the locomotives in service between 1869 and 1925. Also included are the number of engines in service for that particular year:

YEAR	NUMBER OF LOCOMOTIVES	AVERAGE TRACTIVE FORCE PER LOCOMOTIVE	PER CENT INCREASE OVER 1896	
			Number of Locomotives	Tractive Force
1896	990	15,764	. . . .	. . . .
1900	1081	16,927	9.3	7.3
1905	1349	22,346	36.3	41.7
1910	1598	25,737	61.5	63.1
1915	1725	30,606	74.5	94.2
1920	1884	34,500	90.5	118.6
1925	1977	37,021	99.7	134.8

On any large railroad system the distribution and the effective use of motive power becomes a major problem. With over 10,000 miles of line to service, this problem becomes especially important if efficient and economical operation is to be maintained. The greater part of the Burlington System is located on level country, and heavy mountain grades are nowhere encountered,

R-5A, engine No. 2062 on local freight run at Weaver, Iowa. —Wilson Lemberger.

either on mainlines or on branches. There are some marked variations in the profiles of several important divisions, nevertheless, and this fact along with the varying character of weights and speeds of some of the passenger and freight trains was carefully considered in assigning and distributing steam motive power. The volume of passenger traffic on the System varies throughout the season. As the road serves many vacation areas, including the National parks in Colorado and Wyoming, the passenger traffic during the summer months in past years placed increased demands upon its steam power.

The mainline of the Burlington from Denver to Chicago extends a distance of 1,034 miles via Council Bluffs, Iowa, or 1,039 miles via Plattsmouth, Nebraska. From the standpoint of passenger motive power, this distance is divided as follows:

Chicago, Illinois to Burlington, Iowa_____206 miles

Burlington, Iowa to Lincoln Nebraska____ | 345 miles via Council Bluffs
                                           | 350 miles via Plattsmouth

Lincoln, Nebraska to McCook, Nebraska_____228 miles

McCook, Nebraska to Denver, Colorado_____255 miles

Throughout its entire length, the line was protected by automatic signals of the color-light and lower-quadrant, semaphore types. Today the Chicago-Denver line is equipped mainly with C.T.C., with automatic blocks used primarily between Red Oak, Iowa and Galesburg, Ill. Passenger trains were allowed a maximum speed of 60 mph east of Burlington, Iowa; 55 mph between Burlington and Mt. Pleasant, a distance of 28 miles; and 50 mph west of Mt. Pleasant. Fast mail trains were allowed to operate at speeds 5 mph greater than passenger trains.

The country between Chicago and Burlington is quite level, and nowhere along the line does the grade exceed 37 feet per mile. The mail and express trains, and the majority of the fast passenger trains were scheduled at speeds exceeding 40 mph. The heaviest of these trains were hauled by Pacific-type locomotives of the S-3 Class.

An R-3 Prairie coasts into the Somonauk, Ill. station in 1905.   —L. L. Torey.

Between Burlington and Lincoln the grade conditions on the line become more trying, especially where the track crosses the rolling country in southern Iowa. West-bound, the principal grades are as shown in the accompanying table:

LOCATION	LENGTH OF GRADE, MILES	PER CENT
Burlington to West Burlington..............	4	1.00 maximum*
West of Rome.........	4	0.36 to 0.66
Dudley to Maxon.......	11	Maximum 0.88, average about 0.46
Tyrone to Russell.......	13	Maximum 0.88; 3 miles of 0.65
West of Woodburn......	6	Maximum 1.03; greater part 0.60 to 0.66
West of Villisca.........	5	0.62 to 0.66
West of Malvern........	4	0.51 to 0.66
West of Omaha.........	2¼	0.75 to 1.25
Ralston...............	2½	0.90 to 1.25
Chalco Junction........	3	0.55 to 1.00

* Helper used on tonnage freight trains.

The final 24 miles from Ashland, Nebr. to Lincoln are practically level. The principal grades east-bound are as follows:

LOCATION	LENGTH OF GRADE, MILES	PER CENT
Approaching Gretna.....	5½	0.40 to 1.00
Approaching Ralston....	2½	0.15 to 1.00
Approaching South Omaha.........	2½	1.00 to 1.42
Approaching Balfour....	6½	0.18 to 0.66
East of Red Oak........	6	0.45 to 0.66
East of Prescott........	3	0.32 to 0.66
Approaching Harrison...	2¾	0.91 to 1.30
Halpin to Albia........	4½	0.60 to 0.65
East of Ottumwa......	4¾	0.54 to 0.66
Ketcham..............	3	0.62 to 0.66

An early Burlington stock train crosses over the Wabash near Coin, Iowa on the Villisca branch.

—M. D. Lomas

The curvature on this line is light, and exclusive of a few sharp curves in the vicinity of Omaha and Council Bluffs, few curves exceed 3 degrees, and the majority are less than 2 degrees.

East-bound trains that operated through Plattsmouth (rather than through Council Bluffs) approached the Missouri River Bridge, after leaving the Plattsmouth Station, on a one-mile grade which reaches a maximum of 1 percent. Of several sharp curves on this grade, the sharpest is 12 degrees. West-bound, the bridge is approached by a straight grade of 1 percent.

On this run, through passenger trains of 11 cars or less were handled by Pacific-type locomotives. The heaviest work was performed by Class S-3 engines, Class S-1 and S-1A Pacifics being used on lighter trains. For 12 cars or more, Mountain-type engines of the B-1A Class were employed. Crews were changed, and ash pans were dumped at Creston, Iowa, 187 miles west of Burlington.

On the runs already discussed, the engines burned southern Illinois coal. A typical analysis of this fuel is as follows:

Grade of coal	Mine run
Moisture	7.97 per cent
Volatile matter	33.18 "
Fixed carbon	48.23 "
Ash	10.62 "
Sulphur	1.97 "
B.T.U. per pound	11,556

Some of the most interesting operating problems on the mainline were encountered between Lincoln, Nebr. and Denver, a distance of 483 miles. All west-bound trains, and the lighter east-bound trains, changed engines at McCook, Nebr., 228 miles from Lincoln. Between McCook and Lincoln, lighter trains (11 cars or less) were handled by Class S-1 or S-1A Pacifics, and between

B-1A, No. 7011 and Mikado No. 5346 double head through Lincoln, Nebr. in Nov., 1952.
—Dick Rumbolz.

McCook and Denver Class S-1A or S-3 locomotives were used. On this latter run northern Colorado sub-bituminous coal (lignite) was burned. Before the installation of automatic stokers, this fuel was successfully hand-fired. A typical analysis of lignite is as follows:

Grade of coal	1¼" round and 4" square egg
Moisture	19.12 per cent
Volatile matter	33.74 "
Fixed carbon	42.24 "
Ash	4.72 "
Sulphur	0.29 "
B.T.U. per pound	10,075

Between Lincoln and McCook the mainline runs through prairie country which is practically level. However, west of McCook the conditions become more severe. Here the prairie rises gradually, and in the 143-mile distance between McCook and Akron, Nebr., the elevation increases by 2,150 feet. This represents an average grade of 15 feet per mile. In the 55.3-mile distance between Wray and Akron, the increase in elevation is 1,140 feet; this represents an average of 21.4 feet per

Ten-Wheeler No. 637, a Class K-2, was hauling 10 cars of nursery stock from Shenandoah to Red Oak, Iowa. She was making a run for a grade that lay ahead.

—B. G. Corbin.

—153—

mile, the maximum grade being 0.60 percent or 31.7 feet per mile. The Wray-to-Akron line is almost straight, the maximum curvature being 2 degrees. One section is tangent for a distance of 25 miles.

These forementioned grade conditions were not in themselves particularly severe. Considering that at times the heaviest trains were composed of 21 or 22 cars, and that the fastest schedule, with lighter trains, was in excess of an average speed of 40 mph, a difficult operation in assigning steam power was presented. Trains of 12 or more cars were handled by 4-8-2 type locomotives of either the B-1 or B-1A Class. These engines worked west-bound out of McCook to Denver, and after a short lay-over they ran east-bound to Lincoln on a through-run of 483 miles. At Lincoln they were returned on a west-bound train and ran as far as McCook, where a change in locomotives was made. This run was equivalent to a round trip of nearly 1,000 miles. Boilers were washed at McCook during each lay-over, as it was found necessary to start out with a clean boiler and fresh water to meet the challenge of the hard westward run.

When the Mountain types were first placed in service on this run, it was intended to burn lignite as fuel. Due to the severe operating requirements it was found that steam failures were likely to occur; hence, the engines were converted to burn Walsenburg Colorado coal with great success. This fuel ran high in ash, but it had a higher heating value compared to lignite. The Walsenburg coal was clean to handle, and threw but a small amount of cinders. When properly fired, it produced very little smoke.

On these long runs, engine crews were changed (east-bound) at Akron, McCook, and Hastings, this last location being 97 miles west of Lincoln. At McCook the locomotive grates were shaken and the ash pan was dumped. On west-bound runs, crews were changed at Hastings and Akron; and as has been previously noted, locomotives and crews were changed at McCook. The engines in this service made about 9,000 miles per month, and motive power was assigned so that each locomotive handled trains that were within its capacity. Thus double heading was necessary on exceptional occasions only.

The following table outlines the operation of trains No. 1 and 6, and No. 2 and 3, used in mainline service. In their day trains 2 and 3 were the heaviest on the road, and were frequently made up, during the tourist season, of 21 or 22 cars. No helpers were used on any of these runs.

The snow-drifted prairie near McLean, Neb. was shadowed by the smoke from a
Burlington 2-6-2 and an Atlantic which were teaming together behind a rotary plow.   —O. H. Smith.

Train No. 1—Denver Limited

Between	Distance Miles	Class of Locomotive Used	No. of Cars	Weight of Train Back of Tender — Tons	Running Time	No. of Inter-mediate Stops	Average Speed, Miles per Hour
					Hrs. Mins.		
Chicago and Burlington..............	206	S–3	11	786	4 — 57	5	41.7
Burlington and Lincoln (via Plattsmouth)..	350	S–3	11	758	9 — 55	9	35.9*
Lincoln and McCook.................	228	S–1–A	11	731	5 — 36	4	40.7
McCook and Denver..................	255	S–1–A	11	786	6 — 29	4	39.4

* Allowing 10 minutes for long station stop.

Train No. 6—Chicago Limited

Between	Distance Miles	Class of Locomotive Used	No. of Cars	Weight of Train Back of Tender — Tons	Running Time	No. of Inter-mediate Stops	Average Speed, Miles per Hour
					Hrs. Mins.		
Denver and Lincoln..................	483	B–1 and B–1-A	11	731	12 — 10	8	40.9*
Lincoln and Burlington (via Plattsmouth)..	350	S–3	11	786	9 — 47	15	36.9**
Burlington and Chicago................	206	S–3	11	758	5 — 13	7	39.5

* Allowing 22 minutes for long station stops.
**   "   18   "   "   "   "   "

Train No. 3—Overland Express

Between	Distance Miles	Class of Locomotive Used	No. of Cars	Weight of Train Back of Tender — Tons	Running Time	No. of Inter-mediate Stops	Average Speed, Miles per Hour
					Hrs. Mins.		
Chicago and Burlington..............	206	S–3	15	1080	5 — 39	7	36.5
Burlington and Lincoln (via Council Bluffs).	345	B–1-A	20	1480	12 — 35	33	29.2*
Lincoln and McCook.................	228	B–1 and B–1-A	22	1584	6 — 25	6	39.1**
McCook and Denver..................	255	B–1-A	18	1296	7 — 30	5	34.0

* Allowing 45 minutes for long station stops.
**   "   35   "   "   "   "   "

Train No. 2—Overland Express

Between	Distance Miles	Class of Locomotive Used	No. of Cars	Weight of Train Back of Tender — Tons	Running Time	No. of Inter-mediate Stops	Average Speed, Miles per Hour
					Hrs. Mins.		
Denver and Lincoln..................	483	B–1	20 to 22	1480 to 1584	13 — 5	14	38.4*
Lincoln and Burlington (via Plattsmouth)..	350	B–1-A	18	1296	11 — 24	17	32.4**
Burlington and Chicago................	206	S–3	15	1080	5 — 29	4	37.6

* Allowing 30 minutes for long station stops.
**   "   35   "   "   "   "   "

Engine No. 5601 moves a time freight west out of Red Oak on a warm summer evening in July, 1942.

—B. G. Corbin

Freight traffic on the Burlington mainline is diversified. It consists of livestock, grain, food products, manufactured articles, and miscellaneous commodities. This traffic was handled mainly by Class 0-1 and 0-1A Mikado-type locomotives, except on the Creston Division in Iowa, where due to grade conditions, engines of the Classes 0-2, 0-2A, and 0-4 were used. Local freight was handled largely by Prairie-type locomotives of the R-4 and R-5 Classes.

East of Hastings, Nebr., Illinois coal was used for fuel. Stock and preference freight trains that were hauled by locomotives of the Prairie or light-Mikado types were allowed a maximum speed of 40 mph. Other freight trains, using head-end power of the heavier Mikado engines, were allowed speeds of 35 mph. West of Hastings the slower speed applied to all freight trains. On this section of the line, Colorado lignite was used for fuel. The following table shows the tonnage of freight locomotives used on the mainline:

BETWEEN	DISTANCE MILES	RULING GRADE PER CENT		CLASS OF LOCOMOTIVE	TRACTIVE FORCE POUNDS	TONNAGE RATING	
		West Bound	East Bound			West Bound	East Bound
Chicago and Mendota........................	83	.80	.66	0-1-A	58,090	3500	4500
Mendota and Galesburg....................	79	.80	.66	0-1-A	58,090	2600	3800
Galesburg and Burlington.................	42	.66	.66	0-2-A	63,300	4500	3500
Burlington and Ottumwa...................	74	.66	.66	0-2-A	63,300	3100	3100
Ottumwa and Osceola......................	80	.66	.66	0-2-A	63,300	2600	3000
Osceola and Creston.......................	33	.66	.66	0-2-A	63,300	3000	2450
Creston and Villisca.......................	35	.66	.66	0-4	60,000	4000	3000
Villisca and Pacific Junction.............	47	.66	.66	0-4	60,000	3000	3000
Pacific Junction and Lincoln.............	76	.40	.40	R-4 and R-5	35,600	2700	4250
				0-1	58,090	4000	5900
				0-1-A	58,090	4400	6395
				0-2	60,000	4500	6500
				0-4	60,000	4500	6500
Lincoln and Hastings......................	97	.50	.60	0-1	58,090	2800	4800
				0-1-A	58,090	3000	5000
Hastings and McCook......................	131	.50	.60	R-4 and R-5	35,600	2250	2000
				0-1-A	58,090	3500	3100
McCook and Denver........................	255	.80	.70	R-4 and R-5	35,600	2000	2500
				0-1-A	58,090	3200	4600

The ratings for Classes 0-1 and 0-1-A are based on a boiler pressure of 200 lb., and for Class 0-2-A on a boiler pressure of 190 lb.

No. 919 was cruising along at 25 mph west of Altwan, Wyo. with six cars in Dec. 1954.
—Jim Ehernberger.

The Beardstown Division is an important feeder to the mainline. This division covers the southern Illinois coal fields and handles a great deal of heavy traffic. Coal trains made up at Beardstown and other points along the line are hauled northbound to Galesburg, where the cars are humped and distributed for movement to different points. The Beardstown Division is located on level country, and the maximum grades do not exceed 0.3 percent. The coal trains were hauled by 2-10-2 type engines of the M-2, M-2A, and M-3 Classes (and later by Class M-4, 2-10-4 types), which handled from 90 to 100 loaded cars, weighing from 6000 to 7000 tons per train. The speed of these heavy trains were limited to 30 mph. The great majority of the 2-10-2 type locomotives on the Burlington System were at one time concentrated on this division, and they turned in an excellent service record. The M-3 locomotives were later leased to the Colorado and Southern along with a number of M-2A engines.

The two branches of the Burlington System which extend northwest through Wyoming, and terminate on the Northern Pacific at Billings, Montana, pass through areas which are rich in natural resources. These two branches play an important part in handling summer tourist traffic. The more easterly of these two lines terminates at Lincoln, on the mainline, and is composed of the Lincoln, Alliance, and Sheridan divisions. It traverses the northeastern part of Wyoming, an area rich in deposits of lignite. The line formed an important link in the handling of through-passenger traffic between the far Northwest and Kansas City and St. Louis, and to some extent Chicago. This service was furnished by two through trains in each direction per day. An average speed of about 30 mph between Lincoln and Billings, a distance of 841 miles, was maintained. The more important of these trains were No. 41, the Puget Sound Limited, west-bound; and No 42, the Mississippi Valley Limited, east-bound. The locomotive districts on these runs were as follows:

Lincoln to Ravenna, Nebraska_____128 miles
Ravenna to Alliance, Nebraska_____238 miles
Alliance, Nebraska to Sheridan, Wyoming_____333 miles
Sheridan, Wyoming to Billings, Montana_____142 miles

This was the third attempt to open the line west of Campstool, Wyo. in Feb., 1955.
The track had been snow-bound for a week. Engine No. 919 was pushing a wedge plow
mounted on a gondola.   —Jim Ehernberger.

Trains 41 and 42 were at times made up of as many as 15 cars, and were pulled by locomotives of the Class B-1 and B-1A Mountain type, except between Sheridan and Billings where Class S-3 Pacifics were employed. The greater part of this section is relatively level; hence, these engines had sufficient capacity for meeting the schedules.

The most difficult part of this run was between Sheridan, Wyoming and Edgemont, S. D., a distance of 223 miles on the Sheridan-Alliance section. The profile is varied in nature, and shows a succession of ascending and descending grades. Many of them are 0.8 to 1.0 percent; and the maximum grade, which is 1.6 percent and located just south of Sheridan station, stretches for about 1½ miles. Class B-1A locomotives were used on this run; they could handle 14 cars out of Sheridan station and up the grade without assistance.

Lignite was used for fuel on the Sheridan and Alliance Divisions, and was successfully burned in the 4-8-2 type engines, as the service requirements were not so severe as on the mainline run between McCook and Denver. A typical analysis of the Sheridan lignite is as follows:

Grade of coal	Mine run
Moisture	23.10 per cent
Volatile matter	37.73 "
Fixed carbon	35.32 "
Ash	3.85 "
Sulphus	0.41 "
B.T.U.	9,501

A vacationers' special in the Black Hills in May, 1910. The engines are No. 3112, Class D-4A and No. 800, a Class K-5.   —Bostwick Studio.

Burlington passenger train No. 30, eastbound, moves along its run amidst the grandeur of Wyoming's Wind River canyon. The engine is Pacific No. 2808. Burlington Route.

This fuel was comparatively light with respect to its bulk, and it disintegrated rapidly when exposed to the weather. Under a heavy draft lignite literally danced on the grate, and like a wood fire, emitted quantities of fine sparks. For this reason, locomotives burning this type of fuel had all openings in the ash pan carefully screened, and a long smokebox with a large area of fine netting was employed.

In service on the Sheridan and Alliance Divisions, the lignite burning engines steamed freely and emitted practically no smoke. On heavy hauls, with the stoker in continuous operation, the scoop was used to a limited extent to keep the fire properly leveled. When drifting down long grades, the fire could be allowed to burn nearly out, as the lignite ignited very quickly and the fire could again be readily rebuilt. On the run between Sheridan and Alliance, crews were changed at Edgemont, and the fire was cleaned at this point.

Between Lincoln and Billings, through freight was handled mainly by Class 0-1A, 0-2, and 0-2-A Mikado-type locomotives. A number of 2-10-2, Class M-2A engines were also used in this section. On the branch line extending north from Edgemont, and through the Black Hills of South Dakota to Deadwood, a number of Class T-2 Mallets were in service. This line is dominated by relatively steep grades and sharp curves; and here the Mallet engines, with their short rigid wheel base and large hauling capacity, were used to advantage.

The Casper Division lies to the west of the Sheridan and Alliance Divisions. It forms part of a line 672 miles in length which connects Denver to Billings. The section from Denver to Wendover, Wyo., a distance of 243 miles, constitutes part of the Colorado and Southern Railway. Most of the country through which this line runs is sparsely populated. Passenger traffic is handled by one through train per day in each direction. The locomotive districts on this run are as follows:

Denver, Colorado, to Casper Wyoming_____342 miles
Casper, Wyoming, to Greybull, Wyoming_____203 miles
Greybull, Wyoming, to Billings, Montana_____127 miles

Between Denver and Casper these trains were pulled by Class S-3 Pacifics. The engines had initially been built for the C.B.&Q. but were later assigned to the C.&S. North of Casper, locomotives of the S-1 and S-2 Classes were used. Casper is located in a rich oil-producing area, and all steam locomotives used on this run burned oil for fuel.

Barreling through Red Oak, Iowa in 1936 at 65 mph on train No. 38, Hudson No. 3007 was caught in classic pose.

—B. G. Corbin.

No. 5350 at So. Omaha in May, 1949. —Wm. Kratville.

With opened throttle, No. 5359 moves north from Ashland, Nebr. in Dec., 1954.
—Wm. Kratville.

The Casper Division plays an important part in handling the tourist traffic to Yellowstone National Park. From Frannie, Wyo., 72 miles from Billings and 600 miles north of Denver, a branch line runs west to Cody, a distance of 42 miles. Cody is located near the eastern entrance to Yellowstone. Through sleepers were operated from Denver to Cody and also from Cody to Billings. At this point they were distributed for movement to Chicago, Glacier Park, and other destinations. A heavy night train was run in each direction between Cody and Billings, and during the tourist season it was composed of as many as 13 cars, 11 of which were Pullmans. Class S-1 Pacifics were assigned to this service, and because of fairly heavy grade conditions, assistance was given by a 4-6-0, Class K-4 engine between Cody and Duff, a distance of 54 miles.

The Denver-Billings line also handles tourist traffic to and from Rocky Mountain National Park (also known as Estes Park). This park is located in northern Colorado, and is reached from the stations of Longmont and Loveland, 44 and 61 miles from Denver respectively.

The freight traffic on the Casper Division consists chiefly of oil, livestock, grain, and sugar beets. The heavy work was done by Class O-2 and 0-4 Mikados, and the lighter work by Prairie-type locomotives of the R-4 and R-5 Classes.

One of the most important lines in the Burlington System is that which connects Chicago with the "Twin Cities" of St. Paul and Minneapolis. The distance between Chicago and St. Paul is 431 miles. North of Savanna, Ill. the road follows the Mississippi River and is known as the "Burington's Scenic Line." This route handles the "North Coast Limited" of the Northern Pacific and the "Oriental Limited" of the Great Northern Railway. In addition a heavy night train operates in each direction between Chicago and the Twin Cities. At the height of its career, this train was composed of from 12 to 15 cars, and was hauled by Pacific-type engines of the S-1A and S-2A Classes. Freight traffic over this line had been handled primarily by 2-6-2 type locomotives of the R-4 and R-5 Classes.

The network of lines of the Burlington System traversing the states of Iowa, Missouri, and Nebraska, south of the east-west mainline, pass through land rich in livestock and grain. These lines handled through-passenger traffic from St. Louis and Kansas City to locations to the north and west. In addition a large amount of local and branch-line traffic was handled in this area. Relatively light engines of the Mogul and Ten-Wheeler types were used in this service. During the mid 1920's, engines of the A-2 Class were also seen doing their share of this branch-line work.

No. 5632 makes a movie run for delighted railfans at Altona, Ill., in April, 1959.

—Burdell L. Bulgrin.

A meet at Ralston, Nebr. in the summer of 1956. An O-1A Mikado heads into a siding while No. 5344 hold the main. Wm. Kratville.

An important segment of the Burlington's passenger business is the suburban traffic in and out of Chicago. Today this amounts to about 19,000 passengers each way per day. The suburban runs terminate at either Downers Grove or Aurora, which are 21 and 38 miles respectively from the Chicago Union Station. On the three tracks between Chicago and Aurora, the middle track is used for east-bound trains in the morning and west-bound trains in the evening. In past years the majority of these suburban runs were handled by 4-6-0 type engines of the K-1 and K-2 Classes. Later the K-10 Ten Wheelers assumed a segment of this duty; and in the closing years of steam operation on the System, down-graded Class S-1A and S-2A Pacifics performed these chores. Some of the suburban express trains, making only a few stops between Chicago and Aurora, were handled by Class P-6 and P-6A Atlantics.

The following table shows the growth in mileage of the Burlington System, and in the volume of freight handled over the years from 1860 to 1925.

YEAR	MILEAGE OF ROADS OPERATED	TONS OF FREIGHT CARRIED	TONS CARRIED ONE MILE	AVERAGE DISTANCE HAULED (MILES)	FREIGHT TRAIN MILES
1860	310	407,314	50,133,472	123.08	433,112
1870	603	775,829	147,409,207	190.00	1,506,606
1880	2,772	6,639,186	Not Available		
1890	6,331	11,201,873	1,978,896,694	176.66	13,126,619
1900	7,545	15,393,217	3,793,008,334	246.40	19,190,694
1905	8,561	20,399,557	5,188,952,589	254.36	14,198,894
1910	9,023	27,867,618	7,435,144,216	266.80	18,595,294
1915	9,339	31,758,791	8,527,444,254	268.51	16,490,454
1920	9,371	47,233,256	14,130,364,374	299.16	20,929,164
1925	9,399	43,308,852	12,298,287,741	283.97	17,789,818

By comparison, in 1955 the C.B.&Q. was comprised of 8,806 miles of track (since 1917 the System has abandoned 886 miles of unprofitable line); the tons of freight carried was 49,183,080; the revenue ton-miles was 16.1 billion; and the average distance that freight was hauled was 327 miles.

From 1860 to 1900 the tons of freight carried per train increased from 115 to 198, or an increase of 72 percent in 40 years. From 1900 to 1925 the tons per train increased from 198 to 692, or 244 percent in only 25 years. The increased hauling capacity of the locomotives were directly responsible for these statistics. The accompanying table indicates the number of freight engines on the road, their total tractive force, and the average tractive force per engine from the year, 1900 to 1925.

YEAR	NUMBER OF FREIGHT LOCOMOTIVES	TOTAL TRACTIVE FORCE POUNDS	AVERAGE TRACTIVE FORCE PER LOCOMOTIVE	
			Pounds	Per Cent Increase over 1900
1900	307	6,712,820	21,865	. . . .
1905	482	13,243,340	27,473	25
1910	778	24,216,240	31,126	42
1915	945	34,776,420	36,800	68
1920	1025	41,867,920	40,846	86
1925	976	41,563,820	42,582	95

It is evident that from 1900 to 1925 the average tractive force per freight engine increased by 95 percent, yet the revenue tons carried per train increased by 244 percent during this same period. This was mainly due to the increased capacity of freight cars together with their lower frictional resistance, the reduction of grades and curves, the improvement of track and roadbed, and the use of more advanced methods of train loading.

BIBLIOGRAPHY — SECTION 2
The material in Section 2 was derived, for the most part, from the following publication:
"The Locomotives of the Chicago, Burlington and Quincy Railroad" by Paul T. Warner, The Baldwin Locomotive Works, Philadelphia, Pa., 1936.
OTHER REFERENCES
1. "Locomotives of the C.B. & Q. Railroad", Railway & Locomotive Historical Society, Inc., Bulletin of September, 1936.
2. Locomotive Elevation Drawings issued to roundhouse foremen by C.B. & Q. Railroad.

C&S engine No. 902 with an auxiliary tender emerges from tunnel No. 1 just west of Guernsey, Wyo. while pulling 32 cars of iron ore at 25 mph in Sept., 1958.

—Jim Ehernberger.

LOCOMOTIVES OF THE COLORADO AND SOUTHERN

The spark arrestor on Narrow Guage No. 6, a 2-6-0, was a means of getting cinders back on the roadbed.

—H. E. High.

The top of the boiler was the only place with room enough to mount the air tanks on No. 70, a B-4D. Denver, Colo.,—Oct., 1940.

—L. E. Griffith.

No. 74, a Class B-4F, was ready for a hard winter when this photo was taken at Leadville, Colo. in Sept., 1941.

—L. E. Griffith.

Class A-3E2, No. 236.
Denver, Colo. in
May, 1941.

—Al Holck.

No. 233 at Denver,
Colo.—May, 1937.

—H. E. High.

No. 455, a Class B-4F,
at Denver, Colo. in
1938.

—L. E. Griffith.

No. 644 was an oil
burner and was
classed as B-4R1.
Denver, Colo.—
May, 1939.

—Al Holck.

Class B-4R, No. 641, at Denver, in Sept., 1938.

—L. E. Griffith.

No. 528 was away from home territory when it was switching at Pacific Junction, Iowa in Nov., 1937.

—B. G. Corbin.

No. 610, Class B-4R, was built by Richmond in 1902. Denver, Colo. in May, 1941.

—L. E. Griffith.

No. 802, Class E-4A, was making some road tests near Denver in about 1920.

—L. E. Griffith.

Plenty of piping was the keynote of Mikado No. 801, a Class E-4A. Caught working at North Kansas City, Mo. in Oct., 1947.

—Al Holck.

No. 800, an oil burner, stands at Cheyenne, Wyo. in Oct. 1955.

—Al Holck.

No. 5506 still carried its Burlington number when in service on the C & S at Horse Creek, Wyo. in Oct., 1957.

—Jim Ehernberger.

No. 902, an E-5A, was fitted with a Worthington feedwater heater. Denver, Colo. in Sept., 1947.

—Al Holck.

No. 907, a U.S.R.A. engine, was classed as E-5B on the C&S.

—B. G. Corbin. Collection.

Class E-5C, No. 910 has just come in from a hard day's work. Denver—Aug., 1939.

—L. E. Griffith.

No. 905 was hauling tonnage through Denver in 1938.

—H. E. High.

—171—

Class E-5A, No. 904 was similar to the Burlington's M-2A locomotives. Fort Collins, Colo., Nov., 1956.

—Al Holck.

Denver, Colo.

Engine No. 309, a Class C-3E, was heading a milk train at Union Station in Denver in 1927.

—H. E. High.

Pacific No. 370, an F-3B, was ex CB&Q No. 2970. Denver—July, 1936.

—Al Holck.

C&S No. 371 was ex CB&Q No. 2973. Denver, Colo. in July, 1938.

—L. E. Griffith.

A load of timber passes French Gulch tank on the Leadville-to-Climax line.

—Jim Ehernberger.

C&S No. 323 was used on the Black Hills line. Edgemont, S. D. in 1932.

—Lad Arend.

Early days on the Colorado & Southern. Pacific No. 350 heads some varnish over the great plains of Colorado in about 1912.

—B. G. Corbin. Collection

No. 352, Class F-3A, waits at the Union Station at Denver in 1925.

—H. E. High.

No. 644 was on a sugar-beet run at Fort Collins in Dec., 1957.   —Jim Ehernberger.

Narrow-gauge engine No. 73, a 2-8-0, climbs Kenosha Pass west of Webster, Colo.
with 12 cars at 5 mph on July 14, 1938.   —R. H. Kindig

Sanding her flues, engine No. 804 blast through Fort Collins, Colo. in the fall of 1958.
—Jim Ehernberger.

C&S engines No. 903 and 902 doublehead on a southbound freight at Altus, Wyo. in Oct., 1957.
—Jim Ehernberger.

LOCOMOTIVES OF THE FORT WORTH AND DENVER

A builder's photo of 2-6-0, No. 21. Built in 1886.　　　　　—Schenectady.

This 4-4-0, No. 38,
was still in service at
Wichita Falls, Texas
in April, 1938.

—Jim Ehernberger

No. 50 was built by
Schenectady in 1908.
Manchester terminal
at Houston, Texas in
Dec., 1938.

—Charles Keifner

—177—

Switcher No. 68 at Fort Worth Texas in Dec., 1934.

—Robert Graham

No. 206 was built by Rhode Island in 1903. Wichita Falls, Texas in April, 1942.

—W. R. McGee

Slide-valved No. 250 was at Amarillo, Texas on Sept. 3, 1938.

—Robert Graham

No. 310 at Wichita
Falls, Texas in
March, 1942.

—W. R. McGee

Consolidation No. 312,
Class B-4R1, was at
Childress, Texas in
Jan., 1957.

—Al Holck

No. 409, a 2-8-2, was
on a local freight at
Wichita Falls in the
spring of 1956.

—Jim Ehernberger

No. 410 at Wichita
Falls in Sept., 1956.

—Jim Ehernberger

Class E-4A2, No. 453,
at Wichita Falls in
April, 1942.

—W. R. McGee

No. 454, a USRA
Mikado, was at Fort
Worth, Texas in
Aug., 1956.

—Al Holck

Mikado No. 456 waits
for dispatch orders at
Fort Worth in Sept.,
1956.

—Jim Ehernberger

Pacific No. 501 at
Amarillo, Texas in
Sept., 1938.

—Robert Graham.

No. 552, Class F-3A1,
was pulling the Texas
Zephyr at Dallas in
Dec., 1947.

—Al Holck.

No. 556 at
Wichita Falls
in April, 1942.
—W. R. McGee.

HISTORIC SCENES ON THE BURLINGTON ROUTE

The Burlington roundhouse at Galesburg, Ill. in 1869.　　　—Burlington Route.

Twenty-five engines blow their whistles for the adoption of standard time at Creston, Iowa, at 12-noon on Nov. 18, 1883.
—Burlington Route.

Section 3

LOCOMOTIVE PLANS AND SPECIFICATIONS

The locomotive specifications given in this section are based on the information included in the Burlington's erection prints for engines. The specifications in the text of Section 2, for the most part, are based on the data given in past Baldwin Locomotive Works publications. Any observed differences, therefore, are due to the builder's ratings as compared to the road's rating of its motive power.

The following locomotive plans can be readily reproduced to any desired scale by noting the 10-foot measure included on the drawing. In a number of cases several engines used the same tender. Where this has occurred, the tender plan has been shown only once and reference to this fact has been noted on the page of specifications.

A Class E-1, 0-4-0 engine and two G-4A switchers, No. 1390 and 1423, take time out with their crews for a photograph at Pacific, Junction, Iowa in the early 1900's.

—B. G. Corbin Collection

Class A-2, No. 414, was rebuilt from A-1, No. 101, in 1916. Photo taken at Burlington, Iowa in 1925.

—B. G. Corbin Collection

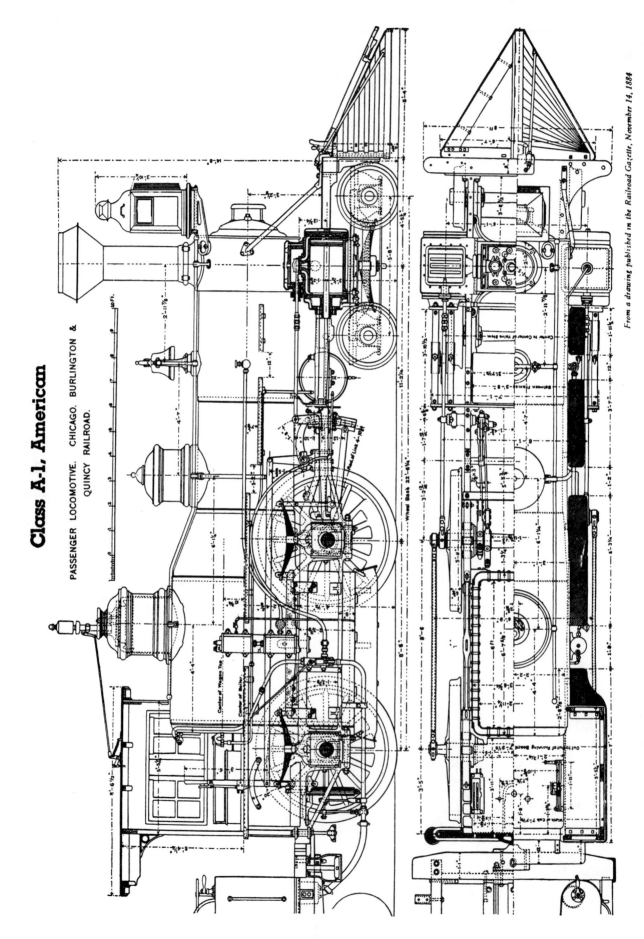

Class A-1, American

PASSENGER LOCOMOTIVE. CHICAGO. BURLINGTON & QUINCY RAILROAD.

From a drawing published in the Railroad Gazette, November 14, 1884

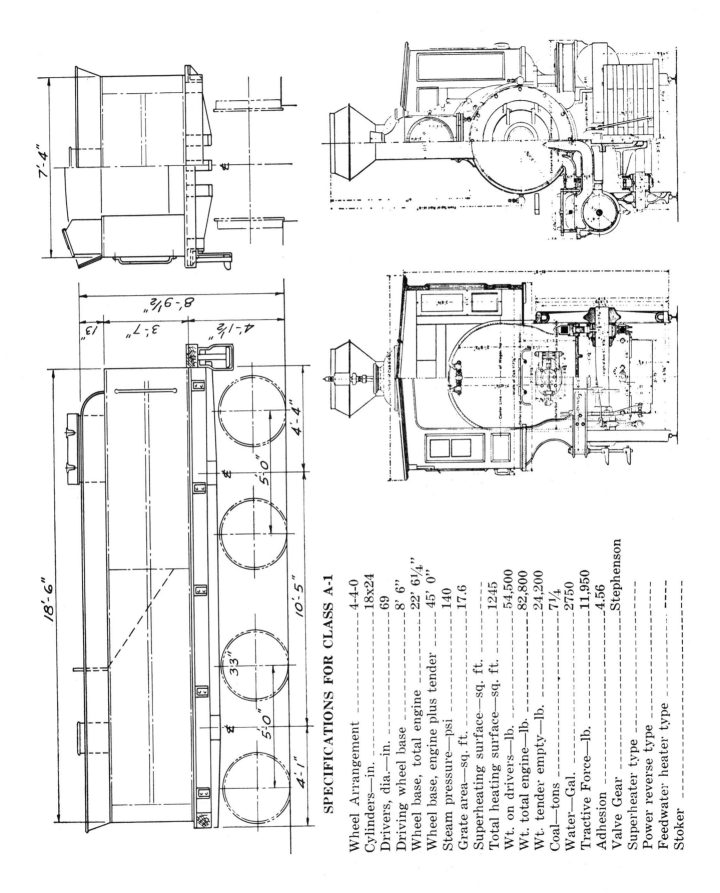

SPECIFICATIONS FOR CLASS A-1

Wheel Arrangement	4-4-0
Cylinders—in.	18x24
Drivers, dia.—in.	69
Driving wheel base	8' 6"
Wheel base, total engine	22' 6¼"
Wheel base, engine plus tender	45' 0"
Steam pressure—psi	140
Grate area—sq. ft.	17.6
Superheating surface—sq. ft.	
Total heating surface—sq. ft.	1245
Wt. on drivers—lb.	54,500
Wt. total engine—lb.	82,800
Wt. tender empty—lb.	24,200
Coal—tons	7¼
Water—Gal.	2750
Tractive Force—lb.	11,950
Adhesion	4.56
Valve Gear	Stephenson
Superheater type	
Power reverse type	
Feedwater heater type	
Stoker	

Class G-3, Switcher

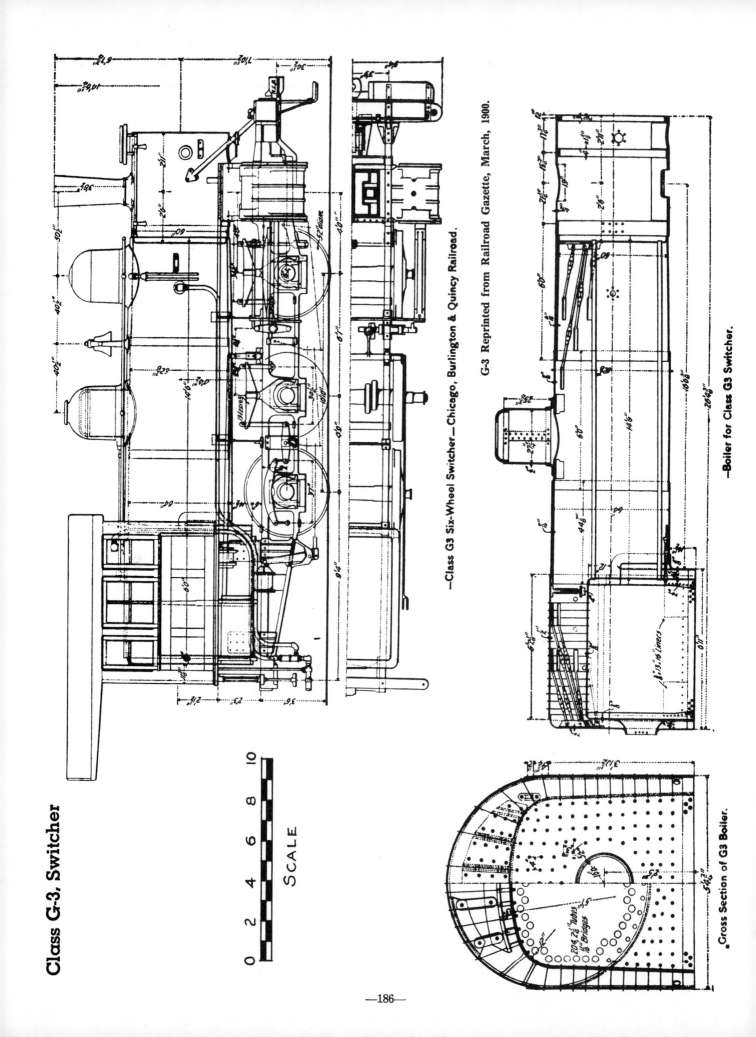

SCALE

—Class G3 Six-Wheel Switcher—Chicago, Burlington & Quincy Railroad.

G-3 Reprinted from Railroad Gazette, March, 1900.

—Boiler for Class G3 Switcher.

*Cross Section of G3 Boiler.

Tender Plan

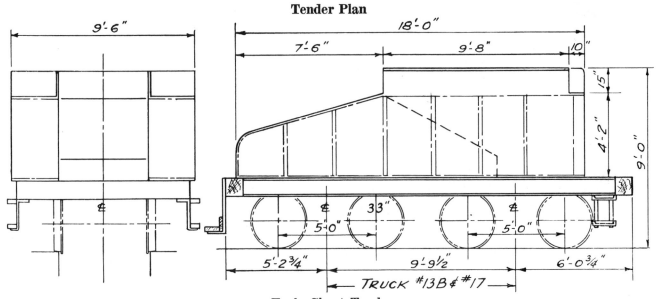

Early Short Tender

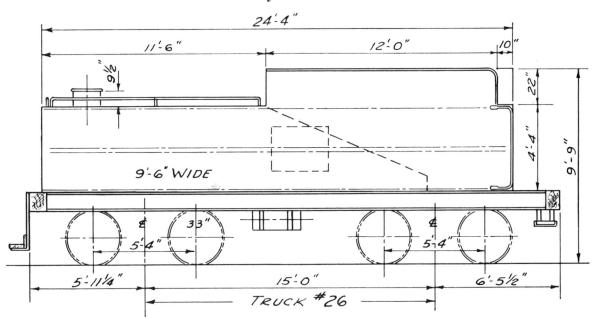

Tender used after 1910.

SPECIFICATIONS FOR CLASS G-3

Wheel Arrangement	0-6-0	
Cylinders—in.	20x24	
Drivers, dia.—in.	52	
Driving Wheel base	10' 10"	
Wheel base, total engine	10' 10"	
Wheel base, engine plus tender	39' 6¾" / 45' 4"	
Steam pressure—psi	180	
Grate area—sq. ft.	27.1	
Superheating surface—sq. ft.	---- / 338.0	
Total heating surface—sq. ft.	1849.6 / 1660.75	
Wt. on drivers—lb.	122,500	
Wt. total engine—lb.	122,500	

Wt. tender empty—lb.	28,500 / 46,500	
Coal—tons	6 / 8	
Water—Gal.	3900 / 6000	
Tractive Force—lb.	28,200	
Adhesion	4.35	
Valve Gear	Stephenson	
Superheater type	---- / Emerson	
Power reverse type		
Feedwater heater type		
Stoker	----	

Class G-5, Switcher

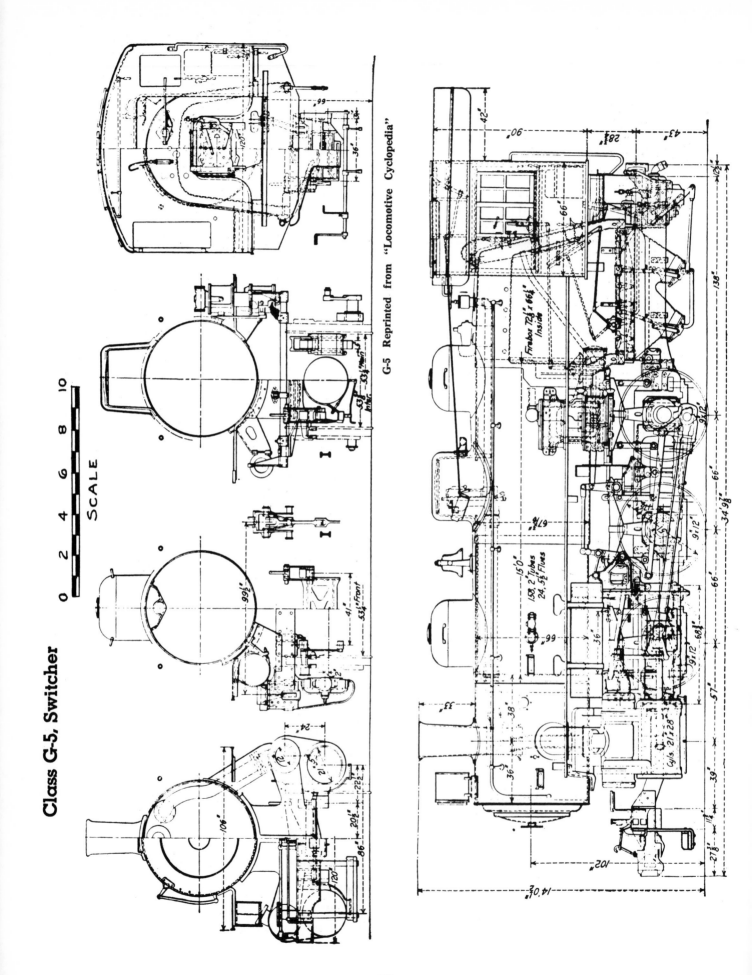

SCALE

G-5 Reprinted from "Locomotive Cyclopedia"

Tender plan for G-5A engine.
For G-5 tender, see Class F-1.

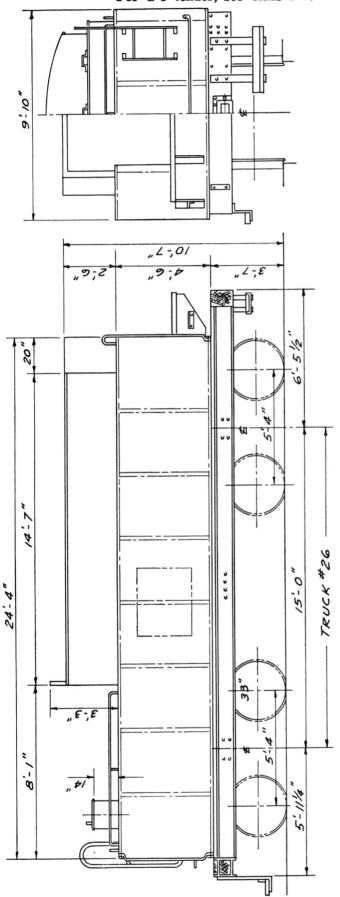

SPECIFICATIONS FOR CLASS G-5

Wheel Arrangement	0-6-0
Cylinders—in.	21x28
Drivers, dia.—in.	52
Driving Wheel base	11' 0"
Wheel base, total engine	11' 0"
Wheel base, engine plus tender	49' 9¼"
Steam pressure—psi	190
	200
Grate area—sq. ft.	33.2
Superheating surface—sq. ft.	409.0
Total heating surface—sq. ft.	2303.0
Wt. on drivers—lb	165,000
Wt. total engine—lb.	165,000
Wt. tender empty—lb.	60,150
	70,040*
Coal—tons	16
Water—Gal.	8000
Tractive Force—lb.	38,350
	40,370
Adhesion	4.30
	4.09
Valve Gear	Baker
Superheater type	Schmidt-A
Power reverse type	Mellin
Feedwater heater type	....
Stoker	....

* Original U.S.R.A. Tender design

Class F-1, Switcher

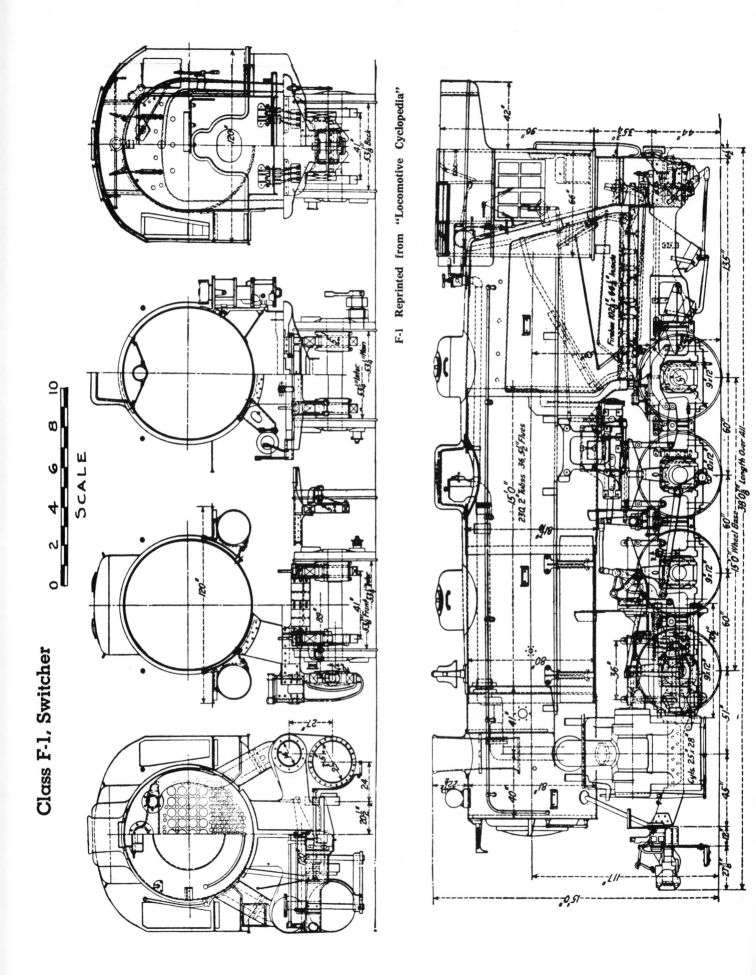

F-1 Reprinted from "Locomotive Cyclopedia"

SCALE

0 2 4 6 8 10

Tender Plan

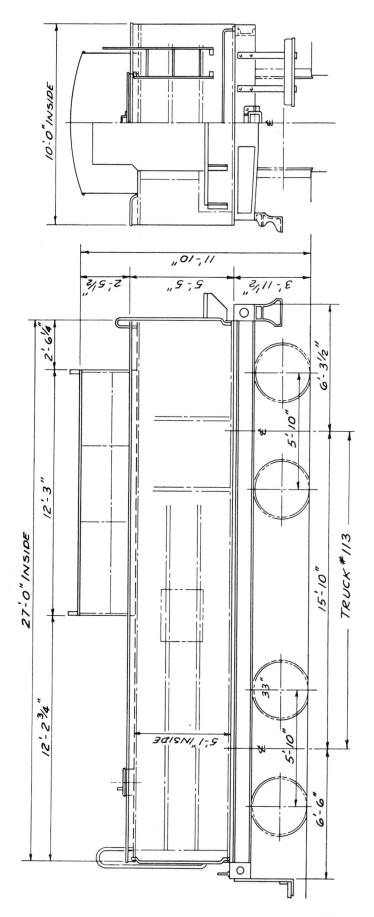

SPECIFICATIONS FOR CLASS F-1

Wheel Arrangement	0-8-0
Cylinders—in.	25x28
Drivers, dia.—in.	52
Driving Wheel base	15' 0"
Wheel base, total engine	15' 0"
Wheel base, engine plus tender	53' 0½"
Steam pressure—psi	175 / 190
Grate area—sq. ft.	47.0
Superheating surface—sq. ft.	614.0
Total heating surface—sq. ft.	3395.0
Wt. on drivers—lb.	214,000 / 219,940
Wt. total engine—lb.	214,000 / 219,940
Wt. tender empty—lb.	69,100
Coal—tons	16
Water—Gal.	8000
Tractive Force—lb.	51,000 / 54,350
Adhesion	4.19 / 4.05
Valve Gear	Baker
Superheater type	Loco. S.H. Co. / Schmidt-A
Power reverse type	Lewis
Feedwater heater type	Alco
Stoker	

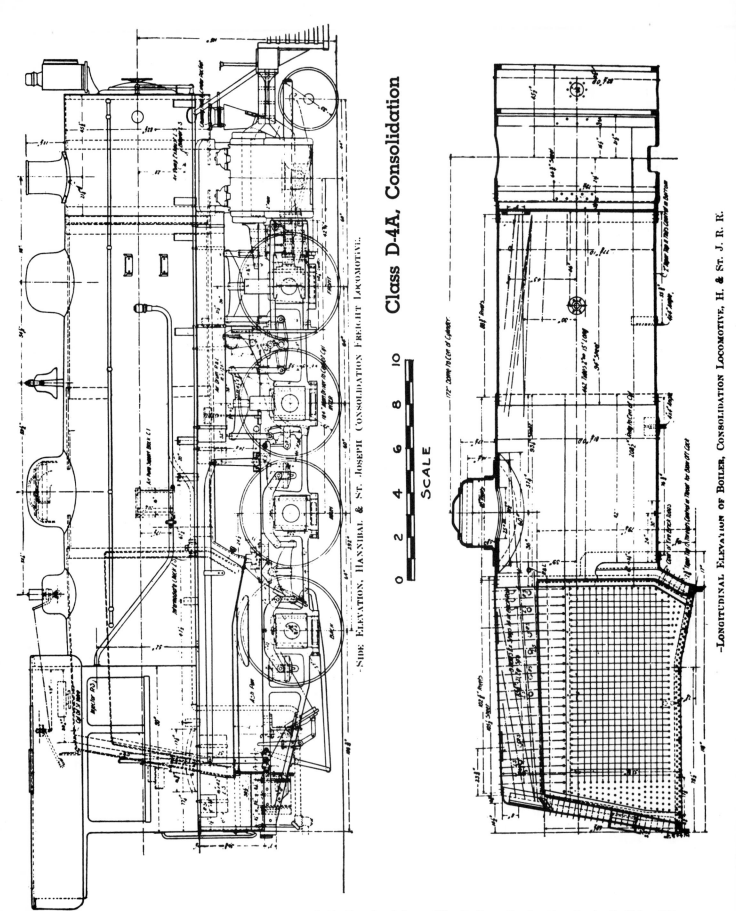

Class D-4A, Consolidation

SCALE

0   2   4   6   8   10

—Side Elevation, Hannibal & St. Joseph Consolidation Freight Locomotive.

—Longitudinal Elevation of Boiler, Consolidation Locomotive, H. & St. J. R. R.

D-4A Reprinted from "The Railway Engineering Review", Feb., 1903.

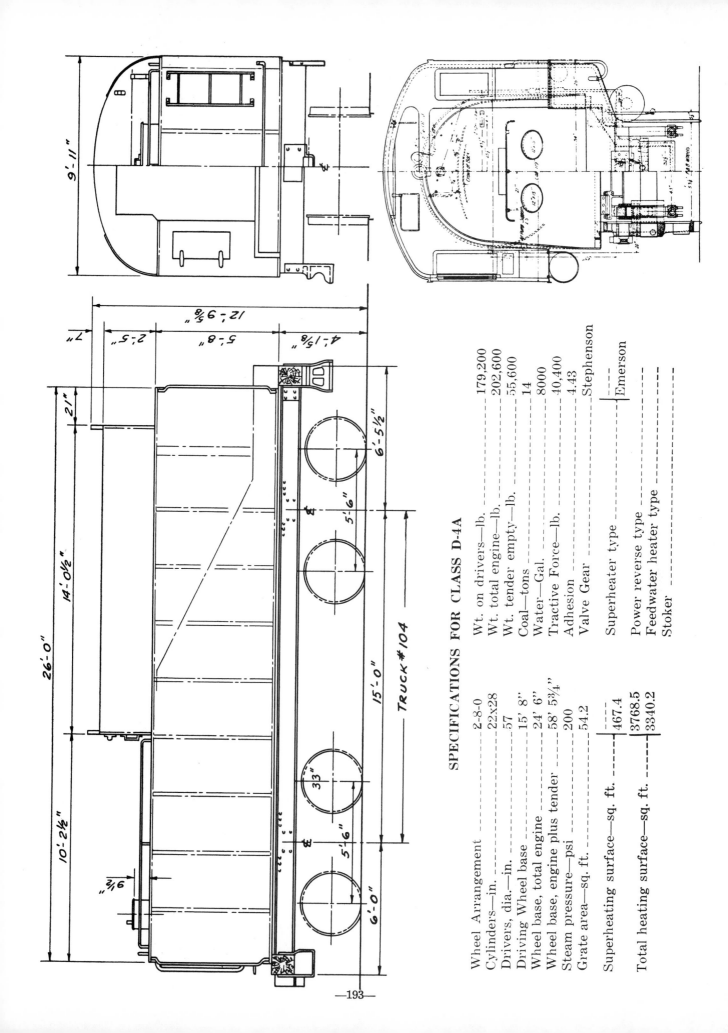

SPECIFICATIONS FOR CLASS D-4A

Wheel Arrangement	2-8-0	
Cylinders—in.	22x28	
Drivers, dia.—in.	57	
Driving Wheel base	15' 8"	
Wheel base, total engine	24' 6"	
Wheel base, engine plus tender	58' 5¾"	
Steam pressure—psi	200	
Grate area—sq. ft.	54.2	
Wt. on drivers—lb.	179,200	
Wt. total engine—lb.	202,600	
Wt. tender empty—lb.	55,600	
Coal—tons	14	
Water—Gal.	8000	
Tractive Force—lb.	40,400	
Adhesion	4.43	
Valve Gear	Stephenson	
Superheater type	Emerson	
Power reverse type		
Feedwater heater type		
Stoker		
Superheating surface—sq. ft.	467.4	
Total heating surface—sq. ft.	3768.5	
	3340.2	

TRUCK #104

Class H-4, Moqul

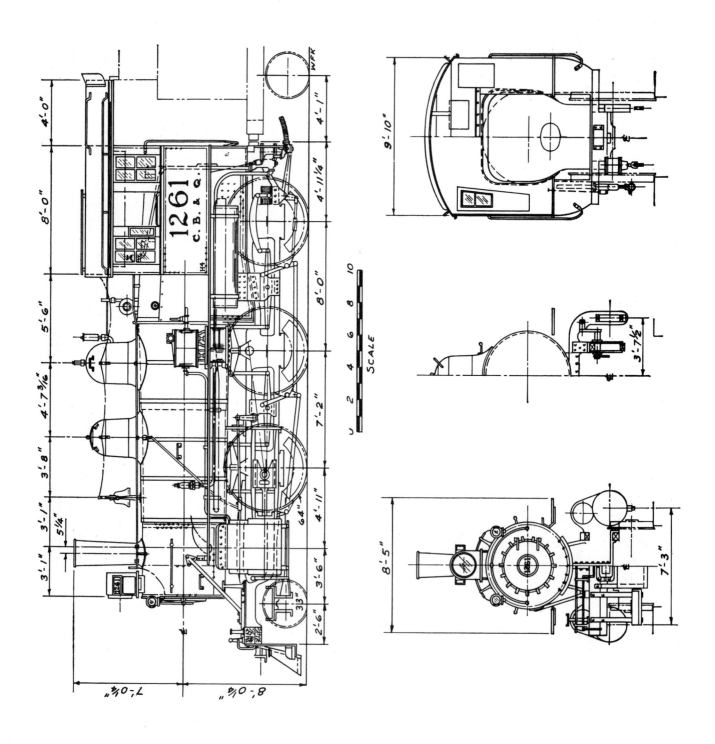

Tender Plan

For original tender see Class K-2

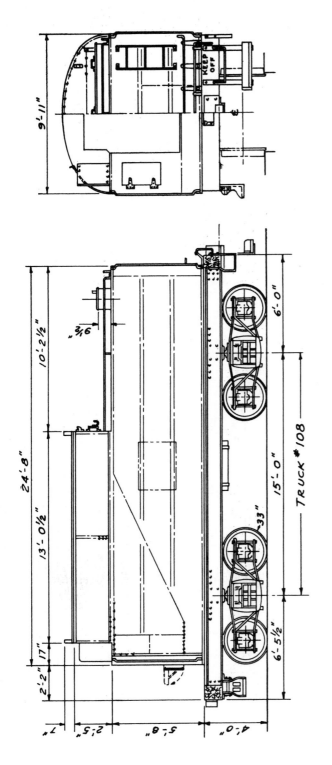

SPECIFICATIONS FOR CLASS H-4

Wheel Arrangement	2-6-0	Wt. total engine—lb.	143,500
Cylinders—in.	19x26	Wt. tender empty—lb.	35,000
Drivers, dia.—in.	64	Coal—tons	9
Driving Wheel base	15' 2"	Water—Gal.	5000
Wheel base, total engine	23' 7"	Tractive Force—lb.	24,900
Wheel base, engine plus tender	48' 7¼"	Adhesion	4.88
Steam pressure—psi	200	Valve Gear	Stephenson
Grate area—sq. ft.	30	Superheater type	
Superheating surface—sq. ft.		Power reverse type	
Total heating surface—sq. ft.	2036.0 / 2052.0	Feedwater heater type	
Wt. on drivers—lb.	121,500	Stoker	

Class K-2, Ten Wheeler

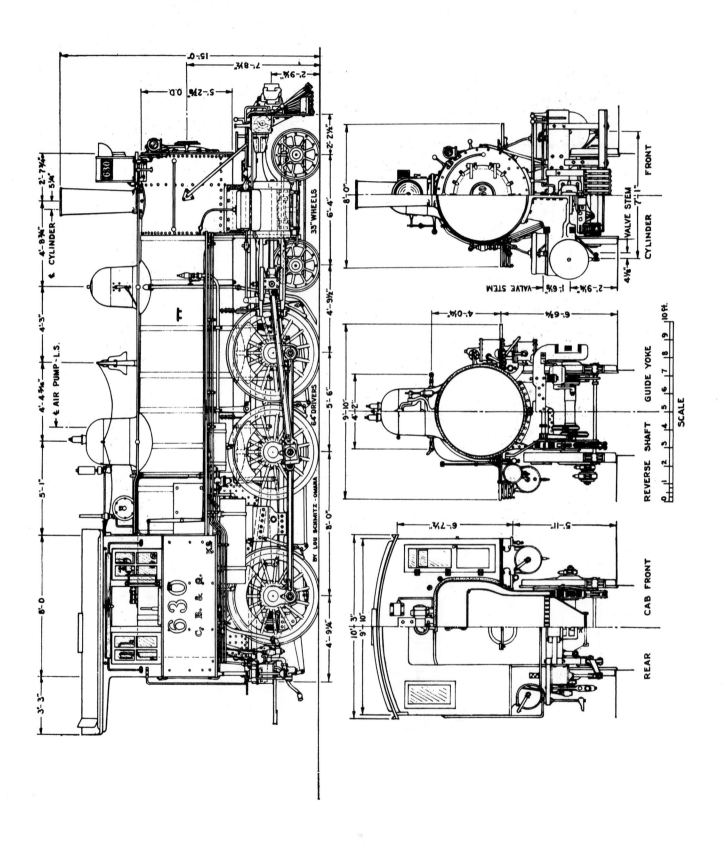

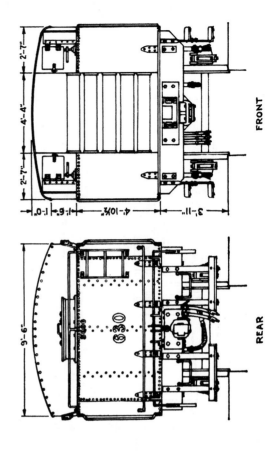

5000 GAL. TENDER

FRONT

REAR

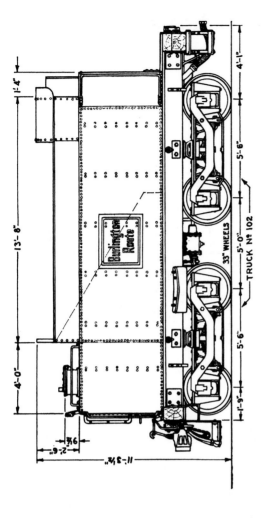

SPECIFICATIONS FOR CLASS K-2

Wheel Arrangement	4-6-0
Cylinders—in.	19x24
Drivers, dia.—in.	64
Driving Wheel base	13' 6"
Wheel base, total engine	24' 7½"
Wheel base, engine plus tender	49' 5¾"
Steam pressure—psi	180
Grate area—sq. ft.	31.5
Superheating surface—sq. ft.	
Total heating surface—sq. ft.	1891.7
Wt. on drivers—lb.	100,700
Wt. total engine—lb.	129,550
Wt. tender empty—lb.	35,000
Coal—tons	9
Water—Gal.	5000
Tractive Force—lb.	20,700
Adhesion	4.86
Valve Gear	Stephenson
Superheater type	
Power reverse type	
Feedwater heater type	
Stoker	

Class K-4, Ten Wheeler

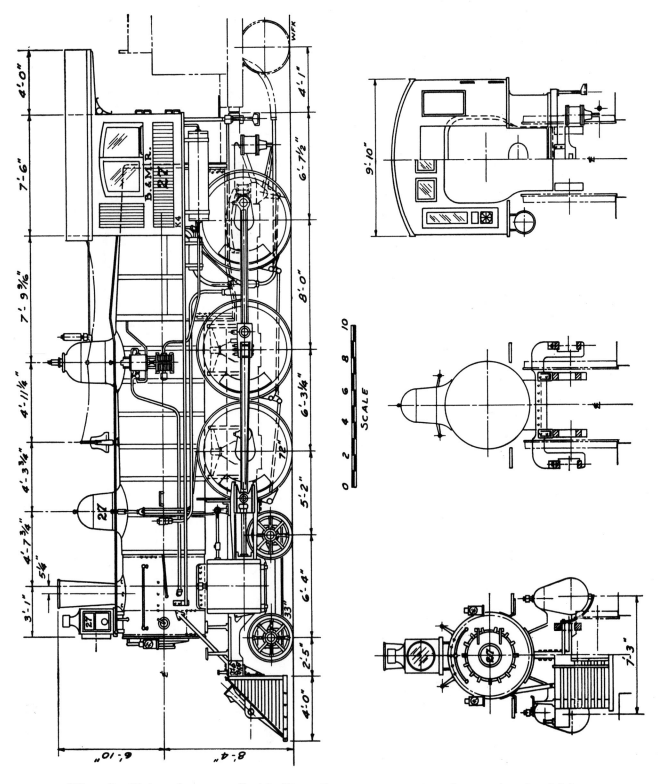

When the K-4 engines were first built, no flanges were used on the center pair of drivers.

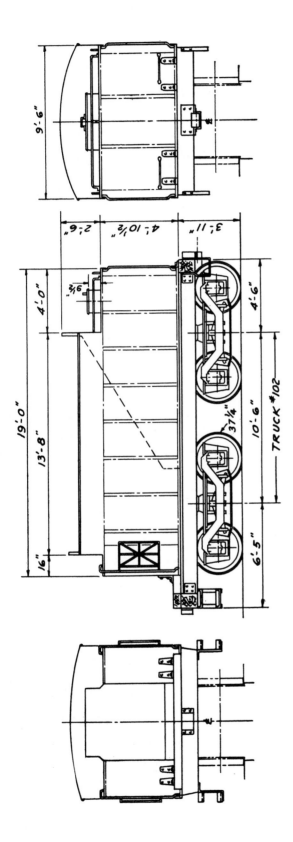

SPECIFICATIONS FOR CLASS K-4

Wheel Arrangement	4-6-0
Cylinders—in.	18x26
	19x26
Drivers, dia.—in.	72
	64
Driving Wheel base	14' 3¼"
Wheel base, total engine	25' 9¼"
Wheel base, engine plus tender	52' 5¾"
Steam pressure—psi	200
Grate area—sq. ft.	30
Superheating surface—sq. ft.	2378.2
Total heating surface—sq. ft.	2394.3
Wt. on drivers—lb.	121,400

Wt. total engine—lb.	156,600
Wt. tender empty—lb.	35,000
Coal—tons	9
Water—Gal.	5000
Tractive Force—lb.	19,890*
	25,000
Adhesion	6.10*
	4.85
Valve Gear	Stephenson
Superheater type	
Power reverse type	
Feedwater heater type	
Stoker	

*Minimum
Maximum

Class N-1, Columbia

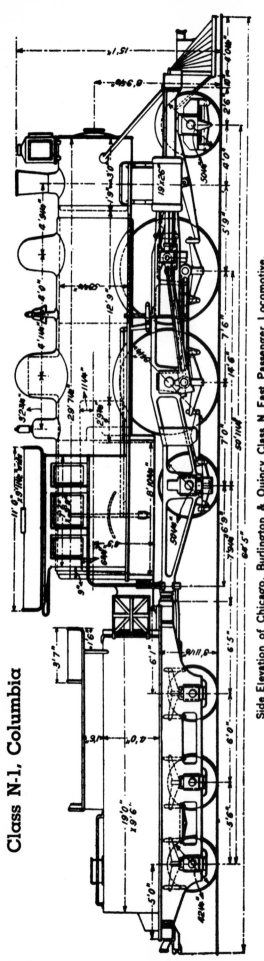

Side Elevation of Chicago, Burlington & Quincy Class N Fast Passenger Locomotive.

N-1 Reprinted from "Railroad Gazette", December, 1895.

SCALE

0 2 4 6 8 10

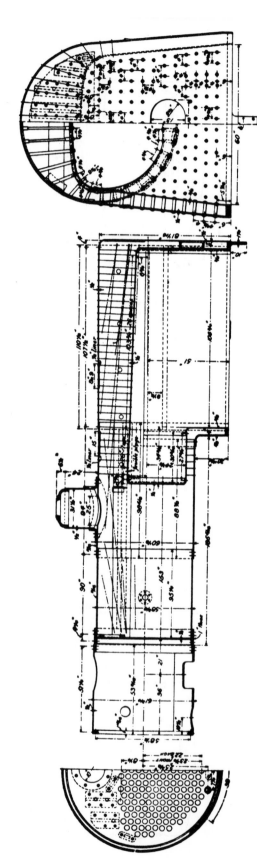

Details of Boiler and Firebox—C., B. & Q. Fast Passenger Locomotive.

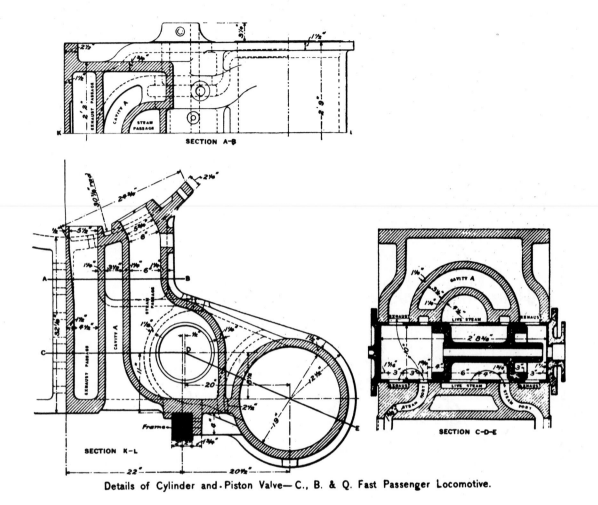

Details of Cylinder and Piston Valve— C., B. & Q. Fast Passenger Locomotive.

SPECIFICATIONS FOR CLASS N-1

Wheel Arrangement	2-4-2	Wt. total engine—lb.	138,000
Cylinders—in.	19x26	Wt. tender empty—lb.	41,000
Drivers, dia.—in.	84¼	Coal—tons	7
Driving Wheel base	7' 6"	Water—Gal.	4200
Wheel base, total engine	24' 3"	Tractive Force—lb.	19,000
Wheel base, engine plus tender	50' 11¼"	Adhesion	4.54
Steam pressure—psi	200	Valve Gear	Stephenson
Grate area—sq. ft.	44.4	Superheater type	
Superheating Surface—sq. ft.		Power reverse type	
Total Heating Surface—sq. ft.	1580	Feedwater heater type	
Wt. on drivers—lb.	86,200	Stoker	

Class P-1-C, Atlantic

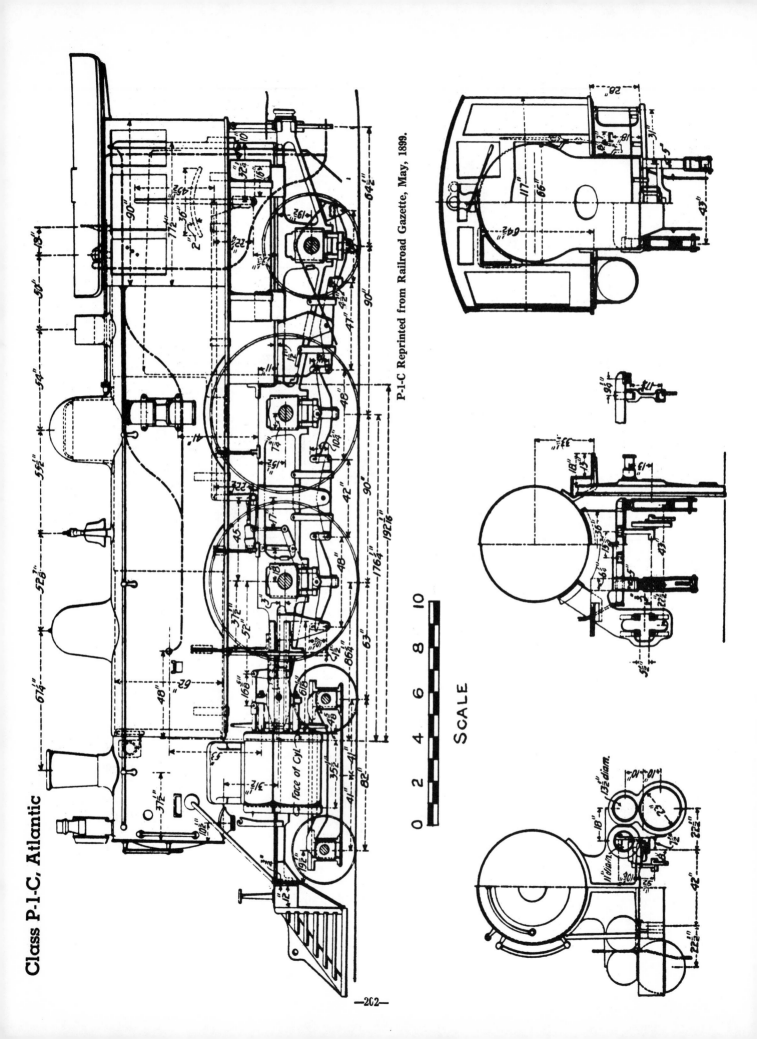

P-1-C Reprinted from Railroad Gazette, May, 1899.

SCALE

0 2 4 6 8 10

Class P-I-C, No. 1591 is shown with its six-wheel tender of European influence in design. This type of tender truck frame was not in use very long and all were changed to the four-wheeled, two-truck style before or during rebuilding the engines to P-1 simples.
—B. G. Corbin Collection.

For tender plan see P-3-C Class

SPECIFICATIONS FOR CLASS P-1-C

Wheel Arrangement	4-4-2
Cylinders—in.	13½&23x26
Drivers, dia.—in.	84¼
Driving Wheel base	7' 6"
Wheel base, total engine	27' 1"
Wheel base, engine plus tender	51' 4¾"
Steam pressure—psi	210
Grate area—sq. ft.	33.6
Superheating surface—sq. ft.	----
Total heating surface—sq. ft.	2511
Wt. on drivers—lb.	85,850
Wt. total engine—lb.	159,050
Wt. tender empty—lb.	41,000
Coal—tons	8¾
Water—Gal.	5000
Tractive Force—lb.	16,400
Adhesion	5.23
Valve Gear	Stephenson
Superheater type	----
Power reverse type	----
Feedwater heater type	----
Stoker	----

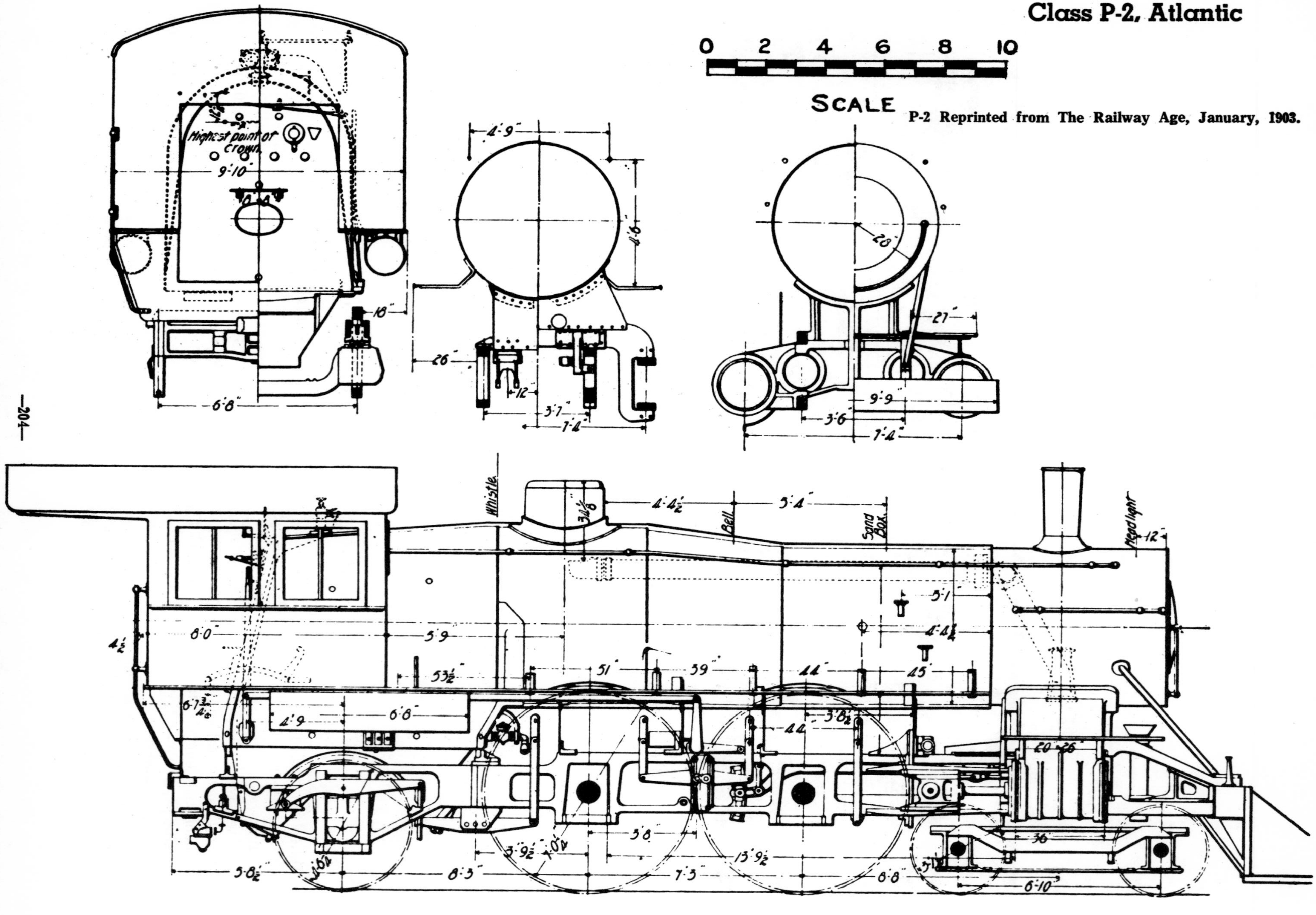

P-2 Reprinted from The Railway Age, January, 1903.

SCALE

0 2 4 6 8 10

This Class P-2 engine, No. 2542, was ex St. Louis, Keokuk and Northwestern No. 783. The high-drivered Atlantic is shown at the Brookfield, Mo. division terminal in June, 1928. She was built by Rogers in 1903 and retired in Dec., 1930. —O. H. Means.

For tender plan see P-3-C Class

SPECIFICATIONS FOR CLASS P-2

Wheel Arrangement	4-4-2	Wt. tender empty—lb.	46,400
Cylinders—in.	20x26	Coal—tons	12
Drivers, dia.—in.	78	Water—Gal.	6000
Driving Wheel base	7' 3"		
Wheel base, total engine	27' 7"	Tractive Force—lb.	22,660 / 23,800
Wheel base, engine plus tender	55' 0¾"		
Steam pressure—psi	200 / 210	Adhesion	4.02 / 3.83
Grate area—sq. ft.	44.1	Valve Gear	Stephenson
Superheating surface—sq. ft.		Superheater type	
Total heating surface—sq. ft.	2990.0	Power reverse type	
Wt. on drivers—lb.	91,250	Feedwater heater type	
Wt. total engine—lb.	187,000	Stoker	

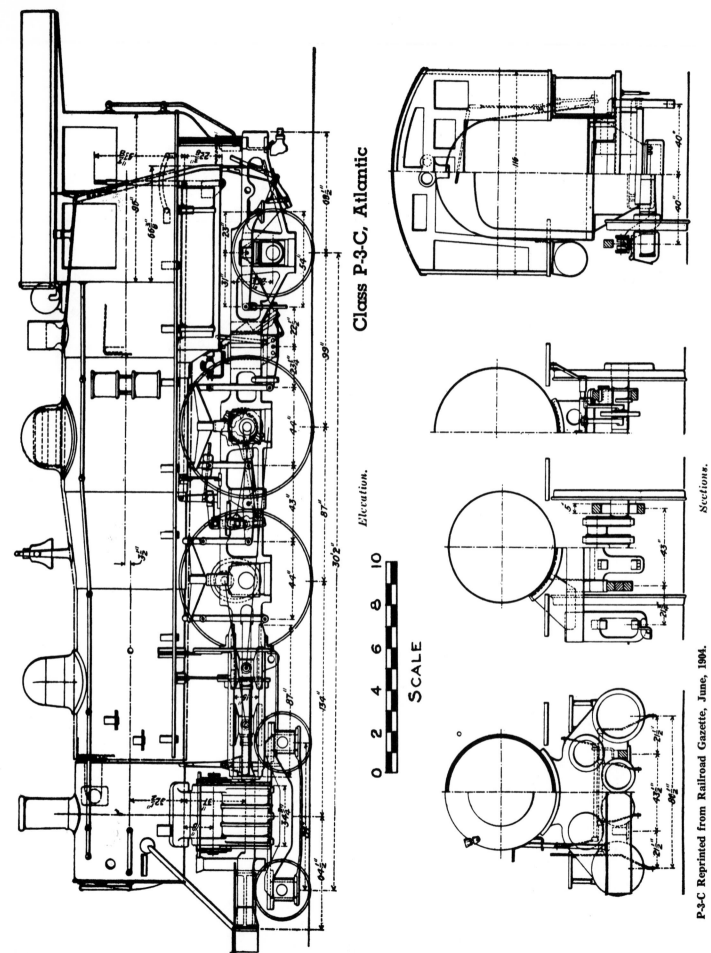

Class P-3-C, Atlantic

Elevation.

SCALE

0 2 4 6 8 10

Sections.

P-3-C Reprinted from Railroad Gazette, June, 1904.

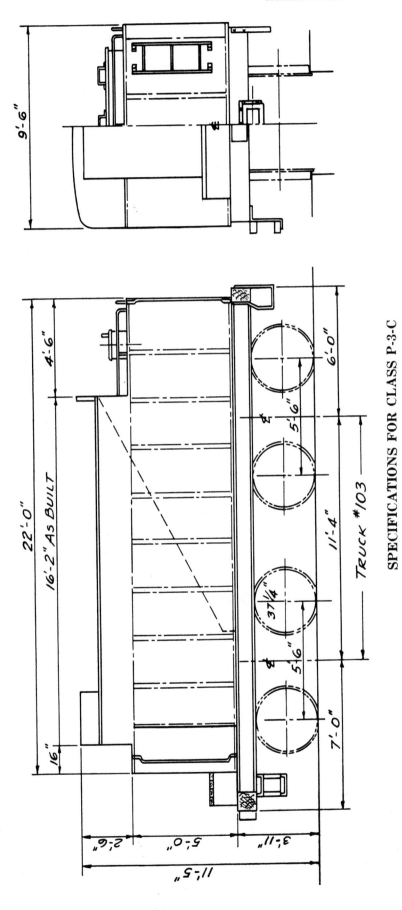

SPECIFICATIONS FOR CLASS P-3-C

Wheel Arrangement	4-4-2
Cylinders—in.	15 & 25x26
Drivers, dia.—in.	74 / 78
Driving Wheel base	7' 3"
Wheel base, total engine	30' 2"
Wheel base, engine plus tender	57' 8¼"
Steam pressure—psi	210
Grate area—sq. ft.	44.1
Superheating surface—sq. ft.	
Total heating surface—sq. ft.	3208.2
Wt. on drivers—lb.	101,200
Wt. total engine—lb.	196,600
Wt. tender empty—lb.	46,400
Coal—tons	12
Water—Gal.	6000
Tractive Force—lb.	22,600 / 21,400
Adhesion	4.47 / 4.72
Valve Gear	Stephenson
Superheater type	
Power reverse type	
Feedwater heater type	
Stoker	

Class R-1, Prairie

R-1 Reprinted from "Railway Gazette", March, 1900.

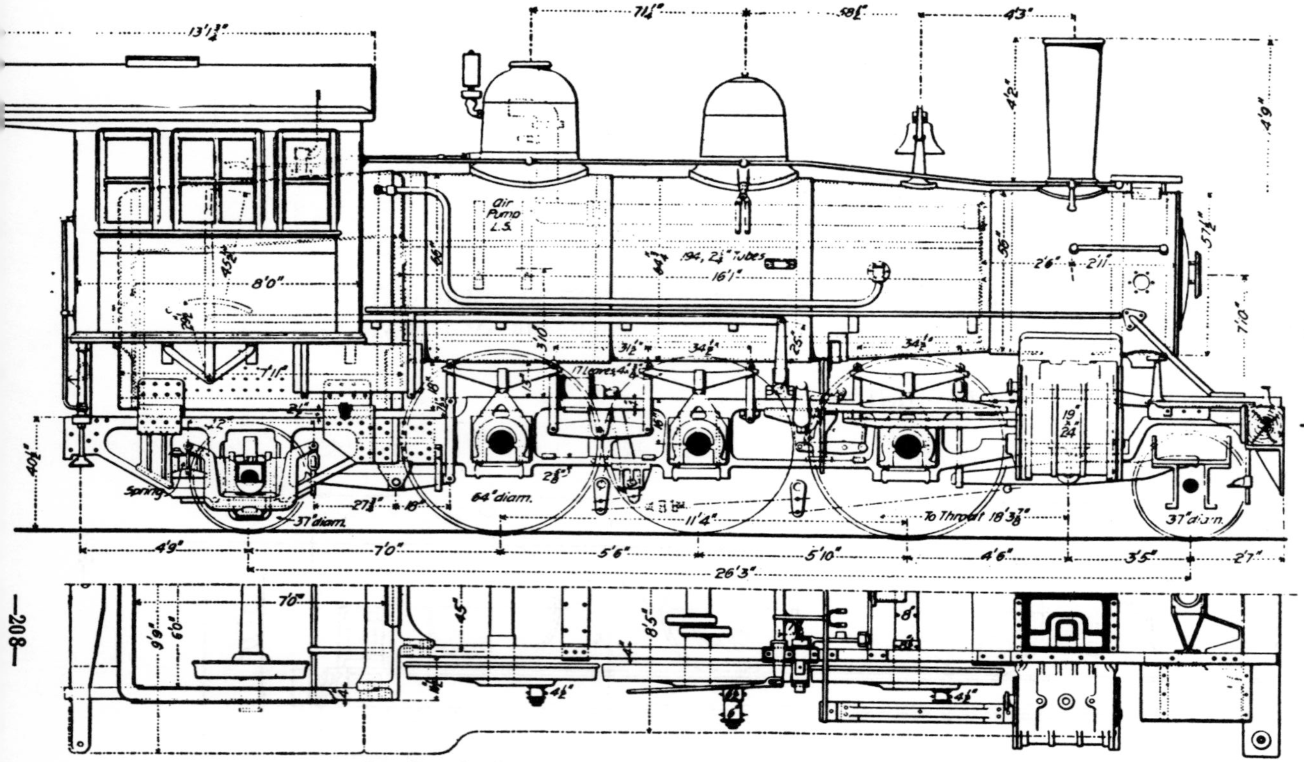

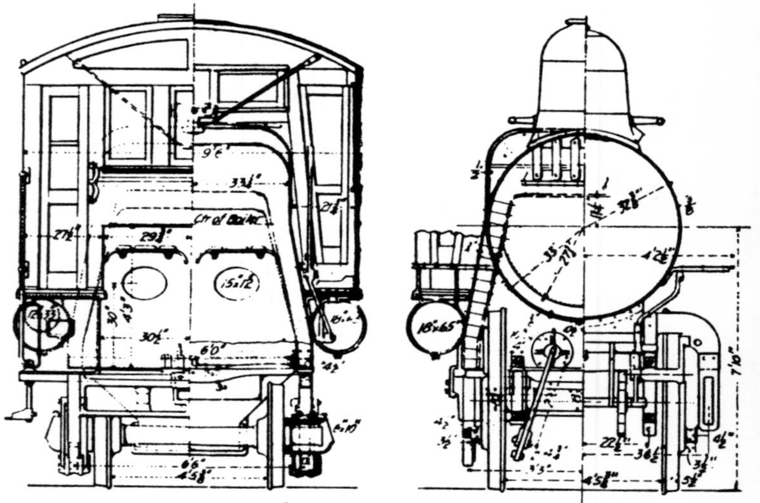

—Sections. Class R Locomotive.

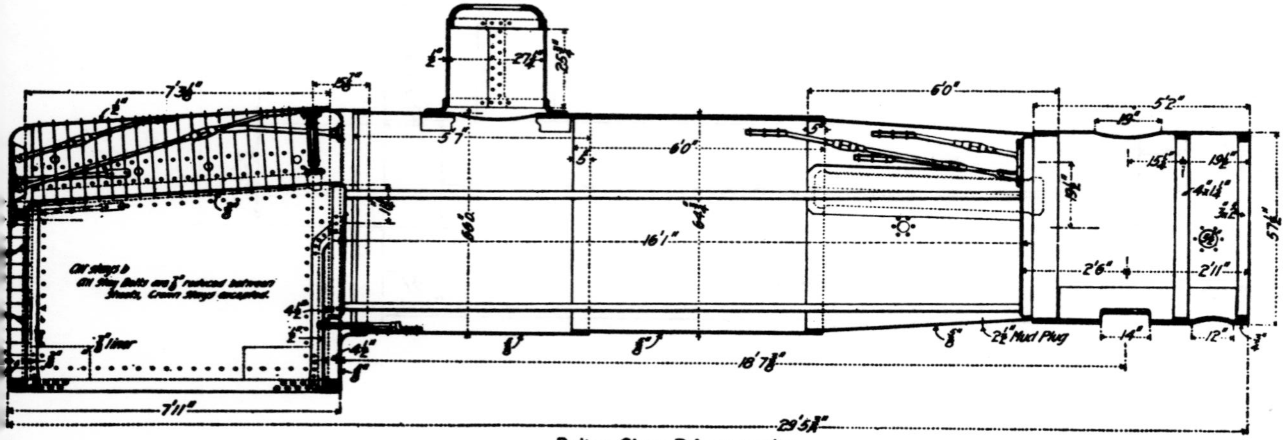

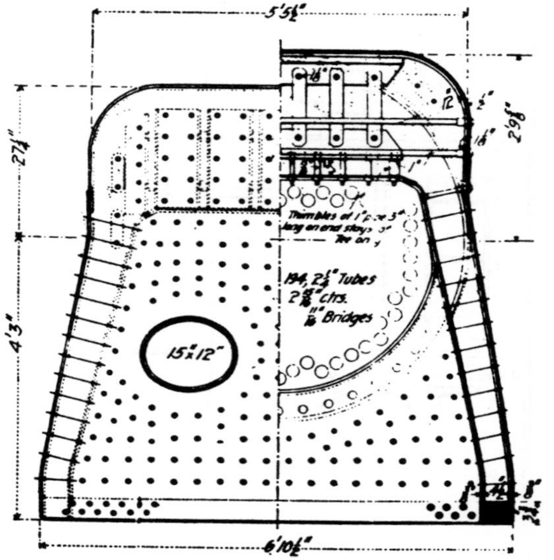

Cross Section, Class R Boiler

— New Class R " Prairie Type " Locomotive—Chicago, Burlington & Quincy Railroad.

—Boiler, Class R Locomotive.

SCALE

0 2 4 6 8 10

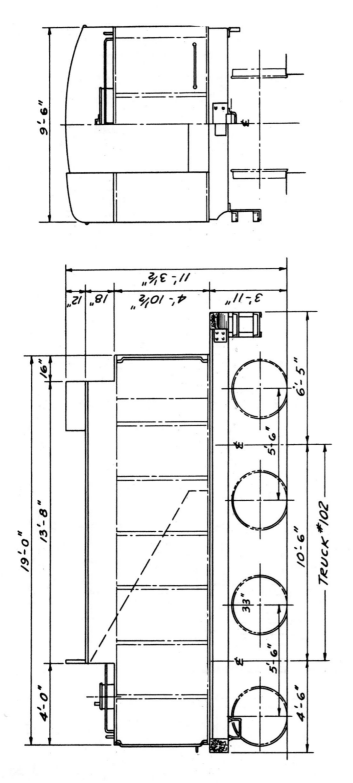

SPECIFICATIONS FOR CLASS R-1

Wheel Arrangement	2-6-2
Cylinders—in.	19x24
Drivers, dia.—in.	64
Driving Wheel base	11' 4"
Wheel base, total engine	26' 3"
Wheel base, engine plus tender	51' 8½"
Steam pressure—psi	190
Grate area—sq. ft.	42.0
Superheating surface—sq. ft.	1957.3
Total heating surface—sq. ft.	
Wt. on drivers—lb.	110,270
Wt. total engine—lb.	151,220
Wt. tender empty—lb.	35,000
Coal—tons	9
Water—Gal.	5000
Tractive Force—lb.	21,900
Adhesion	5.03
Valve Gear	Stephenson
Superheater type	
Power reverse type	
Feedwater heater type	
Stoker	

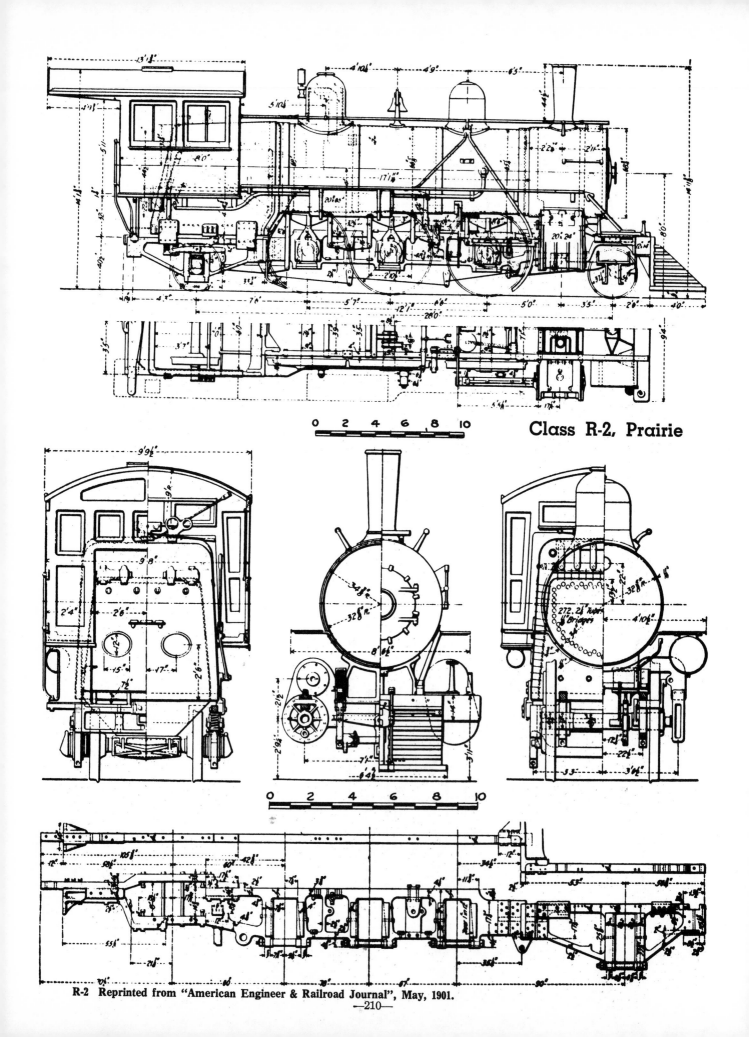

Class R-2, Prairie

R-2 Reprinted from "American Engineer & Railroad Journal", May, 1901.

—210—

Tender Plan

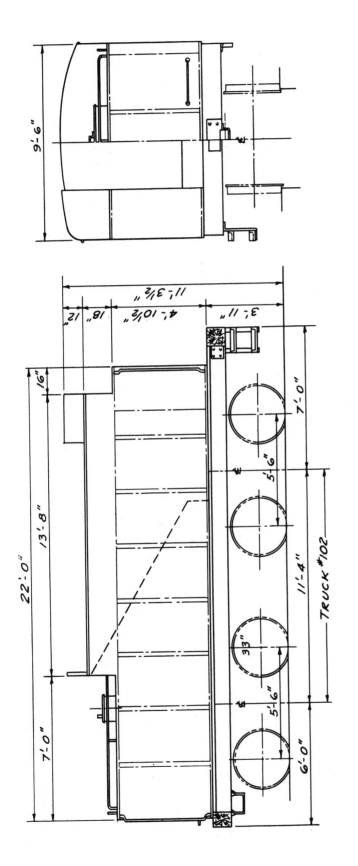

SPECIFICATIONS FOR CLASS R-2

Wheel Arrangement	2-6-2
Cylinders—in.	20x24
Drivers, dia.—in.	64
Driving Wheel base	12' 1"
Wheel base, total engine	28' 0"
Wheel base, engine plus tender	54' 6"
Steam pressure—psi	200
Grate area—sq. ft.	42.0
Superheating surface—sq. ft.	2884.1
Total heating surface—sq. ft.	2884.1
Wt. on drivers—lb.	130,550

Wt. total engine—lb.	170,000
Wt. tender empty—lb.	46,400
Coal—tons	12
Water—Gal.	6000
Tractive Force—lb.	25,500
Adhesion	5.11
Valve Gear	Stephenson
Superheater type	
Power reverse type	
Feedwater heater type	
Stoker	

—211—

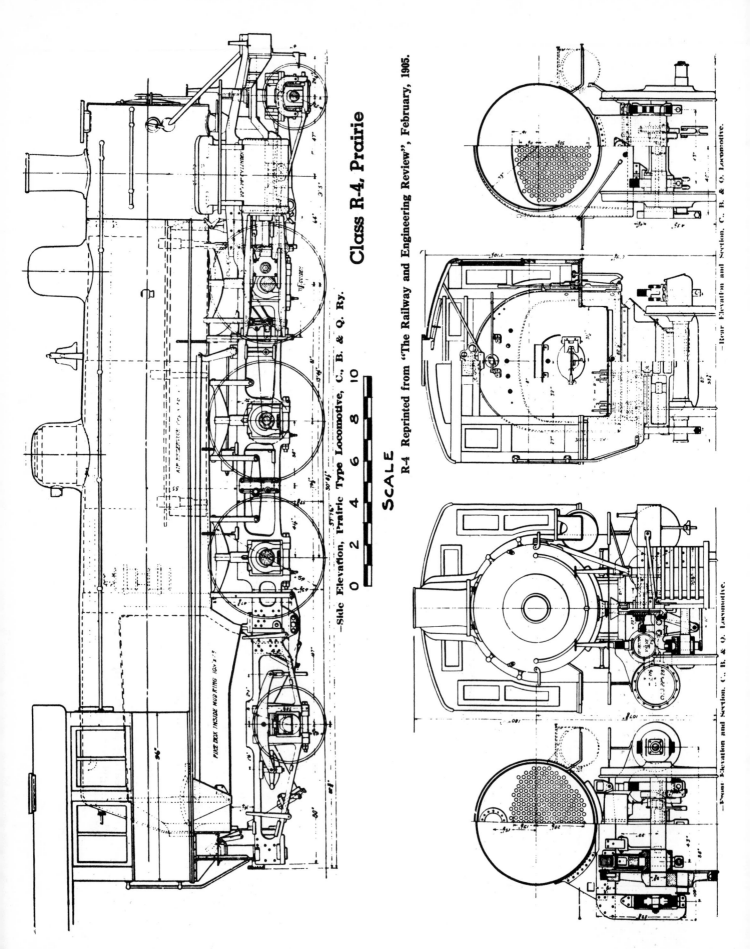

Class R-4, Prairie

—Side Elevation, Prairie Type Locomotive, C., B. & Q. Ry.

SCALE

0   2   4   6   8   10

R-4 Reprinted from "The Railway and Engineering Review", February, 1905.

—Rear Elevation and Section, C., B. & Q. Locomotive.

—Front Elevation and Section, C., B. & Q. Locomotive.

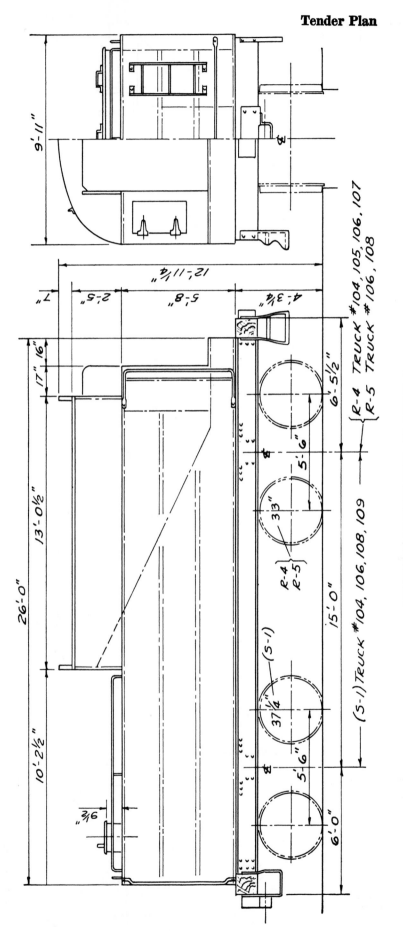

SPECIFICATIONS FOR CLASS R-4

Wheel Arrangement	2-6-2
Cylinders—in.	25x28 / 22x28
Drivers, dia.—in.	69
Driving Wheel base	13' 4½"
Wheel base, total engine	30' 8½"
Wheel base, engine plus tender	62' 2¾"
Steam pressure—psi.	165 / 200
Grate area—sq. ft.	54.2
Superheating Surface—sq. ft.	--- / 596.0
Total Heating surface—sq. ft.	3442.3 / 3310.4
Wt. on drivers—lb.	151,000
Wt. total engine—lb.	210,000
Wt. tender empty—lb.	55,600
Coal—tons	13
Water—Gal.	8000
Tractive Force—lb.	35,600 / 33,400
Adhesion	4.24 / 4.54
Valve Gear	Stephenson
Superheater type	Emerson / Schmidt-A
Power reverse type	---
Feedwater heater type	---
Stoker	---

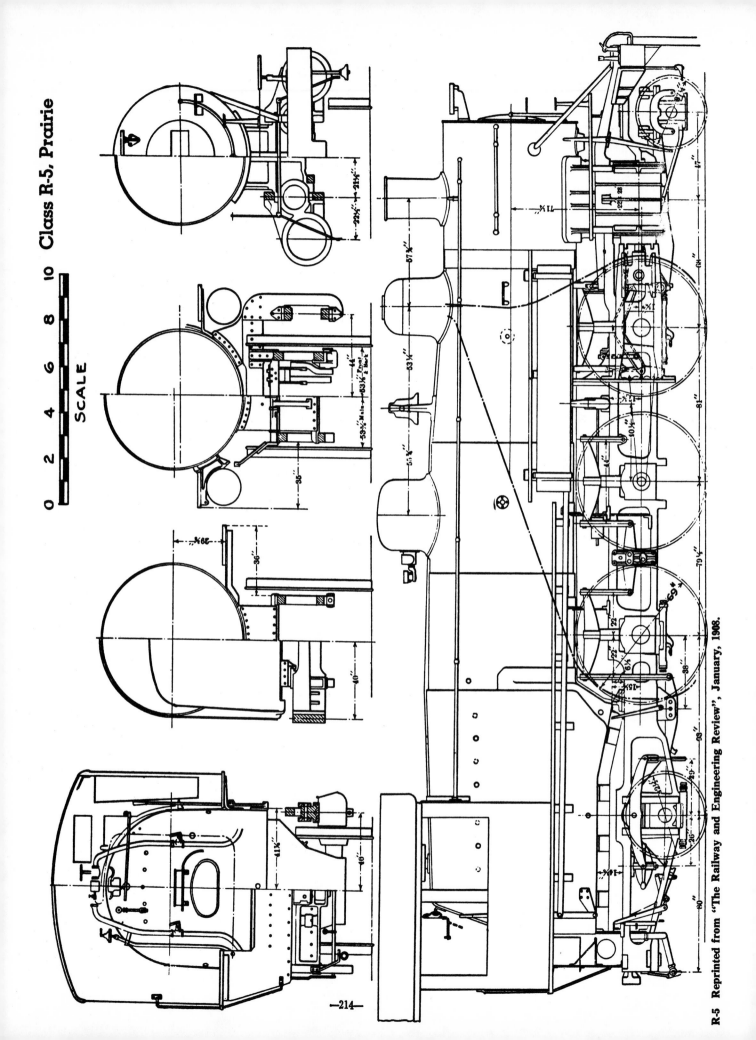

Class R-5, Prairie

SCALE

0 2 4 6 8 10

—214—

R-5 Reprinted from "The Railway and Engineering Review", January, 1908.

No. 2170 was switching at E. St. Louis, Ill. yards in May, 1939. These Prairie-type engines served a multitude of duties and were found wide-spread over the System.

—Al Holck.

For tender plans see R-4 Class

SPECIFICATIONS FOR CLASS R-5

Wheel Arrangement	2-6-2	Wt. on drivers—lb.	152,000
Cylinders—in.	25x28 / 22x28	Wt. total engine—lb.	216,000
		Wt. tender empty—lb.	55,600
Drivers, dia.—in.	69	Coal—tons	13
Driving Wheel base	13' 4½"	Water—Gal.	8000
Wheel base, total engine	30' 8½"		
Wheel base, engine plus tender	62' 2¾"	Tractive Force—lb.	27,600* / 35,600
Steam pressure—psi.	165 to 200	Adhesion	5.51* / 4.27
Grate area—sq. ft.	54.2	Valve Gear	Stephenson
Superheating Surface—sq. ft.	---- / 596.0 / 682.0	Superheater type	---- / Emerson / Schmidt-A
Total heating surface—sq. ft.	3489.0 / 3388.1 / 3504.0	Power reverse type	----
		Feedwater heater type	----
		Stoker	----

* Minimum
 Maximum

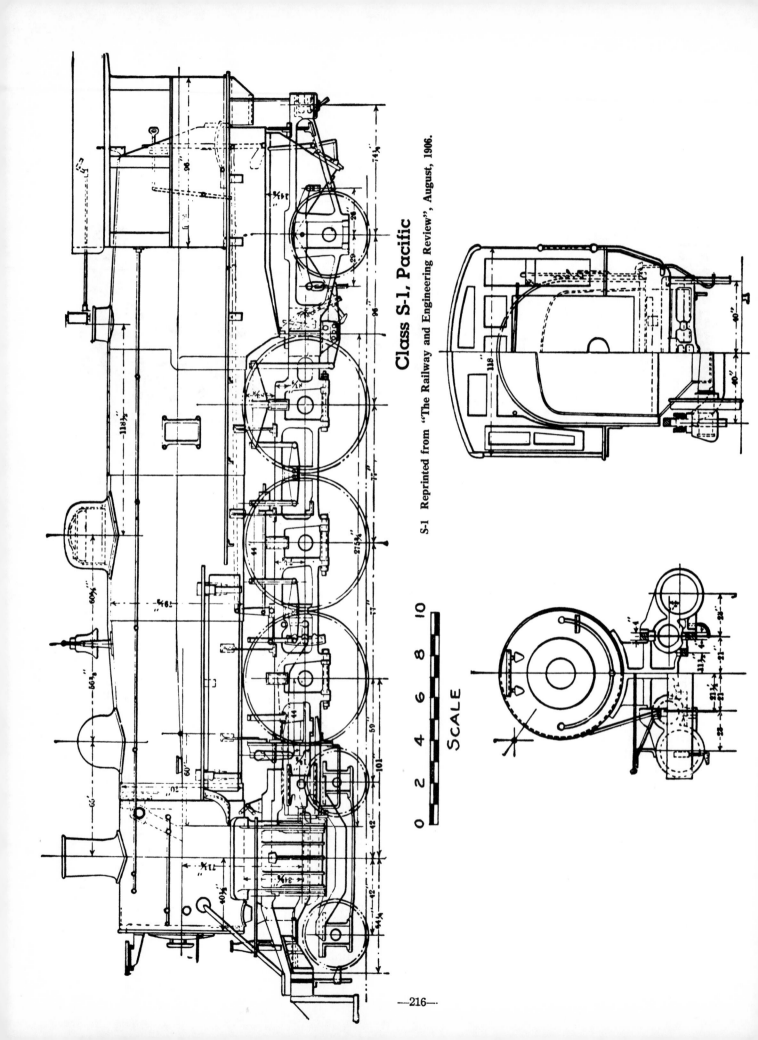

Class S-1, Pacific

S-1   Reprinted from "The Railway and Engineering Review", August, 1906.

SCALE

0   2   4   6   8   10

No. 2801 was in commuter service between Downers Grove and Chicago in July, 1932. This S-1 engine is shown with a rebuilt cab. The single-stage air compressor that was originally mounted on the left side has been replaced with the cross-compound type. The locomotive was never rebuilt to an S-1A, but was dismantled in Nov., 1939.

—Al Holck.

For tender plans see R-4 Class

SPECIFICATIONS FOR CLASS S-1 (2800-2844)

Wheel Arrangement	4-6-2	Wt. total engine—lb.	230,940
Cylinders—in.	22x28	Wt. tender empty—lb.	55,600
Drivers, dia.—in.	74	Coal—tons	13
Driving Wheel base	12' 10"	Water—Gal.	8000
Wheel base, total engine	32' 9"	Tractive Force—lb.	32,700
Wheel base, engine plus tender	64' 3¾"	Adhesion	4.63
Steam pressure—psi	210	Valve Gear	Stephenson
Grate area—sq. ft.	54.2	Superheater type	
Superheating Surface—sq. ft.		Power reverse type	
Total Heating surface—sq. ft.	3922	Feedwater heater type	
Wt. on drivers—lb.	151,290	Stoker	

Class S-3. Pacific (2950-2964)

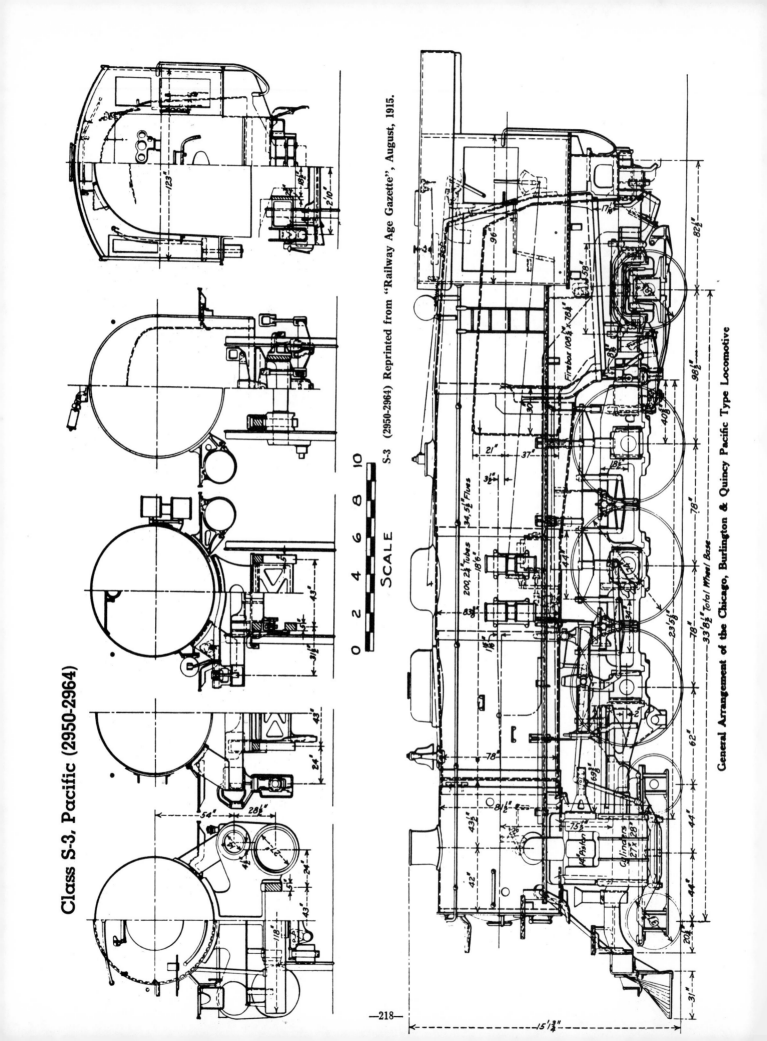

SCALE

0 2 4 6 8 10

S-3 (2950-2964) Reprinted from "Railway Age Gazette", August, 1915.

General Arrangement of the Chicago, Burlington & Quincy Pacific Type Locomotive

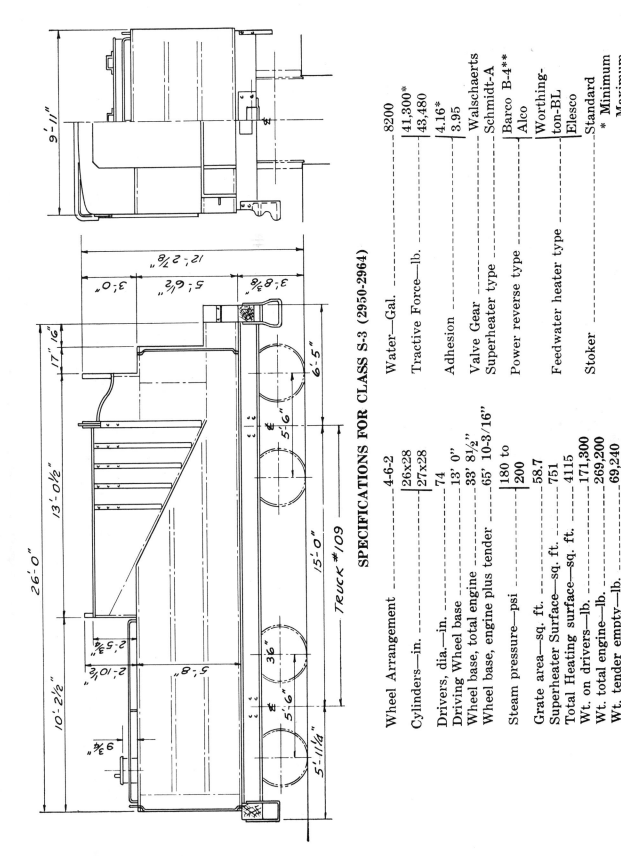

SPECIFICATIONS FOR CLASS S-3 (2950-2964)

Wheel Arrangement	4-6-2
Cylinders—in.	26x28 / 27x28
Drivers, dia.—in.	74
Driving Wheel base	13' 0"
Wheel base, total engine	33' 8½"
Wheel base, engine plus tender	65' 10-3/16"
Steam pressure—psi	180 to 200
Grate area—sq. ft.	58.7
Superheater Surface—sq. ft.	751
Total Heating surface—sq. ft.	4115
Wt. on drivers—lb.	171,300
Wt. total engine—lb.	269,200
Wt. tender empty—lb.	69,240
Coal—tons	13
Water—Gal.	8200
Tractive Force—lb.	41,300* / 43,480
Adhesion	4.16* / 3.95
Valve Gear	Walschaerts
Superheater type	Schmidt-A
Power reverse type	Barco B-4** / Alco
Feedwater heater type	Worthington-BL / Elesco
Stoker	Standard
	* Minimum
	Maximum

**Originally used Ragonnet

Class S-3, Pacific (2965-2974)

Cross Section, Pacific Type Locomotive, Chicago Burlington & Quincy R. R.

SCALE

0   2   4   6   8   10

Elevation, Pacific Type Locomotive, Chicago Burlington & Quincy R. R.

S-3—(2965-2974) Reprinted from "Railway Review", July, 1918.

Tender Plan

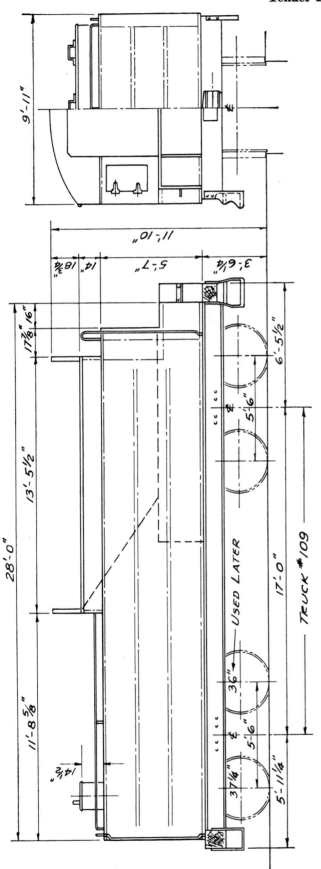

SPECIFICATIONS FOR CLASS S-3 (2965-2974)

Wheel Arrangement	4-6-2
Cylinders—in.	26x28
	27x28
Drivers, dia.—in.	74
Driving Wheel base	13' 0"
Wheel base, total engine	33' 8½"
Wheel base, engine plus tender	68' 3-15/16"
Steam pressure—psi	180 to
	200
Grate area—sq. ft.	58.7
Superheating Surface—sq. ft.	751
Total Heating surface—sq. ft.	4163
Wt. on drivers—lb.	171,300
Wt. total engine—lb.	269,200
Wt. tender empty—lb.	69,240
Coal—tons	**13**

Water—Gal.	8200
Tractive Force—lb.	**41,300***
	43,480
Adhesion	4.16*
	3.95
Valve Gear	Walschaerts
Superheater type	**Schmidt-A**
Power reverse type	**Barco B-4****
	Alco
Feedwater heater type	Worthing-ton-BL
	Elesco
Stoker	Standard
	* Minimum
	Maximum

**Originally used Ragonnet

—221—

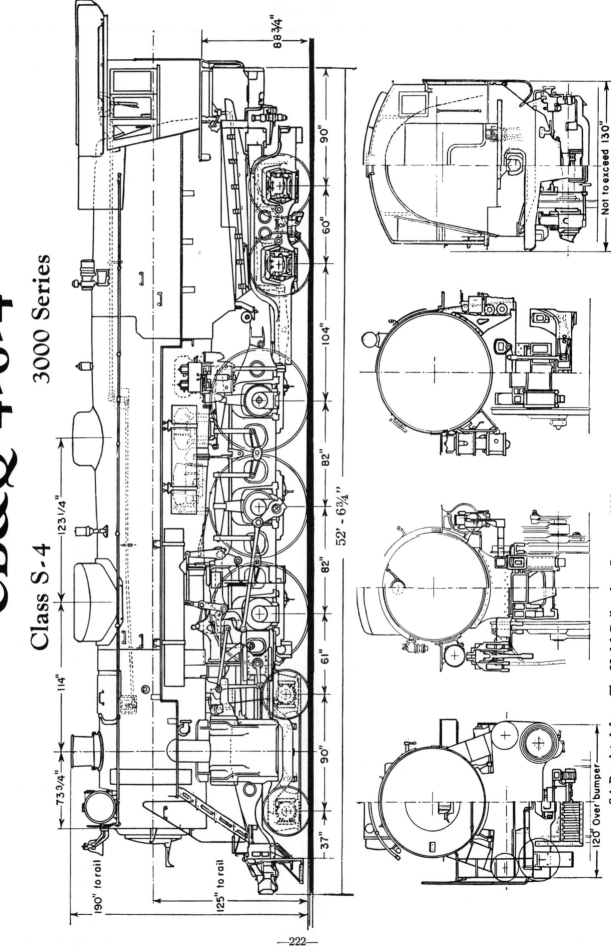

CB&Q 4-6-4

Class S-4

3000 Series

8 3/4"
90"
60"
104"
82"
82"
61"
90"
37"
52' - 6 3/4"

123 1/4"
114"
73 3/4"
190" to rail
125" to rail

Not to exceed 130"
120" Over bumper

S-4 Reprinted from The Model Railroader, January, 1944.

Tender Plan

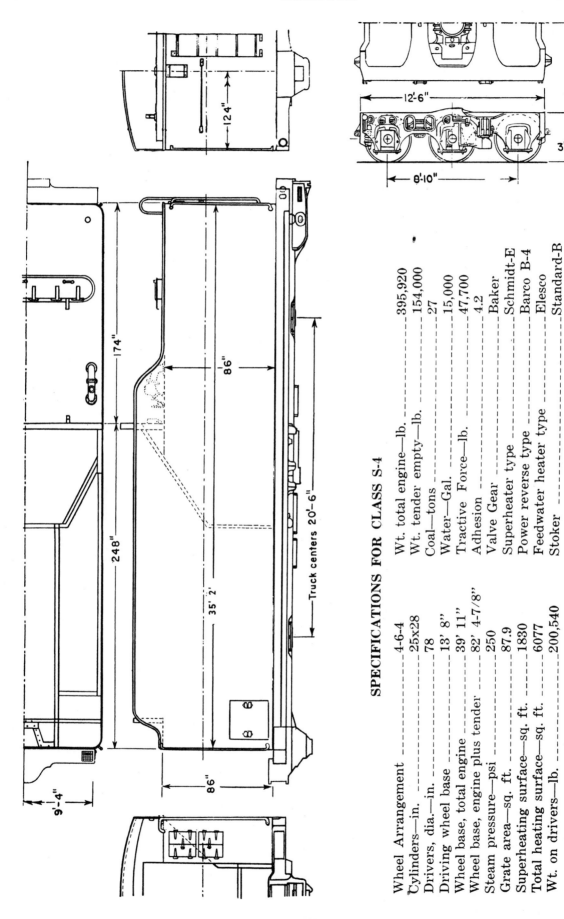

SPECIFICATIONS FOR CLASS S-4

Wheel Arrangement	4-6-4
Cylinders—in.	25x28
Drivers, dia.—in.	78
Driving wheel base	13' 8"
Wheel base, total engine	39' 11"
Wheel base, engine plus tender	82' 4-7/8"
Steam pressure—psi	250
Grate area—sq. ft.	87.9
Superheating surface—sq. ft.	1830
Total heating surface—sq. ft.	6077
Wt. on drivers—lb.	200,540
Wt. total engine—lb.	395,920
Wt. tender empty—lb.	154,000
Coal—tons	27
Water—Gal.	15,000
Tractive Force—lb.	47,700
Adhesion	4.2
Valve Gear	Baker
Superheater type	Schmidt-E
Power reverse type	Barco B-4
Feedwater heater type	Elesco
Stoker	Standard-B

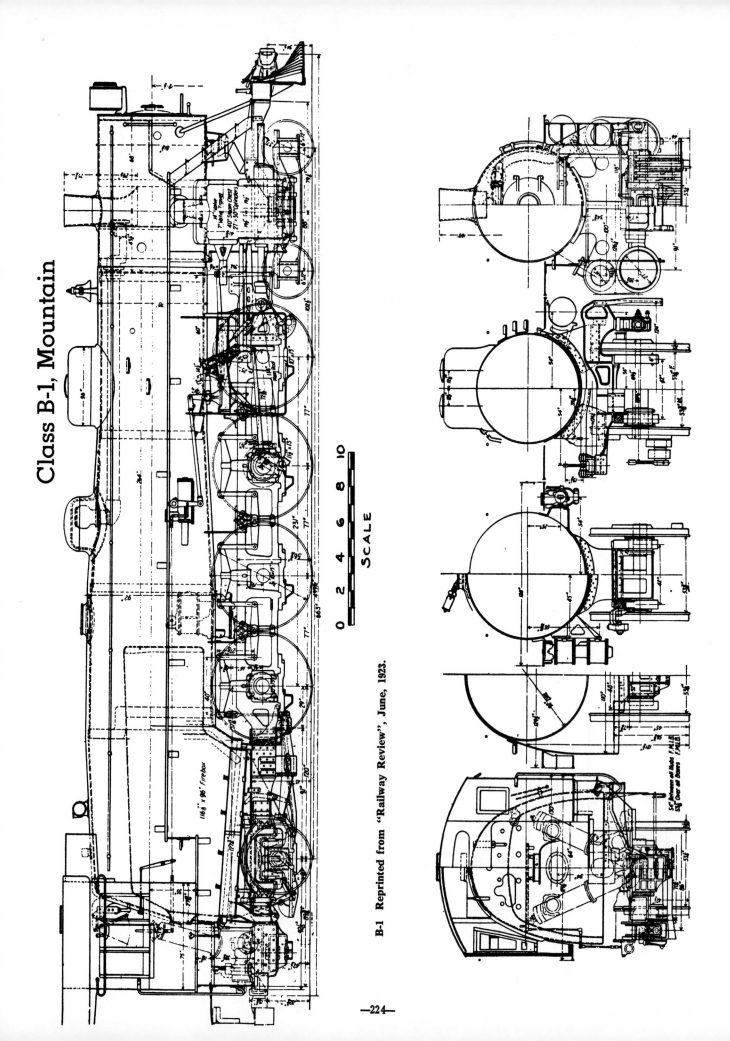

Class B-1, Mountain

SCALE

0 2 4 6 8 10

B-1 Reprinted from "Railway Review", June, 1923.

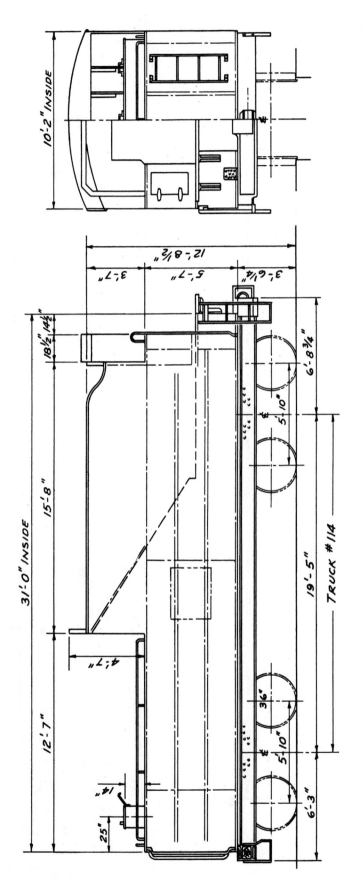

SPECIFICATIONS FOR CLASS B-1

Wheel Arrangement	4-8-2
Cylinders—in.	27x30
Drivers, dia.—in.	74
Driving Wheel base	19' 3"
Wheel base, total engine	41' 7½"
Wheel base, engine plus tender	79' 5"
Steam pressure—psi	210
Grate area—sq. ft.	78.25
Superheating surface—sq. ft.	1172
Total heating surface—sq. ft.	5527.7
Wt. on drivers—lb.	235,500
Wt. total engine—lb.	350,000
Wt. tender empty—lb.	82,000
Coal—tons	20
Water—Gal.	10,000
Tractive Force—lb.	52,750
Adhesion	4.46
Valve Gear	Walschaerts
Superheater type	Schmidt-A
Power reverse type	Barco
Feedwater heater type	Worthington-BL
Stoker	Duplex

Class 0-1, Mikado

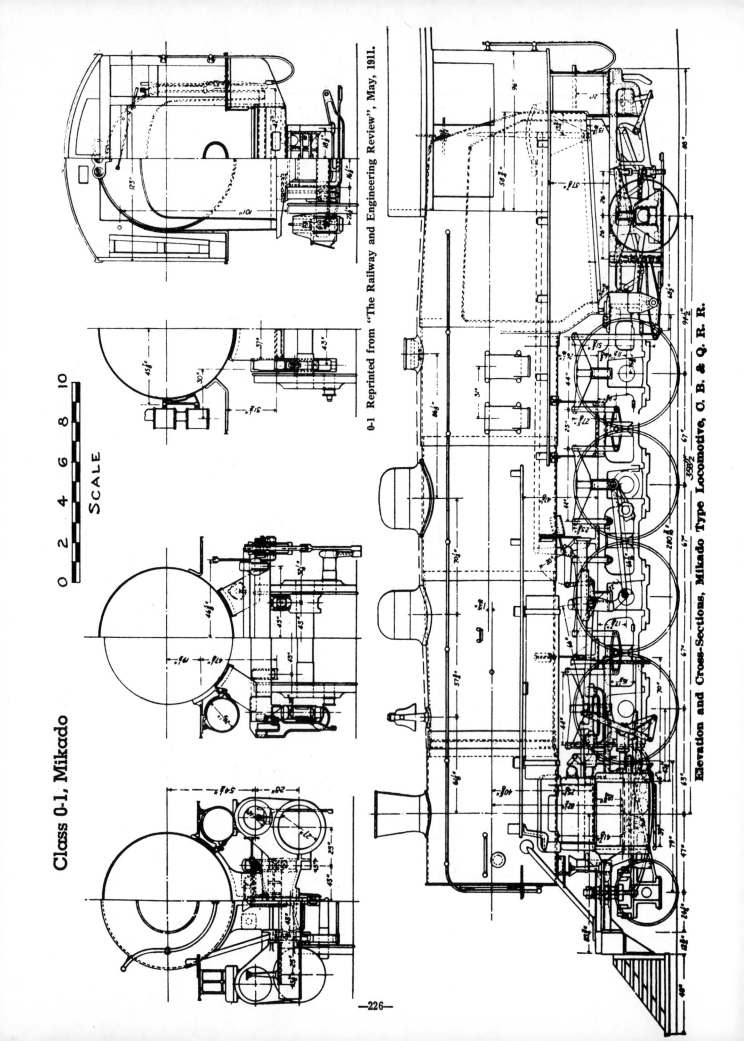

SCALE

0   2   4   6   8   10

0-1 Reprinted from "The Railway and Engineering Review", May, 1911.

Elevation and Cross-Sections, Mikado Type Locomotive, C. B. & Q. R. R.

Tender Plan

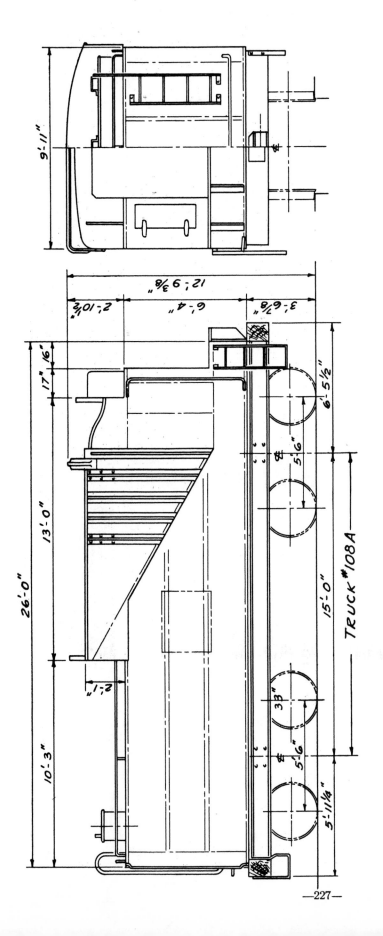

SPECIFICATIONS FOR CLASS O-1

Wheel Arrangement	2-8-2
Cylinders—in.	27x30
Drivers, dia.—in.	64
Driving Wheel base	16' 9"
Wheel base, total engine	33' 9½"
Wheel base, engine plus tender	66' 2-15/16"
Steam pressure—psi	200
Grate area—sq. ft.	54.2
Superheating surface—sq. ft.	679
Total heating surface—sq. ft.	4357.4
Wt. on drivers—lb.	223,450
Wt. total engine—lb.	288,140
Wt. tender empty—lb.	67,000
Coal—tons	13
Water—Gal.	9200
Tractive Force—lb.	58,090
Adhesion	3.84
Valve Gear	Walschaerts
Superheater type	Emerson
Power reverse type	Ragonnet
Feedwater heater type	———
Stoker	———

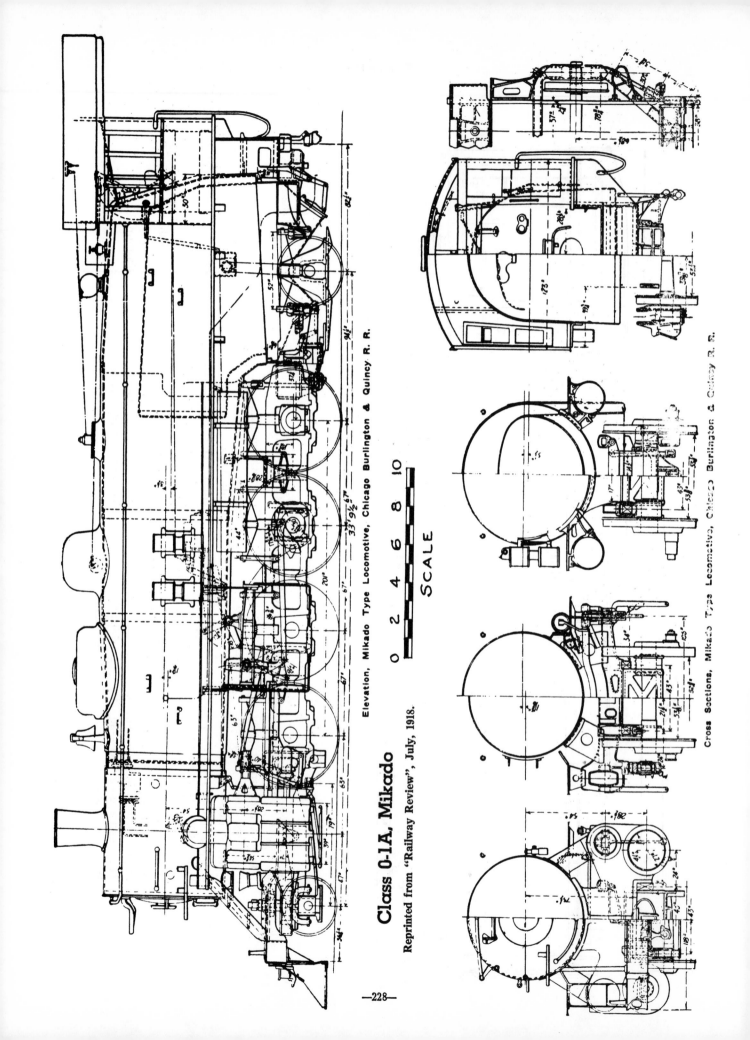

Class 0-1A, Mikado

Reprinted from "Railway Review", July, 1918.

Elevation, Mikado Type Locomotive, Chicago Burlington & Quincy R. R.

Cross Sections, Mikado Type Locomotive, Chicago Burlington & Quincy R. R.

SCALE

0   2   4   6   8   10

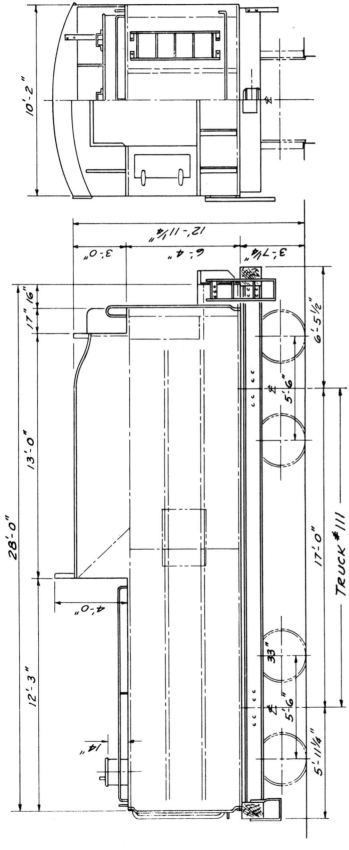

SPECIFICATIONS FOR CLASS 0-1A

Wheel Arrangement	2-8-2
Cylinders—in.	27x30
Drivers, dia.—in.	64
Driving Wheel base	16' 9"
Wheel base, total engine	33' 9½"
Wheel base, engine plus tender	70' 0"
Steam pressure—psi	200
Grate area—sq. ft.	58.8
Superheating surface—sq. ft.	769
Total heating surface—sq. ft.	4178
Wt. on drivers—lb.	233,850
Wt. total engine—lb.	310,780
Wt. tender empty—lb.	74,000
Coal—tons	19
Water—Gal.	10,000
Tractive Force—lb.	58,090
Adhesion	3.85
Valve Gear	Walschaerts
Superheater type	Schmidt-A
Power reverse type	Ragonnet
Feedwater heater type	Worthington BL
	Elesco
Stoker	Standard BK
	Martin

Class 0-2, Mikado

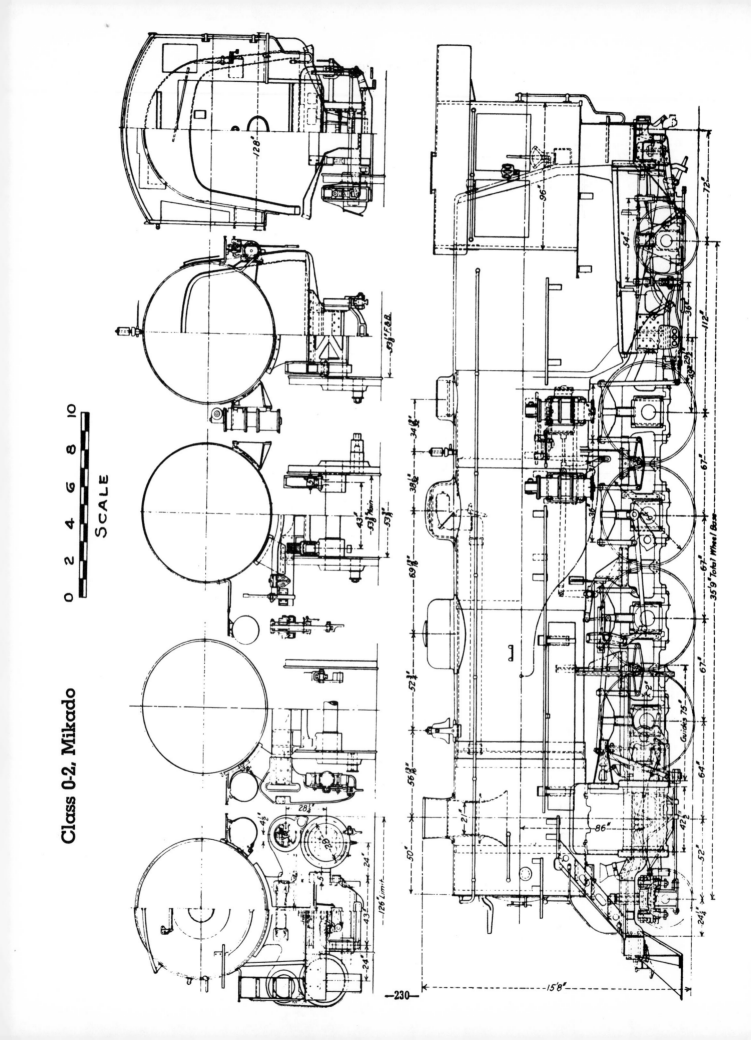

SCALE

0 2 4 6 8 10

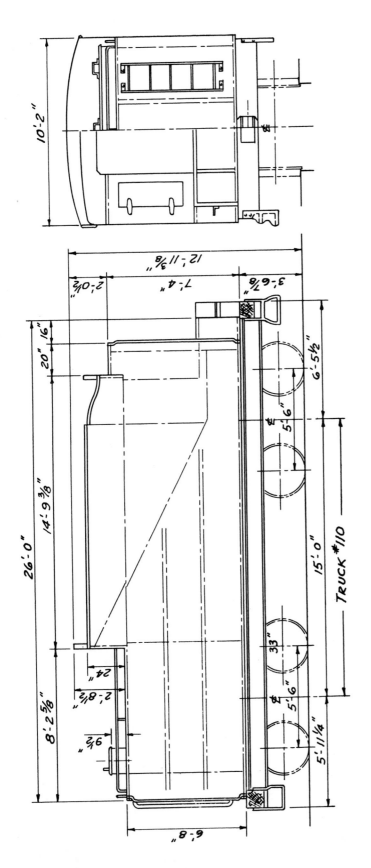

SPECIFICATIONS FOR CLASS 0-2

Wt. total engine—lb.	310,000
Wt. tender empty—lb.	70,350
Coal—tons	14
Water—Gal.	9200
Tractive Force—lb.	60,000
	61,965
Adhesion	3.78
	3.67
Valve Gear	Walschaerts
Superheater type	Emerson
Power reverse type	Ragonnet
Feedwater heater type	Elesco
Stoker	Duplex

Wheel Arrangement	2-8-2
Cylinders—in.	28x32
Drivers, dia.—in.	64
Driving Wheel base	16' 9"
Wheel base, total engine	35' 9"
Wheel base, engine plus tender	67' 6"
Steam pressure—psi	180
	200 (27")
	(Cyl.)
Grate area—sq. ft.	78
Superheating surface—sq. ft.	961
Total heating surface—sq. ft.	5618
Wt. on drivers—lb.	227,000

Class 0-4, Mikado

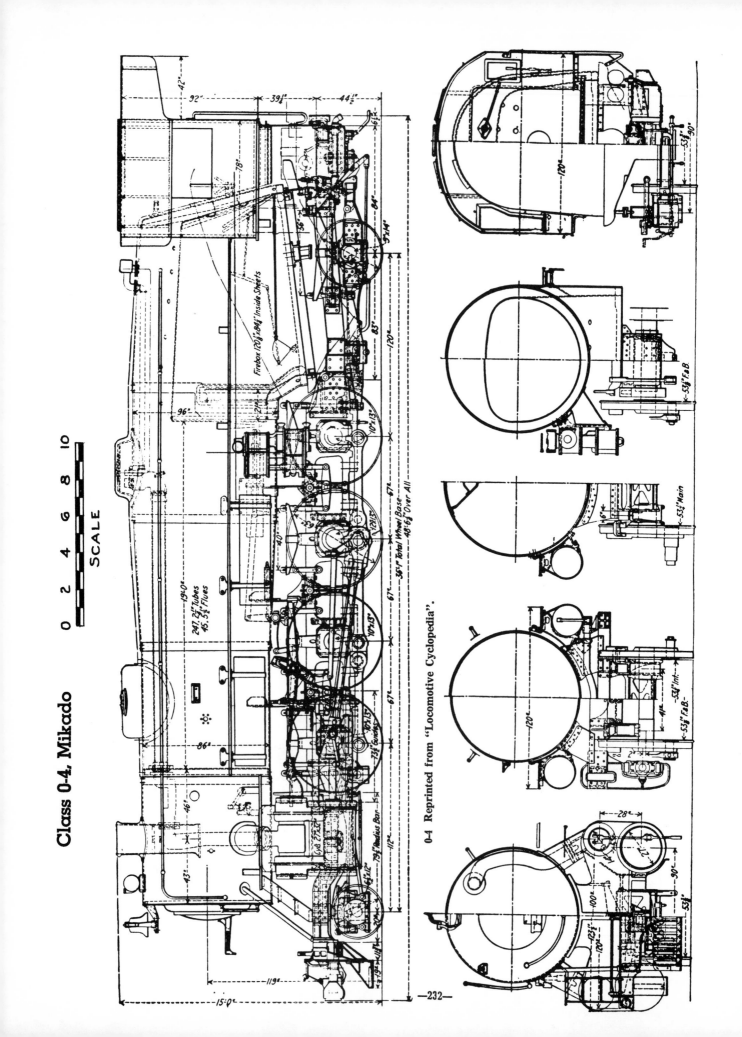

Firebox 120⅛"x94¾" Inside Sheets

247 2¼" Tubes
45 5½" Flues

36'-1" Total Wheel Base
48'-6⅞" Over All

0-4 Reprinted from "Locomotive Cyclopedia".

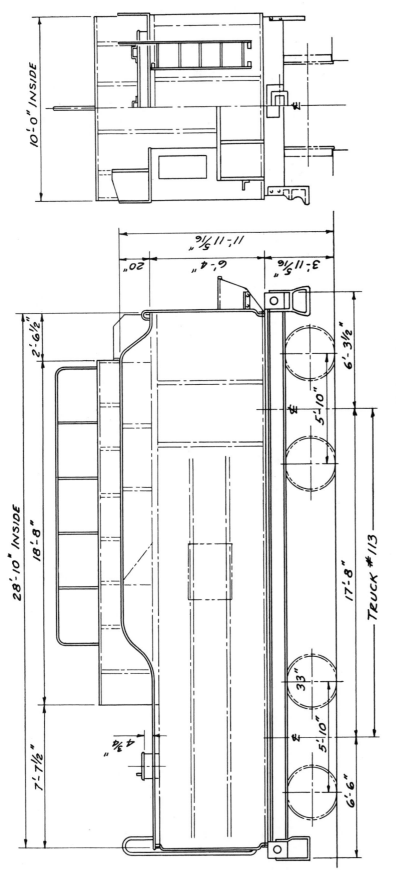

SPECIFICATIONS FOR CLASS 0-4

Wheel Arrangement	2-8-2
Cylinders—in.	27x32
Drivers, dia.—in.	63
Driving Wheel base	16' 9"
Wheel base, total engine	36' 1"
Wheel base, engine plus tender	71' 8½"
Steam pressure—psi	190
	200
Grate area—sq. ft.	70.3
Superheating surface—sq. ft.	993
Total heating surface—sq. ft.	5284
Wt. on drivers—lb.	238,260
Wt. total engine—lb.	320,950
Wt. tender empty—lb.	72,350
Oil—Gal.	5635
Water—Gal.	10,000
Tractive Force—lb.	59,850
	62,950
Adhesion	3.98
	3.78
Valve Gear	Walschaerts
Superheater type	Schmidt
Power reverse type	Lewis
Feedwater heater type	Worthington BL
	Elesco
Stoker	Oil Fired

Class 0-5A, Northern (5621-5635)

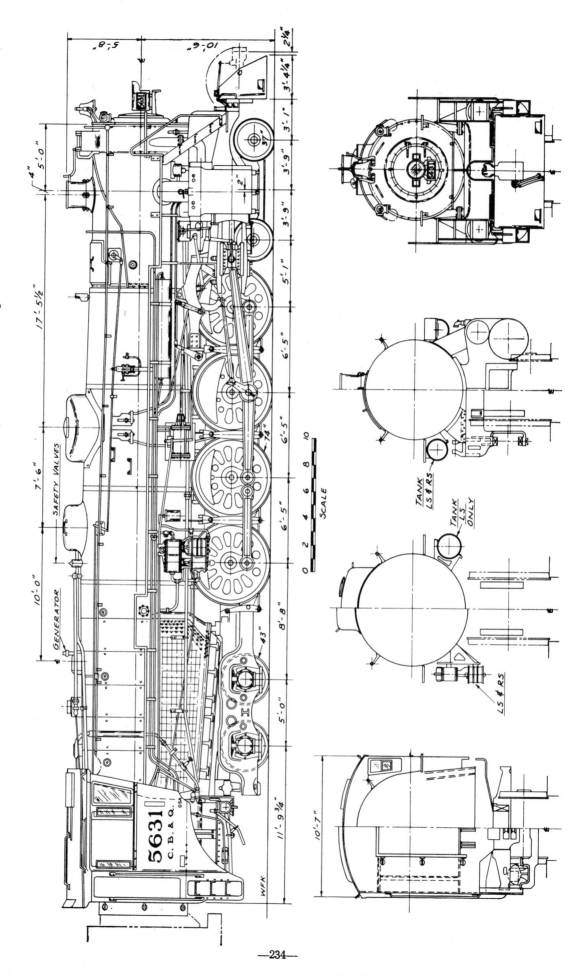

SAFETY VALVES

GENERATOR

SCALE

TANK LS & RS

TANK LS ONLY

LS & RS

5631
C. B. & Q.

Tender Plan

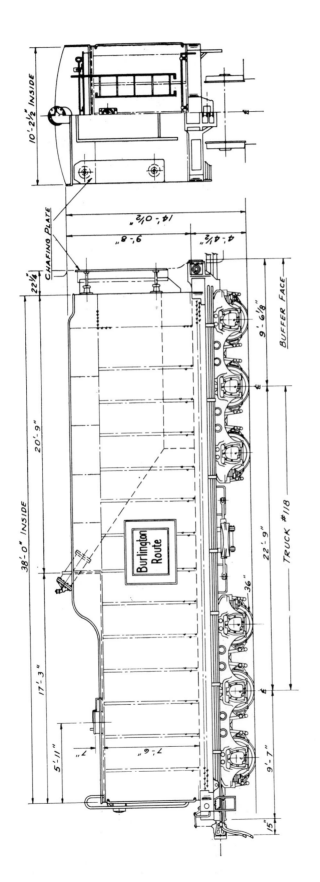

SPECIFICATIONS FOR CLASS O-5A (5621-5635)

Wheel Arrangement	4-8-4
Cylinders—in.	28x30
Drivers, dia.—in.	74
Driving Wheel base	19' 3"
Wheel base, total engine	45' 6"
Wheel base, engine plus tender	94' 0-1/8"
Steam pressure—psi	250
Grate area—sq. ft.	106.5
Superheating surface—sq. ft.	2403.0
Total heating surface—sq. ft.	7628
Wt. on drivers—lb.	281,410
Wt. total engine—lb.	476,050

Wt. tender empty—lb.	158,000
Coal—tons	27
Water—Gal.	18,000
Tractive Force—lb.	67,500
Adhesion	4.16
Valve Gear	Baker
Superheater type	Schmidt-E
Power reverse type	Alco-L
Feedwater heater type	Worthington-S
Stoker	Standard Modified-B

Class M-1, Santa Fe Type

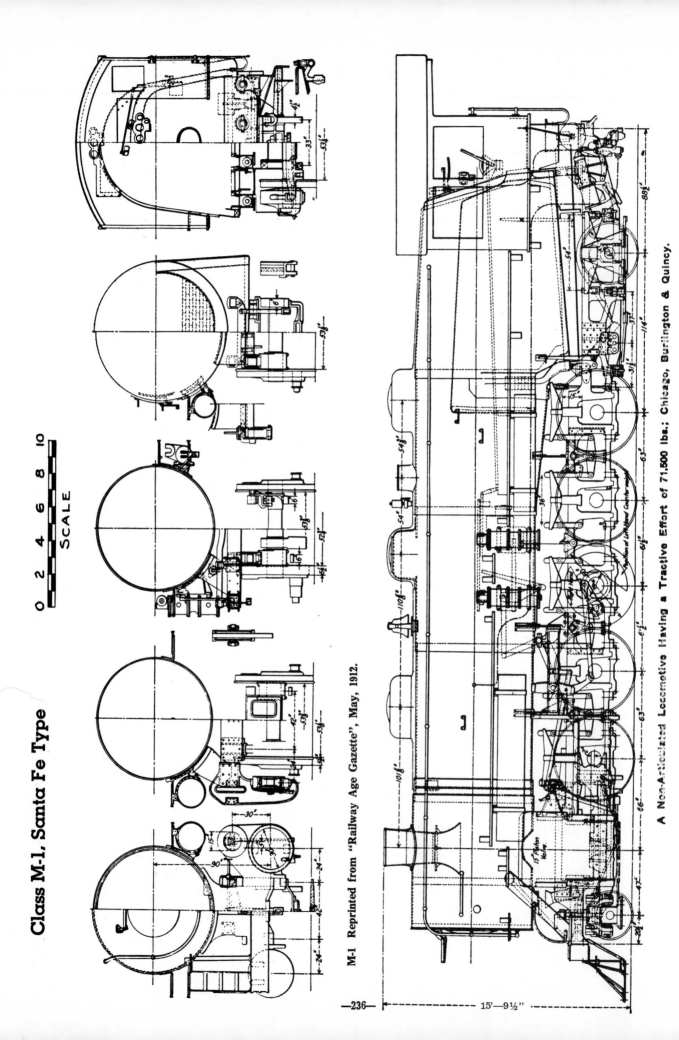

SCALE

M-1 Reprinted from "Railway Age Gazette", May, 1912.

A Non-Articulated Locomotive Having a Tractive Effort of 71,500 lbs.; Chicago, Burlington & Quincy.

—236—

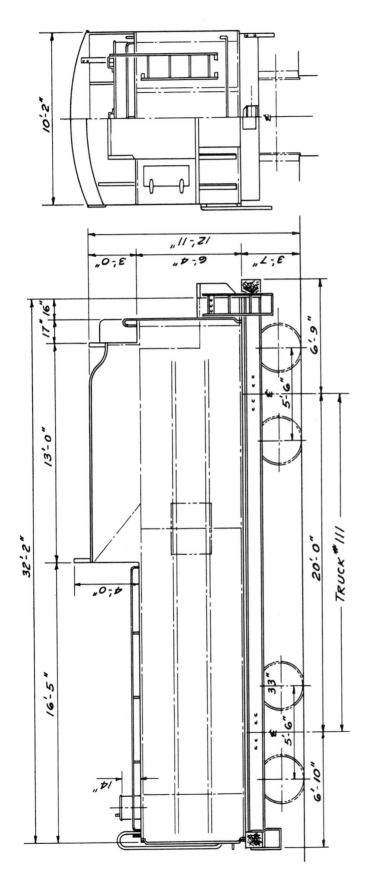

SPECIFICATIONS FOR CLASS M-1

Wheel Arrangement	2-10-2
Cylinders—in.	30x32
Drivers, Dia.—in.	59
Driving Wheel base	20' 9"
Wheel base, total engine	39' 8"
Wheel base, engine plus tender	78' 0-15/16"
Steam pressure—psi	200
Grate area—sq. ft.	88
Superheating surface—sq. ft.	1232
Total heating surface—sq. ft.	6555
Wt. on drivers—lb.	301,800
Wt. total engine—lb.	378,700
Wt. tender empty—lb.	79,500
Coal—tons	20.8
Water—Gal.	12,000
Tractive Force—lb.	83,000
Adhesion	3.64
Valve Gear	Walschaerts
Superheater type	Schmidt-A
Power reverse type	Ragonnet
Feedwater heater type	Worthington BL
	Elesco
	Standard BK
Stoker	Duplex

Class M-2, Santa Fe Type

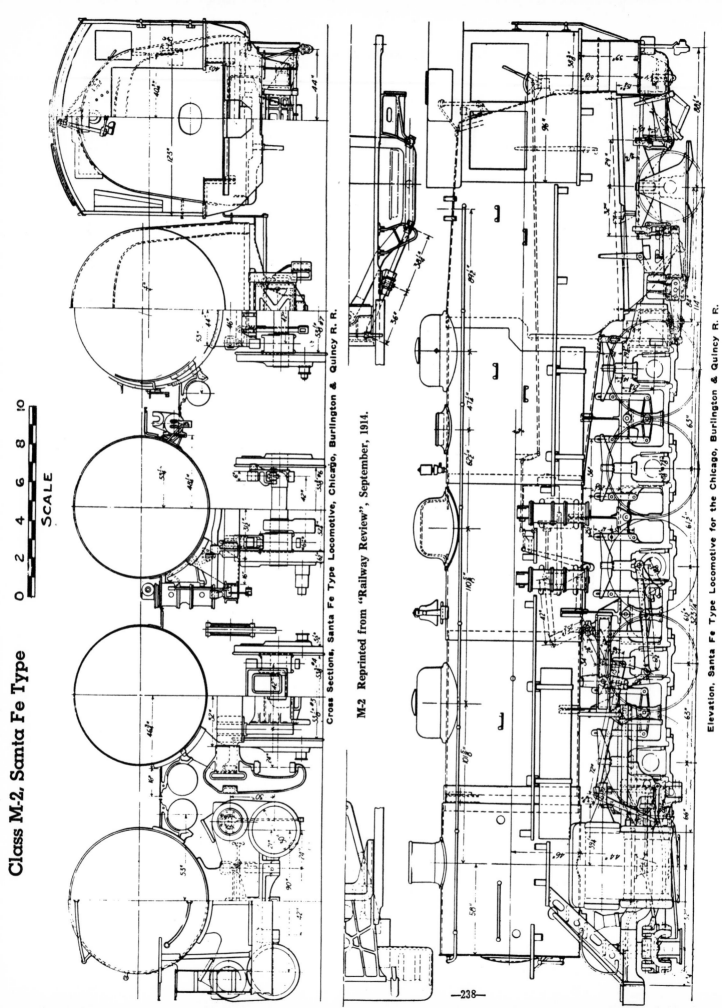

SCALE
0 2 4 6 8 10

Cross Sections, Santa Fe Type Locomotive, Chicago, Burlington & Quincy R. R.

M-2 Reprinted from "Railway Review", September, 1914.

Elevation, Santa Fe Type Locomotive for the Chicago, Burlington & Quincy R. R.

The Class M, Santa Fe types, were first built with 60" drivers with no flanges on the center pair. The tires were later turned down to 59". The original tenders were also lengthened to increase their capacity. No. 6126, a Class M-2A, was coaling up at Brookfield, Mo. in June, 1928.

—B. G. Corbin Collection.

For Tender Plan see M-1 Class

SPECIFICATIONS FOR CLASS M-2

Wheel Arrangement	2-10-2	Coal—tons	20.8
Cylinders—in.	30x32	Water—Gal.	12,000
Drivers, dia.—in.	59	Tractive Force—lb.	83,000
Driving Wheel base	20' 9"	Adhesion	3.62
Wheel base, total engine	40' 1"	Valve Gear	Walschaerts
Wheel base, engine plus tender	78' 5-15/16"	Superheater type	Schmidt-A
Steam pressure—psi	200	Power reverse type	Ragonnet
Grate area—sq. ft.	88	Feedwater heater type	Worthington BL Elesco
Superheating surface—sq. ft.	1232		
Total heating surface—sq. ft.	6576.3		
Wt. on drivers—lb.	300,700	Stoker	Standard MB, BK Duplex
Wt. total engine—lb.	377,100		
Wt. tender empty—lb.	79,500		

Class M-3, Santa Fe Type

SCALE

0 2 4 6 8 10

M-3 Reprinted from "Locomotive Cyclopedia".

—240—

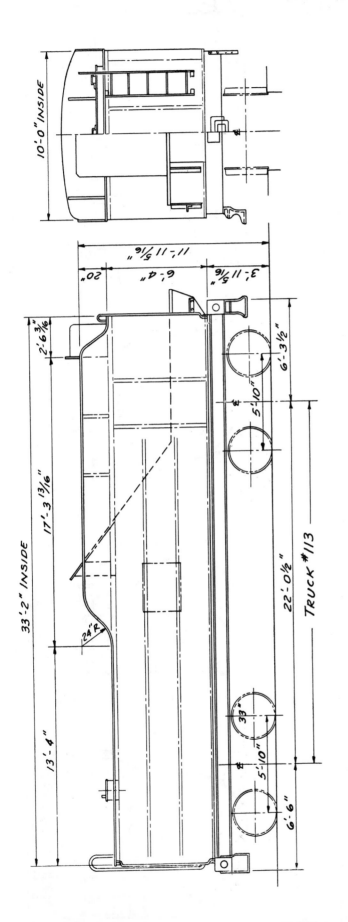

SPECIFICATIONS FOR CLASS M-3

Wheel Arrangement	2-10-2
Cylinders—in.	30x32
Drivers, dia.—in.	63
Driving Wheel base	22' 4"
Wheel base, total engine	42' 2"
Wheel base, engine plus tender	82' 10"
Steam pressure—psi	190 / 200
Grate area—sq. ft.	88.2
Superheating surface—sq. ft.	1208
Total heating surface—sq. ft.	6381
Wt. on drivers—lb.	293,000
Wt. total engine—lb.	380,000
Wt. tender empty—lb.	74,100
Coal—tons	16
Water—Gal.	12,000
Tractive Force—lb.	73,830 / 77,710
Adhesion	3.97 / 3.77
Valve Gear	Southern
Superheater type	Schmidt
Power reverse type	Mellin
Feedwater heater type	Worthington BL / Elesco
Stoker	Duplex

Class M-4, Texas Type

SCALE

0 2 4 6 8 10

M-4 Reprinted from "Locomotive Cyclopedia".

—242—

Tender Plan

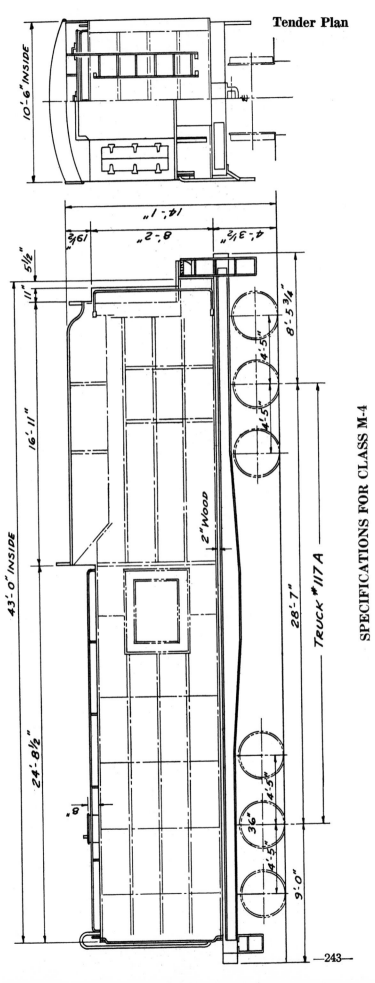

SPECIFICATIONS FOR CLASS M-4

Wheel Arrangement	2-10-4
Cylinders—in.	31x32
Drivers, dia.—in.	64
Driving Wheel base	22' 4"
Wheel base, total engine	45' 6"
Wheel base, engine plus tender	95' 11¾"
Steam pressure—psi	250
Grate area—sq. ft.	106.5
Superheating surface—sq. ft.	2487
Total heating surface—sq. ft.	8391
Wt. on drivers—lb.	353,820
Wt. total engine—lb.	512,770
Wt. tender empty—lb.	158,600
Coal—tons	24
Water—Gal.	21,500
Tractive Force—lb.	90,000
Adhesion	3.93
Valve Gear	Baker
Superheater type	Schmidt-E
Power reverse type	Barco B-4
Feedwater heater type	Worthington BL Elesco
Stoker	Standard Duplex

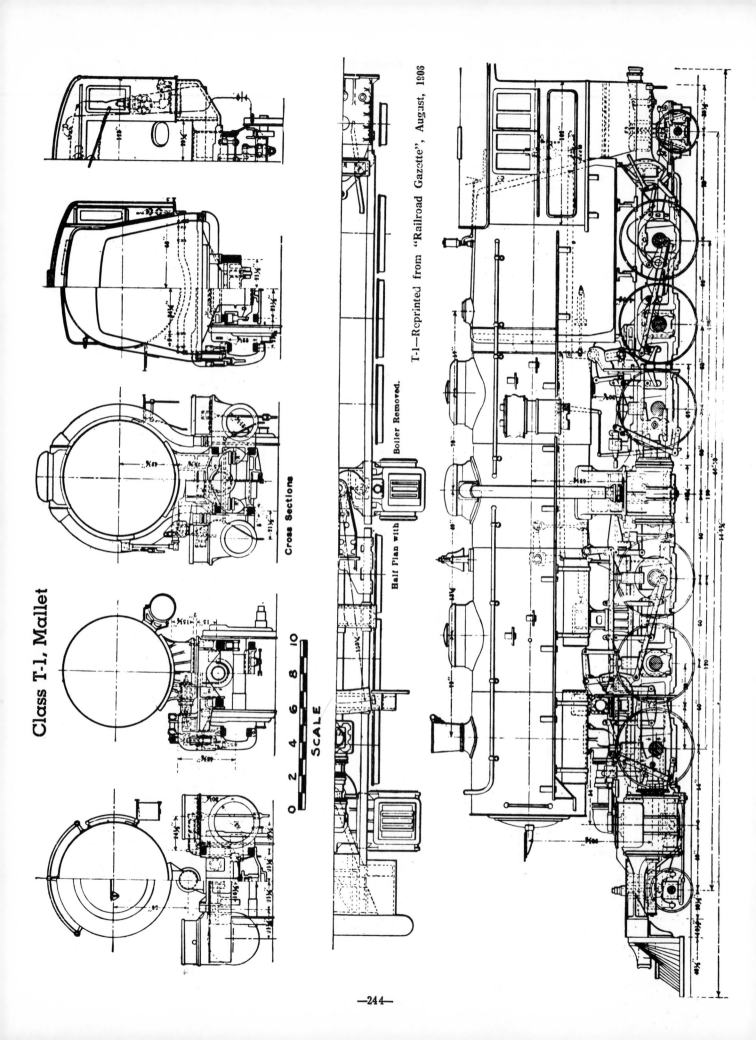

Class T-1, Mallet

Cross Sections

SCALE
0 2 4 6 8 10

Half Plan with Boiler Removed.

T-1—Reprinted from "Railroad Gazette", August, 1905

—244—

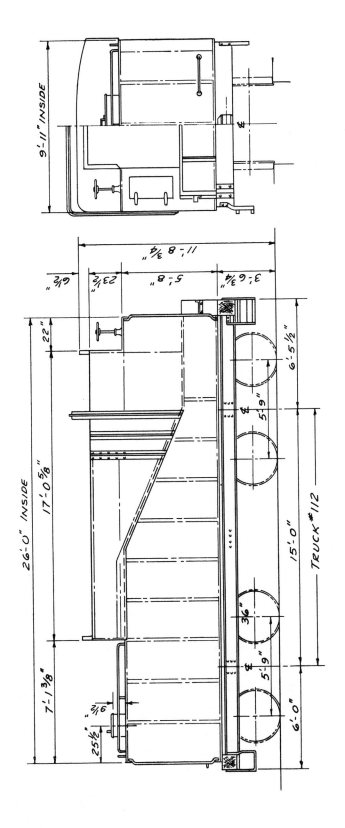

SPECIFICATIONS FOR CLASS T-1

Wheel Arrangement	2-6-6-2
Cylinders—in.	21½&33x32
Drivers, dia.—in.	56
Driving Wheel base	10' 0"
Wheel base, total engine	44' 10"
Wheel base, engine plus tender	73' 3¼"
Steam pressure—psi	200
Grate area—sq. ft.	78
Superheating surface—sq. ft.	
Total heating surface—sq. ft.	5662.0
Wt. on drivers—lb.	311,600
Wt. total engine—lb.	354,500
Wt. tender empty—lb.	55,600
Coal—tons	13
Water—Gal.	8000
Tractive Force—lb.	70,500
Adhesion	4.42
Valve Gear	Walschaerts
Superheater type	
Power reverse type	Ragonnet
Feedwater heater type	
Stoker	

Class T-2. Mallet

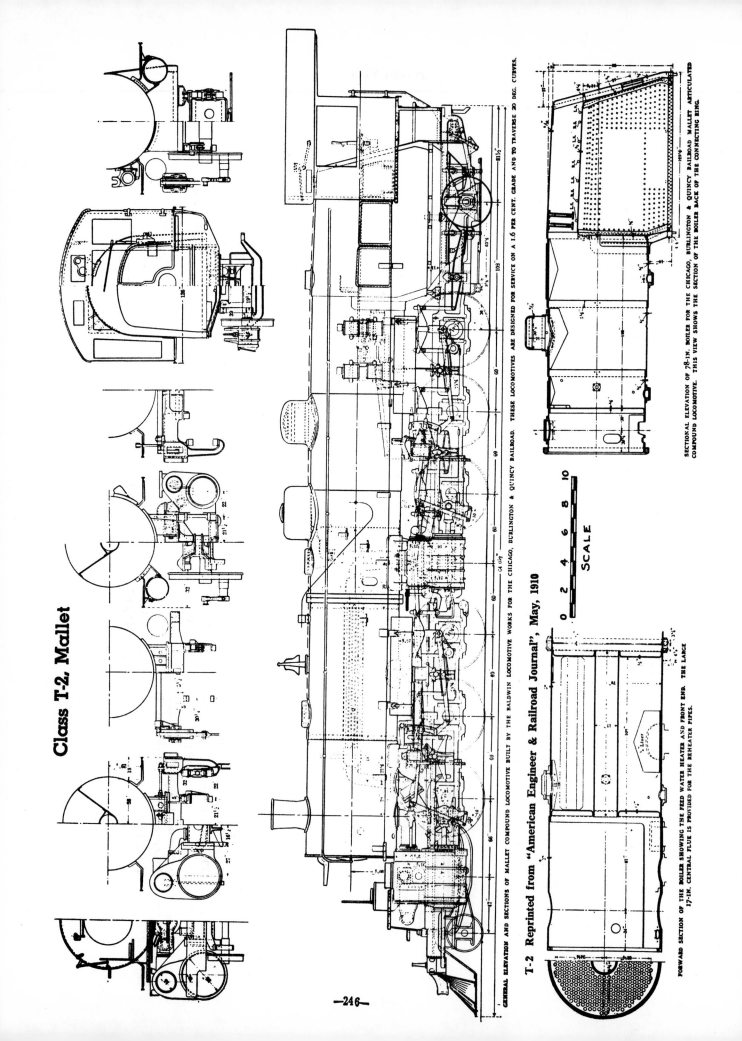

GENERAL ELEVATION AND SECTIONS OF MALLET COMPOUND LOCOMOTIVE BUILT BY THE BALDWIN LOCOMOTIVE WORKS FOR THE CHICAGO, BURLINGTON & QUINCY RAILROAD. THESE LOCOMOTIVES ARE DESIGNED FOR SERVICE ON A 1.6 PER CENT. GRADE AND TO TRAVERSE 20 DEG. CURVES.

T-2 Reprinted from "American Engineer & Railroad Journal", May, 1910

SCALE

0 2 4 6 8 10

SECTIONAL ELEVATION OF 78-IN. BOILER FOR THE CHICAGO, BURLINGTON & QUINCY RAILROAD MALLET ARTICULATED COMPOUND LOCOMOTIVE. THIS VIEW SHOWS THE SECTION OF THE BOILER BACK OF THE CONNECTING RING.

FORWARD SECTION OF THE BOILER SHOWING THE FEED WATER HEATER AND FRONT END. THE LARGE 17-IN. CENTRAL FLUE IS PROVIDED FOR THE REHEATER PIPES.

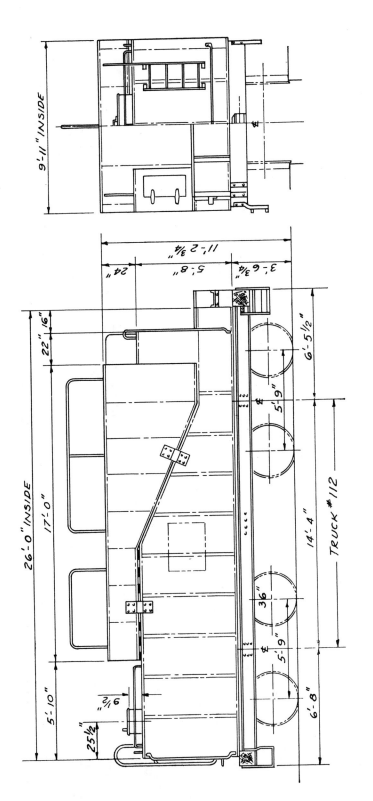

SPECIFICATIONS FOR CLASS T-2

Wheel Arrangement	2-6-6-2
Cylinders—in.	23 & 35x32
Drivers, dia.—in.	64
Driving Wheel base	11' 6"
Wheel base, total engine	51' 5"
Wheel base, engine plus tender	83' 0"
Steam pressure—psi	200
Grate area—sq. ft.	65.2
Superheating surface—sq. ft.	569.0
Total heating surface—sq. ft.	5692.5
Wt. on drivers—lb.	314,850
Wt. total engine—lb.	379,650
Wt. tender empty—lb.	55,500
Coal—tons	13*
Water—Gal.	8000
Tractive Force—lb.	70,500
Adhesion	4.46
Valve Gear	Walschaerts
Superheater type	Emerson
Power reverse type	Ragonnet
Feedwater heater type	Elesco
Stoker	

* Later converted to oil.

Class T-3, Mallet

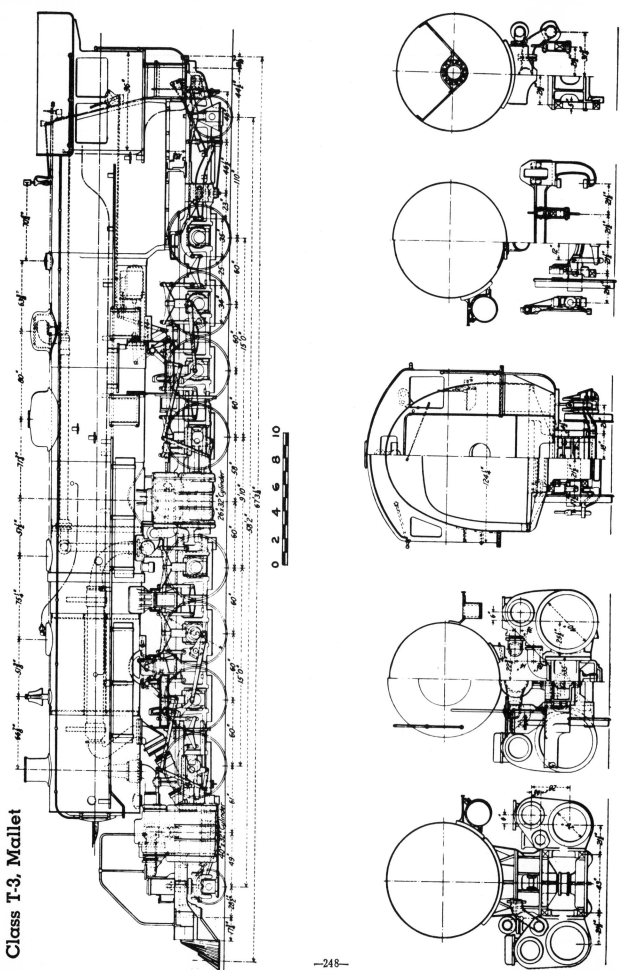

T-3—Reprinted from "Railway Age Gazette", August, 1911

Tender Plan

For original tender see Class 0-1.

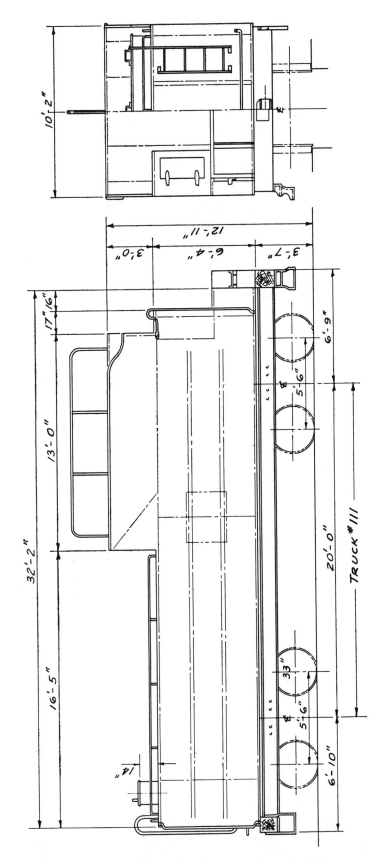

SPECIFICATIONS FOR CLASS T-3

Wheel Arrangement	2-8-8-2
Cylinders—in.	26 & 40x32
Drivers, dia.—in.	56
Driving Wheel base	15' 0"
Wheel base, total engine	58' 2"
Wheel base, engine plus tender	92' 5-11/16"
Steam pressure—psi	200
Grate area—sq. ft.	84.0
Superheating surface—sq. ft.	
Total heating surface—sq. ft.	5283.0*
Wt. on drivers—lb.	399,900
Wt. total engine—lb.	441,400
Wt. tender empty—lb.	79,500
Oil—Gal.	4365
Water—Gal.	12,000
Tractive Force—lb.	93,000
Adhesion	4.3
Valve Gear	Walschaerts
Superheater type	
Power reverse type	Ragonnet
Feedwater heater type	
Stoker	Oil-Fired

* Rating after boiler was rebuilt to single section.

This type of tender was used on the Class 0-1, 0-2, and S-3 engines. The coal pusher used on this tender was of novel design in that it lifted the rear of the bunker, which was hinged at the front, so that the coal would slide forward.

TENDER TRUCK SPECIFICATIONS

Number	Type	Capacity-lb.	Journal Size-in.	Weight-lb.
13 B	Arch Bar	50,000	4¼x8	5515
17	Arch Bar	60,000	4¼x8	5625
26	Arch Bar	80,000	5x9	7200
102	Pedestal	80,000	5x9	----
103	Pedestal	80,000	5x9	8700
104	Pedestal	100,000	5½x10	----
105	Bettendorf Cast Steel	100,000	5½x10	----
106	Arch Bar	100,000	5½x10	8700
107	Bettendorf Cast Steel	100,000	5½x10	----
108	Arch Bar	100,000	5½x10	8700
108 A	Arch Bar	100,000	5½x10	8700
109	Pedestal	100,000	5½x10	----
110	Arch Bar	100,000	5½x10	----
111	Arch Bar	140,000	6x11	----
112	Pedestal	100,000	5½x10	----
113	Andrews Cast Steel	140,000	6x11	----
114	Pedestal	140,000	6x11	----
117 A	Commonwealth Cast Steel	300,000	6½x12	----
118	General Steel Casting	300,000	----	----

Section 4

ROSTERS AND ASSIGNMENT SHEETS
LOCOMOTIVE ROSTER OF THE CHICAGO, BURLINGTON & QUINCY RAILROAD
1904 — 1959

In 1898 the Burlington System consisted of the Chicago, Burlington and Quincy; the Burlington and Missouri River in Nebraska; the Kansas City, St. Joseph and Council Bluffs; the Hannibal and St. Joseph; the St. Louis, Keokuk and Northwestern; the Chicago, Burlington and Kansas City; the Chicago, Burlington and Northern; and two narrow-gauge lines, the Burlington and Western, and the Burlington and Northwestern. Each of these roads had its own locomotives and system of numbering. Because at several locations two or more of these roads used the same terminals and tracks, it became advisable to adopt a new system of numbering that would avoid duplication of engine numbers. This was done by assigning a certain set of numbers to each road as follows:

B. & M.R. in Nebraska	1	to	500
K. C. St. J. & C. B.	501	to	600
H. & St. J.	601	to	700
St. L. K. & N. W.	701	to	800
C. B. & K. C.	801	to	900
C. B. & N.	901	to	999
C. B. & Q.	1000	to	2000

Since the B.&M.R. in Nebraska had already been using the same engine numbers that were assigned to it, no changes in its numbering system were necessary. The engines of the B. & M.R. in Nebraska had a large number painted on the tender and the letters, B. & M. R., on the cab. The engines of the original B. & M.R., before the road was absorbed by the C.B.&Q. in 1872, had the letters, B.&M.R.R.R., on the tender and the name of the engine on the cab.

In 1898 the C.B.&Q. engines were renumbered by adding 1000 to each number. On the remaining five roads, the numbers were changed considerably, and during the years from 1898 to 1904 numerous other changes were made. Although there was much inter-changing of engines among the various roads between 1898 and 1904, each engine retained its own number, and at no time after 1898 was there a duplication of numbers.

As the B.&M.R. began receiving new engines, it found that its assigned numbers, 1 to 500, were inadequate. Therefore, in 1903 the road began numbering its new engines in the 3000 series. Some of the older engines were also numbered in this series, but before the complete change had been made, the road was integrated with the C.B.&Q. in 1904.

When the controlled C.B.&N. was purchased outright in 1899, its engines were lettered with the initials of the C.B.&Q., but the numbers were continued in the 900 series until 1904. The engines of the Keokuk and Western[1] were taken over in 1898 when this road was purchased. The engines retained their original numbers until 1903 when they were assigned to the 800 series. A number of K. & W. engines were transferred to the C.B.&Q. in 1903, but they carried their Keokuk and Western numbers until the general change in 1904.

As the C.B.&Q. began receiving new engines between 1898 and 1904 many of the older engines were transferred to its subsidiary roads. These engines were re-lettered and renumbered to the series assigned to the road receiving them.

---

[1] The Keokuk and Western was organized on August 19, 1886 by the purchasers of the Missouri Iowa and Nebraska Railway Co. The K. & W. extended from Keokuk, Iowa to Van Wert, a distance of 148 miles. Of this, 5.2 miles was on St. L.K.&N.W. tracks. In 1895 the K. & W. purchased the Des Moines & Kansas City, a 112-mile, narrow gauge line extending from Des Moines to Cainesville. This latter road was widened to standard gauge in 1897.

In 1898 the two narrow-gauge lines, the Burlington and Western and the Burlington and Northwestern, were also given new engine numbers. The engines numbered from 1 to 10 were given double numbers; for example, No. 4 became No. 44, etc. No. 10 became No. 100. C.B.&Q. engines were used on these roads after the lines were converted to standard gauge in 1902.

The present locomotive - classification system was adopted in 1898. Little is known of the old system, but in the new system the class letter denotes the wheel arrangement, and the class number denotes the order in which new groups of engines were added to each class. The sub-classes were noted with a letter after the class number. Rebuilt engines were in some cases given a sub-classification. For instance, the rebuilt R-5 engines were classed as R-5A. When rebuilding of an engine was extensive, a new class number was sometimes assigned. The rebuilt P-2-C Atlantics were classed as P-5, for example. When an engine was rebuilt to a different wheel arrangement, it was given the class letter of that wheel arrangement. Thus, when some of the Class R engines were rebuilt to 0-6-0 switchers, they became Class G. In more recent years, there were four cases in which engines of different wheel arrangements were given the same class letter. The 2-6-6-2 and 2-8-8-2 types were both Class T. The 4-6-4 engines built in 1930 were given the same class letter as the 4-6-2 types, and the 4-8-4 and 2-8-2 locomotives were designated as Class 0. Also the 2-10-2 and 2-10-4 types were classed as M.

In 1904 the Burlington System, in order to make a more practical and a more efficiently operated organization, merged all of its controlled roads into one road under the name of the Chicago, Burlington and Quincy. Consequently, several roads which had operated under their original names for many years lost their identities; for instance, the H. & St. J. had operated under its corporate name since 1859. Some of these roads had been owned outright by the Burlington from an early date. Others had been controlled either by lease or by stock control, but by 1904 all were owned directly.

As these roads became a physical part of the C.B.&Q., all of their equipment were re-lettered with the initials of the parent road. In all, there were 1323 locomotives on the combined roads and these were renumbered according to class. This was the second general change of numbers made on the locomotives of the Burlington System, the first having been made in 1898.

The locomotives of the Colorado and Southern, and of the Fort Worth and Denver City had their own numbers and classification system. The engine rosters of these two roads are, therefore, listed separately. The acquired engines of the Quincy, Omaha and Kansas City were soon retired and all traffic on this road was handled by C.B.&Q. engines.

The following schedule was issued by the Burlington for renumbering in 1904. In later years, as the need arose, several changes were made in this listing.

Class			Class			Class			
	A-1	1-199		K-5	800- 899		R-1		1700-1709
	A-2	200-399		K-6	900- 909		R-2		1710-1799
	A-3	400-439		K-7	910- 919		R-3		1800-1899
	A-4	440-459		K-8	920- 939		R-4		1900-____
	A-5	460-469		K-9	940- 999		N-1		2400-____
	A-6	470-489		H-1	1000-1119		P-1	comp	2500-2509
	A-7	490-499		H-2	1120-1199		P-2	comp	2510-2519
	I-1	500-529		H-3	1200-1219		P-2		2520-2599
Narrow Gauge		530-549		H-4	1220-1269		P-3	comp	2700-____
Class	E	550-589		H-5	1270-1299		D-2		2980-2999
Class	L	590-599		G-1	1300-1389		D-3		3000-3009
Class	K-1	600-629		G-2	1390-1399		D-5		3010-3019
	K-2	630-675		G-3	1400-1599		D-6		3020-3029
	K-3	676-699		G-4	1600-1689		D-7		3030-3099
	K-4	700-799		G-5	1690-1699		D-4		3100-____

Class A—4-4-0; D—2-8-0; E—0-4-0; G—0-6-0; H—2-6-0; I—0-6-2T; K—4-6-0; L—0-10-0; N—2-4-2; P—4-4-2; R—2-6-2.

The Hannibal shops built this American-type engine for the H.&St.J. in 1886 as No. 22. She was classed as A-1 in 1898, renumbered to C.B.&Q. No. 45 in 1904, and rebuilt to Class A-2, No. 455, in 1916. The engine is shown being serviced at West Burlington, Iowa in Oct., 1914 —O. H. Means

Condition, Dimensions and Weight of Engines bel

NAME OF ENGINE.	BY WHOM MANUFACTURED.	KIND OF FUEL USED.	HOW CONNECTED.	CYLINDERS.		DRIVERS.			BOILERS.			
				Diam. in.	Stroke. in.	No.	Diam. Ft.	in.	Length. Ft.	in.	Diam. Ft.	in.
Stag Hound,	Amoskeag Manufacturing Co.	Wood.	Inside.	16	20	4	5	6	17	8	3	
Fox Hound	"	"	"	16	20	4	5	6	17	8	3	
Grey Hound,	" " "	"	"	16	20	4	5	8	17	8	3	
West Wind	Manchester Loc. Works.	"	"	16	20	4	5	6	17	8	3	
North Wind	" " "	"	"	16	20	4	5	6	17	8	3	
Grey Eagle	" " "	"	"	16	20	4	5	6	17	8	3	
Golden Eagle,	" " "	"	"	16	20	4	5	6	17	8	3	
Antelope,	Amoskeag Manufacturing Co.	"	"	16	20	4	6	0	17	0	3	
Reindeer,	" " "	"	"	16	20	4	5	8	17	0	3	
Panther,	" " "	"	"	16	20	4	6	0	17	0	3	
Roebuck	" " "	"	"	16	20	4	5	6	17	0	3	
Troubadour,	Manchester Loc. Works.	"	Outside.	15	20	4	5	8	18	0	3	
Talisman,	" " "	"	"	15	20	4	5	0	18	0	3	
Cossack,	" " "	"	"	15	20	4	5	0	18	0	3	
Arab,	" " "	"	"	15	20	4	5	0	18	0	3	
Corsair,	" " "	"	"	15	20	4	5	0	18	0	3	
Tartar,	" " "	"	"	15	20	4	5	0	18	0	3	
Whirlwind,	Amoskeag Manufacturing Co.	"	Inside.	16	22	4	5	0	17	5	3	
Hurricane,	" " "	"	"	16	20	4	6	0	17	5	3	
Tornado,	" " "	"	"	16	20	4	5	0	17	5	3	
Tempest,	" " "	"	"	16	22	4	5	0	17	5	3	
Garden City,	Chicago Locomotive Works.	"	Outside.	15	22	4	5	0	17	6	3	
Stranger,	" " "	Coal.	"	15	22	4	5	0	18	0	3	
No. 58,	R. K. & G., New Jersey.	Wood.	"	15	22	4	5	0	18	2	3	
No. 57,	" " "	"	"	14½	22	4	5	0	18	2	3	
No. 56,	Manchester Loc. Works.	Coal.	"	15	24	4	5	0	19	0	3	
No. 55,	" " "	"	"	15	24	4	5	0	19	0	3	
No. 54,	" " "	"	"	15	24	4	5	0	19	0	3	
No. 53,	" " "	"	"	15	24	4	5	0	19	0	3	
No. 52,	" " "	"	"	16	24	4	4	9	19	0	3	
No. 51,	" " "	"	"	16	24	4	4	9	19	0	3	1
No. 50,	" " "	"	"	16	24	4	4	9	19	0	3	1
No. 49,	" " "	"	"	16	24	4	4	9	19	0	3	1
No. 48,	" " "	"	"	16	24	4	4	9	19	0	3	1
No. 47,	" " "	"	"	16	24	4	4	9	19	0	3	1
Wataga,	" " "	"	"	15	22	4	4	6	19	0	3	
Aurora,	Amoskeag Manufacturing Co.	"	"	15	22	4	4	8	18	10	3	
Batavia,	" " "	Wood.	"	15	22	4	4	6	17	10	3	
Excelsior,	" " "	"	"	15	22	4	4	6	17	10	3	
Little Indian,	" " "	Coal.	"	15	22	4	4	6	18	10	3	
Lion,	" " "	Wood.	Inside.	16	20	6	3	10	17	1	3	
Tiger,	" " "	"	"	16	20	6	3	10	17	1	3	
Samson,	" " "	"	"	16	20	6	3	10	17	1	3	
Brown Bear,	" " "	"	"	16	20	6	3	10	17	1	3	
White Bear,	" " "	"	"	16	20	6	3	10	17	1	3	
Black Bear,	" " "	"	"	16	20	6	3	10	17	1	3	
Titan,	" " "	"	"	16	20	6	3	10	16	10	3	
No. 59,	Detroit Locomotive Works.	"	"	16	20	6	3	10	17	0	3	
No. 60,	" " "	"	"	16	20	6	3	10	17	0	3	
Challenge,	Amoskeag Manufacturing Co.	"	Outside.	16	22	4	4	8	19	6	3	10
Invincible,	" " "	Coal.	"	16	22	4	4	8	19	6	3	10
Starlight,	New Jersey Loc. Works.	"	Inside.	16	20	4	4	10	19	9	3	10
Moonlight,	" " " "	"	"	16	20	4	4	8	19	9	3	10
Daylight,	" " " "	Wood.	"	16	20	6	3	10	18	8	3	8
Erastus Corning,	Schenectady Loc. Works.	"	Outside.	14½	22	4	5	0	17	0	3	4
Rocket,	Hinckley, Drury & others.	"	Inside.	15	18	4	5	0	14	0	3	4
Pigeon,	M. W. Baldwin.	"	Outside.	13	16	2	5	0	14	7	3	4
No. One,	Amoskeag Manufacturing Co.	"	Inside.	14	20	4	4	0	16	10	3	4

Flues			Fire Box						When Built	Weight in Tons	Condition	Remarks
Length. Ft. in.	Diam. in.	No.	Length. Ft. in.		Width. Ft. in.		Height. Ft. in.		Year.			
10 6	2	146	4 1		3 0		5 3		1855	28	In Shop,	Having slight repairs.
10 6	2	146	4 1		3 0		5 3		1855	28	Running order,	Steam Chests and Valve Seats, needs repairs.
10 6	2	146	4 1		3 0		5 3		1855	28	Good order,	
10 6	2	152	4 1		3 2		5 3		1855	28	Running order,	Needs slight repairs.
10 6	2	152	4 1		3 2		5 3		1855	28	Rebuilding,	Had new Cylinders,
10 6	2	152	4 1		3 2		5 3		1855	28	Good order,	
10 6	2	152	4 1		3 2		5 3		1855	28	In shop,	At Galesburg. General repairs.
10 1	2	147	3 11		3 2		4 10		1853	26	Running order,	Has brick arch for burning coal.
10 1	2	147	3 10		3 1		4 10		1853	26	"	Needs general repairs.
10 1	2	147	3 10		3 1		4 7		1853	26	In shop,	At Galesburg. Wants general repairs.
10 1	2	149	3 10		3 1		4 10		1853	26	Running order,	Needs repairs.
11 5	2	118	3 8½		3 1		4 8		1855	27	Good order,	
11 5	2	118	3 8½		3 1		4 8		1855	27	"	
11 5	2	118	3 8½		3 1		4 8		1855	26	"	
11 5	2	118	3 8½		3 1		4 8		1855	26	"	
11 5	2	118	3 8½		3 1		4 8		1855	26	Running order,	Needs repairs.
10 2	2	132	3 11		3 1½		5 0		1853	25	Good order,	
10 2	2	132	3 11		3 1½		5 0		1853	25	Wants general repairs,	
10 2	2	132	3 11		3 1½		5 0		1853	25	Running order,	
10 2	2	132	3 11		3 1½		5 0		1853	25	Good order,	
10 11	2	151	3 9		3 2		4 6		1854	26	Running order,	
10 11	2	136	4 9		3 2		5 0		1854	26	In shop at Aurora,	Having new coal Fire Box, new Tires, &c.
11 0	2	144	4 0		3 0		4 9		1855	26	Good order,	
11 0	2	144	4 0		3 0		4 9		1854	26	"	
11 0	2¼	126	4 9		3 6		4 5		1856	29	Running order,	Needs new Fire Box.
11 0	2¼	126	4 9		3 6		3 5		1856	29	In shop,	Having flues repaired.
11 0	2¼	126	4 9		3 6		3 5		1856	29	Good order,	
11 0	2¼	126	4 9		3 6		3 5		1856	29	"	
10 6	2¼	126	4 8		3 3		3 5		1857	30	"	
10 6	2¼	126	4 8		3 3		3 5		1857	30	"	
10 6	2¼	126	4 8		3 3		3 5		1857	30	"	
10 6	2¼	126	4 8		3 3		3 5		1857	30	"	
10 6	2¼	126	4 8		3 3		3 5		1857	30	"	
11 0	2	121	4 8		3 6		3 5		1855	28	"	Rebuilt at Galesburg.
11 0	2	140	4 8		3 5		4 9		1853	25	"	Rebuilt at Aurora.
11 0	2	140	3 10		3 2		4 9		1853	24	Running order,	
11 0	2	140	3 10		3 2		4 9		1853	24	Good order,	
7 0	2	136	4 8		3 2		5 0		1853	25	Rebuilding.	Having new Coal Fire Box and New Tires.
10 7	2	144	4 0		3 1		4 6		1855	28	Good order,	
10 7	2	144	4 0		3 1		4 6		1855	28	In shop,	Having Steam Chests and Valves repaired.
10 7	2	144	4 0		3 1		4 6		1855	28	Running order,	
10 7	2	144	4 0		3 1		4 6		1855	28	Good order,	
10 7	2	144	4 0		3 1		4 6		1855	28	"	
10 7	2	144	4 0		3 1		4 6		1855	28	"	
11 6	2	146	3 10		3 2		4 6		1854	27	Running order,	
10 6	2	143	3 10		3 4		4 5		1855	28	Good order,	
11 2	2	145	3 10		3 0		4 9		1853	28	In shop,	For new Drivers, Tires, Stack and Heater.
11 2	2	145	5 0		2 11		3 5		1853	29	Good order,	Had new Fire Box and general repairs.
11 ¾	2	142	5 0		3 3		3 8½		1857	32	"	Rebuilt at Galesburg.
11 ¾	2¼	141	4 9		3 3		3 6		1856	32	Running order,	Needs new Fire Box.
11 ¾	2	147	4 1		3 4		4 8		1854	28	"	Needs overhauling.
10 10	2	136	3 7		3 2		4 2		1852	22	Good order,	Had new Drivers and Tires, and gen'l repairs.
9 0	2	120	2 10		3 1		4 0		1846	19	Running order,	
10 0	2	118	3 4		3 3		4 0		1837	14	Laid up.	Wants rebuilding.
11 3	2	126	3 0		3 1		4 0		1851	19	Good order,	Rebuilt at Aurora.

C. G. HAMMOND, Gen'l Sup't.

Class A-1.   4-4-0

New CB&Q No. 1904	Original	No.	Builder	B. No.	Date	No Change 1898		Changes 1898 to 1904		Disposition	
1	CB&Q	96	Galesburg		1880	CB&Q	1096			Retired	
2	StL. K&NW	15	Aurora		1882	St'NW	740			Ret. 1910	
3	KCStJ&CB	6	St. Joseph		1883	KC'CB	537			Retired	
4	KCStJ&CB	41	Manchester		1883	KS'CB	541			Reb. to A-2	454
5	StLK&NW	23	Hinkley		1883	St'NW	723			Reb. to A-2	472
6	KCStJ&CB	2	St. Joseph		1884	KC'CB	527			Reb. to A-2	470
7	H&StJ	38	Aurora		1884	H&StJ	638			Retired 12-22	
8	H&StJ	39	Aurora		1884	H&StJ	639			Prob. reb. to A-2	
9	StLK&NW	21	Aurora		1884	St'NW	721			Retired	
10	StLK&NW	9	Aurora		1884	St'NW	734			Retired 1911	
11	CB&Q	205	Aurora		1884	CB&Q	1205			Reb. to A-2	395
12	B&MR	104	Aurora		1884	B&MR	104			Retired	
13	B&MR	131	Manch.	1229	1885	B&MR	131			Reb. to A-2	387
14	B&MR	132	Manch.	1230	1885	B&MR	132			Reb. to A-2	444
15	B&MR	133	Manch.	1231	1885	B&MR	133			Retired	
16	B&MR	135	Manch.	1233	1885	B&MR	135			Reb. to A-2	453
17	B&MR	136	Manch.	1234	1885	B&MR	136			Retired 12-22	
18	B&MR	137	Manch.	1235	1885	B&MR	137			Reb. to A-2	449
19	B&MR	138	Manch.	1236	1885	B&MR	138			Retired	
20	CB&Q	33	Aurora		1885	CB&Q	1033			Reb. to A-2	477
21	CB&Q	143	Aurora		1885	CB&Q	1143			Reb. to A-2	478
22	CB&Q	149	Galesburg		1885	CB&Q	1149			Retired	
23	CB&Q	153	Galesburg		1885	CB&Q	1153			Reb. to A-2	464
24	CB&Q	210	W. B. Shops		1885	CB&Q	1210			Reb. to A-2	375
25	CB&Q	295	W. B. Shops		1885	CB&Q	1295			Reb. to A-2	396
26	CB&Q	305	Galesburg		1885	CB&Q	1305			Reb. to A-2	374
27	CB&Q	363	W. B. Shops		1885	CB&Q	1363			Retired 12-22	
28	CB&Q	376	W. B. Shops		1885	CB&Q	1376			Retired 12-22	
29	KCStJ&SB	5	Aurora		1885	KC'CB	532			Reb. to A-2	474
30	CB&Q	412	Manch.	1218	1885	CB&Q	1412	KCStJ&CB	543	Reb. to A-2	397
31	CB&Q	28	Aurora		1885	CB&Q	1028	KCStJ&CB	548	Retired 1911	
32	H&StJ	23	Aurora		1885	H&StJ	623			Retired	
33	H&StJ	31	Manchester		1885	H&StJ	631			Retired	
34	H&StJ	37	Hannibal		1885	H&StJ	637			Retired 1-23	
35	H&StJ	41	Hannibal		1885	H&StJ	641			Retired	
36	H&StJ	57	Aurora		1885	H&StJ	657			Reb. to A-2	398
37	H&StJ	65	Hannibal		1885	H&StJ	665			Retired 1911	
38	H&StJ	67	Manchester		1885	H&StJ	667			Reb. to A-2	476
39	StLK&NW	3	Aurora		1885	St'NW	729			Retired	
40	StLK&NW	17	Aurora		1885	St'NW	742			Retired	
41	StLK&NW	20	Aurora		1885	St'NW	745			Retired	
42	CB&Q	288	Aurora		1885	CB&Q	1288	StLK&NW	749	Retired	
43	CB&KC	2	Manchester		1885	CB&KC	822			Retired	
44	CB&N	60	Rhd I	1617	1886	CB&N	938	CB&Q	938		
								KCStJ&CB	546	Reb. to A-2	471
45	H&StJ	22	Hannibal		1886	H&StJ	622			Reb. to A-2	455
46	H&StJ	24	Hannibal		1886	H&StJ	624			Retired	
47	H&StJ	30	Hannibal		1886	H&StJ	630			Retired	
48	H&StJ	34	Aurora		1886	H&StJ	634			Retired 1909	
49	H&StJ	35	Aurora		1886	H&StJ	635			Reb. to A-2	399
50	H&StJ	44	Hannibal		1886	H&StJ	644	KCStJ&CB	644	Retired 1911	
51	H&StJ	15	Aurora		1886	H&StJ	675			Retired	
52	H&StJ	16	Aurora		1886	H&StJ	676			Retired	
53	H&StJ	19	Aurora		1886	H&StJ	679			Retired 1910	
54	H&StJ	20	Aurora		1886	H&StJ	680			Reb. to A-2	400
55	StLK&NW	24	Hannibal		1886	St'NW	724			Reb. to A-2	473
56	StLK&NW	25	Hannibal		1886	St'NW	725			Retired 1911	
57	StLK&NW	2	Aurora		1886	St'NW	728			Reb. to A-2	401
58	StLK&NW	16	Aurora		1886	St'NW	741			Reb. to A-2	456
59	CB&N	68	Rhd. I	1625	1886	CB&N	946	CB&Q 946			
								StLK&NW	748	Reb. to A-2	402
60	KCStJ&CB	10	St. Joseph		1886	KC'CB	542	K&W 21, K&W 827		Retired	
61	CB&N	61	Rhd. I.	1618	1886	CB&N	939	CB&Q 939			
								KCStJ&CB 547			
								K&W 30, K&W 830		Retired	
62	CB&N	1	Rhd. I.	1579	1886	CB&N	916	CB&Q	916	Reb. to A-2	376
63	CB&N	2	Rhd. I.	1580	1886	CB&N	917	CB&Q	917	Retired 1900	
64	CB&N	3	Rhd. I.	1630	1886	CB&N	918	CB&Q	918	Reb. to A-2	379
65	CB&N	4	Rhd. I.	1631	1886	CB&N	919	CB&Q	919	Reb. to A-2	403
66	CB&N	5	Rhd. I.	1632	1886	CB&N	920	CB&Q	920	Reb. to A-2	469
67	CB&N	6	Rhd. I.	1633	1886	CB&N	921	CB&Q	921	Reb. to A-2	404
68	CB&N	7	Rhd. I.	1634	1886	CB&N	922	CB&Q	922	Retired	
69	CB&N	8	Rhd. I.	1635	1886	CB&N	923	CB&Q	923	Reb. to A-2	377
70	CB&N	9	Rhd. I.	1636	1886	CB&N	924	CB&Q	924	Reb. to A-2	457

K. C. St. J. & C. B. 41 probably Manchester 1148, Orig. CB&Q 286
H. & St. J. 31 probably Manchester 1227, Orig. H. & St. J. 3
H. & St. J. 67 probably Manchester 1228, Orig. H. & St. J. 5
C. B. & K. C. 2 probably Manchester 1220, Orig. C. B. & Q. 427

Class A-1, 4-4-0

New CB&Q No. 1904	Original	No.	Builder	Date	No Change 1898	Changes 1898 to 1904	
71	CB&N	10	Rhd. I. 1637	1886 CB&N	925	CB&Q 925	Reb. to A-2 462
72	CB&N	50	Rhd. I. 1581	1886 CB&N	928	CB&Q 928	Reb. to A-2 405
73	CB&N	51	Rhd. I 1582	1886 CB&N	929	CB&Q 929	Reb. to A-2 406
74	CB&N	52	Rhd. I. 1583	1886 CB&N	930	CB&Q 930	Retired
75	CB&N	53	Rhd. I. 1604	1886 CB&N	931	CB&Q 931	Reb. to A-2 468
76	CB&N	54	Rhd. I. 1605	1886 CB&N	932	CB&Q 932	Retired
77	CB&N	55	Rhd. I. 1606	1886 CB&N	933	CB&Q 933	Retired
78	CB&N	56	Rhd. I. 1613	1886 CB&N	934	CB&Q 934	Retired
79	CB&N	57	Rhd. I. 1614	1886 CB&N	935	CB&Q 935	Retired 6-24
80	CB&N	58	Rhd. I. 1615	1886 CB&N	936	CB&Q 936	Reb. to A-2 407
81	CB&N	59	Rhd. I. 1616	1886 CB&N	937	CB&Q 937	Reb. to A-2 408
82	CB&N	62	Rhd. I. 1619	1886 CB&N	940	CB&Q 940	Reb. to A-2 475
83	CB&N	63	Rhd. I. 1620	1886 CB&N	941	CB&Q 941	Reb. to A-2 409
84	CB&N	64	Rhd. I. 1621	1886 CB&N	942	CB&Q 942	Retired 12-22
85	CB&N	65	Rhd. I. 1622	1886 CB&N	943	CB&Q 943	Retired
86	CB&N	66	Rhd. I. 1623	1886 CB&N	944	CB&Q 944	Retired 4-23
87	CB&N	67	Rhd. I. 1624	1886 CB&N	945	CB&Q 945	Reb. to A-2 463
88	CB&N	69	Rhd. I. 1626	1886 CB&N	947	CB&Q 947	Retired 4-23
89	CB&N	70	Rhd. I. 1627	1886 CB&N	948	CB&Q 948	Reb. to A-2 410
90	CB&N	71	Rhd. I. 1628	1886 CB&N	949	CB&Q 949	Retired
91	CB&N	72	Rhd. I. 1629	1886 CB&N	950	CB&Q 950	Reb. to A-2 411
92	CB&Q	90	Aurora	1886 CB&Q	1090		Reb. to A-2 412
93	CB&Q	130	Aurora	1886 CB&Q	1130		Reb. to A-2 413
94	CB&Q	138	Aurora	1886 CB&Q	1138		Retired
95	CB&Q	191	Aurora	1886 CB&Q	1191		Retired
96	CB&Q	256	W. B. Shops	1886 CB&Q	1256		Retired 4-23
97	CB&Q	259	W. B. Shops	1886 CB&Q	1259		Retired
98	CB&Q	292	W. B. Shops	1886 CB&Q	1292		Reb. to A-2 380
99	CB&Q	357	W. B. Shops	1886 CB&Q	1357		Reb. to A-2 381
100	CB&Q	378	Aurora	1886 CB&Q	1378		Retired
101	CB&Q	619	Aurora	1886 CB&Q	1619		Reb. to A-2 414
102	CB&Q	620	Aurora	1886 CB&Q	1620		Reb. to A-2 415
103	CB&Q	50	Aurora	1887 CB&Q	1050		Retired
104	CB&Q	148	W. B. Shops	1887 CB&Q	1148		Retired
105	CB&Q	194	W. B. Shops	1887 CB&Q	1194		Reb. to A-2 467
106	CB&Q	282	W. B. Shops	1887 CB&Q	1282		Retired 1912
107	CB&Q	358	W. B. Shops	1887 CB&Q	1358		Reb. to A-2 416
108	CB&N	11	Rhd. I. 1638	1886 CB&N	926	CB&Q 1362, 8-98	Retired 1911
109	CB&N	12	Rhd. I. 1639	1886 CB&N	927	CB&Q 1373, 8-98	Retired
110	CB&Q	610	Aurora	1887 CB&Q	1610		Reb. to A-2 417
111	CB&Q	616	Aurora	1887 CB&Q	1616		Reb. to A-2 382
112	KCStJ&CB	3	Aurora	1887 KC'CB	528		Retired 4-23
113	KCStJ&CB	4	St. Joseph	1887 KC'CB	531		Reb. to A-2 466
114	KCStJ&CB	9	Co. Shops	1887 KC'CB	539		Reb. to A-2 465
115	H&StJ	21	Hannibal	1887 H&StJ	621		Reb. to A-2 418
116	H&StJ	25	Aurora	1887 H&StJ	625		Retired 1910
117	H&StJ	26	Hannibal	1887 H&StJ	626		Retired 6-24
118	H&StJ	27	Hannibal	1887 H&StJ	627		Reb. to A-2 458
119	H&StJ	29	Hannibal	1887 H&StJ	629		Retired 1910
120	H&StJ	18	Hannibal	1887 H&StJ	678		Retired
121	StLK&NW	22	Hannibal	1887 St'NW	722		Reb. to A-2 419
122	B&MR	163	W. B. Shops	1887 B&MR	163		Reb. to A-2 452
123	B&MR	164	W. B. Shops	1887 B&MR	164		Reb. to A-2 420
124	B&MR	157	Aurora	1887 B&MR	157		Reb. to A-2 445
125	B&MR	158	Aurora	1887 B&MR	158		Reb. to A-2 421
126	B&MR	160	Aurora	1887 B&MR	160		Retired
127	B&MR	161	Aurora	1887 B&MR	161		Reb. to A-2 446
128	B&MR	165	W. B. Shops	1887 B&MR	165		Retired
129	B&MR	167	W. B. Shops	1887 B&MR	167		Reb. to A-2 388
130	B&MR	203	Manch. 1390	1888 B&MR	203		Reb. to A-2 422
131	B&MR	204	Manch. 1391	1888 B&MR	204		Retired
132	B&MR	205	Manch. 1376	1888 B&MR	205		Reb. to A-2 450
133	B&MR	206	Manch. 1377	1888 B&MR	206		Reb. to A-2 389
134	B&MR	207	Manch. 1378	1888 B&MR	207		Reb. to A-2 423
135	B&MR	211	Manch. 1382	1888 B&MR	211		Reb. to A-2 451
136	B&MR	212	Manch. 1383	1888 B&MR	212		Retired
137	B&MR	23	Plattsmouth	1888 B&MR	23		Reb. to A-2 424
138	H&StJ	45	Hannibal	1888 H&StJ	652	StLK&NW 652	Reb. to A-2 425
139	H&StJ	42	Aurora	1888 H&StJ	642		Reb. to A-2 383
140	H&StJ	43	Aurora	1888 H&StJ	643		Retired
141	H&StJ	68	Aurora	1888 H&StJ	668		Reb. to A-2 459
142	B&MR	221	Rhd. I. 2178	1889 B&MR	221		Retired
143	B&MR	222	Rhd. I. 2179	1889 B&MR	222		Reb. to A-2 442
144	B&MR	224	Rhd. I. 2181	1889 B&MR	224		Retired
145	B&MR	225	Rhd. I. 2182	1889 B&MR	225		Reb. to A-2 426
146	B&MR	226	Rhd. I. 2183	1889 B&MR	226		Reb. to A-2 427
147	B&MR	227	Rhd. I. 2184	1889 B&MR	227		Retired
148	B&MR	228	Rhd. I. 2185	1889 B&MR	228		Retired 6-27

Class A-1, 4-4-0

New CB&Q No. 1904	Original	No. Builder	Date	No Change 1898		Changes 1898 to 1904	
149	B&MR	229 Rhd. I. 2186	1889	B&MR	229		Reb. to A-2 428
150	H&StJ	40 Hannibal	1890	H&StJ	640		Retired 1909
151	H&StJ	54 Hannibal	1890	H&StJ	654	StLK&NW 654	Reb. to A-2 460
152	H&StJ	62 Hannibal	1890	H&StJ	662		Reb. to A-2 429
153	CB&Q	157 Co. Shops	1881	CB&Q	1157		Retired 12-22

Cyls.	Drs.	Wt., Drs.	Total	T.E.	B.P.
18"x24"	69"	54,500 lbs.	82,800 lbs.	13,900 lbs.	145 lbs.
18"x24"	64"	54,500 lbs.	82,800 lbs.	14,900 lbs.	145 lbs.

Class A-2, 4-4-0

New CB&Q No. 1904	Original	No. Builder	Date	No Change 1898	Changes 1898 to 1904	
200	*CB&Q	247 Manch. 110	1868	CB&Q	1247	Retired 1910
201	*CB&Q	248 Manch. 128	1868	CB&Q	1248	Retired
202	*CB&Q	252 Manch. 141	1869	CB&Q	1252	Retired 4-23
203	CB&Q	217 Hinkley, Wms.	1870	CB&Q	1217	Retired
204	CB&Q	218 Hinkley, Wms.	1870	CB&Q	1218	Retired
205	*CB&Q	372 Lancaster	1870	CB&Q	1372	Retired
206	*CB&Q	289 Manchester	1871	CB&Q	1289	Retired
207	*CB&Q	300 Manchester	1872	CB&Q	1300	Retired
208	CB&Q	214 Manch. 507	1873	CB&Q	1214	Retired 1910
209	CB&Q	228 Manch. 680	1874	CB&Q	1228	Retired
210	CB&Q	229 Manch. 681	1874	CB&Q	1229	Retired 1910
211	CB&Q	8 Aurora	1878	CB&Q	1008	Retired
212	CB&Q	16 Aurora	1878	CB&Q	1016	Retired
213	CB&Q	72 Aurora	1878	CB&Q	1072	Retired 5-17
214	CB&Q	101 Aurora	1878	CB&Q	1101	Retired
215	CB&Q	308 Aurora	1878	CB&Q	1308	Retired
216	CB&Q	311 Manch. 749	1878	CB&Q	1311	Retired
217	CB&Q	313 Manch. 758	1878	CB&Q	1313	Retired
218	I&StL	2 Baldwin	1878	Acq'd	1903	Retired
219	StLK&NW	19 Baldwin	1879	St'NW	744	Retired 12-22
220	CB&Q	340 Bald. 4773	1879	CB&Q	1340 StLK&NW 750 CB&KC 750	Retired 9-18
221	CB&Q	323 Bald. 4705	1879	CB&Q	1323 CB&KC 824	Retired 1909
222	CB&Q	59 Aurora	1879	CB&Q	1059	Retired
223	CB&Q	66 W. B. Shops	1879	CB&Q	1066	Retired 1911
224	CB&Q	118 Galesburg	1879	CB&Q	1118	Retired 1912
225	CB&Q	175 Co. Shops	1879	CB&Q	1175	Retired
226	CB&Q	309 Aurora	1879	CB&Q	1309	Retired 1910
227	CB&Q	310 Aurora	1879	CB&Q	1310	Retired
228	CB&Q	318 Bald. 4697	1879	CB&Q	1318	Retired 12-22
229	CB&Q	319 Bald. 4698	1879	CB&Q	1319	Retired
230	CB&Q	320 Bald. 4700	1879	CB&Q	1320	Retired 10-17
231	CB&Q	321 Bald. 4701	1879	CB&Q	1321	Reb. to A-2 384
232	CB&Q	322 Bald. 4702	1879	CB&Q	1322	Retired 1910
233	CB&Q	327 Manch. 763	1879	CB&Q	1327	Retired
234	CB&Q	329 Manch. 765	1879	CB&Q	1329	Sold 9-13-12
235	CB&Q	330 Manch. 766	1879	CB&Q	1330	Retired 1910
236	CB&Q	331 Manch 767	1879	CB&Q	1331	Reb. to A-2 385
237	CB&Q	333 Manch. 769	1879	CB&Q	1333	Retired 9-18
238	CB&Q	337 Bald. 4769	1879	CB&Q	1337	Retired
239	CB&Q	339 Bald. 4771	1879	CB&Q	1339	Reb. to A-2 386
240	CB&Q	341 Bald. 4777	1879	CB&Q	1341	Retired 1909
241	CB&Q	13 Galesburg	1880	CB&Q	1013	Retired 1910
242	CB&Q	30 Co. Shops	1880	CB&Q	1030	Reb. to A-2 430
243	CB&Q	34 Co. Shops	1880	CB&Q	1034	Retired
244	CB&Q	38 Aurora	1880	CB&Q	1038	Retired 1909
245	*CB&Q	360 Aurora	1880	CB&Q	1360	Retired 1912
246	*CB&Q	375 Aurora	1880	CB&Q	1375	Retired 5-18
247	B&MR	43 Manchester	1880	B&MR	43	Retired
248	B&MR	49 Manchester	1880	B&MR	49	Retired 8-05
249	CB&Q	41 Galesburg	1881	CB&Q	1041	Retired
250	CB&Q	151 Co. Shops	1881	CB&Q	1151	Retired
252	CB&Q	158 Aurora	1881	CB&Q	1158	Retired 1910
253	*CB&Q	366 Co. Shops	1881	CB&Q	1366	Retired 1909

* No. 247 from original B. & M. R. in 1875. Engine "Abraham Lincoln."
No. 248 from original B. & M. R. in 1875. Engine "General Grant."
No. 252 from original B. & M. R. in 1875. Engine "F. W. Grimes."
No. 289 and No. 300 from original B. & M. R. in 1875. Names unknown.
No. 372 from St. Louis, Rock Island & Chicago about 1879. Was No. 22.
No. 360 from St. L. R. I. & C. Built originally by Danforth Cooke 1869. No. 10.
No. 375 from St. L. R. I. & C. Built originally by Danforth Cooke 1870. No. 25.
St. L. K. & N. W. No. 19 formerly C. B. & Q. engine.
No. 234 (1904 No.) sold to Q. O. & K. C. R. R. Became Q. O. & K. C. No. 12.
* No. 366 from St. L. R. I. & C., original builder Danforth Cooke 1869. Was No. 16.
No No. 251 listed in 1904.

Class A-2, 4-4-0

New CB&Q No. 1904	Original	No. Builder	Date No Change 1898	Changes 1898 to 1904	
254	*CB&Q	368 Aurora	1881 CB&Q 1368		Retired 1910
255	*CB&Q	377 Galesburg	1881 CB&Q 1377		Retired 1911
256	CB&Q	399 Manch. 887	1881 CB&Q 1399		Retired 1911
257	CB&Q	400 Manch. 888	1881 CB&Q 1400		Retired 1909
258	CB&Q	401 Manch. 889	1881 CB&Q 1401		Retired
259	CB&Q	403 Manch. 891	1881 CB&Q 1403		Retired
260	CB&Q	404 Manch. 892	1881 CB&Q 1404		Retired 1910
261	CB&Q	406 Manch. 894	1881 CB&Q 1406		Retired 10-18
262	CB&Q	407 Manch. 885	1881 CB&Q 1407		Retired
263	CB&Q	408 Change to			
	StLK&NW	18 Mancn. 886	1881 St'NW 743	CB&KC 743	Retired
264	CB&Q	405 Manch. 893	1881 CB&Q 1405	StLK&NW 751, CB&KC 751	Retired
265	KCStJ&CB	1 St. Joseph	1882 KC'CB 526		Retired
266	CB&Q	116 Aurora	1882 CB&Q 1116	KCStJ&CB 551	Retired 1910
267	K&W	27 Pittsburgh	1882 Acq'd 1903		Retired
268	K&W	29 Pittsburgh	1882 Acq'd 1903		Retired
269	CB&Q	55 Galesburg	1882 CB&Q 1055		Retired 1909
270	CB&Q	154 Co. Shops	1882 CB&Q 1154		Retired 12-22
271	CB&Q	155 Co. Shops	1882 CB&Q 1155		Retired 1910
272	CB&Q	169 Co. Shops	1882 CB&Q 1169		Retired 7-18
273	CB&Q	427 Manchester	1882 CB&Q 1427		Reb. to A-2 431
274	CB&Q	428 Manch. 1150	1883 CB&Q 1428		Retired 1911
275	CB&Q	604 Pittsburgh	1882 CB&Q 1604		Retired
276	CB&Q	605 Pittsburgh	1882 CB&Q 1605		Retired
277	CB&Q	606 Pittsburgh	1882 CB&Q 1606		Retired
278	CB&Q	607 Pittsburgh	1882 CB&Q 1607		Retired
279	B&MR	80 Manchester	1882 B&MR 80		Retired
280	B&MR	81 Manchester	1882 B&MR 81		Retired 5-18
281	CB&Q	437 Changed '84 to			
	B&MR	130 Hinkley	1883 B&MR 130		Retired
282	CB&Q	142 Aurora	1883 CB&Q 1142		Retired 1910
283	CB&Q	152 Aurora	1883 CB&Q 1152		Retired
284	CB&Q	156 Aurora	1883 CB&Q 1156		Reb. to A-2 432
285	CB&Q	209 Aurora	1883 CB&Q 1209		Retired 1911
286	CB&Q	237 W. B. Shops	1883 CB&Q 1237		Retired 1909
287	CB&Q	429 Manch. 1151	1883 CB&Q 1429		Retired
288	CB&Q	430 Manch 1152	1883 CB&Q 1430		Reb. to A-2 433
289	CB&Q	432 Manch. 1154	1883 CB&Q 1432		Retired
290	KCStJ&CB	40 Manchester	1883 KC'CB 540		Retired 1910
291	CB&Q	431 Manch. 1153	1883 CB&Q 1431	StLK&NW 752, CB&KC 752	Retired 1910
292	CB&Q	433 Manch 1155	1883 CB&Q 1433	CB&KC 825	Retired 1910
293	K&W	24 Pittsburgh	1884	K&W 836, 1903	Retired 1910
294	CB&Q	40 Galesburg	1884 CB&Q 1040		Reb. to A-2 434
295	CB&Q	137 W. B. Shops	1884 CB&Q 1137		Reb. to A-2 435
296	*CB&Q	280 W. B. Shops	1884 CB&Q 1280		Retired 1910
297	*CB&Q	365 Co. Shops	1884 CB&Q 1365		Retired
298	CB&Q	618 Aurora	1884 CB&Q 1618		Sold 8-13-12
299	B&MR	108 Manchester	1884 B&MR 108		Retired
300	B&MR	109 Manchester	1884 B&MR 109		Retired 6-05
301	B&MR	110 Manchester	1884 B&MR 110		Reb. to A-2 390
302	B&MR	111 Manchester	1884 B&MR 111		Retired
303	B&MR	112 Manchester	1884 B&MR 112		Reb. to A-2 436
304	B&MR	113 Manchester	1884 B&MR 113		Retired
305	B&MR	116 Manchester	1884 B&MR 116		Reb. to A-2 447
306	B&MR	123 Hinkley	1884 B&MR 123		Reb. to A-2 437
307	B&MR	100 Aurora	1884 B&MR 100		Retired
308	B&MR	101 Aurora	1884 B&MR 101		Retired 4-27-06
309	B&MR	102 Aurora	1884 B&MR 102		Reb. to A-2 391
310	B&MR	105 Aurora	1884 B&MR 105		Retired 1911
311	B&MR	118 Aurora	1884 B&MR 118		Retired 10-05
312	B&MR	119 Aurora	1884 B&MR 119		Retired 8-07
313	B&MR	120 Aurora	1884 B&MR 120		Retired
314	B&MR	124 Hinkley	1884 B&MR 124		Retired
315	B&MR	125 Hinkley	1884 B&MR 125		Retired
316	B&MR	126 Hinkley	1884 B&MR 126		Retired 1910
317	B&MR	127 Hinkley	1884 B&MR 127		Reb. to A-2 392
318	B&MR	128 Hinkley	1884 B&MR 128		Retired 9-19
319	CB&Q	436 Hinkley	1884 B&MR 129	(9-84)	Retired 1911
320	CB&Q	438 Hinkley	1884 B&MR 145	(5-86)	Reb. to A-2 438
321	CB&Q	440 Hinkley	1884 B&MR 152	(6-86)	Reb. to A-2 439
322	CB&Q	442 Hinkley	1884 B&MR 153	(6-86)	Retired

No. 368 from St. L. R. I. & C., original builder Lancaster 1870. Was No. 18.
No. 377 from St. L. R. I. & Co., original builder Danforth Cooke 1870. Was No. 27.
No. 604 to No. 607 probably from Humeston & Shenandoah R. R. acquired 1896.
K. C. St. J. & C. B. No. 40 probably Manchester No. 1149 original C. B. & Q. No. 414.
* No. 365 from St. L. R. I. & Co., original builder, Danforth Cooke 1869. Was No. 15.
No. 280 probably from original B.&M.R. in 1875.

Class A-2, 4-4-0

New CB&Q No. 1904	Original	No. Builder	Date	No Change 1898	Changes 1898 to 1904	
323	CB&Q	443 Hinkley	1884 B&MR	154 (7-86)		Retired 9-05
324	CB&Q	445 Hinkley	1884 B&MR	156 (7-86)		Reb. to A-2 440
325	B&MR	140 Manch. 1238	1885 B&MR	140		Retired
326	CB&Q	436 Manch. 1221	1885 B&MR	146 (5-86)		Retired 8-19
327	CB&Q	437 Manch. 1222	1885 B&MR	149 (5-86)		Reb. to A-2 441
328	CB&Q	434 Manch. 1156	1883 B&MR	150 (5-86)		Retired 8-19
329	CB&Q	79 Hinkley	1885 CB&Q	1079		Retired 1910
330	CB&Q	119 Manch. 1216	1885 CB&Q	1119		Retired
331	CB&Q	253 Hinkley	1885 CB&Q	1253		Retired 1909
332	CB&Q	356 Hinkley	1885 CB&Q	1356		Retired
333	CB&Q	458 Manch. 1223	1885 CB&Q	1458		Retired 1911
334	K&W	22 CB&Q Shops	1885		K&W 22 to 1904	Retired
335	K&W	26 CB&Q Shops	1885		K&W 26 to 1904	Retired
336	CB&Q	132 Aurora	1885 CB&Q	1132	CB&KC 823	Retired 1911
337	K&W	10 Pittsburgh	1885		K&W 832, 1903	Retired
338	K&W	11 Pittsburgh	1885		K&W 833, 1903	Retired
339	B&MR	20 Plattsmouth	1899 B&MR	20		Retired
340	CB&Q	240 W. B. Shops	1886 CB&Q	1240		Retired 7-18

No numbers listed from 340 to 248 on 1904 list.

New CB&Q No. 1904	Original	No. Builder	Date	No Change 1898	Changes 1898 to 1904	
348	CB&Q	167 W. B. Shops	1887 CB&Q	1167		Retired
349	B&MR	168 W. B. Shops	1887 B&MR	168		Retired
350	B&MR	208 Manch. 1379	1888 B&MR	208		Reb. to A-2 448
351	B&MR	19 Plattsmouth	1889 B&MR	19		Reb. to A-2 393
352	CB&Q	121 Aurora	1889 CB&Q	1121		Retired
353	H&StJ	64 Hannibal	1889 H&StJ	664		Reb. to A-2 461
354	H&StJ	58 Hannibal	1890 H&StJ	658		Retired
355	H&StJ	50 Hannibal	1891 H&StJ	650	CB&KC 650	Retired 1911
356	H&StJ	53 Hannibal	1891 H&StJ	663		Reb. to A-2 443
357	StLK&NW	4 Hannibal	1891 St'NW	730		Retired 6-21
358	K&W	6 Pitts. 1268	1891		K&W 831, 1903	Retired
359	H&StJ	66 Aurora	1892 H&StJ	666		Reb. See note.
360	StLK&NW	26 Hannibal	1892 St'NW	726		Retired 4-28
361	K&W	14 Pitts. 1344	1892		K&W 834, 1903	Retired
362	StLK&NW	27 Hannibal	1893 St'NW	727		Retired 4-28
363	CB&Q	100 Aurora	1896 CB&Q	1100		Retired 9-29
364	CB&Q	168 Aurora	1896 CB&Q	1168		Retired 12-27
365	J&StL	9 Baldwin	1896		Acquired, 1903	Retired 1909
366	B&MR	24 Manchester	1878 B&MR	24		Retired 4-28
367	B&MR	69 Manchester	1881 B&MR	69		Retired 12-28
368	B&MR	72 Manchester	1881 B&MR	72		Retired 4-28
369	B&MR	34 Plattsmouth	1880 B&MR	34		Retired 12-29
370	B&MR	5 Manchester	1870 B&MR	5		Retired 11-27
371	B&MR	7 Manchester	1870 B&MR	7		Retired 4-27
372	B&MR	57 Unknown	B&MR	57		Retired 8-27
373	SC&W	238 Rhd. Island	1890		Acquired, 1907	Retired 7-18

K. & W. No. 22 and No. 26 transferred to C. B. & Q. in 1903 but retained K. & W. numbers until 1904. No. 298 (1904 No.) became Q. O. & K. C. No. 13.

No. 359 rebuilt at Denver, 6-32, for exhibition at the Century of Progress and lettered B. & M. R. No. 35.

The records are not clear on B. & M. R. 24, 69, 72, 34, 5, 7 and 57. These engines were either replaced by new engines or were rebuilt at the Havelock Shops in 1897.

The Sioux City & Western Sioux City to Ashland, Nebr., with a branch to O'Neil was purchased by the Burlington in 1907.

Rebuilt Class A-2

New No.	Old No.	Rebuilt	Date	Retired	New No.	Old No.	Rebuilt	Date	Retired
374	A-1 26		1915	5-27	390	A-2 301	Havelock	1915	9-29
375	A-1 24		1915	9-28	391	A-2 309	Havelock	1915	10-27
376	A-1 62	Aurora	1915	1-28	392	A-2 317	Havelock	1915	4-28
377	A-1 69	Aurora	1915	12-27	393	A-2 351	Havelock	1915	12-31
378	A-1 ?		1915	12-27	394	A-1	St. Joseph	1916	12-27
379	A-1 64	Galesburg	1916	Sold			(Probably rebuilt from No. 8)		
	6-29 to Atlantic & Northern				395	A-1 11	Creston	1916	5-27
380	A-1 98		1915	2-29	396	A-1 25	Creston	1916	8-29
381	A-1 99		1915	1927	397	A-1 30	Creston	1916	8-30
382	A-1 111	Aurora	1915	9-29	398	A-1 36	W. Burlington	1916	2-28
383	A-1 139	Creston	1915	Sold	399	A-1 49	Aurora	1916	3-29
	7-28 to Galesburg Great Eastern				400	A-1 54	W. Burlington	1916	9-28
384	A-2 231	St. Joseph	1915	6-27	401	A-1 57	Aurora	1916	9-28
385	A-2 236	Aurora	1915	12-27	402	A-1 59	Aurora	1916	7-31
386	A-2 239	Grand Crossing	1915	3-30.	403	A-1 65	W. Burlington	1916	1927
387	A-1 13	Havelock	1915	12-31	404	A-1 67	W. Burlington	1916	5-29
388	A-1 129	Havelock	1915	12-31	405	A-1 72	Aurora	1916	3-30
389	A-1 133	Havelock	1915	11-33	406	A-1 73	Aurora	1916	2-29

The former number of No. 378 is not on record. It was built originally by Rhode Island Works in 1886.

Rebuilt Class A-2

New No.	Old No.		Rebuilt	Date	Retired		New No.	Old No.		Rebuilt	Date	Retired
407	A-1	80	Beardstown	1916	7-29		443	A-2	356	Hannibal	1916	6-28
408	A-1	81	Beardstown	1916	10-30		444	A-1	14	Havelock	1917	4-30
409	A-1	83	W. Burlington	1916	7-29		445	A-1	124	Havelock	1918	8-28
410	A-1	89	W. Burlington	1916	12-31		446	A-1	127	Havelock	1918	3-33
411	A-1	91	Aurora	1915	9-28		447	A-2	305	Havelock	1918	4-28
412	A-1	92	Aurora	1916	3-29		448	A-2	350	Havelock	1918	12-28
413	A-1	93	Aurora	1916	3-33		449	A-1	18	Havelock	1917	7-28
414	A-1	101	Hannibal	1916	8-28		450	A-1	132	Havelock	1917	6-27
415	A-1	102	Aurora	1915	7-29		451	A-1	135	Havelock	1918	8-31
416	A-1	107	Aurora	1916	9-27		452	A-1	122	Havelock	1918	3-33
417	A-1	110	Aurora	1916	12-35		453	A-1	16	Havelock	1918	9-29
418	A-1	115	W. Burlington	1916	11-30		454	A-1	4	Havelock	1918	6-28
419	A-1	121	Grand Crossing	1916	8-27		455	A-1	45	Aurora	1918	7-33
420	A-1	123	Havelock	1916	6-27		456	A-1	58	Aurora	1917	2-31
421	A-1	125	Havelock	1916	9-29		457	A-1	70	Aurora	1918	6-28
422	A-1	130	Havelock	1915	9-27		458	A-1	118	W. Burlington	1917	5-27
423	A-1	134	Havelock	1916	12-28		459	A-1	141	Aurora	1918	12-29
424	A-1	137	Havelock	1916	4-28		460	A-1	151	Aurora	1918	3-28
425	A-1	138	St. Joseph	1917	8-29		461	A-2	353	Hannibal	1917	9-29
426	A-1	145	Havelock	1917	4-28		462	A-1	71	W. Burlington	1917	10-30
427	A-1	146	Havelock	1917	5-29		463	A-1	87	Hannibal	1917	3-31
428	A-1	149	Havelock	1916	7-28		464	A-1	23	Hannibal	1917	9-27
429	A-1	152	Hannibal	1916	8-29		465	A-1	114	Hannibal	1917	8-27
430	A-2	242	Aurora	1916	4-29		466	A-1	113	Hannibal	1917	10-30
431	A-2	273	Grand Crossing	1916	10-35		467	A-1	105	Beardstown	1918	12-31
432	A-2	284	Aurora	1916	2-29		468	A-1	75	Beardstown	1917	12-30
433	A-2	288	Creston	1916	8-27		469	A-1	66	Aurora	1918	7-30
434	A-2	294	W. Burlington	1916	6-27		470	A-1	6	Hannibal	1918	3-33
435	A-2	295	Aurora	1915	6-28		471	A-1	44	Hannibal	1918	4-30
436	A-2	303	Havelock	1916	4-28		472	A-1	5	Grand Crossing	1918	6-28
437	A-2	306	Havelock	1917	9-27		473	A-1	55	St. Joseph	1917	5-29
438	A-2	320	Havelock	1916	8-30		474	A-1	29	St. Joseph	1917	9-27
439	A-2	321	Havelock	1916	1927		475	A-1	82	W. Burlington	1917	6-35
440	A-2	324	Havelock	1916	7-26		476	A-1	38	W. Burlington	1917	2-31
441	A-2	327	Havelock	1916	6-27		477	A-1	20	Aurora	1917	3-28
442	A-1	143	Havelock	1916	11-29		478	A-1	21	W. Burlington	1917	7-28

Cyls.	Drs	Wt., Drs.	Total	T. E.	B. P.
17"x24"	69"	57,100 lbs.	94,000 lbs.	13,700 lbs.	160 lbs.
17"x24"	64"	57,100 lbs.	94,000 lbs.	14,500 lbs.	160 lbs.

Class A-3, 4-4-0

New CB&Q No. 1904	Original	No.	Builder	Date	No Change 1898		Changes 1898 to 1904	
400	I&StL	3	Baldwin				Acquired 03	Retired 5-24-07
401	CB&Q	281	Manchester	1870	CB&Q	1281		Retired
402	CB&Q	379	Danforth C	1870	CB&Q	1379		Retired
403	CB&Q	380	Danforth C	1870	CB&Q	1380		Retired
404	CB&Q	161	Manchester	1871	CB&Q	1161		Retired
405	CB&Q	287	Manchester	1871	CB&Q	1287		Retired
406	CB&Q	198	Manchester	1872	CB&Q	1198		Retired
407	CB&Q	212	Manch. 505	1873	CB&Q	1212		Retired
408	CB&Q	12	Galesburg	1874	CB&Q	1012		Retired
409	CB&Q	227	Manchester	1874	CB&Q	1227		Retired
410	CB&Q	109	Co. Shops	1877	CB&Q	1109		Retired 1912
411	CB&Q	26	Co. Shops	1878	CB&Q	1026		Retired
412	CB&Q	70	Galesburg	1878	CB&Q	1070		Retired 1912
413	CB&Q	200	Co. Shops	1878	CB&Q	1200		Retired
414	B&MR	26	Plattsmouth	1878	B&MR	26	B&MR 3200, '03	Retired 1912
415	CB&Q	362	Co. Shops	1879	CB&N	915	CB&Q 915, '99	Retired
416	CB&Q	44	Co. Shops	1879	CB&Q	1044		Retired
417	CB&Q	74	Co. Shops	1879	CB&Q	1074		Retired
418	CB&Q	56	Galesburg	1882	CB&Q	1056		Retired
419	CB&Q	242	Co. Shops	1882	CB&Q	1242		Ch. to 160, '16 Retired
420	B&MR	79	Manchester	1882	B&MR	79		Retired 6-05
421	CB&Q	53	Co. Shops	1884	CB&Q	1053		Retired
422	B&MR	115	Manchester	1884	B&MR	115		Retired
423	B&MR	139	Manch. 1237	1885	B&MR	139		Retired
424	CB&Q	86	Co. Shops	1885	CB&Q	1086		Retired
425	CB&Q	370	Beardstown	1886	CB&Q	1370	Reb. Aurora '01	Ch. to 161, '16 Retired 6-24
426	CB&Q	188	Co. Shops	1887	CB&N	913	CB&Q 913, '09	Retired

No. 281, No. 287 and No. 242 from the original B. & M. R. in 1875, No. 242 built originally by Manchester, Shop No. 74, 1866. Name, J. G. Reid. Was Class A-2 but later changed to A-3.

No. 379, No. 380, No. 362 and No. 370 from St. L. R. I. & C. originally. No. 362 built by Danforth Cooke in 1870 and No. 370 built by Lancaster in 1870.

No. 400, No. 401, No. 402 and No. 415 had B. P., 130 lbs.

Class A-4, 4-4-0

New CB&Q No. 1904	Original	No.	Builder	Date	No Change 1898	Changes 1898 to 1904	
440	CB&Q	129	Baldwin	1869	CB&Q 1129	Retired	
441	CB&Q	250	Manch. 130	1868	CB&Q 1250	Retired	
442	CB&Q	58	Co. Shops	1869	CB&Q 1058	Retired	
443	B&MR	18	Havelock	1897	B&MR 18	Retired	
444	B&MR	54	Havelock	1897	B&MR 54	Retired	

No. 250, engine Gen. Sherman from original B. & M. R. B. & M. R. No. 18 was Rogers engine from Nebr. R. R. and No. 54 was from A. & N. R. R. Both engines rebuilt at Havelock in 1897.

Class A-5, 4-4-0

New CB&Q No. 1904	Original	No.	Builder	Date	No Change 1898	Changes 1898 to 1904	
460	CB&Q	602	Hinkley		CB&Q 1602	Retired 1909	
461	CB&Q	361	Co. Shops	1879	CB&Q 1361	Retired	
462	CB&Q	78	Co. Shops	1884	CB&Q 1078	Retired 1909	
463	CB&Q	139	Aurora	1885	CB&Q 1139	Retired	
464	CB&Q	97	Aurora	1896	CB&Q 1197	Ch. to No. 190, '16 Retired 6-24	

No. 361 from St. L. R. I. & C., original builder Danforth Cooke, 1869.

Class A-6, 4-4-0

New CB&Q No. 1904	Original	No.	Builder	Date	No Change 1898	No Change 1916	Retired
470	CB&Q	612	Aurora	1892	CB&Q 1612	191	12-21
417	CB&Q	617	Aurora	1892	CB&Q 1617	192	5-29
472	CB&Q	550	Rogers 4849	1893	CB&Q 1550	193	12-22
				Change '98 to '04			
473	H&StJ	633	Pitts. 1829	1898	KC'CB 633	194	7-28
474	H&StJ	636	Pitts 1830	1898	KC'CB 636	195	7-29
475	H&StJ	645	Pitts 1831	1898	KC'CB 645	196	6-27
476	H&StJ	653	Pitts 1832	1898	KC'CB 653	197	12-22
477	StLK&NW	746	Pitts 1833	1898		198	8-27
478	StLK&NW	747	Pitts 1834	1898		199	6-27
479	DRI&NW	2	Baldwin 18650	1901	Acquired 1903	200	4-23

As the numbers of the rebuilt Class A-2 engines were extended to 478 it became necessary to renumber Class A-6 engines as well as the two Class A-3 and one A-5 still in service in 1916.

The D.R.I.&N.W. engine was not built to the same design as the standard A-6. The standard A-6 engines were originally known as Class M.

Class A-7, 4-4-0

I&StL No. 1 acquired in 1903 and changed to No. 491, in 1904. No further record.

Class I-1, 0-6-2-T
Suburban

New CB&Q No. 1904	Original	No.	Builder	Date	No Change 1898	
500	CB&Q	83				
	6-90 to 500		Aurora	1889	CB&Q 1500	Retired 1911
501	CB&Q	501	Aurora	1890	CB&Q 1501	Retired 1910
502	CB&Q	502	Aurora	1890	CB&Q 1502	Retired 1910
503	CB&Q	503	Aurora	1891	CB&Q 1503	Retired 1910
504	CB&Q	504	Aurora	1893	CB&Q 1504	Retired 1910

Narrow Gauge

New CB&Q No. 1904	Original	No.	Builder	Date	Change 1901	
530	BH&FtP	2	Porter	1882	B&MR 493	Sold Fitzhugh Co. 12-04
531	BH&FtP	4	Porter	1890	B&MR 491	Sold Fitzhugh Co. 12-04
532	BH&FtP	5	Baldwin	1883	B&MR 490	Scrapped 1911
533	BH&FtP	7	Baldwin	1901	B&MR 488	Scrapped 11-30
534	BH&FtP	6	Baldwin	1900	B&MR 489	Scrapped 11-30
535	DC	3	Baldwin	1891	B&MR 498	Scrapped 1910
536	BH&FtP	3	Baldwin	1883	B&MR 492	Scrapped 4-24
537	DC	5	Baldwin	1896	B&MR 496	Scrapped 9-39
538	DC	6	Baldwin	1900	B&MR 495	Scrapped 12-30
539	DC	2	Baldwin	1884	B&MR 499	Scrapped 1910
	DC	1	Baldwin	1888	B&MR 500	Sold Fitzhugh Co. 5-03
	DC	4	Baldwin	1889	B&MR 497	Scrapped 6-03
	BH&FtP	1	Baldwin	?	B&MR 494	Scrapped 11-02

D. C. No. 1, No. 2 and No. 4, six drivers. No. 3, No. 5 and No. 6, eight drivers.
B. H. & Ft. P. No. 1, No. 2 and No. 4, six drivers. No. 3 and No. 8 eight drivers.
No data on No. 6 and No. 7.
D. C. No. 2 was Denver, Utah & Pacific No. 6, 1884 to 1890.
D. C. No. 4 was Denver, Utah & Pacific No. 3, 1889 to 1894.

Deadwood Central and Black Hills & Ft. Pierre, both three foot gauge, were acquired by the B. & M. R. in 1901.

Several of these narrow gauge engines were used on the Burlington's line from Englewood to Spearfish, S. D. in later years. This line was abandoned about 1930.

An interesting note in the records. "Deadwood Central engine No. 1 was taken into Deadwood with mule teams, Sept., 1888."

Class E-1, 0-4-0

New CB&Q No. 1904	Original	No.	Builder	Date	No Change 1898		Changes 1898 to 1904	Date Retired
550	CB&Q	351	McKay & Aldus	1869	CB&Q	1351		1912
551	CB&Q	62	Co. Shops	1874	CB&Q	1062		No. Rec.
552	CB&Q	222	Aurora	1874	CB&Q	1222		No. Rec.
553	CB&Q	19	Aurora	1875	CB&Q	1019		to No. 574 11-27
554	CB&Q	23	Aurora	1875	CB&Q	1023		No. Rec.
555	CB&Q	63	Aurora	1875	CB&Q	1063		No. Rec.
556	CB&Q	24	Aurora	1876	CB&Q	1024		No. Rec.
557	CB&Q	65	Aurora	1876	CB&Q	1065		No. Rec.
558	CB&Q	5	Aurora	1878	CB&Q	1005		No. Rec.
559	CB&Q	343	Aurora	1879	CB&Q	1343		No. Rec.
560	CB&Q	14	Aurora	1879	CB&Q	1014	KCStJ&CB 518	No. Rec.
561	CB&Q	381	Aurora	1880	CB&Q	1381		1910
562	CB&Q	411	Aurora	1881	CB&Q	1411		No. Rec.
563	KCStJ&CB	39	Aurora	1881	KC'CB	509		No. Rec.
564	CB&Q	426	Aurora	1882	CB&Q	1426		1912
565	B&MR	93	Plattsmouth	1882	B&MR	93		No. Rec.
566	CB&Q	4	Aurora	1883	CB&Q	1004		1910
567	CB&Q	354	Aurora	1883	CB&Q	1354		No. Rec.
568	CB&Q	374	Aurora	1883	CB&Q	1374		1-26
569	CB&Q	448	Aurora	1884	CB&Q	1448		7-21
570	B&MR	99	Plattsmouth	1884	B&MR	99		12-16
571	H&StJ	6	Aurora	1885	H&StJ	606	StLK&NW 606	2-17
572	B&MR	141	Plattsmouth	1886	B&MR	141		Sold 3-28
573	CB&N	101	Rhd. I. 1599	1886	CB&N	902	CB&Q 902	No. Rec.
574	CB&N	103	Rhd. I. 1601	1886	CB&N	904	CB&Q 904	No. Rec.
575	CB&N	105	Rhd. I. 1603	1886	CB&N	906	CB&Q 906	No. Rec.
576	CB&Q	61	W. B. Shops	1887	CB&Q	1061		1912
577	CB&Q	186	Co. Shops	1888	CB&Q	1186		

C. B. & Q. No. 351 was originally St. Louis, Rock Island and Chicago No. 1, acquired by C. B. &Q. in 1879. K. C. St. J. & C. B. No. 39 was probably built originally for the C. B. & Q.

Class L-1, 0-10-0

New CB&Q No. 1904	Original	No.	Builder	Date		
590	B&MR	273	Rogers 4504	1891		10-16
591	B&MR	274	Rogers 4505	1891		10-16
592	B&MR	275	Rogers 4525	1891		10-16

NEW LOCOMOTIVES ASSIGNED TO 500 SERIES
1919 and 1921
Class G-5, 0-6-0

No.	Builder	Date	Shop No.		No.	Builder	Date	Shop No.	
500	Cooke	1919	61380	Scrapped 3-53	505	Cooke	1919	61385	Scrapped 2-54
501	Cooke	1919	61381	Scrapped 12-53	506	Cooke	1919	61386	Scrapped 4-54
502	Cooke	1919	61382	Scrapped 5-54	507	Cooke	1919	61387	Scrapped 5-54
503	Cooke	1919	61383	Scrapped 2-54	508	Cooke	1919	61388	Scrapped 3-54
504	Cooke	1919	61384	Sold for Scrap 12-54	509	Cooke	1919	61389	Scrapped 5-54

Class G-5A, 0-6-0

No.	Builder	Date	Shop No.		No.	Builder	Date	Shop No.	
510	Baldwin	1921	53983	Sold to French Lick Hotel 12-57	517	Baldwin	1921	54134	Sold for Scrap 3-53
					518	Baldwin	1921	54190	Sold for Scrap 4-54
511	Baldwin	1921	53976	Sold for Scrap 4-55	519	Baldwin	1921	54191	Sold for Scrap 10-53
512	Baldwin	1921	54048	Sold for Scrap 4-55	520	Baldwin	1921	53979	Sold for Scrap 3-54
513	Baldwin	1921	54049	Sold for Scrap 3-53	521	Baldwin	1921	53980	Sold for Scrap 4-54
514	Baldwin	1921	54050	Sold for Scrap 5-54	522	Baldwin	1921	53982	Sold for Scrap 10-53
515	Baldwin	1921	54232	Sold for Scrap 12-54	523	Baldwin	1921	54195	Sold for Scrap 5-54
516	Baldwin	1921	54133	Sold for Scrap 5-55	524	Baldwin	1921	54196	Sold for Scrap 3-53

Class F-1, 0-8-0

No.	Builder	Date	Shop No.		No.	Builder	Date	Shop No.	
540	Brooks	1919	61233	Sold for Scrap 4-54	545	Brooks	1919	61238	Sold for Scrap 8-56
541	Brooks	1919	61234	Sold for Scrap 11-53	546	Brooks	1919	61230	Sold for Scrap 4-55
542	Brooks	1919	61235	Sold for Scrap 2-54	547	Brooks	1919	61240	Sold for Scrap 5-54
543	Brooks	1919	61236	Sold for Scrap 8-56	548	Brooks	1919	61241	Sold for Scrap 2-54
544	Brooks	1919	61237	Sold for Scrap 4-54	549	Brooks	1919	61242	Sold for Scrap 8-56

Class G-5 and F-1 were built in accordance with the standards of the United States Railroad Administration. Class G-5A were built to the same design as G-5 with certain details revised, the most notable change being the omission of the superheater.

REBUILT LOCOMOTIVES ASSIGNED TO 500 SERIES
1926 to 1930
Class F-2, 0-8-0, Rebuilt From Class T-1, 2-6-6-2

550 Rebuilt from No. 4003 9-26	Baldwin No. 33986	1909	Scrapped 2-46
551 Rebuilt from No. 4006 3-27	Baldwin No. 34021	1909	Sold for Scrap 11-48
552 Rebuilt from No. 4005 5-27	Baldwin No. 34020	1909	Sold for Scrap 12-48
553 Rebuilt from No. 4002 7-27	Baldwin No. 32724	1908	Sold for Scrap 12-48
554 Rebuilt from No. 4007 8-27	Baldwin No. 34029	1909	Scrapped 8-47
555 Rebuilt from No. 4000 8-27	Baldwin No. 32722	1908	Scrapped 11-46
556 Rebuilt from No. 4004 12-27	Baldwin No. 33987	1909	Scrapped 12-46

Class G-10, 0-6-0, Rebuilt From Class R-4, 2-6-2

560 Rebuilt from No. 1950 12-28	Brooks No. 30406	1905	Sold for Scrap 11-53
561 Rebuilt from No. 1981 12-28	Brooks No. 30437	1905	Sold for Scrap 10-53
562 Rebuilt from No. 2034 12-28	Baldwin No. 27419	1906	Sold for Scrap 4-54
563 Rebuilt from No. 1905 12-28	Baldwin No. 24463	1904	Sold for Scrap 7-51
564 Rebuilt from No. 1920 12-28	Baldwin No. 24496	1904	Sold for Scrap 4-55
565 Rebuilt from No. 1908 7-29	Baldwin No. 24466	1904	Sold 7-59
566 Rebuilt from No. 2006 7-29	Baldwin No. 27250	1906	Sold for Scrap 4-54
567 Rebuilt from No. 2021 8-29	Baldwin No. 27357	1906	Sold for Scrap 3-51
568 Rebuilt from No. 1902 8-29	Baldwin No. 24457	1904	Sold for Scrap 5-54
569 Rebuilt from No. 1976 8-29	Brooks No. 30432	1905	Sold for Scrap 12-53
570 Rebuilt from No. 2042 8-29	Baldwin No. 27497	1906	Sold for Scrap 12-54
571 Rebuilt from No. 1973 10-29	Brooks No. 30429	1905	Sold for Scrap 7-52
572 Rebuilt from No. 1900 11-29	Baldwin No. 24436	1904	Sold for Scrap 4-54
573 Rebuilt from No. 1969 11-29	Brooks No. 30425	1905	Sold for Scrap 2-53
574 Rebuilt from No. 2009 11-29	Baldwin No. 27272	1906	Sold for Scrap 4-55
575 Rebuilt from No. 1913 12-29	Baldwin No. 24486	1904	Sold for Scrap 7-51
576 Rebuilt from No. 1944 1-30	Brooks No. 30400	1905	Sold for Scrap 4-54
577 Rebuilt from No. 1936 4-30	Baldwin No. 24568	1904	Sold for Scrap 4-54
578 Rebuilt from No. 1945 12-29	Brooks No. 30401	1905	Sold for Scrap 5-55
579 Rebuilt from No. 2004 12-29	Baldwin No. 27248	1906	Sold for Scrap 12-54
580 Rebuilt from No. 1906 12-29	Baldwin No. 24464	1904	Sold for Scrap 12-54
581 Rebuilt from No. 2040 12-29	Baldwin No. 27459	1906	Sold for Scrap 12-54
582 Rebuilt from No. 1989 3-30	Brooks No. 30445	1905	Sold for Scrap 3-54
583 Rebuilt from No. 2041 3-30	Baldwin No. 27496	1906	Sold for Scrap 10-53
584 Rebuilt from No. 2035 3-30	Baldwin No. 27421	1906	Sold for Scrap 4-54
585 Rebuilt from No. 2031 3-30	Baldwin No. 27403	1906	Sold for Scrap 7-52
586 Rebuilt from No. 2048 4-30	Baldwin No. 27540	1906	Sold for Scrap 4-53
587 Rebuilt from No. 2001 4-30	Baldwin No. 27245	1906	Sold for Scrap 3-54
588 Rebuilt from No. 1932 4-30	Baldwin No. 24542	1904	Sold for Scrap 6-54
589 Rebuilt from No. 1921 4-30	Baldwin No. 24497	1904	Sold for Scrap 5-54
590 Rebuilt from No. 1926 4-30	Baldwin No. 24513	1904	Sold for Scrap 5-54
591 Rebuilt from No. 2032 8-30	Baldwin No. 27418	1906	Sold for Scrap 5-54
592 Rebuilt from No. 2047 8-30	Baldwin No. 27539	1906	Sold for Scrap 5-54
593 Rebuilt from No. 1923 8-30	Baldwin No. 24506	1904	Sold for Scrap 5-51
594 Rebuilt from No. 1929 11-30	Baldwin No. 24529	1904	Sold for Scrap 8-51

Class K-1, 4-6-0

New CB&Q No. 1904	Orig. No.	Builder	Date		
600	B&MR 253	Baldwin	11496	1891	Retired 7-26
601	B&MR 254	Baldwin	11497	1891	Retired 12-21
602	B&MR 255	Baldwin	11498	1891	Retired 2-33
603	B&MR 256	Baldwin	11503	1891	Retired 2-33
604	B&MR 257	Baldwin	11506	1891	Retired 12-31
605	B&MR 258	Baldwin	11514	1891	Retired 4-31
606	B&MR 259	Baldwin	11515	1891	Retired 7-34
607	B&MR 260	Baldwin	11527	1891	Retired 5-33
608	B&MR 276	Rogers	4662	3-92	Retired 11-39
609	B&MR 277	Rogers	4663	3-92	Retired 12-31
610	B&MR 278	Rogers	4664	3-92	Retired 8-29
611	B&MR 279	Rogers	4665	3-92	Retired 12-31
612	B&MR 280	Rogers	4666	3-92	Retired 7-36
613	B&MR 281	Rogers	4678	3-92	Retired 3-31
614	B&MR 282	Rogers	4679	3-92	Retired 2-33
615	B&MR 283	Rogers	4680	3-92	Sold 6-37—STL&H
616	B&MR 284	Rogers	4681	3-92	Retired 8-31
617	B&MR 285	Rogers	4682	3-92	Retired 9-37
618	B&MR 286	Rogers	4683	4-92	Retired 1-33
619	B&MR 287	Rogers	4684	4-92	Retired 5-33
620	B&MR 288	Rogers	4685	4-92	Retired 12-31
621	B&MR 289	Rogers	4686	4-92	Retired 12-33
622	B&MR 290	Rogers	4687	4-92	Retired 7-35

623	B&MR	291	Rogers	4688	4-92	Retired 2-28
624	B&MR	292	Rogers	4693	4-92	Retired 10-33
625	B&MR	293	Rogers	4694	4-92	Retired 6-39
626	B&MR	294	Rogers	4697	5-92	Retired 12-31
627	B&MR	295	Rogers	4702	5-92	Retired 7-37

No change of numbers made on these engines in 1898.

Class K-2, 4-6-0

New CB&Q No. 1904	Orig. No.		Builder	Date		
630	B&MR	302	Rogers	4766	9-92	Retired 11-46
631	B&MR	303	Rogers	4767	9-92	Retired 4-34
632	B&MR	304	Rogers	4768	9-92	Sold for Srap 7-51
633	B&MR	305	Rogers	4772	10-92	Retired 7-41
634	B&MR	306	Rogers	4773	10-92	Retired 11-39
635	B&MR	307	Rogers	4774	10-92	Retired
636	B&MR	308	Rogers	4787	11-92	Retired 4-47
637	B&MR	309	Rogers	4788	11-92	Donated—Aurora, Ill. 6-63
638	B&MR	310	Rogers	4789	11-92	Retired 1-41
639	B&MR	311	Rogers	4799	12-92	Retired 10-46
640	B&MR	312	Rogers	4800	12-92	Retired 11-46
641	B&MR	313	Rogers	4801	12-92	Retired 1-41
642	B&MR	314	Rogers	4805	12-92	Retired 1-41
643	B&MR	315	Rogers	4806	12-92	Retired 7-47
644	B&MR	316	Rogers	4807	12-92	Sold for Scrap 11-51
645	B&MR	317	Rogers	4817	1-93	Retired 7-30
646	B&MR	318	Rogers	4818	1-93	Sold for Scrap 7-52
647	B&MR	319	Rogers	4819	1-93	Retired 10-46
648	B&MR	320	Rogers	4826	2-93	Retired 1-33
649	B&MR	321	Rogers	4827	2-93	Retired 9-39
650	B&MR	322	Rogers	4828	2-93	Retired 10-39
651	B&MR	323	Rogers	4829	2-93	Retired 8-43
652	B&MR	324	Rogers	4830	2-93	Retired 2-53
653	B&MR	325	Rogers	4831	2-93	Retired 11-46
654	B&MR	326	Rogers	4832	2-93	Sold for Scrap 6-51
655	B&MR	327	Grant		1893	Dismantled 6-42 Boiler to 665
656	B&MR	328	Grant		1893	Retired 5-48
657	B&MR	329	Grant		1893	Retired 3-43
658	B&MR	4	Havelock		1895	Retired 1-33
659	B&MR	6	Havelock		1895	Retired 10-46
660	B&MR	8	Havelock		1895	Sold 6-42 to EWF&G
661	B&MR	9	Havelock		1895	Retired 1-41
662	B&MR	12	W. B. Shops		1896	Retired 6-39
663	B&MR	13	W. B. Shops		1896	Retired 9-31
664	B&MR	14	W. B. Shops		1896	Retired 10-46
665	B&MR	52	W. B. Shops		1896	Retired 12-46
666	B&MR	55	W. B. Shops		1896	Retired 1-41
667	B&MR	330	Havelock		1896	Retired 7-35
668	B&MR	331	Havelock		1896	Retired 5-33
669	B&MR	332	Havelock		1896	Retired 12-31

Class K-3, 4-6-0

New CB&Q No. 1904	Orig. No.		Builder	Date		No. Change 1898		No. Change 1899		
676	CB&N	150	Hinkley	1710	1887	CB&N	976	CB&Q	976	Retired
677	CB&N	153	Hinkley	1713	1887	CB&N	977	CB&Q	977	Retired 10-16
678	CB&N	155	Hinkley	1715	1887	CB&N	978	CB&Q	978	Retired 1911
679	CB&N	158	Hinkley	1718	1887	CB&N	979	CB&Q	979	Retired 1911
680	CB&N	163	Hinkley	1723	1887	CB&N	980	CB&Q	980	Retired
681	CB&N	151	Hinkley	1711	1887	CB&N	981	CB&Q	981	Retired
682	CB&N	152	Hinkley	1712	1887	CB&N	982	CB&Q	982	Retired 1911
683	CB&N	154	Hinkley	1714	1887	CB&N	983	CB&Q	983	Retired 1911
684	CB&N	156	Hinkley	1716	1887	CB&N	984	CB&Q	984	Retired 1912
685	CB&N	157	Hinkley	1717	1887	CB&N	985	CB&Q	985	Retired
686	CB&N	159	Hinkley	1719	1887	CB&N	986	CB&Q	986	Retired
687	CB&N	160	Hinkley	1720	1887	CB&N	987	CB&Q	987	Retired
688	CB&N	161	Hinkley	1721	1887	CB&N	988	CB&Q	988	Retired 1911
689	CB&N	162	Hinkley	1722	1887	CB&N	989	CB&Q	989	Retired 1912
690	CB&N	164	Hinkley	1724	1887	CB&N	990	CB&Q	990	Retired 12-22

There is evidence that some of these engines were used on the B. & M. R. about 1895 and had temporary numbers in 500 series. Also of a Class K-3 No. 691 owned in later years but no definite record is shown for these.

Class K-4, 4-6-0

New CB&Q No. 1904	Orig. No.		Builder	Date	No. Change 1903	No. Change 1951	
700	B&MR	1	Havelock	1900		900	Sold for scrap 10-53
701	B&MR	15	Havelock	1900		901	Sold for scrap 11-53
702	B&MR	27	Havelock	1900			Retired 4-47
703	B&MR	29	Havelock	1900		903	Sold for scrap 12-52
704	B&MR	59	Havelock	1900		904	Sold for scrap 7-51
705	B&MR	74	Havelock	1900			Sold for scrap 5-51
706	B&MR	75	Havelock	1900		906	Sold for scrap 3-53

707	B&MR	90	Havelock	1901			Dismantled 2-51
708	B&MR	41	Havelock	1901			Retired 12-31
709	B&MR	63	Havelock	1901		909	Sold for scrap 11-53
710	B&MR	31	Havelock	1901		910	Donated Lincoln, Neb. 12-54
711	B&MR	33	Havelock	1901			Sold for scrap 1-51
712	B&MR	30	Havelock	1901			Retired 7-35
713	B&MR	39	Havelock	1901			Retired 9-39
714	B&MR	70	Havelock	1901		914	Sold for scrap 8-51
715	B&MR	44	Havelock	1901		915	Held 12-57
716	B&MR	96	Havelock	1902			Retired 10-31
717	B&MR	64	Havelock	1902			Retired 1-41
718	B&MR	38	Havelock	1902	B&MR 3686	918	Sold for scrap 3-52
719	B&MR	40	Havelock	1903	B&MR 3687	919	Held
720	B&MR	47	Havelock	1903	B&MR 3688		Rebuilt to K-4-B. Retired
721	B&MR	3689	Havelock	1903		921	Sold for scrap 7-52
722	B&MR	3690	Havelock	1903		922	Sold for scrap 7-51
723	B&MR	3691	Havelock	1904			Retired 2-51

Class K-5, 4-6-0

	Orig. No.	Builder	Date	
CB&Q	800	Havelock	1904	Retired 7-27
CB&Q	801	Havelock	1904	Retired 7-27
CB&Q	802	Havelock	1904	Changed to No. 808, Wymore 11-28, Retired 5-29
CB&Q	803	Havelock	1904	Retired 7-27
CB&Q	804	Havelock	1905	Retired
CB&Q	805	Havelock	1905	Retired 6-27
CB&Q	806	Havelock	1905	Retired 7-27
CB&Q	807	Havelock	1905	Retired 7-30

Class K-6, 4-6-0

New CB&Q No. 1904	Orig. No.		Builder		Date	Change 1903		
900	K&W	18	Rogers	5186	1897	K&W	845	
901	K&W	19	Rogers	5187	1897	K&W	846	
902	K&W	20	Rogers	5188	1897	K&W	847	

Class K-7, 4-6-0

910	K&W	15	Rogers	5148	1896	K&W	848	
911	K&W	16	Rogers	5149	1896	K&W	849	Sold 1907 to Fitzhugh Luther Co.
912	K&W	17	Rogers	5150	1896	K&W	850	Sold 1907 to Fitzhugh Luther Co.

Class K-9, 4-6-0

940	J&StL	7	Rhode Island	1890
941	J&StL	8	Rhode Island	1890

	Cyls.	Drs.
K-6	16"x24"	54"
K-7	17"x24"	56"
K-9	18"x24"	56"

No other data available. These engines were not built to Burlington standards. All were retired prior to 1917.

Jacksonville and St. Louis engines were acquired by the Burlington about 1903.

Class K-10, 4-6-0 Rebuilt From Class H-4, 2-6-0

			Rebuilt		Original Builder		
950	Rebuilt from 1245	Aurora	8-08	Rogers 5507	1900	Ret. 11-46
951	Rebuilt from 1258	Aurora	9-08	Rogers 5513	1900	Sold for scrap 10-53
952	Rebuilt from 1256	Aurora	10-08	Rogers 5511	1900	Ret. 4-47
953	Rebuilt from 1253	Aurora	10-08	W. B. Shops	1900	Sold for scrap 2-54
954	Rebuilt from 1244	Aurora	11-08	Rogers 5506	1900	Sold for scrap 4-54
955	Rebuilt from 1251	Aurora	12-08	W. B. Shops	1900	Sold for scrap 7-52
956	Rebuilt from 1259	Aurora	1-09	Rogers 5514	1900	Sold for scrap 8-50
957	Rebuilt from 1250	Aurora	2-09	W. B. Shops	1900	Sold for scrap 5-54
958	Rebuilt from 1249	Aurora	4-09	Aurora	1900	Sold for scrap 7-52
959	Rebuilt from 1222	Aurora	5-09	Bald. 17002	1899	Sold for scrap 7-52
960	Rebuilt from 1238	Havelock	8-08	Rogers 5525	1900	Sold for scrap 9-53
961	Rebuilt from 1243	Aurora	9-09	Rogers 5505	1900	Sold for scrap 8-53
962	Rebuilt from 1247	Aurora	9-09	Aurora	1900	Sold for scrap 12-52
963	Rebuilt from 1252	Aurora	11-09	W. B. Shops	1900	Ret. 9-31
964	Rebuilt from 1246	Aurora	12-09	Aurora	1900	Ret. 1-33
965	Rebuilt from 1221	Havelock	10-14	Bald. 17001	1899	Ret. 6-42. Boiler to 967
966	Rebuilt from 1231	Havelock	10-14	Bald. 16970	1899	Sold for scrap 12-51
967	Rebuilt from 1229	Havelock	10-14	Bald. 16950	1899	Sold 4-55 to H. Warp, Minden, Nebr.
968	Rebuilt from 1239	Havelock	10-14	Rogers 5526	1900	Dismantled 6-42

Class H-1, 2-6-0

New CB&Q No. 1904		Builder		Date	No Change 1898		Changes 1898 to 1904		Date Retired
1000	CB&Q	135	Aurora	1888	CB&Q	1135	H&StJ. 683		Sold 9-12
1001	CB&Q	73	Aurora	1888	CB&Q	1073	H&StJ. 682,		
							KCStJ&CB 682		9-27

New CB&Q No. 1904	Original	No.	Builder	Date	No. Change 1898		Changes 1898 to 1904	Date Retired
1002	CB&Q	202	W. B. Shops	1888	CB&Q	1202	H&StJ 684	No Record
1003	CB&Q	128	Aurora	1888	CB&Q	1128	StLK&NW 761	9-28
1004	CB&Q	125	Aurora	1888	CB&Q	1125	StLK&NW 763	1-26
1005	CB&Q	32	Aurora	1888	CB&Q	1032		No Record
1006	CB&Q	92	Co. Shops	1888	CB&Q	1092		8-27
1007	CB&Q	123	Aurora	1888	CB&Q	1123		No Record
1008	CB&Q	196	W. B. Shops	1888	CB&Q	1196		4-26
1009	CB&Q	141	W. B. Shops	1888	CB&O	1141		Sold 9-12
1010	CB&Q	145	W. B. Shops	1889	CB&Q	1145		5-27
1011	CB&Q	163	Aurora	1889	CB&Q	1163		7-24
1012	CB&Q	178	W. B. Shops	1889	CB&Q	1178		9-27
1013	CB&Q	219	W. B. Shops	1889	CB&Q	1219		6-26
1014	CB&Q	234	W. B. Shops	1889	CB&O	1234		7-28
1015	CB&Q	238	W. B. Shops	1889	CB&Q	1238		No Record
1016	B&MR	236	Aurora	1889	B&MR	236		No Record
1017	B&MR	237	Co. Shops	1889	B&MR	237		2-26
1018	B&MR	238	W. B. Shops	1889	B&MR	238		10-20
1019	B&MR	231	Rhd. Is. 2188	1889	B&MR	231		1-11
1020	B&MR	232	Rhd. I. 2189	1889	B&MR	232		No Record
1021	B&MR	233	Rhd. I. 2190	1889	B&MR	233		7-26
1022	B&MR	234	Rhd. I. 2191	1889	B&MR	234		11-17
1023	B&MR	235	Rhd. I. 2192	1889	B&MR	235		11-17
1024	B&MR	239	Aurora	1898	B&MR	239		8-29
1025	B&MR	240	Co. Shops	1889	B&MR	240		No Record
1026	B&MR	241	Bald. 11137	1889	B&MR	241		6-26
1027	B&MR	242	Bald. 11138	1889	B&MR	242		No Record
1028	B&MR	243	Bald. 11139	1889	B&MR	243		6-23
1029	B&MR	244	Bald. 11140	1889	B&MR	244		6-23
1030	B&MR	245	Bald. 11151	1889	B&MR	245		No Record
1031	B&MR	246	Bald. 11148	1889	B&MR	246		6-23
1032	B&MR	247	Bald. 11177	1889	B&MR	247		11-20
1033	B&MR	248	Bald. 11178	1889	B&MR	248		No Record
1034	CB&Q	207	W. B. Shops	1889	CB&Q	1207	KCStJ&CB 567	No Record
1035	CB&Q	235	W. B. Shops	1889	CB&Q	1235	KCStJ&CB 568	1-26
1036	CB&Q	290	W. B. Shops	1889	CB&O	1290	KCStJ&CB 569	12-22
1037	CB&Q	302	W. B. Shops	1889	CB&Q	1302	StLK&NW 766	1-26
1038	CB&Q	164	Co. Shops	1890	CB&Q	1164	KCStJ&CB 565	12-22
1039	CB&Q	179	Bald 11209	1890	CB&Q	1179	KCStJ&CB 566	7-19
1040	H&StJ	28	Co. Shops	1890	H&StJ	628		1-26
1041	H&StJ	10	Co. Shops	1890	H&StJ	648		3-27
1042	H&StJ	12	Co. Shops	1890	H&StJ	651		11-28
1043	H&StJ	11	Co. Shops	1890	H&StJ	656		1-26
1044	H&StJ	17	Co. Shops	1890	H&StJ	677		10-28
1045	CB&Q	304	Aurora	1890	CB&Q	1304	H&StJ 681	6-23
1046	CB&Q	243	Co. Shops	1890	CB&O	1243	StLK&NW 760	6-23
1047	CB&Q	3	Aurora	1890	CB&O	1003		6-24
1048	CB&Q	48	Aurora	1890	CB&O	1048		Sold 9-12
1049	CB&Q	75	Aurora	1890	CB&O	1075		11-29
1050	CB&Q	134	W. B. Shops	1890	CB&O	1134		3-27
1051	CB&Q	144	Aurora	1890	CB&O	1144		7-26
1052	CB&Q	232	W. B. Shops	1890	CB&O	1232		2-27
1053	CB&Q	312	Aurora	1890	CB&Q	1312		8-27
1054	CB&Q	414	Bald. 11210	1890	CB&Q	1414		3-28
1055	B&MR	21	Aurora	1890	BM&R	21		8-27
1056	B&MR	261	Rogers 4506	1891	B&MR	261		9-29
1057	B&MR	262	Rogers 4507	1891	B&MR	262		11-29
1058	B&MR	263	Rogers 4508	1891	B&MR	263		7-29
1059	B&MR	264	Rogers 4509	1891	B&MR	264		1-27
1060	B&MR	265	Rogers 4521	1891	B&MR	265		1-27
1061	B&MR	266	Rogers 4522	1891	B&MR	266		7-27
1062	B&MR	267	Rogers 4523	1891	B&MR	267		No Record
1063	B&MR	268	Rogers 4524	1891	B&MR	268		10-27
1064	B&MR	269	Rogers 4533	1891	B&MR	269		1-30
1065	B&MR	270	Rogers 4534	1891	B&MR	270		No Record
1066	B&MR	271	Rogers 4535	1891	B&MR	271		11-28
1067	B&MR	272	Rogers 4536	1891	B&MR	272		5-28
1068	CB&Q	47	Rogers 4620	1891	CB&Q	1047		8-28
1069	CB&Q	99	Rogers 4566	1891	CB&Q	1099		12-27
1070	CB&Q	208	Rogers 4623	1891	CB&Q	1208		9-27
1071	CB&Q	254	W. B. Shops	1891	CB&Q	1254		8-27
1072	CB&Q	324	Co. Shops	1891	CB&Q	1324		11-28
1073	CB&Q	336	Aurora	1891	CB&Q	1336		Sold 4-09
1074	CB&Q	398	Rogers 4595	1891	CB&Q	1398		1-27
1075	CB&Q	37	Rogers 4565	1891	CB&Q	1037	KCStJ&CB 561	Sold 9-12
1076	CB&Q	43	Rogers 4619	1891	CB&O	1043	KCStJ&CB 562	No Record
1077	CB&Q	51	Rogers 4621	1891	CB&Q	1051	KCStJ&CB 563	6-23
1078	CB&Q	107	Rogers 4594	1891	CB&O	1107	KCStJ&CB 564	11-28
1079	H&StJ	14	Rogers 4543	1891	H&StJ	632		12-27
1080	H&StJ	46	Rogers 4544	1891	H&StJ	646		12-22
1081	H&StJ	47	Rogers 4545	1891	H&StJ	647		6-26
1082	H&StJ	76						
	Ch. to	69	Rogers 4573	1891	H&StJ	669		5-27
1083	H&StJ	70	Rogers 4546	1891	H&StJ	670		5-27
1084	H&StJ	72	Rogers 4596	1891	H&StJ	672		Sold 9-12

New CB&Q No. 1904	Original	No.	Builder	Date	No. Change 1898	Changes 1898 to 1904	Date Retired
1085	H&StJ	73	Rogers 4597	1891	H&StJ 673		8-27
1086	H&StJ	·74	Rogers 4572	1891	H&StJ 674		6-27
1087	CB&Q	203	W. B. Shops	1891	CB&Q 1203	StLK&NW 762	7-26
1088	CB&Q	131	Rogers 4622	1891	CB&Q 1131	StLK&NW 764	8-28
1089	CB&Q	35	Rogers 4624	1891	CB&Q 1035	KCStJ&CB 560	5-27
1090	CB&Q	484	Rogers 4671	1892	CB&Q 1484	KCStJ&CB 574	1-26
1091	CB&Q	496	Rogers 4705	1892	CB&Q 1496	KCStJ& CB 575	5-26
1092	CB&Q	495	Rogers 4704	1892	CB&Q 1495	H&StJ 686	6-27
1093	CB&Q	408	Co. Shops	1892	CB&Q 1408	H&StJ 687	6-27
1094	CB&Q	491	Rogers 4692	1892	CB&Q 1491	StLK&NW 765	2-27
1095	CB&Q	483	Rogers 4657	1892	CB&Q 1483	K&W 31, K&W 839, StLK&NW 839	7-28
1096	CB&Q	150	Aurora	1892	CB&Q 1150		5-27
1097	CB&Q	480	Rogers 4654	1892	CB&Q 1480		7-26
1098	CB&Q	481	Rogers 4655	1892	CB&Q 1481		Sold 9-12
1099	CB&Q	482	Rogers 4656	1892	CB&Q 1482		3-28
1100	CB&Q	485	Rogers 4672	1892	CB&Q 1485		7-29
1101	CB&Q	486	Rogers 4675	1892	CB&Q 1486		2-27
1102	CB&Q	487	Rogers 4676	1892	CB&Q 1487		3-26
1103	CB&Q	488	Rogers 4689	1892	CB&Q 1488		4-27
1104	CB&Q	489	Rogers 4690	1892	CB&Q 1489		6-24
1105	CB&Q	490	Rogers 4691	1892	CB&Q 1490		4-27
1106	CB&Q	492	Rogers 4698	1892	CB&Q 1492		11-27
1107	CB&Q	493	Rogers 4699	1892	CB&Q 1493		1-27
1108	CB&Q	494	Rogers 4703	1892	CB&Q 1494		4-26
1109	CB&Q	498	Rogers 4707	1892	CB&Q 1498		5-28
1110	CB&Q	499	Rogers 4708	1892	CB&Q 1499		7-30
1111	CB&Q	497	Rogers 4706	1892	CB&Q 1497		7-19
1112	CB&Q	211	Aurora	1805	CB&Q 1211		8-27
1113	CB&Q	364	Aurora	1805	CB&Q 1364	B&MR 385 ('01)	7-27
1114			Rhode Island	1890			
1115			Rhode Island	1890			11-16

No. 1114 and No. 1115 do not appear on the 1904 list but do appear on later lists. There is no data on these engines on the records.

C. B. & Q. No. 211 and No. 364 were built as Class H-2 with Richmond compound cylinders. These were later changed to Class H-1, probably when simpled.

No. 1073 was sold to the Wapello Coal Co. for a former Class G-1 engine and a cash consideration.

The following engines were sold to the Q. O. & K. C. R. R. in 1912. Numbers assigned by Q. O. & K. C. are as shown.

C. B. & Q. No. 1000	Q. O. & K. C. No. 40
C. B. & Q. No. 1009	Q. O. & K. C. No. 41
C. B. & Q. No. 1048	Q. O. & K. C. No. 42
C. B. & Q. No. 1075	Q. O. & K. C. No. 43
C. B. & Q. No. 1084	Q. O. & K. C. No. 44
C. B. & Q. No. 1098	Q. O. & K. C. No. 45

Class H-2, 2-6-0

New CB&Q No. 1904	Original	No.	Builder	Date	No. Change 1898	Changes 1898 to 1904	Date Retired
1120	CB&Q	83	Rogers 4745	1892	CB&Q 1083		7-29
1121	CB&Q	91	Rogers 4746	1892	CB&Q 1091		3-29
1122	CB&Q	510	Rogers 4747	1892	CB&Q 1510		6-27
1123	CB&Q	511	Rogers 4748	1892	CB&Q 1511		3-30
1124	CB&Q	512	Rogers 4753	1892	CB&Q 1512		4-28
1125	CB&Q	514	Rogers 4761	1892	CB&Q 1514		1-28
1126	CB&Q	515	Rogers 4781	1892	CB&Q 1515		4-28
1127	CB&Q	516	Rogers 4782	1892	CB&Q 1516		5-27
1128	CB&Q	517	Rogers 4783	1892	CB&Q 1517		4-27
1129	CB&Q	518	Rogers 4792	1892	CB&Q 1518		3-28
1130	CB&Q	519	Rogers 4793	1892	CB&Q 1519		2-28
1131	CB&Q	520	Rogers 4794	1892	CB&Q 1520		8-27
1132	CB&Q	521	Rogers 4803	1892	CB&Q 1521		7-30
1133	CB&Q	522	Rogers 4804	1892	CB&Q 1522		12-31
1134	CB&Q	523	Rogers 4811	1892	CB&Q 1523		12-27
1135	CB&Q	524	Rogers 4812	1892	CB&Q 1524		8-27
1136	H&StJ	49	Rogers 4784	1892	H&StJ 649		11-28
1137	H&StJ	55	Rogers 4802	1892	H&StJ 655		1-30
1138	H&StJ	71	Rogers 4813	1892	H&StJ 671		6-27
1139	CB&Q	513	Rogers 4754	1892	CB&Q 1513	H&StJ 688	7-28
1140	H&StJ Ch. to	77 60	Rogers 4835	1893	H&StJ 660		3-30
1141	CB&Q	530	Rogers 4825	1893	CB&Q 1530	H&StJ 689	3-28
1142	CB&Q	525	Rogers 4820	1893	CB&Q 1525		11-29
1143	CB&Q	526	Rogers 4821	1893	CB&Q 1526		1-30
1144	CB&Q	527	Rogers 4822	1893	CB&Q 1527		11-29
1145	CB&Q	528	Rogers 4823	1893	CB&Q 1528		3-33
1146	CB&Q	529	Rogers 4824	1893	CB&Q 1529		8-29
1147	CB&Q	531	Rogers 4833	1893	CB&Q 1531		8-29
1148	CB&Q	532	Rogers 4834	1893	CB&Q 1532		7-29
1149	CB&Q	80	Aurora	1895	CB&Q 1080		11-28
1150	CB&Q	140	Aurora	1895	CB&Q 1140		5-29

New CB&Q No. 1904	Orig. No.		Builder	Date	No. Change 1898		Changes 1898 to 1904	Date Retired
1151	CB&Q	165	W. B. Shops	1895	CB&Q	1165		8-27
1152	CB&Q	170	W. B. Shops	1893	CB&Q	1170		12-30
1153	CB&Q	189	Aurora	1895	CB&Q	1189		5-30
1154	CB&Q	201	W. B. Shops	1895	CB&Q	1201		4-31
1155	CB&Q	106	Aurora	1895	CB&Q	1106	B&MR 384	5-27
1156	H&StJ	61	Co. Shops	1895	H&StJ	661		6-27
1157	CB&Q	36	Co. Shops	1896	CB&Q	1036		4-27
1158	CB&Q	46	Aurora	1896	CB&Q	1046		10-29
1159	CB&Q	76	Co. Shops	1896	CB&Q	1076		8-29
1160	CB&Q	77	Aurora	1896	CB&Q	1077		10-29

Class H-2, 2-6-0
Built Subsequent to Number Change of 1898

New CB&Q No. 1904	Builder	Date	Original No.		Retired Date
1161	Pitts 1827	1898	CB&Q	1021	5-27
1162	Pitts. 1823	1898	CB&Q	1031	4-27
1163	Aurora	1898	CB&Q	1039	10-27
1164	Pitts. 1828	1898	CB&Q	1045	5-29
1165	Aurora	1898	CB&Q	1054	8-29
1166	Pitts. 1818	1898	CB&Q	1166	3-28
1167	Aurora	1898	CB&Q	1103	5-28
1168	Pitts. 1824	1898	CB&Q	1108	8-29
1169	Aurora	1898	CB&Q	1114	7-29

Class H-2, 2-6-0

New CB&Q No. 1904	Original No.		Builder	Date	Retired
1170	CB&Q	1159	Pitts. 1825	1898	8-27
1171	CB&Q	1067	Pitts. 1817	1898	11-28
1172	CB&Q	1172	Co. Shops	1898	7-29
1173	CB&Q	1225	W. B. Shops	1898	1-28
1174	CB&Q	1174	Pitts. 1826	1898	11-27
1175	CB&Q	1126	Pitts. 1815	1898	8-30
1176	CB&Q	1230	W. B. Shops	1898	4-27
1177	CB&Q	1236	Pitts. 1821	1898	1-30
1178	CB&Q	1262	Aurora	1898	11-28
1179	CB&Q	1283	Pitts. 1816	1898	3-27
1180	CB&Q	1303	Pitts. 1819	1898	7-29
1181	CB&Q	1181	Pitts. 1820	1898	3-27
1182	CB&Q	1299	Pitts. 1822	1898	11-28

No. 1145 built by Pittsburg Works was built as a cross compound.

Class H-3, 2-6-0

1200	CB&Q	1193	W. Burlington	1898	12-31
1201	CB&Q	1294	W. Burlington	1898	9-29
1202	CB&Q	1533	W. Burlington	1898	2-31
1203	CB&Q	1534	W. Burlington	1898	3-30
1204	CB&Q	1535	W. Burlington	1898	12-30
1205	CB&Q	1536	W. Burlington	1898	9-29
1206	CB&Q	1537	W. Burlington	1898	11-29
1207	CB&Q	1538	W. Burlington	1898	11-33
1208	CB&Q	1539	W. Burlington	1898	10-30
1209	CB&Q	1540	W. Burlington	1898	12-31
1210	CB&Q	1541	Aurora	1899	7-31
1211	CB&Q	1542	Aurora	1899	10-29
1212	CB&Q	1543	Aurora	1899	3-33
1213	CB&Q	1544	Aurora	1899	9-29
1214	CB&Q	1545	W. Burlington	1899	12-29
1215	CB&Q	1546	Aurora	1899	5-33
1216	CB&Q	1547	Aurora	1899	7-33
1217	CB&Q	1548	Aurora	1899	12-30

Class H-4, 2-6-0

New CB&Q No. 1904	Orig. No.		Builder	Date	Changes 1898 to 1904	Retired
1220	CB&Q	1551	Bald. 17000	1899		Sold for scrap 5-49
1221	CB&Q	1552	Bald. 17001	1899		Reb. to K-10 965 '14
1222	CB&Q	1553	Bald. 17002	1899		Reb. to K-10 959 '09
1223	CB&Q	1554	Bald. 17003	1899		Retired 3-47
1224	CB&Q	1555	Bald. 17004	1899		Retired 11-46
1225	B&MR	339	Bald. 16914	1899		Retired 11-46
1226	B&MR	340	Bald. 16915	1899		Retired 8-30
1227	B&MR	341	Bald. 16948	1899		Retired 6-35
1228	B&MR	342	Bald. 16949	1899		Retired 1-41
1229	B&MR	343	Bald. 16950	1899		Reb. to K-10 967 '14
1230	B&MR	344	Bald. 16951	1899		Retired 11-46
1231	B&MR	345	Bald. 16970	1899		Reb. to K-10 966 '14
1232	B&MR	346	Bald. 16971	1899		Retired 11-46
1233	B&MR	347	Bald. 16972	1899		Retired 10-46

New CB&Q No. 1904	Orig. No.		Builder		Date	1898 to 1904 Changes	Retired
1234	B&MR	348	Bald. 16973		1899		Sold to StL&H 3-19-35
1235	B&MR	11	Rogers 5524		1900		Sold for scrap 5-51
1236	B&MR	25	Rogers 5522		1900		Retired 10-46
1237	B&MR	37	Rogers 5523		1900		
1238	B&MR	56	Rogers 5525		1900		Reb. to K-10 960 '08
1239	B&MR	58	Rogers 5526		1900		Reb. to K-10 968 '14
1240	CB&Q	1566	Rogers 5502		1900		Retired 11-46
1241	CB&Q	1557	Rogers 5503		1900		Sold for scrap 10-48
1242	CB&Q	1558	Rogers 5504		1900		Retired 2-41
1243	CB&Q	1559	Rogers 5505		1900		Reb. to K-10 961 '09
1244	CB&Q	1560	Rogers 5506		1900		Reb. to K-10 954 '08
1245	CB&Q	1561	Rogers 5507		1900		Reb. to K-10 950 '08
1246	CB&Q	1562	Aurora		1900		Reb. to K-10 964 '09
1247	CB&Q	1563	Aurora		1900		Reb. to K-10 962 '09
1248	CB&Q	1564	Aurora		1900		Retired 11-46
1249	CB&Q	1565	Aurora		1900		Reb. to K-10 958 '09
1250	CB&Q	1566	W. B. Shops		1900		Reb. to K-10 957 '09
1251	CB&Q	1567	W. B. Shops		1900		Reb. to K-10 955 '08
1252	CB&Q	1568	W. B. Shops		1900		Reb. to K-10 963 '09
1253	CB&Q	1569	W. B. Shops		1900		Reb. to K-10 953 '08
1254	KCStJ&CB	521	Rogers 5509		1900	H&StJ 521	Retired 5-47
1255	KCStJ&CB	522	Rogers 5510		1900	H&StJ 522	Retired 2-43
1256	KCStJ&CB	523	Rogers 5511		1900	H&StJ 523	Reb. to K-10 952 '08
1257	KCStJ&CB	524	Rogers 5512		1900	H&StJ 524	Retired 11-46
1258	KSStJ&CB	525	Rogers 5513		1900	H&StJ 525	Reb. to K-10 951 '08
1259	KCStJ&CB	529	Rogers 5514		1900	H&StJ 529	Reb. to K-10 956 '09
1260	KCStJ&CB	538	Rogers 5515		1900	H&StJ 538	Retired 12-29
1261	KCCtJ&CB	544	Rogers 5516		1900	H&StJ 544	Retired 4-47
1262	CB&Q	1562	Rogers 5508		1900	KCStJ&CB 545 H&StJ 545	Retired 4-47

The first C. B. & Q. No. 1562, built by Rogers, was transferred to K. C. & St. J. & C. B. in 1900 and a new engine built at Aurora the same year was assigned this number.

Class H-5, 2-6-0

New CB&Q No. 1904	Orig. No.		Builder	Date	Change 1902		
1270	KC&O	27	Rome	1887	B&MR	427	
1271	KC&O	28	Rome	1887	B&MR	428	
1272	KC&O	29	Rome	1887	B&MR	429	No. 1270 to No. 1279
1273	KC&O	30	Rome	1887	B&MR	430	all retired prior to
1274	KC&O	31	Rome	1887	B&MR	431	1917
1275	KC&O	32	Rome	1887	B&MR	432	
1276	KC&O	33	Rome	1887	B&MR	433	
1277	KC&O	34	Rome	1887	B&MR	434	
1278	KC&O	35	Rome	1887	B&MR	435	
1279	KC&O	36	Rome	1887	B&MR	436	
1280	I&StL	5	Hinkley	1871	Acquired 1903		Rebuilt to G-1 1382

Class G-1, 0-6-0

New CB&Q No. 1904	Orig. No.		Builder	Date	No. Change 1898		Changes 1898 to 1904	Retired
1300	Unknown		Unknown		KC'CB	501		No Record
1301	H&StJ	36	Unknown		H&StJ	604	StLK&NW 604	No Record
1302	H&StJ	9	Unknown		H&StJ	609	KCStJ&CB 609	No Record
1303	H&StJ	48	Unknown		H&StJ	610	KCStJ&CB 610	No Record
1304	H&StJ	56	Unknown		H&St J	611	KCStJ&CB 611	No Record
1305	H&StJ	32	Unknown		H&StJ	614	KCStJ&CB 614	No Record
1306	CB&Q	162	Co. Shops	1885	CB&Q	1162		No Record
1307	CB&Q	459	Aurora	1886	CB&Q	1459		12-29
1308	CB&Q	461	Aurora	1886	CB&Q	1461		Sold 1914
1309	CB&Q	462	Aurora	1886	CB&Q	1462		3-31
1310	CB&Q	463	Aurora	1886	CB&Q	1463		No Record
1311	B&MR	143	Plattsmouth	1886	B&MR	143		No Record
1312	B&MR	144	Plattsmouth	1886	B&MR	144		No Record
1313	CB&Q	460	Aurora	1886	CB&Q	1460	KCStJ&CB 557	6-17
1314	CB&Q	231	Co. Shops	1887	CB&Q	1231	KCStJ&CB 507 H&StJ 507	5-26
1315	KCStJ&CB	42	Co. Shops	1887	KC'CB	510		Sold 9-27
1316	H&StJ	2	Co. Shops	1887	H&StJ	602	KCStJ&CB 602	No Record
1317	CB&Q	464	Aurora	1887	CB&Q	1464	K&W 13, K&W 803	12-22
1318	B&MR	169	Plattsmouth	1887	B&MR	169		No Record
1319	B&MR	170	Plattsmouth	1887	B&MR	170		No Record
1320	CB&Q	224	W. B. Shops	1887	CB&Q	1224		4-31
1321	CB&Q	233	W. B. Shops	1887	CB&Q	1233		No Record
1322	CB&Q	291	W. B. Shops	1887	CB&Q	1291		9-27
1323	CB&Q	297	W. B. Shops	1887	CB&Q	1297		6-24
1324	CB&Q	465	Aurora	1887	CB&Q	1465		3-29
1325	CB&Q	467	Aurora	1887	CB&Q	1467		4-31
1326	CB&Q	468	Aurora	1887	CB&Q	1468		No Record
1327	CB&Q	469	Aurora	1887	CB&Q	1469		2-27
1328	CB&Q	94	W. B. Shops	1888	CB&Q	1094		4-30

No. 1308 Became DRI&NW No. 22. Scrapped 1927.

New CB&Q No. 1904	Orig. No.		Builder	Date	Change 1898		Changes 1899 to 1904	Date Retired
1329	CB&Q	466	Aurora	1887	CB&Q	1466		5-27
1330	H&StJ	1	W. B. Shops	1888	H&StJ	601		1-26
1331	B&MR	171	Plattsmouth	1888	B&MR	171		Sold 7-16
1332	B&MR	172	Plattsmouth	1888	B&MR	172		11-29
1333	B&MR	213	Bald. 9602	1888	B&MR	213		No Record
1334	B&MR	214	Bald. 9604	1888	B&MR	214		No Record
1335	B&MR	215	Bald. 9605	1888	B&MR	215		12-30
1336	B&MR	216	Bald. 9603	1888	B&MR	216		4-26
1337	B&MR	217	Bald. 9608	1888	B&MR	217		No Record
1338	B&MR	218	Bald 9609	1888	B&MR	218		3-17
1339	B&MR	219	Bald. 9612	1888	B&MR	219		No Record
1340	B&MR	220	Bald. 9613	1888	B&MR	220		1-17
1341	B&MR	17	Plattsmouth	1889	B&MR	17		3-30
1342	H&StJ	3	W. B. Shops	1889	H&StJ	603	KCStJ&CB 603	6-19
1343	CB&Q	293	W. B. Shops	1889	CB&Q	1293		No Record
1344	CB&Q	298	W. B. Shops	1889	CB&Q	1298		8-21
1345	CB&Q	192	Bald. 11164	1890	CB&Q	1192		Sold 1914
1346	CB&Q	206	Bald. 11163	1890	CB&Q	1206		5-28
1347	CB&Q	255	Aurora	1890	CB&Q	1255		8-27
1348	CB&Q	470	Bald. 11165	1890	CB&Q	1470		Sold 1914
1349	CB&Q	471	Bald. 11167	1890	CB&Q	1471		No Record
1350	CB&Q	472	Bald. 11168	1890	CB&Q	1472		No Record
1351	CB&Q	473	Bald. 11195	1890	CB&Q	1473		9-31
1352	B&MR	22	Plattsmouth	1890	B&MR	22		6-21
1353	B&MR	249	Bald. 11161	1891	B&MR	249		4-17
1354	B&MR	250	Bald. 11175	1891	B&MR	250		No Record
1355	B&MR	251	Bald. 11176	1891	B&MR	251		8-30
1356	B&MR	252	Bald. 11162	1891	B&MR	252		1-25
1357	CB&Q	204	Aurora	1891	CB&Q	1204		5-27
1358	CB&N	106	Rogers 4741	1892	CB&N	909	CB&Q 909	9-27
1359	CB&N	107	Rogers 4742	1892	CB&N	910	CB&Q 910	12-27
1360	CB&Q	474	Bald. 12468	1892	CB&Q	1474		5-27
1361	CB&Q	475	Bald. 12469	1892	CB&Q	1475		10-27
1362	CB&Q	478	Bald. 12471	1892	CB&Q	1478		10-30
1363	CB&Q	479	Bald. 12475	1892	CB&Q	1479		1-28
1364	CB&Q	476	Bald. 12470	1892	CB&Q	1476	B&MR 337, 8-98	No Record
1365	CB&Q	477	Bald. 12474	1882	CB&Q	1477	B&MR 338, 8-98	7-28
1366	B&MR	296	Bald. 12476	1892	B&MR	296		5-17
1367	B&MR	297	Bald. 12477	1892	B&MR	297		9-31
1368	B&MR	298	Bald. 12485	1892	B&MR	298		Sold 5-05
1369	B&MR	299	Bald. 12486	1892	B&MR	299		No Record
1370	B&MR	300	Bald. 12491	1892	B&MR	300		9-29
1371	B&MR	301	Bald. 12493	1892	B&MR	301		No Record
1372	H&StJ	7	Rogers 4739	1892	H&StJ	607	StLK&NW 607	12-27
1373	H&StJ	8	Rogers 4740	1892	H&StJ	608	StLK&NW 608	Sold 1916
1374	CB&Q	115	Aurora	1893	CB&Q	1115		11-31
1375	CB&Q	213	Aurora	1893	CB&Q	1213		No Record
1376	CB&Q	335	Aurora	1893	CB&Q	1335		11-28
1377	B&MR	16	Havelock	1898	B&MR	16		No Record
1378	B&MR	48	Havelock	1898	B&MR	48		12-31
1379	B&MR	28	Havelock	1898	B&MR	28		2-27
1380	B&MR	32	Havelock	1898	B&MR	32		2-27
1381	I&StL	6	Unknown		Acq'd 1903			1911
1382			Hinkley	1871	Rebuilt from H 5 1280			1911
1383			Baldwin	1892	Formerly 1368			1912

No. 1345 Became DRI&NW No. 24 Scrapped 1927.
No. 1348 Became DRI&NW No. 23 Scrapped 1926.
No. 1315 Sold to Hooppole, Yorktown & Tampico R. R.
No. 1331 Sold to Moffet Coal Co.
No. 1368 was sold to Wapello Coal Co. in 1905 and taken back again in 1909 as part payment for a Class H-1 engine being given the new number. No. 1373 sold to Q. O. & K. C. R. R. and became No. 50 on that road.

Class G-2, 0-6-0

					Change 1901	
1390	CB&Q	1476	Co. Shops	1899		Sold 7-26
1391	CB&KC	801	Co. Shops	1899	StLK&NW 801	Sold 11-26

No. 1390 became D. R. I. & N. W. No. 47. No. 1391 became D. R. I. & N. W. No. 48.

Class G-3, 0-6-0

New CB&Q No. 1904	Orig. No.		Builder	Date		
1400	KCStJ&CB	508	Changed to			Reb. to Shop Switcher No. 300 3-31
	H&StJ	508	Aurora	1900		
1401	CB&Q	1650	Aurora	1900		Retired 11-30
1402	CB&Q	1651	Aurora	1900		Retired 12-31
1403	CB&Q	1652	Aurora	1900		Retired 3-31
1404	CB&Q	1653	Aurora	1901		Retired 4-33
1405	CB&Q	1654	Aurora	1901		Retired 3-31
1406	CB&Q	1655	Aurora	1901		Retired 1-30
1407	CB&Q	1656	Aurora	1901		Retired 1-33

New CB&Q No. 1904	Orig. No.		Builder	Date	Changes 1903	Retired
1408	CB&Q	1657	Aurora	1901		Retired 8-33
1409	CB&Q	1658	Aurora	1901		Retired 4-31
1410	CB&Q	1659	Aurora	1901		Retired 7-30
1411	CB&Q	1660	Aurora	1901		Retired 9-29
1412	CB&Q	1661	Aurora	1901		Retired 12-28
1413	CB&Q	1662	Aurora	1901		Reb. to Shop Switcher 301 3-31
1414	CB&Q	1663	Aurora	1902		Retired 7-33
1415	CB&Q	1664	Aurora	1902		Retired 12-31
1416	CB&Q	1665	Aurora	1902		Retired 4-33
1417	CB&Q	1666	Aurora	1902		Reb. to Shop Switcher 302-3-31 **Ret. 10-35**
1418	CB&Q	1667	Aurora	1902		Retired 4-31
1419	CB&Q	1668	Aurora	1902		Retired 1-30
1420	CB&Q	1669	Aurora	1902		Retired 11-30
1421	CB&Q	1670	Aurora	1902		Retired 9-29
1422	CB&Q	1671	Aurora	1902		Retired 7-33
1423	CB&Q	1672	Aurora	1902		Retired 7-30
1424	CB&Q	1673	W. B. Shops	1902		Retired 5-33
1425	CB&Q	1674	W. B. Shops	1902		Retired 10-35
1426	CB&Q	1675	W. B. Shops	1902		Retired 8-33
1427	CB&Q	1676	W. B. Shops	1902		Retired 12-31
1428	CB&Q	1677	Aurora	1902		Retired 7-30
1429	CB&Q	1678	Aurora	1902		Retired 6-39
1430	CB&Q	1679	Aurora	1902		Retired 7-31
1431	CB&Q	1680	Aurora	1902		Retired 8-29
1432	KCStJ&CB	519	W. B. Shops	1903		Retired 12-31
1433	KCStJ&CB	520	W. B. Shops	1903		Retired 1-33
1434	StLK&NW	703 Changed to				
	KCStJ&CB	530	W. B. Shops	1903		Retired 12-30
1435	KCStJ&CB	534	W. B. Shops	1903		Retired 12-31
1436	KCStJ&CB	535	W. B. Shops	1903		Retired 2-33
1437	KCStJ&CB	542	W. B. Shops	1903		Retired 12-31
1438	KCStJ&CB	547	W. B. Shops	1903		Retired 8-31
1439	KCStJ&CB	550	W. B. Shops	1903		Retired 12-31
1440	KCStJ&CB	556	W. B. Shops	1903		Retired 5-33
1441	CB&KC	802 Changed to				
	StLK&NW	802	W. B. Shops	1903		Retired 12-31
1442	CB&Q	1647	Aurora	1903		Retired 2-33
1443	CB&Q	1648	Aurora	1903		Reb. to Shop Switcher 303 3-31
1444	CB&Q	1649	Aurora	1903		Retired 3-31
1445	CB&Q	1681	Aurora	1903		Retired 10-30
1446	CB&Q	1682	Aurora	1903		Retired 2-33
1447	CB&Q	1683	Aurora	1903		Retired 9-31
1448	CB&Q	1684	W. B. Shops	1903		Retired 12-31
1449	CB&Q	1685	W. B. Shops	1903		Retired 9-31
1450	CB&Q	1686	W. B. Shops	1903		Retired 2-33
1451	CB&Q	1687	W. B. Shops	1903		Retired 12-30
1452	CB&Q	1688	Aurora	1903		Retired 9-31
1453	CB&Q	1689	Aurora	1903		Retired 12-31
1454	CB&Q	1690	Aurora	1903		Retired 5-33
1455	CB&Q	1691	Aurora	1903		Retired 7-33
1456	CB&Q	1692	Aurora	1903		Retired 4-31
1457	CB&Q	1694	W. B. Shops	1903		Retired 12-30
1458	CB&Q	1695	W. B. Shops	1903		Retired 7-31
1459	B&MR	67	Havelock	1903	B&MR 3050	Reb. to Shop Switcher 314 Ret. 6-47
1460	B&MR	69	Havelock	1903	B&MR 3051	Reb. to Shop Switcher 304 3-31
1461	B&MR	91	Havelock	1903	B&MR 3052	Reb. to Shop Switcher 305 3-31
1462	B&MR	71	Havelock	1903	B&MR 3053	Retired 2-33
1463	B&MR	2	Havelock	1903	B&MR 3054	Retired 9-31
1464	B&MR	95	Havelock	1903	B&MR 3055	Retired 12-30
1465	CB&Q	1693	Aurora	1904		Retired 11-46
1466	CB&Q	1696	Aurora	1904		Retired 7-33
1467	CB&Q	1697	Aurora	1904		Retired 7-23
1468	CB&Q	1698	Aurora	1904		Retired 12-31

The change of numbers on K. C. St. J. & C. B. No. 508, St. L. K. & N. W. No. 703 and C. B. & K. C. No. 802 was made shortly after the engines were built. St. L. K. & N. W. No. 703 carried the original lettering after being transferred to K. C. St. J. & C. B.

Class G-3 Built Subsequent to 1904

No.	Builder	Date	
1469	Havelock	1907	Retired 10-30
1470	Havelock	1907	Retired 11-30
1471	Havelock	1907	Rebuilt to Shop Switcher No. 306 3-31
1472	Havelock	1907	Retired 8-31
1473	W. B. Shops	1907	Retired 12-31
1474	W. B. Shops	1907	Retired 7-29
1475	W. B. Shops	1907	Retired 11-34
1476	Aurora	1907	Retired 11-30
1477	Aurora	1907	Retired 2-33
1478	Aurora	1907	Retired 10-30

No.	Builder	Date	
1479	Aurora	1909	Retired 12-30
1480	Aurora	1909	Rebuilt to Shop Switcher No. 307 3-31. Ret. 10-39.
1481	Aurora	1909	Retired 10-30
1482	Aurora	1909	Rebuilt to Shop Switcher No. 308 3-31
1483	Aurora	1909	Retired 2-33
1484	W. B. Shops	1909	Retired 8-31
1485	W. B. Shops	1909	Retired 10-34
1486	W. B. Shops		
1487	W. B. Shops	1909	Retired 8-31
1488	W. B. Shops	1909	Retired 8-31
1489	Aurora	1910	Retired 8-33
1490	Aurora	1910	Retired 12-30
1491	Aurora	1910	Retired 12-30
1492	Aurora	1910	Rebuilt to Shop Switcher No. 309 3-31. Ret. 7-40.
1493	Aurora	1910	Retired 8-31
1494	Aurora	1910	
1495	Aurora	1910	Retired 9-33
1496	W. B. Shops	1910	Retired 10-33
1497	W. B. Shops	1910	Retired 8-31
1498	W. B. Shops	1910	Retired 12-30
1499	W. B. Shops	1910	Retired 12-33
1500	W. B. Shops	1910	Rebuilt to Shop Switcher No. 310 3-31. Ret. 6-47.
1501	W. B. Shops	1910	Retired 12-31
1502	W. B. Shops	1910	Retired 2-33
1503	W. B. Shops	1910	Retired 7-33
1504	W. B. Shops	1910	Retired 3-33
1505	W. B. Shops	1910	Retired 3-33
1506	Havelock	1910	Retired 10-34
1507	Havelock	1910	Retired 8-30
1508	Havelock	1910	Retired 12-31
1509	Havelock	1910	Retired 6-42
1510	Havelock	1910	Sold for scrap 6-51
1511	Havelock	1910	Rebuilt to Shop Switcher No. 311 3-31
1512	Havelock	1910	Retired 2-33
1513	Havelock	1910	Retired 9-33
1514	Aurora	1910	Retired 4-33
1515	Aurora	1910	Sold to DRI&NW
1516	Aurora	1910	Retired 8-33
1517	Aurora	1910	Retired 12-30
1518	Aurora	1910	Sold to DRI&NW 2-29 DRI &NW No. 52
1519	Aurora	1910	Retired 7-30
1520	Aurora	1913	Retired 6-35
1521	Aurora	1913	Retired 3-33
1522	Aurora	1913	Sold to Midland Elec. Coal Co.
1523	Aurora	1913	Retired 8-33
1524	Aurora	1913	Retired 12-31
1525	Havelock	1913	Retired 1-33
1526	Havelock	1913	Retired 3-31
1527	Havelock	1913	Retired 6-33
1528	Havelock	1913	Retired 11-39
1529	Havelock	1913	Retired 3-33
1530	Bald. 38682	1912	Retired 8-31
1531	Bald. 38683	1912	Retired 11-40
1532	Bald. 38684	1912	Retired 11-46
1533	Bald. 38685	1912	Retired 3-33
1534	Bald. 38686	1912	Retired 8-33
1535	Bald. 38687	1912	Retired 7-33
1536	Bald. 38688	1912	Retired 9-33
1537	Bald. 38689	1912	Retired 8-29
1538	Bald. 38690	1912	Retired 6-42
1539	Bald. 38691	1912	Retired 12-30
1540	Bald. 38815	1912	Sold to DRI&NW 3-29 DRI&NW No. 53
1541	Bald. 38816	1912	Sold to DRI&NW 11-29 DRI&NW No. 55
1542	Bald. 38817	1912	Retired 10-33
1543	Bald. 38818	1912	Retired 3-33
1544	Bald. 38823	1912	Sold to Franklin Co. Coal Corp. 7-41
1545	Bald. 38824	1912	Sold for scrap 12-50
1546	Bald. 38825	1912	Retired 9-33
1547	Bald. 38826	1912	Rebuilt to Shop Switcher No. 312. Renumbered back to 1547 6-39. Sold to Midland Elec. Coal Co. 7-41
1548	Bald. 38838	1912	Sold to Midland Elec. Coal Co. 1-42
1549	Bald. 38839	1912	Sold to Midland Elec. Coal Co. 6-41
1550	Bald. 39002	1912	Retired 8-31
1551	Bald. 39003	1912	Retired 8-31
1552	Bald. 39023	1912	Retired 8-31
1553	Bald. 39024	1912	Held 12-57 Sold for scrap 12-60
1554	Bald. 39025	1912	Retired 1-32
1555	Bald. 39559	1913	Retired 9-33
1556	Bald. 39560	1913	Sold to DRI&NW 5-29 DRI&NW No. 54
1557	Bald. 39646	1913	Retired 6-42
1558	Bald. 39647	1913	Retired 9-33
1559	Bald. 39648	1913	Sold to DRI&NW 1-30 DRI&NW No. 58
1560	Bald. 39649	1913	Retired 12-31
1561	Bald. 39650	1913	Retired 10-30
1562	Bald. 39651	1913	Retired 4-33

Class G-3 Built Subsequent to 1904

No.	Builder		Date	
1563	Bald.	39704	1913	Sold for scrap 7-52
1564	Bald.	39705	1913	Retired 4-33
1565	Bald.	39706	1913	Retired 12-31
1566	Bald.	39707	1913	Retired 4-47
1567	Bald.	39708	1913	Sold to Midland Elec. Coal Corp. 7-33
1568	Bald.	39709	1913	Retired 11-46
1569	Bald.	39710	1913	Retired 9-33
1570	Bald.	39711	1913	Retired 3-33
1571	Bald.	39712	1913	Retired 4-33
1572	Bald.	39713	1913	Retired 9-33
1573	Bald.	39739	1913	Retired 4-47
1574	Bald.	39740	1913	Sold for scrap 12-52
1575	Bald.	39741	1913	Retired 12-30
1576	Bald.	39742	1913	
1577	Bald.	39743	1913	Retired 3-33
1578	Bald.	39748	1913	Retired 2-33
1579	Bald.	39749	1913	Retired 4-31

Class G-4-A, 0-6-0

New CB&Q No. 1904	Orig. No.		Builder		Date	No. Change 1898		Changes		
1600	CB&Q	326	Bald.	4682	1879	KCStJ&CB	511	StLK&NW	511	Retired
1601	CB&Q	325	Bald.	4683	1879	H&StJ	615	StLK&NW	615	Retired
1602	CB&Q	345	Bald.	5146	1880	CB&Q	1345	KCStJ&CB	504	Retired
1603	CB&Q	349	Bald.	5202	1880	CB&Q	1349	StLK&NW	701	Retired
1604	CB&Q	346	Bald.	5150	1880	CB&Q	1346			Retired
1605	CB&Q	347	Bald.	5179	1880	CB&Q	1347			Retired 1911
1606	CB&Q	348	Bald.	5181	1880	CB&Q	1348			Retired
1607	CB&Q	350	Bald.	5203	1880	CB&Q	1350			Retired
1608	CB&Q	389	Bald.	5692	1881	CB&Q	1389			Retired 5-16
1609	CB&Q	390	Bald.	5696	1881	CB&Q	1390			Retired
1610	CB&Q	391	Bald.	5717	1881	CB&Q	1391			Retired
1611	CB&Q	392	Bald.	5719	1881	CB&Q	1392			Retired 8-21
1612	CB&Q	393	Bald.	5729	1881	CB&Q	1393			Retired
1613	CB&Q	394	Bald.	5734	1881	CB&Q	1394			Retired
1614	CB&Q	395	Bald.	5749	1881	CB&Q	1395			Retired
1615	CB&Q	396	Bald.	5752	1881	CB&Q	1396			Retired
1616	CB&Q	415	Bald.	6298	1882	CB&Q	1415			Retired
1617	CB&Q	418	Bald.	6313	1882	CB&Q	1418			Retired
1618	CB&Q	420	Bald.	6327	1882	CB&Q	1420			Retired
1619	CB&Q	422	Bald.	6348	1882	CB&Q	1422			Retired
1620	CB&Q	423	Bald.	6347	1882	CB&Q	1423			Retired
1621	CB&Q	414	Bald.	6296	1882	B&MR	97	(10-82)		Retired 12-17
1622	CB&Q	417	Bald.	6308	1882	CB&Q	1417	KCStJ&CB	506	Retired
1623	CB&Q	416	Bald.	6301	1882	CB&Q	1416	KCStJ&CB	514	
								StLK&NW	514	Retired 1910
1624	CB&Q	421	Bald.	6328	1882	CB&Q	1421	KCStJ&CB	515	Retired
1625	H&StJ	51	No Rec	5759		H&StJ	612	StLK&NW	612	Retired
1626	H&StJ	52	No Rec	5762		H&StJ	613	KCStJ&CB	613	Retired
1627	CB&Q	456	Bald.	7351	1884	CB&Q	1456	KCStJ&CB	517	Retired 7-16
1628	CB&Q	455	Bald.	7352	1884	CB&Q	1455	H&StJ	616	
								KCStJ&CB	616	Retired
1629	CB&Q	449	Bald.	7327	1884	CB&Q	1449			Retired 5-27
1630	CB&Q	450	Bald.	7328	1884	CB&Q	1450			Retired 1-26
1631	CB&Q	451	Bald.	7331	1884	CB&Q	1451			Retired
1632	CB&Q	453	Bald.	7337	1884	CB&Q	1453			Retired 11-28
1633	CB&Q	454	Bald.	7342	1884	CB&Q	1454			Retired 1909
1634	CB&Q	457	Bald.	7359	1884	CB&Q	1457			Retired 1910
1635	CB&Q	458	Bald.	7361	1884	B&MR	122	(8-84)		Retired
1636	CB&Q	452	Bald.	7343	1884	CB&Q	1452	B&MR 381	(3-01)	Retired
1637	CB&Q	419	Bald.	6315	1882	CB&Q	1419	B&MR 382	(3-01)	Retired
1638	CB&Q	434	Rhd. I.	1664	1886	CB&Q	1434			Retired 1-26
1639	CB&Q	435	Rhd. I.	1665	1886	CB&Q	1435			Retired 5-27
1640	CB&Q	436	Rhd. I.	1666	1886	CB&Q	1436			Retired 5-16
1641	CB&Q	438	Rhd. I.	1668	1886	CB&Q	1438			Retired 3-28
1642	CB&Q	440	Rhd. I.	1670	1886	CB&Q	1440			Retired
1643	CB&Q	441	Rhd. I.	1671	1886	CB&Q	1441			Retired
1644	CB&Q	442	Rhd. I.	1672	1886	CB&Q	1442			Retired
1645	CB&Q	443	Rhd. I.	1673	1886	CB&Q	1443			Retired
1646	CB&Q	444	Rhd. I.	1674	1886	CB&Q	1444			Retired 8-28
1647	CB&Q	445	Rhd. I.	1675	1886	CB&Q	1445	KCStJ&CB	505	Retired 6-16
1648	CB&Q	437	Rhd. I.	1667	1886	KC'CB	512			Retired
1649	CB&Q	439	Rhd. I.	1669	1886	CB&Q	1439	KCStJ&CB	516	
								StLK&NW	516	Retired 1911
1650	CB&Q	190	Aurora		1888	CB&Q	1190	KCStJ&CB	503	Sold for scrap 3-52
1651	CB&Q	126	W. B. Shops		1888	CB&Q	1126	KCStJ&CB	513	Retired 12-16
1652	CB&Q	89	W. B. Shops		1888	CB&Q	1089			Retired 12-22
1653	CB&Q	127	W. B. Shops		1888	CB&Q	1127			Retired 5-27
1654	CB&Q	227	W. B. Shops		1888	CB&Q	1277			Retired 7-27

No. 1650 is shown as Class G-4-C in late lists.

Class G-4, 0-6-0 Rebuilt From Class D-2, 2-8-0
Rebuilt prior to 1904

New CB&Q No. 1904	Orig. No.		Builder		Date	No. Change 1903		
1655	B&MR	195	Bald.	9636	1888			Retired 4-26
1656	B&MR	197	Bald.	9639	1888			Retired 3-26
1657	B&MR	201	W. B. Shops		1888			Retired 6-27
1658	B&MR	173	Bald.	8939	1888	B&MR	3162	Retired 3-26
1659	B&MR	181	Bald.	8995	1888	B&MR	3167	Retired 8-27
1660	B&MR	175	Bald.	8943	1888	B&MR	3168	Retired 5-28
1661	B&MR	184	Bald.	9001	1888	B&MR	3164	Retired 12-27
1662	B&MR	191	Bald.	9075	1888	B&MR	3161	Retired 4-26
1663	B&MR	192	Bald.	9084	1888	B&MR	3163	Retired 4-26
1664	B&MR	186	Bald.	9064	1888	B&MR	3165	Retired 4-23
1665	B&MR	189	Bald.	9069	1888	B&MR	3166	Retired 10-27
1666	B&MR	193	Bald.	9633	1888	B&MR	3160	Retired 2-27

Class G-4, 0-6-0 Rebuilt From Class D-2, 2-8-0
Rebuilt subsequent to 1904

New No.	D-2 No.	Orig. B&MR No.	Original Builder		
1667	2996	202	W. B. Shops	1888	Retired 1-27
1668	2992	190	Bald. 9074	1888	Retired 11-39
1669	2995	200	W. B. Shops	1888	Retired 7-28
1670	2994	199	W. B. Shops	1888	Retired 2-27
1671	2989	185	Bald. 9063	1888	Retired 1-26
1672	2991	188	Bald. 9066	1888	Retired
1673	2984	178	Bald. 8991	1888	Retired 5-27
1674	2987	182	Bald. 8996	1888	Retired 5-26
1675	2997	194	Bald. 9640	1888	Retired 6-27
1676	2985	179	Bald. 8992	1888	Retired 12-27
1677	2986	180	Bald. 8993	1888	Retired 5-27
1601	2980	383	Aur. Shops	1884	Retired 10-30
1602	2981	174	Bald. 8942	1888	Retired 7-29
1603	2982	176	Bald. 8951	1888	Sold to FW&DC 8-29
1647	2983	177	Bald. 8990	1888	Retired 5-26
1651	2986	183	Bald. 8998	1888	Retired 3-26

B. & M. R. No. 383 was C. B. & Q. No. 1397 to 3-1-01.
No. 1667 to No. 1677 were rebuilt prior to 1910.
No. 1601 to No. 1603 were rebuilt in 1921.
No. 1647 and No. 1651 were rebuilt in 1918.
New numbers were assigned at the time of rebuilding. No. 1601, No. 1602, No. 1603, No. 1647 and No. 1651 should not be confused with engines of the same numbers listed on previous pages, as they were assigned these numbers after the older engines had been retired. As all numbers in the 1600 series above 1677 had been assigned to Class G-6 by the time these five engines were rebuilt, it became necessary to use numbers which had been vacated.
All engines from No. 1655 to No. 1677 were Class G-4-B except No. 1668. No. 1647 and No. 1651 were also Class G-4-B. No. 1668, No. 1601 to No. 1603 were Class G-4-C.

Class G-5, 0-6-0

New CB&Q No. 1904	Orig. No.	
1690	K&W	12

There is no data to be had on this engine. No doubt it was retired shortly after 1904. It should not be confused with the Class G-5 built in later years.

Class G-6, 0-6-0

No. Change 1910	Orig. No.	Builder	Date	
	1678	Aurora	1910	Retired 11-46
	1679	Aurora	1910	Sold for Scrap 9-55
1680	1500	W. B. Shops	1905	Retired 2-47
1681	1501	W. B. Shops	1905	Retired 6-40
1682	1502	W. B. Shops	1905	Retired 12-31
1683	1503	W. B. Shops	1905	Retired 11-40
1684	1504	W. B. Shops	1905	Retired 11-38
1685	1505	W. B. Shops	1905	Retired 11-46
1686	1506	Havelock	1905	Sold for Scrap 1-51
1687	1507	Havelock	1905	Sold for Scrap 4-54
1688	1508	Havelock	1905	Retired 12-46
1689	1509	Havelock	1905	Sold for scrap 9-48
1690	1510	W. B. Shops	1906	Sold 5-40 Old Ben Coal Corp.
1691	1511	W. B. Shops	1906	Retired 9-46
1692	1512	W. B. Shops	1906	Retired 12-31
1693	1513	W. B. Shops	1906	Retired 11-33

Class G-6, 0-6-0

No Change 1910	Original No.	Builder	Date	
1694	1514	W.B. Shops	1906	
1695	1515	Aurora	1906	Retired 1-33
1696	1516	Aurora	1906	
1697	1517	Aurora	1906	
1698	1518	Aurora	1906	Retired 6-33
1699	1519	Aurora	1906	

The number change in 1910 was made necessary by the numbers of Class G-3 being extended to 1500 series in that year.

Class R-1, 2-6-2

New CB&Q No. 1904	Orig. No.		Builder	Date	Change 1903	
1700	CB&Q	1700	W. B. Shops	1900		Retired 6-29
1701	CB&Q	1701	W. B. Shops	1900		Retired 7-30
1702	CB&Q	1702	W. B. Shops	1900		Reb. to G7- .Ret. 8-31
1703	B&MR	62	W. B. Shops	1900	CB&Q 1699 (5-03)	Reb. to G-7. Ret. 3-33

Class R-2, 2-6-2

New CB&Q 1904	Orig. No.		Builder	Date	Date Rebuilt to Class G-8	
1710	CB&Q	1710	W. B. Shops	1901	1918	Sold 7-41 U. S. Gov.
1711	CB&Q	1711	W. B. Shops	1901	1920	Retired 1-41
1712	CB&Q	1712	W. B. Shops	1901	1917	Retired 5-38
1713	CB&Q	1713	Bald. 19489	1901	1920	Retired 4-41
1714	CB&Q	1714	Bald. 19490	1901	1918	Retired 4-47
1715	CB&Q	1715	Bald. 19491	1901	1918	Retired 2-38
1716	CB&Q	1716	Bald. 19492	1901	1918	Retired 11-46
1717	CB&Q	1717	Bald. 19493	1901	1918	Retired 9-47
1718	CB&Q	1718	Bald. 19494	1901	1918	Retired 11-46
1719	CB&Q	1719	Bald. 19495	1901	1918	Retired 5-41
1720	CB&Q	1720	Bald. 19496	1901	1918	Sold for scrap 10-48
1721	CB&Q	1703	Bald. 18951	1901	1918	Sold for scrap 12- 48
1722	CB&Q	1704	Bald. 18952	1901	1918	Sold for Scrap 1-51
1723	CB&Q	1705	Bald. 18953	1901	1918	Retired 10-46
1724	CB&Q	1706	W. B. Shops	1901	1918	Retired 1-41
1725	CB&Q	1707	W. B. Shops	1901	1918	Retired 6-40
1726	CB&Q	1708	W. B. Shops	1901	1918	Retired 4-44
1727	CB&Q	1709	W. B. Shops	1901	1920	Retired 11-46
1728	H&StJ	570	Bald. 18794	1901	1920	Retired 12-46
1729	H&StJ	571	Bald. 18795	1901	1918	Retired 12-46
1730	H&StJ	572	Bald. 18796	1901	1918	Sold for Scrap 3-51
1731	H&StJ	573	Bald. 18797	1901	1918	Retired 12-46
1732	H&StJ	685	Bald. 18822	1901	1918	Retired 10-39
1733	H&StJ	840	Bald. 18823	1901	1918	Retired 6-47
1734	H&StJ	841	Bald. 18824	1901	1918	Sold for scrap 9-48
1735	H&StJ	842	W. B. Shops	1901	1918	Sold for Scrap 6-51
1736	H&StJ	843	W. B. Shops	1901	1918	Retired 3-38
1737	H&StJ	844	W. B. Shops	1901	1918	Retired 11-46
1738	B&MR	349	Bald. 18825	1901	1924	Retired 4-47
1739	B&MR	350	Bald. 18845	1901	1924	Retired 3-38
1740	B&MR	351	Bald. 18846	1901	1918	Retired 10-46
1741	B&MR	352	Bald. 18847	1901	1929	Sold for Scrap 6-51
1742	B&MR	353	Bald. 18848	1901	1920	Retired 3-42
1743	B&MR	354	Bald. 18867	1901	1923	Retired 11-46
1744	B&MR	355	Bald. 18868	1901	1918	Retired 9-39
1745	B&MR	356	Bald. 18869	1901	1925	Retired 11-46
1746	B&MR	357	Bald. 18870	1901	1918	Sold for Scrap 2-51
1747	B&MR	358	Bald. 18871	1901	1924	Sold 7-41 U. S. Gov.
1748	B&MR	359	Bald. 18872	1901	1918	Retired 11-46
1749	B&MR	360	Bald. 18873	1901	1918	Retired 10-46
1750	B&MR	361	Bald. 18874	1901	1918	Sold for Scrap 1-51
1751	B&MR	362	Bald. 18875	1901	1918	Retired 11-46
1752	B&MR	363	Bald. 18876	1901	1919	Retired 7-39
1753	B&MR	364	Bald. 18877	1901	1924	Retired 7-47
1754	B&MR	365	Bald. 18878	1901	1925	Retired 1-41
1755	B&MR	366	Bald. 18954	1901	1918	Sold for scrap 8-49
1756	B&MR	367	Bald. 18955	1901	1920	Retired 11-46
1757	B&MR	368	Bald. 18956	1901	1920	Retired 12-35
1758	B&MR	369	Bald. 19513	1901	1923	Retired 11-46
1759	B&MR	370	Bald. 19520	1901	1924	Sold for scrap 4-49
1760	B&MR	371	Bald. 19521	1901	1925	Retired 4-47
1761	B&MR	372	Bald. 19522	1901	1925	Retired 5-41
1762	B&MR	373	Bald. 19523	1901	1919	Retired 6-39
1763	B&MR	374	Bald. 19524	1901	1923	Retired 6-40
1764	B&MR	375	Bald. 19525	1901	1923	Retired 5-41
1765	B&MR	376	Bald. 19526	1901	1921	Retired 4-41
1766	B&MR	377	Bald. 19574	1901	1918	Sold for Scrap 2-51

1767	B&MR	378	Bald.	19575	1901	1918	Retired 12-46
1768	B&MR	379	Bald.	19576	1901	1920	Retired 11-46
1769	B&MR	380	Bald.	19577	1901	1920	Retired 3-48

C. B. & Q. No. 1703, No. 1704, No. 1705, B. & M. R. No. 366, No. 367 and No. 368 were built as Vauclain compounds.

H. & St. J. No. 570 to No. 573 were ordered originally as H. & St. J. No. 681 to No. 684. These were changed to K. C. St. J. & C. B. numbers as above but, as the engines were to be used on the H. & St. J., they were lettered with the initials of that road. H. & St. J. No. 840 and No. 841 were ordered as H. & St. J. No. 686 and No. 687. These were changed to C. B. & K. C. numbers as above but were also lettered H. & St. J.

These changes were made at the Baldwin Works before the engines were delivered which explains why the Baldwin Works issued a photograph of H. & St. J. No. 687 while the records show the engine to have been delivered under another number.

Class R-3, 2-6-2

New CB&Q No. 1904	Orig. No.		Builder		Date	
1800	CB&Q	1721	Bald.	20859	1902	Retired 12-28
1801	CB&Q	1722	Bald.	20860	1902	Retired 6-29
1802	CB&Q	1723	Bald.	20861	1902	Retired 6-29
1803	CB&Q	1724	Bald.	20862	1902	Retired 12-28
1804	CB&Q	1725	Bald.	20914	1902	Retired 12-28
1805	CB&Q	1726	Bald.	20915	1902	Rebuilt to G-9-A, 12-27. Sold to U. S. Gov. 2-42
1806	CB&Q	1727	Bald.	20916	1902	Rebuilt to G-9-A, 2-28. Retired 12-46
1807	CB&Q	1728	Bald.	20957	1902	Retired 12-28
1808	CB&Q	1729	Bald.	20958	1902	Rebuilt to G-9-A, 11-28. Sold for Scrap 9-51
1809	CB&Q	1730	Bald.	20959	1902	Retired 11-28
1810	CB&Q	1731	Bald.	20994	1902	Retired 6-29
1811	CB&Q	1732	Bald.	21007	1902	Retired 11-28
1812	CB&Q	1733	Bald.	21015	1902	Rebuilt to G-9-A, 5-28. Retired 10-46
1813	CB&Q	1734	Bald.	21021	1902	Rebuilt to G-9-A, 12-27. Retired 10-47
1814	CB&Q	1735	Bald.	21022	1902	Retired 12-28
1815	CB&Q	1736	Bald.	21023	1902	Rebuilt to G-9-A, 6-28. Retired 4-47
1816	CB&Q	1737	Bald.	21069	1902	Retired 8-30
1817	CB&Q	1738	Bald.	21070	1902	Rebuilt to G-9, 2-26. Retired 8-47
1818	CB&Q	1739	Bald.	21071	1902	Retired 11-29
1819	CB&Q	1740	Bald.	21072	1902	Rebuilt to G-9-A, 9-27. Retired 12-46
1820	CB&Q	1741	Bald.	21073	1902	Retired 12-28
1821	CB&Q	1742	Bald.	21113	1902	Retired 11-28
1822	CB&Q	1743	Bald.	21140	1902	Rebuilt to G-9-A, 7-28 Sold for scrap 3-48
1823	CB&Q	1744	Bald.	21141	1902	Rebuilt to G-9, 11-25. Retired 11-46
1824	CB&Q	1745	Bald.	21142	1902	Retired 8-30
1825	CB&Q	1746	Bald.	21152	1902	Rebuilt to G-9-A, 7-28. Retired 12-46
1826	CB&Q	1747	Bald.	21160	1902	Rebuilt to G-9-A, 8-28. Retired 12-46
1827	CB&Q	1748	Bald.	21161	1902	Rebuilt to G-9, 10-26. Sold for Scrap 8-51
1828	CB&Q	1749	Bald.	21173	1902	Rebuilt to G-9, 8-26. Retired 6-47
1829	CB&Q	1750	Bald.	21205	1902	Retired 6-29
1830	CB&Q	1751	Bald.	21206	1902	Retired 12-28
1831	CB&Q	1752	Bald.	21207	1902	Rebuilt to G-9-A, 2-28. Retired 2-44
1832	CB&Q	1753	Bald.	21208	1902	Rebuilt to G-9-A, 11-28. Retired 10-46
1833	CB&Q	1754	Bald.	21222	1902	Retired 12-28
1834	CB&Q	1755	Bald.	21223	1902	Retired 8-30
1835	CB&Q	1756	Bald.	21224	1902	Retired 6-29
1836	CB&Q	1757	Bald.	21225	1902	Retired 6-29
1837	CB&Q	1758	Bald.	21254	1902	Retired 12-28
1838	CB&Q	1759	Bald.	21255	1902	Retired 12-29
1839	CB&Q	1760	Bald.	21256	1902	Rebuilt to G-9-A, 9-28. Retired 12-46
1840	CB&Q	1761	Bald.	21257	1902	Retired 8-30
1841	CB&Q	1762	Bald.	21288	1902	Retired 11-28
1842	CB&Q	1763	Bald.	21299	1902	Rebuilt to G-9, 3-27 Sold for scrap 10-48
1843	CB&Q	1764	Bald.	21300	1902	Retired 12-28
1844	CB&Q	1765	Bald.	21301	1902	Rebuilt to G-9-A, 9-28. Retired 12-46
1845	CB&Q	1766	Bald.	21302	1902	Rebuilt to G-9-A, 10-28. Retired 5-47
1846	CB&Q	1767	Bald.	21378	1902	Rebuilt to G-9, 1-27. Retired 11-46
1847	CB&Q	1768	Bald.	21379	1902	Retired 11-28
1848	CB&Q	1769	Bald.	21436	1902	Rebuilt to G-9-A, 8-28. Retired 2-44
1849	CB&Q	1770	Bald.	21543	1902	Retired 6-29

Class R-4, 2-6-2

No.	Builder		Date	
1900	Bald.	24436	1904	Rebuilt to G-10 No. 572, 11-29
1901	Bald	24456	1904	Retired 12-32
1902	Bald.	24457	1904	Rebuilt to G-10 No. 568, 8-29
1903	Bald.	24458	1904	Retired 5-33
1904	Bald.	24459	1904	Retired 6-28
1905	Bald.	24463	1904	Rebuilt to G-10 No. 563, 12-28
1906	Bald.	24464	1904	Rebuilt to G-10 No. 580, 12-29
1907	Bald.	24465	1904	Retired 12-46
1908	Bald.	24466	1904	Rebuilt to G-10 No. 565, 7-29
1909	Bald.	24474	1904	Retired 12-31
1910	Bald.	24477	1904	Sold for Scrap 8-50
1911	Bald.	24478	1904	Retired 4-33
1912	Bald.	24485	1904	Rebuilt to R-4-A, 2-24. Retired 12-52
1913	Bald.	24486	1904	Rebuilt to G-10 No. 575, 12-29

Class R-4, 2-6-2

No.	Builder		Date	
1914	Bald.	24487	1904	Retired 5-33
1915	Bald.	24488	1904	Retired 4-47
1916	Bald.	24492	1904	Retired 9-39
1917	Bald.	24493	1904	Retired 12-32
1918	Bald.	24494	1904	Retired 12-29
1919	Bald.	24495	1904	Retired 6-28
1920	Bald.	24496	1904	Rebuilt to G-10 No. 564, 12-28
1921	Bald.	24497	1904	Rebuilt to G-10 No. 589, 4-30
1922	Bald.	24505	1904	Retired 1-33
1923	Bald.	24506	1904	Rebuilt to G-10 No. 593, 8-30
1924	Bald.	24511	1904	Rebuilt to R-4-A, 6-25. Retired 5-46
1925	Bald.	24512	1904	Retired 11-46
1926	Bald.	24513	1904	Rebuilt to G-10 No. 590, 4-30
1927	Bald.	24514	1904	Retired 4-33
1928	Bald.	24528	1904	Retired 5-47
1929	Bald.	24529	1904	Rebuilt to G-10 No. 594, 11-30
1930	Bald.	24537	1904	Retired 11-46
1931	Bald.	24538	1904	Retired 12-32
1932	Bald.	24542	1904	Rebuilt to G-10 No. 588, 4-30
1933	Bald.	24543	1904	Retired 12-32
1934	Bald.	24552	1904	Retired 5-33
1935	Bald.	24557	1904	Retired 12-31
1936	Bald.	24568	1904	Rebuilt to G-10 No. 577, 4-30
1937	Bald.	24569	1904	Rebuilt to R-4-A, 12-24. Retired 8-52
1938	Bald.	24601	1904	Rebuilt to R-4-A, 9-19. Retired 9-53
1939	Bald.	24602	1904	Retired 4-33
1940	Brooks	30396	1-05	Retired 6-33
1941	Brooks	30397	1-05	Retired 12-31
1942	Brooks	30398	1-05	Retired 10-46
1943	Brooks	30399	1-05	Retired 12-33
1944	Brooks	30400	1-05	Rebuilt to G-10 No. 576, 1-30
1945	Brooks	30401	1-05	Rebuilt to G-10 No. 578, 12-29
1946	Brooks	30402	1-05	Retired 6-33
1947	Brooks	30403	1-05	Retired 7-48
1948	Brooks	30404	1-05	Rebuilt to R-4-A, 3-24. Retired 5-46
1949	Brooks	30405	1-05	Rebuilt to R-4-A, 7-24. Retired 10-53
1950	Brooks	30406	1-05	Rebuilt to G-10 No. 560, 12-28
1951	Brooks	30407	1-05	Retired 12-32
1952	Brooks	30408	1-05	Retired 8-34
1953	Brooks	30409	1-05	Retired 6-33
1954	Brooks	30410	1-05	Retired 9-33
1955	Brooks	30411	1-05	Sold for scrap 5-48
1956	Brooks	30412	1-05	Retired 3-41
1957	Brooks	30413	1-05	Retired 7-33
1958	Brooks	30414	1-05	Sold for Scrap 8-50
1959	Brooks	30415	1-05	Retired 7-33
1960	Brooks	30416	2-05	Retired 10-30
1961	Brooks	30417	2-05	Retired 12-32
1962	Brooks	30418	2-05	Retired 10-39
1963	Brooks	30419	2-05	Rebuilt to R-4-A, 4-24. Retired 3-54
1964	Brooks	30420	2-05	Retired 2-41
1965	Brooks	30421	2-05	Retired 11-30
1966	Brooks	30422	2-05	Retired 10-33
1967	Brooks	30423	2-05	Sold to Toledo, Peoria & Western, 10-26
1968	Brooks	30424	2-05	Retired 9-28
1969	Brooks	30425	2-05	Rebuilt to G-10 No. 573, 11-29
1970	Brooks	30426	2-05	Retired 10-31
1971	Brooks	30427	2-05	Sold for Scrap 8-50
1972	Brooks	30428	2-05	Rebuilt to R-4-A, 5-25. Retired 7-51
1973	Brooks	30429	2-05	Rebuilt to G-10 No. 571, 10-29
1974	Brooks	30430	2-05	Retired 10-31
1975	Brooks	30431	2-05	Retired 5-47
1976	Brooks	30432	2-05	Rebuilt to G-10 No. 569, 8-29
1977	Brooks	30433	2-05	Retired 12-31
1978	Brooks	30434	2-05	Retired 12-32
1979	Brooks	30435	2-05	Retired 6-29
1980	Brooks	30436	2-05	Sold to Toledo, Peoria & Western, 10-26
1981	Brooks	30437	2-05	Rebuilt to G-10 No. 561, 12-28
1982	Brooks	30438	2-05	Retired 11-30
1983	Brooks	30439	2-05	Retired 6-28
1984	Brooks	30440	2-05	Retired 7-31
1985	Brooks	30441	2-05	Retired 5-47
1986	Brooks	30442	2-05	Retired 12-30
1987	Brooks	30443	2-05	Rebuilt to R-4-A, 10-24. Retired 4-55
1988	Brooks	30444	2-05	Rebuilt to R-4-A, 12-23. Retired 5-54
1989	Brooks	30445	2-05	Rebuilt to G-10 No. 582, 3-30

Dates given for rebuilding of Class R-4-A are not the dates of this class being assigned to these engines but, the date of principal rebuilding which led up to the class change. This also applies to Class R-5-A. The new classification was given to these engines at a later date.

Class R-4, 2-6-2

No.	Builder		Date	
2000	Bald.	27244	1906	Retired 12-31
2001	Bald.	27245	1906	Rebuilt to G-10 No. 587, 4-30
2002	Bald.	27246	1906	Retired 9-33
2003	Bald.	27247	1906	Retired 9-33
2004	Bald.	27248	1906	Rebuilt to G-10 No. 579, 12-29
2005	Bald.	27249	1906	Rebuilt to R-4-A, 10-25. Ret. 7-52
2006	Bald.	27250	1906	Rebuilt to G-10 No. 566, 7-29
2007	Bald.	27251	1906	Retired 12-31
2008	Bald.	27271	1906	Retired 12-31
2009	Bald.	27272	1906	Rebuilt to G-10 No. 574, 11-29
2010	Bald.	27286	1906	Retired 11-32
2011	Bald.	27287	1906	Retired 12-30
2012	Bald.	27288	1906	Retired 6-28
2013	Bald.	27289	1906	Retired 12-31
2014	Bald.	27290	1906	Retired 7-31
2015	Bald.	27305	1906	Retired 5-31
2016	Bald.	27306	1906	Retired 7-39
2017	Bald.	27307	1906	Retired 4-33
2018	Bald.	27308	1906	Rebuilt to R-4-A, 5-24. Ret. 7-51
2019	Bald.	27309	1906	Retired 12-31
2020	Bald.	27337	1906	Retired 2-33
2021	Bald.	27357	1906	Rebuilt to G-10 No. 567, 8-29
2022	Bald.	27358	1906	Retired 1-30
2023	Bald.	27359	1906	Retired 11-33
2024	Bald.	27371	1906	Retired 9-33
2025	Bald.	27372	1906	Retired 12-31
2026	Bald.	27373	1906	Retired 5-40
2027	Bald.	27374	1906	Rebuilt to R-4-A, 11-24. Ret. 8-51
2028	Bald.	27388	1906	Retired 12-32
2029	Bald.	27389	1906	Sold to Toledo, Peoria & Western, 10-26
2030	Bald.	27390	1906	Retired 11-28
2031	Bald.	27403	1906	Rebuilt to G-10, No. 585, 3-30
2032	Bald.	27418	1906	Rebuilt to G-10, No. 591, 8-30
2033	Bald.	27419	1906	Retired 12-32
2034	Bald.	27420	1906	Rebuilt to G-10 No. 562, 12-28
2035	Bald.	27421	1906	Rebuilt to G-10 No. 584, 3-30
2036	Bald.	27456	1906	Retired 11-28
2037	Bald.	27457	1906	Sold to Toledo, Peoria & Western, 10-26
2038	Bald.	27458	1906	Retired 3-35
2039	Bald.	27459	1906	Rebuilt to R-4-A, 12-24. Ret. 1-51
2040	Bald.	27495	1906	Rebuilt to G-10 No. 581, 12-29
2041	Bald.	27496	1906	Rebuilt to G-10 No. 583, 3-30
2042	Bald.	27497	1906	Rebuilt to G-10 No. 570, 8-29
2043	Bald.	27498	1906	Retired 8-33
2044	Bald.	27509	1906	Retired 12-31
2045	Bald.	27510	1906	Retired 12-30
2046	Bald.	27511	1906	Retired 4-33
2047	Bald.	27539	1906	Rebuilt to G-10 No. 592, 8-30
2048	Bald.	27540	1906	Rebuilt to G-10 No. 586, 4-30
2049	Bald.	27558	1906	Retired 12-31

The four engines sold to T. P. & W. became No. 30 to No. 33 on that road. They were scrapped by the T. P. & W. about 1930.

Class R-5, 2-6-2

No.	Builder		Date	
2050	Bald.	28396	1906	Retired 6-47
2051	Bald.	28397	1906	Retired 12-31
2052	Bald.	28420	1906	Rebuilt to R-5-A, 9-24. Ret. 6-51
2053	Bald.	28421	1906	Rebuilt to R-5-A, 11-24. Ret. 12-52
2054	Bald.	28426	1906	Retired 9-39
2055	Bald.	28427	1906	Retired 8-29
2056	Bald.	28449	1906	Retired 12-28
2057	Bald.	28459	1906	Rebuilt to R-5-A, 9-23. Ret. 7-52
2058	Bald.	28472	1906	Retired 2-51
2059	Bald.	28487	1906	Retired 12-28
2060	Bald.	28490	1906	Retired 4-34
2061	Bald.	28503	1906	Retired 10-46
2062	Bald.	28504	1906	Rebuilt to R-5-A, 2-27. Ret. 12-52
2063	Bald.	28505	1906	Retired 10-31
2064	Bald.	28506	1906	Retired 8-50
2065	Bald.	28507	1906	Retired 12-28
2066	Bald.	28536	1906	Retired 4-47
2067	Bald.	28537	1906	Retired 12-28
2068	Bald.	28538	1906	Retired 1-30
2069	Bald.	28539	1906	Retired 1-30
2070	Bald.	28546	1906	Retired 6-28
2071	Bald.	28547	1906	Retired 8-50
2072	Bald.	28569	1906	Retired 12-30
2073	Bald.	28580	1906	Retired 4-30
2074	Bald.	28590	1906	Retired 4-30
2075	Bald.	28595	1906	Retired 6-40

Class R-5, 2-6-2

No.	Builder		Date	
2076	Bald.	28596	1906	Retired 11-30
2077	Bald.	28597	1906	Retired 5-46
2078	Bald.	28610	1906	Retired 11-30
2079	Bald.	28628	1906	Retired 12-32
2080	Bald.	28647	1906	Retired 7-29
2081	Bald.	28653	1906	Retired 6-40
2082	Bald.	28662	1906	Retired 8-47
2083	Bald.	28672	1906	Retired 6-28
2084	Bald.	28681	1906	Retired 9-50
2085	Bald.	28682	1906	Retired 10-46
2086	Bald.	28703	1906	Retired 6-33
2087	Bald.	28720	1906	Retired 4-33
2088	Bald.	28721	1906	Retired 12-31
2089	Bald.	28722	1906	Retired 1-30
2090	Bald.	28723	1906	Retired 4-47
2091	Bald.	28754	1906	Retired 12-32
2092	Bald.	28755	1906	Retired 4-47
2093	Bald.	28778	1906	Retired 12-31
2094	Bald.	28779	1906	Retired 10-46
2095	Bald.	28798	1906	Retired 4-47
2096	Bald.	28864	1906	Sold for Scrap 8-50
2097	Bald.	28900	1906	Retired 9-31
2098	Bald.	28821	1906	Retired 10-46
2099	Bald.	28831	1906	Rebuilt to R-5-A, 12-23 Sold for scrap 12-48
2100	Brooks	41554	1906	Retired 12-32
2101	Brooks	41555	1906	Retired 7-29
2102	Brooks	41556	1906	Retired 11-46
2103	Brooks	41557	1906	Retired 6-40
2104	Brooks	41558	1906	Retired 1-30
2105	Brooks	41559	1906	Retired 12-46
2106	Brooks	41560	1906	Retired 6-47
2107	Brooks	41561	1906	Sold for scrap 11-48
2108	Brooks	41562	1906	Retired 12-30
2109	Brooks	41563	1906	Retired 12-32
2110	Brooks	41564	1906	Rebuilt to R-5-A, 11-23. Ret. 5-54
2111	Brooks	41565	1906	Retired 6-42
2112	Brooks	41566	1906	Retired 7-29
2113	Brooks	41567	1906	Rebuilt to R-5-A, 6-24. Ret. 9-50
2114	Brooks	41568	1906	Retired 10-31
2115	Brooks	41569	1906	Retired 12-32
2116	Brooks	41570	1906	Retired 12-32
2117	Brooks	41571	1906	Retired 6-40
2118	Brooks	41572	1906	Sold for Scrap 8-51
2119	Brooks	41573	1906	Retired 1-30
2120	Brooks	41574	1906	Retired 1-30
2121	Brooks	41575	1906	Retired 4-47
2122	Brooks	41576	1906	Retired 4-47
2123	Brooks	41577	1906	Retired 11-46
2124	Brooks	41578	1906	Retired 12-31
2125	Brooks	41579	1906	Retired 10-38
2126	Brooks	41580	1906	Retired 4-47
2127	Brooks	41581	1906	Retired 12-28
2128	Brooks	41582	1906	Retired 11-28
2129	Brooks	41583	1906	Retired 11-30
2130	Brooks	41584	1906	Retired 12-31
2131	Brooks	41585	1906	Retired 8-29
2132	Brooks	41586	1906	Retired 5-40
2133	Brooks	41587	1906	Retired 11-30
2134	Brooks	41588	1906	Retired 12-30
2135	Brooks	41589	1906	Retired 11-30
2136	Brooks	41590	1906	Retired 5-40
2137	Brooks	41591	1906	Retired 12-32
2138	Brooks	41592	1906	
2139	Brooks	41593	1906	Retired 12-30
2140	Brooks	41594	1906	Retired 9-29
2141	Brooks	41595	1906	Retired 7-33
2142	Brooks	41596	1906	Retired 12-46 Sold for scrap 10-48
2143	Brooks	41597	1906	Retired 8-33
2144	Brooks	41598	1906	Retired 12-31
2145	Brooks	41599	1906	Retired 6-40
2146	Brooks	41600	1906	Retired 10-33
2147	Brooks	41601	1906	Retired 12-29
2148	Brooks	41602	1906	Retired 8-47
2149	Brooks	41603	1906	Rebuilt to R-5-A, 5-24. Ret. 4-54
2150	Brooks	43490	1907	Retired 7-29
2151	Brooks	43491	1907	Rebuilt to R-5-A, 9-28. Ret. 9-53
2152	Brooks	43492	1907	Sold for Scrap 8-50
2153	Brooks	43493	1907	Retired 7-47
2154	Brooks	43494	1907	Retired 12-32
2155	Brooks	43495	1907	Retired 12-30
2156	Brooks	43496	1907	Retired 7-29
2157	Brooks	43497	1907	Retired 12-30
2158	Brooks	43498	1907	Retired 6-47

No.	Builder		Date	
2159	Brooks	43499	1907	Sold for scrap 5-48
2160	Brooks	43500	1907	Retired 12-30
2161	Brooks	43501	1907	Retired 12-28
2162	Brooks	43502	1907	Retired 12-31
2163	Brooks	43503	1907	Retired 12-31
2164	Brooks	43504	1907	Retired 12-30
2165	Brooks	43505	1907	Retired 5-47
2166	Brooks	43506	1907	Retired 12-31
2167	Brooks	43507	1907	Retired 12-30
2168	Brooks	43508	1907	Retired 12-31
2169	Brooks	43509	1907	Sold for scrap 11-48
2170	Brooks	43510	1907	Retired 10-46
2171	Brooks	43511	1907	Retired 10-30
2172	Brooks	43512	1907	Retired 7-33
2173	Brooks	43513	1907	Retired 9-47
2174	Brooks	43514	1907	Retired 12-30
2175	Brooks	43515	1907	Retired 1-30
2176	Brooks	43516	1907	Retired 11-30
2177	Brooks	43517	1907	Retired 1-30
2178	Brooks	43518	1907	Retired 8-29
2179	Brooks	43519	1907	Retired 6-47
2180	Brooks	43520	1907	Retired 12-32
2181	Brooks	43521	1907	Retired 12-30
2182	Brooks	43522	1907	Retired 4-30
2183	Brooks	43523	1907	Retired 12-32
2184	Brooks	43524	1907	Retired 4-30
2185	Brooks	43525	1907	Retired 10-46
2186	Brooks	43526	1907	Retired 12-30
2187	Brooks	43527	1907	Retired 7-29
2188	Brooks	43528	1907	Retired 8-33
2189	Brooks	43529	1907	Rebuilt to R-5-A, 6-26. Ret. 2-51
2190	Brooks	43530	1907	Retired 12-31
2191	Brooks	43531	1907	Rebuilt to R-5-A, 9-28. Ret. 9-50
2192	Brooks	43532	1907	Retired 7-47
2193	Brooks	43533	1907	Retired 10-39
2194	Brooks	43534	1907	Retired 12-32
2195	Brooks	43535	1907	Retired 7-28
2196	Brooks	43536	1907	Rebuilt to R-5-A, 8-23. Ret. 6-51
2197	Brooks	43537	1907	Sold for Scrap 8-50
2198	Brooks	43538	1907	Sold for Scrap 2-51
2199	Brooks	43539	1907	Retired 4-47
2200	Brooks	43555	1907	Retired 12-36. Boiler to 1938
2201	Brooks	43556	1907	Retired 3-47
2202	Brooks	43557	1907	Sold for Scrap 8-50
2203	Brooks	43558	1907	Retired 9-33
2204	Brooks	43559	1907	Sold for scrap 5-48
2205	Brooks	43560	1907	Retired 10-30
2206	Brooks	43561	1907	Retired 9-29
2207	Brooks	43562	1907	Retired 9-31
2208	Brooks	43563	1907	Retired 4-40
2209	Brooks	43564	1907	Retired 7-33
2210	Brooks	43565	1907	Retired 5-39
2211	Brooks	43566	1907	Retired 6-47
2212	Brooks	43567	1907	Retired 12-31
2213	Brooks	43568	1907	Retired 12-31
2214	Brooks	43569	1907	Retired 8-29
2215	Brooks	43570	1907	Rebuilt to R-5-A, 6-19. Ret. 10-53
2216	Brooks	43571	1907	Retired 7-33
2217	Brooks	43572	1907	Retired 11-46
2218	Brooks	43573	1907	Retired 12-31
2219	Brooks	43574	1907	Rebuilt to R-5-A, 3-24. Ret. 11-53
2220	Brooks	43575	1907	Retired 12-31
2221	Brooks	43576	1907	Retired 7-33
2222	Brooks	43577	1907	Rebuilt to R-5-A, 8-26. Ret. 11-53
2223	Brooks	43578	1907	Retired 12-31
2224	Brooks	43579	1907	Retired 12-31

Class N-1, 2-4-2

New CB&Q No. 1904	Orig. No.	Builder	Date	No. Change 1898
2400	CB&Q 590	Bald. 14410	1895	CB&Q 1590 Reb. to 4-4-2 1905

Class P-4 No. 2599 retired 11-29.

Class P-1-Comp., 4-4-2

New CB&Q No. 1904	Orig. No.	Builder	Date	
2500	CB&Q 1591	Bald. 16547	1899	Reb. to P-1 1913 Retired 1-33
2501	CB&O 1592	Bald. 16548	1899	Reb. to P-1 1914 Retired 1-32
2502	CB&Q 1593	Bald. 18332	1900	Reb. to P-1 1914 Retired 1-33
2503	CB&O 1594	Bald. 18333	1900	Reb. to P-1 1915 Retired 1-33
2504	CB&Q 1595	Bald. 18337	1900	Reb. to P-1 1915 Retired 1-33

Class P-2-Comp., 4-4-2

New CB&Q No. 1904	Orig. No.	Builder	Date			No Change 1924
2510	CB&Q 1854	Bald. 20118	1902	Reb. to P-5 1915		2550
2511	CB&Q 1585	Bald. 20119	1902	Reb. to P-5 1915		2551
2512	CB&Q 1586	Bald. 20120	1902	Reb. to P-5 1916		2552
2513	CB&Q 1587	Bald. 20148	1902	Reb. to P-5 1916		2553
2514	CB&Q 1588	Bald. 20160	1902	Reb. to P-5 1917		2554
2515	CB&Q 1589	Bald. 20161	1902	Reb. to P-5 1917		2555

Class P-2, 4-4-2

New CB&Q No. 1904	Orig. No.		Builder		Date		
2520	CB&Q	1576	Rogers	5875	1903	Rebuilt to P-6-A No. 2594	1928
2521	CB&Q	1577	Rogers	5876	1903	Rebuilt to P 6-A No. 2597	1928
2522	CB&Q	1578	Rogers	5881	1903	Retired 1-32	
2523	CB&Q	1579	Rogers	5883	1903	Rebuilt to P-6-A No. 2591	1927
2524	CB&Q	1580	Rogers	5884	1903	Retired 1-32	
2525	CB&Q	1581	Rogers	5885	1903	Retired 11-30	
2526	CB&Q	1582	Rogers	5886	1903	Retired 12-30	
2527	CB&Q	1583	Rogers	5887	1903	Retired 2-33	
2528	B&MR	3700	Rogers	5852	1902	Retired 4-33	
2529	B&MR	3701	Rogers	5853	1902	Retired 4-33	
2530	B&MR	3702	Rogers	5854	1902	Rebuilt to P-6-A No. 2596	1928
2531	B&MR	3703	Rogers	5855	1902	Rebuilt to P-6-A No. 2590	1927
2532	B&MR	3704	Rogers	5856	1902	Retired 1-33	
2533	B&MR	3705	Rogers	5857	1902	Rebuilt to P-6-A No. 2595	1928
2534	B&MR	3706	Rogers	5858	1902	Retired 2-33	
2535	B&MR	3707	Rogers	5859	1902	Retired 12-31	
2536	B&MR	3708	Rogers	5860	1902	Retired 10-31	
2537	B&MR	3709	Rogers	5861	1902	Retired 2-33	
2538	H&StJ	690	Rogers	5888	1903	Retired 2-33	
2539	StLK&NW	780	Rogers	5916	1903	Retired 7-30	
2540	StLK&NW	781	Rogers	5917	1903	Retired 10-31	
2541	StLK&NW	782	Rogers	5918	1903	Retired 11-30	
2542	StLK&NW	783	Rogers	5922	1903	Retired 12-30	
2543	StLK&NW	784	Rogers	5923	1903	Rebuilt to P-6-A No. 2593	1928
2544	H&StJ	691	Changed 9-03 to				
	StLK&NW	785	Rogers	5889	1903	Rebuilt to P-6-A No. 2592	1927

Class P-3-Comp., 4-4-2
Balanced Compound

No.	Builder		Date			
2700	Bald.	24219	1904	Rebuilt to P-6	2583	1928
2701	Bald.	24644	1904	Rebuilt to P-6	2581	1927
2702	Bald.	24651	1904	Rebuilt to P-5	2558	1927
2703	Bald.	24652	1904	Rebuilt to P-5	2559	1925
2704	Bald.	24672	1904	Rebuilt to P-6	2582	1927
2705	Bald.	24680	1904	Rebuilt to P-5	2561	1925
2706	Bald.	24681	1904	Rebuilt to P-5	2562	1925
2707	Bald.	24682	1904	Rebuilt to P-5	2563	1924
2708	Bald.	24694	1904	Rebuilt to P-5	2564	1926
2709	Bald.	24705	1904	Rebuilt to P-5	2565	1924
2710	Bald.	26735	1905	Rebuilt to P-5	2566	1927
2711	Bald.	26736	1905	Rebuilt to P-5	2567	1927
2712	Bald.	26793	1905	Rebuilt to P-5	2568	1924
2713	Bald.	26794	1905	Rebuilt to P-5	2569	1925
2714	Bald.	26844	1905	Rebuilt to P-6	2584	1928
2715	Bald.	26845	1905	Rebuilt to P-5	2571	1925
2716	Bald.	26910	1905	Rebuilt to P-5	2572	1924
2717	Bald.	26911	1905	Rebuilt to P-6	2580	1927
2718	Bald.	26983	1905	Rebuilt to P-5	2574	1924
2719	Bald.	26984	1905	Rebuilt to P-6	2585	1928

Class P-5, 4-4-2

2550	P-5	Rebuilt	P-2-C	2510	Retired 6-42
2551	P-5	Rebuilt	P-2-C	2511	Retired 10-47
2552	P-5	Rebuilt	P-2-C	2512	Retired 6-42
2553	P-5	Rebuilt	P-2-C	2513	Retired 11-46
2554	P-5	Rebuilt	P-2-C	2514	Retired 6-42
2555	P-5	Rebuilt	P-2-C	2515	Retired 6-42
2556	Number Vacant				
2557	Number Vacant				
2558	P-5	Rebuilt	P-3-C	2702	Retired 6-42
2559	P-5	Rebuilt	P-3-C	2703	Retired 6-42
2560	Number Vacant				
2561	P-5	Rebuilt	P-3-C	2705	Retired 6-42
2562	P-5	Rebuilt	P-3-C	2706	Retired 11-46
2563	P-5	Rebuilt	P-3-C	2707	Retired 6-43
2564	P-5	Rebuilt	P-3-C	2708	Retired 2-54
2565	P-5	Rebuilt	P-3-C	2709	Retired 6-42
2566	P-5	Rebuilt	P-3-C	2710	Retired 6-48

2567	P-5	Rebuilt	P-3-C	2711	Retired 2-54
2568	P-5	Rebuilt	P-3-C	2712	Retired 6-42
2569	P-5	Rebuilt	P-3-C	2713	Retired 10-53
2570	Number Vacant				
2571	P-5	Rebuilt	P-3-C	2715	Sold for Scrap 2-51
2572	P-5	Rebuilt	P-3-C	2716	Retired 5-42
2573	Number Vacant				
2574	P-5	Rebuilt	P-3-C	2718	Retired 5-47
2575	Number Vacant				

Class P-6, 4-4-2

2580	P-6	Rebuilt	P-3-C	2717	Sold for Scrap 10-53
2581	P-6	Rebuilt	P-3-C	2701	Sold for Scrap 7-52
2582	P-6	Rebuilt	P-3-C	2704	Sold for Scrap 8-51
2583	P-6	Rebuilt	P-3-C	2700	Sold for Scrap 12-53
2584	P-6	Rebuilt	P-3-C	2714	Sold for Scrap 12-53
2585	P-6	Rebuilt	P-3-C	2719	Sold for Scrap 2-51

Class P-6-A, 4-4-2

2590	P-6-A	Rebuilt	P-2	2531	Retired 4-47
2591	P-6-A	Rebuilt	P-2	2523	Sold for Scrap 4-54
2592	P-6-A	Rebuilt	P-2	2544	Sold for Scrap 6-51
2593	P-6-A	Rebuilt	P-2	2543	Sold for Scrap 12-51
2594	P-6-A	Rebuilt	P-2	2520	Sold for Scrap 4-54
2595	P-6-A	Rebuilt	P-2	2533	Sold for Scrap 6-51
2596	P-6-A	Rebuilt	P-2	2530	Sold for Scrap 10-53
2597	P-6-A	Rebuilt	P-2	2521	Sold for scrap 12-48

Class S-1, 4-6-2

No.	Builder	Date	Shop No.	
2800	Baldwin	1906	28231	Rebuilt to S-1-A, 1925 Sold for scrap 5-51
2801	Baldwin	1906	28232	Retired 11-39 Running gear to 2848 in 1936
2802	Baldwin	1906	28238	Rebuilt to S-1-A, 1927 Sold for scrap 2-51
2803	Baldwin	1906	28264	Retired 8-33
2804	Baldwin	1906	28281	Rebuilt to S-1-A, 1926 Sold for scrap 3-54
2805	Baldwin	1906	28297	Retired 8-33
2806	Baldwin	1906	28298	Rebuilt to S-1-A, 1926 Ret. 9-39
2807	Baldwin	1906	28299	Retired 6-35
2808	Baldwin	1906	28319	Rebuilt to S-1-A, 1930 Sold for scrap 12-52
2809	Baldwin	1906	28373	Rebuilt to S-1-A, 1929 Sold for scrap 3-51
2810	Baldwin	1906	28374	Retired 8-33
2811	Baldwin	1906	28375	Rebuilt to S-1-A, 1929 Sold for scrap 12-52
2812	Baldwin	1906	28376	Rebuilt to S-1-A, 1925 Sold for scrap 4-51
2813	Baldwin	1906	28402	Rebuilt to S-1-A, 1928 Sold for scrap 10-53
2814	Baldwin	1906	28412	Rebuilt to S-1-A, 1927 Sold for scrap 2-51
2815	Baldwin	1906	29709	Rebuilt to S-1-A, 1926 Sold for scrap 4-51
2816	Baldwin	1906	29710	Rebuilt to S-1-A, 1925 Sold for scrap 12-52
2817	Baldwin	1906	29736	Rebuilt to S-1-A, 1926 Sold for scrap 9-53
2818	Baldwin	1906	29806	Rebuilt to S-1-A, 1925 Retired 7-33
2819	Baldwin	1906	29807	Retired 11-39
2820	Baldwin	1906	29808	Rebuilt to S-1-A, 1924 Sold for scrap 3-51
2821	Baldwin	1906	29847	Rebuilt to S-1-A, 1926 Sold for scrap 3-52
2822	Baldwin	1906	29848	Rebuilt to S-1-A, 1924 Sold for scrap 2-49
2823	Baldwin	1906	29882	Rebuilt to S-1-A, 1923 Sold for scrap 1-51
2824	Baldwin	1906	29883	Rebuilt to S-1-A, 1926 Sold for scrap 12-51
2825	Baldwin	1906	29884	Rebuilt to S-1-A, 1929 Sold for scrap 3-54
2826	Baldwin	1906	29930	Rebuilt to S-1-A, 1925 Sold for scrap 4-51
2827	Baldwin	1906	29931	Rebuilt to S-1-A, 1927 Sold for scrap 1-51
2828	Baldwin	1906	29932	Retired 5-33
2829	Baldwin	1906	30011	Rebuilt to S-1-A, 1927 Sold for scrap 1-51
2830	Schenectady	1907	43475	Rebuilt to S-1-A, 1928 Sold for scrap 2-54
2831	Schenectady	1907	43476	Retired 8-33
2832	Schenectady	1907	43477	Rebuilt to S-1-A, 1927 Sold for scrap 4-51
2833	Schenectady	1907	43478	Rebuilt to S-1-A, 1927 Sold for scrap 10-53
2834	Schenectady	1907	43479	Rebuilt to S-1-A, 1925 Sold for scrap 12-52
2835	Schenectady	1907	43480	Rebuilt to S-1-A, 1925 Sold for scrap 12-48
2836	Schenectady	1907	43481	Rebuilt to S-1-A, 1924 Sold for scrap 3-52
2837	Schenectady	1907	43482	Rebuilt to S-1-A, 1924 Sold for scrap 4-51
2838	Schenectady	1907	43483	Rebuilt to S-1-A, 1925 Sold for scrap 2-51
2839	Schenectady	1907	43484	Rebuilt to S-1-A, 1929 Sold for scrap 12-51
2840	Schenectady	1907	43485	Retired 11-33
2841	Schenectady	1907	43486	Rebuilt to S-1-A, 1927 Sold for scrap 5-54
2842	Schenectady	1907	43487	Retired 11-33
2843	Schenectady	1907	43488	Retired 5-33
2844	Schenectady	1907	43489	Rebuilt to S-1-A, 1929 Sold for scrap 9-53
2845	Baldwin	1909	33441	Retired 11-33
2846	Baldwin	1909	33442	Rebuilt to S-1-A, 1925 Sold for scrap 2-51
2847	Baldwin	1909	33443	Retired 4-36 Running gear to 2801
2848	Baldwin	1909	33444	Rebuilt to S-1-A, 1926 Sold for scrap 3-51
2849	Baldwin	1909	33445	Rebuilt to S-1-A, 1927 Sold for scrap 3-51
2850	Baldwin	1909	33446	Rebuilt to S-1-A, 1924 Sold for scrap 2-51
2851	Baldwin	1909	33447	Rebuilt to S-1-A, 1924 Sold for scrap 8-48
2852	Baldwin	1909	33448	Rebuilt to S-1-A, 1924
2853	Baldwin	1909	33449	Rebuilt to S-1-A, 1925 Retired 4-47

No.	Builder	Date	Shop No.		
2854	Baldwin	1909	33450	Rebuilt to S-1-A, 1925	Sold for scrap 4-51
2855	Baldwin	1909	33451	Rebuilt to S-1-A, 1925	Sold for scrap 12-48
2856	Baldwin	1909	33452	Rebuilt to S-1-A, 1927	Sold for scrap 9-50
2857	Baldwin	1909	33471	Rebuilt to S-1-A, 1927	Ret. 12-41. Running gear to 2862
2858	Baldwin	1909	33472	Rebuilt to S-1-A, 1926	Sold for scrap 9-53
2859	Baldwin	1909	33485	Rebuilt to S-1-A, 1924	Sold for scrap 2-51
2860	Baldwin	1909	33486	Rebuilt to S-1-A, 1924	Sold for scrap 2-51
2861	Baldwin	1909	33487	Rebuilt to S-1-A, 1925	Sold for scrap 12-52
2862	Baldwin	1909	33488	Rebuilt to S-1-A, 1927	Sold for scrap 2-51
2863	Baldwin	1909	33489	Rebuilt to S-1-A, 1924	Sold for scrap 5-55
2864	Baldwin	1909	33490	Rebuilt to S-1-A, 1926	Sold for scrap 3-51
2865	Baldwin	1909	33491	Rebuilt to S-1-A, 1924	Retired 8-47
2866	Baldwin	1909	33492	Rebuilt to S-1-A, 1924	Sold for scrap 2-51
2867	Baldwin	1909	33493	Rebuilt to S-1-A, 1927	Sold for scrap 12-52
2868	Baldwin	1909	33523	Retired 10-39	
2869	Baldwin	1909	33524	Retired 5-33	

Class S-2, 4-6-2

No.	Builder	Date	Shop No.		
2900	Baldwin	1910	34511	Rebuilt to S-2-A, 1926	Retired 3-35
2901	Baldwin	1910	34512	Rebuilt to S-2-A, 1928.	Sold for scrap 3-51
2902	Baldwin	1910	34513	Retired 11-39	
2903	Baldwin	1910	34514	Rebuilt to S-2-A, 1925	Sold for scrap 12-54
2904	Baldwin	1910	34515	Retired 11-34	
2905	Baldwin	1910	34516	Rebuilt to S-2-A, 1927	Sold for scrap 5-55
2906	Baldwin	1910	34583	Retired 11-33	
2907	Baldwin	1910	34584	Rebuilt to S-2-A, 1927	Sold for scrap 2-54
2908	Baldwin	1910	34585	Retired 11-33	
2909	Baldwin	1910	34586	Retired 8-33	
2910	Baldwin	1910	34587	Retired 9-33	
2911	Baldwin	1910	34588	Rebuilt to S-2-A, 1926	Sold for scrap 9-53
2912	Baldwin	1910	34589	Retired 6-35	
2913	Baldwin	1910	34600	Rebuilt to S-2-A, 1926	Sold for scrap 5-51
2914	Baldwin	1910	34605	Rebuilt to S-2-A, 1929	Sold for scrap 4-54
2915	Baldwin	1910	34606	Rebuilt to S-2-A, 1924	Sold for scrap 2-51
2916	Baldwin	1910	34619	Rebuilt to S-2-A, 1927	Sold for scrap 3-52
2917	Baldwin	1910	34620	Retired 8-33	
2918	Baldwin	1910	34621	Retired 12-38	
2919	Baldwin	1910	34622	Rebuilt to S-2-A, 1928	Sold for scrap 10-53
2920	Baldwin	1910	34623	Retired 4-36	
2921	Baldwin	1910	34624	Rebuilt to S-2-A, 1926	Sold for scrap 12-52
2922	Baldwin	1910	34685	Rebuilt to S-2-A, 1929	Sold for scrap 12-52
2923	Baldwin	1910	34686	Rebuilt to S-2-A, 1927	Sold for scrap 1-51
2924	Baldwin	1910	34687	Rebuilt to S-2-A, 1935	Sold for scrap 4-51
2925	Baldwin	1910	34688	Rebuilt to S-2-A, 1924	Sold for scrap 5-51
2926	Baldwin	1910	34689	Rebuilt to S-2-A, 1925	Sold for scrap 12-52
2927	Baldwin	1910	34706	Rebuilt to S-2-A, 1926	Sold for scrap 11-51
2928	Baldwin	1910	34707	Rebuilt to S-2-A, 1925	Sold for scrap 3-51
2929	Baldwin	1910	34736	Rebuilt to S-2-A, 1926	Sold for scrap
2930	Baldwin	1910	34737	Rebuilt to S-2-A, 1927	Sold for scrap 5-51
2931	Baldwin	1910	34738	Rebuilt to S-2-A, 1928	Sold for scrap 4-54
2932	Baldwin	1910	34757	Rebuilt to S-2-A, 1925	Sold for scrap 12-51
2933	Baldwin	1910	34758	Rebuilt to S-2-A, 1925	Sold for scrap 4-51
2934	Baldwin	1910	34759	Rebuilt to S-2-A, 1924	Sold for scrap 6-51
2935	Baldwin	1910	34760	Rebuilt to S-2-A, 1924	Sold for scrap 5-51
2936	Baldwin	1910	34811	Retired 11-39	
2937	Baldwin	1910	34812	Rebuilt to S-2-A, 1924	Sold for scrap 5-51
2938	Baldwin	1910	34850	Rebuilt to S-2-A, 1924	Sold for scrap 6-51
2939	Baldwin	1910	34851	Rebuilt to S-2-A, 1929	Sold for scrap 5-51
2940	Baldwin	1910	34852	Retired 7-34	
2941	Baldwin	1910	34853	Rebuilt to S-2-A, 1924	Sold for scrap 8-51
2942	Baldwin	1910	34854	Retired 2-38	
2943	Baldwin	1910	34855	Rebuilt to S-2-A, 1928	Sold for scrap 12-53
2944	Baldwin	1910	34868	Rebuilt to S-2-A, 1928	Sold for scrap 4-51
2945	Baldwin	1910	34869	Rebuilt to S-2-A, 1928	Sold for scrap 12-53
2946	Baldwin	1910	34913	Rebuilt to S-2-A, 1928	Sold for scrap 12-52
2947	Baldwin	1910	34914	Rebuilt to S-2-A, 1925	Sold for scrap 10-53
2948	Baldwin	1910	34915	Rebuilt to S-2-A, 1924	Sold for scrap 5-51
2949	Baldwin	1910	34916	Rebuilt to S-2-A, 1924	Sold for scrap 6-51

Class S-3, 4-6-2

No.	Builder	Date	Shop No.	
2950	Baldwin	1915	42150	Sold for scrap 7-52
2951	Baldwin	1915	42151	Sold for scrap 7-52
2952	Baldwin	1915	42152	Sold for scrap 9-49
2953	Baldwin	1915	42153	Sold for scrap 12-51
2954	Baldwin	1915	42154	Sold for scrap 7-52
2955	Baldwin	1915	42155	Sold for scrap 9-53
2956	Baldwin	1915	42156	Sold for scrap 8-51
2957	Baldwin	1915	42157	Sold for scrap 12-51
2958	Baldwin	1915	42158	Sold for scrap 10-53
2959	Baldwin	1915	42159	Retired 2-38
2960	Baldwin	1915	42160	Sold for scrap 7-52
2961	Baldwin	1915	42161	Sold for scrap 12-52
2962	Baldwin	1915	42171	Sold for scrap 7-52
2963	Baldwin	1915	42172	Sold for scrap 9-53

No.	Builder	Date	Shop No.	
2964	Baldwin	1915	42173	Sold for scrap 6-52
2965	Baldwin	1918	48261	Sold to Colorado & Southern. C. & S. No. 372
2966	Baldwin	1918	48262	Sold for scrap 12-51
2967	Baldwin	1918	48570	Sold for scrap 12-51
2968	Baldwin	1918	48571	Sold for scrap 7-52
2969	Baldwin	1918	48674	Sold for scrap 7-58
2970	Baldwin	1918	48731	Sold to Colorado & Southern. C. & S. No. 370
2971	Baldwin	1918	48886	Sold for scrap 12-51
2972	Baldwin	1918	48887	Sold for scrap 9-53
2973	Baldwin	1918	49071	Sold to Colorado & Southern. C. & S. No. 371
2974	Baldwin	1918	49075	Sold for scrap 8-51

Class S-4, 4-6-4

No.	Builder	Date	Shop No.		No.	Builder	Date	Shop No.	
3000	Baldwin	1930	61445	Sold for scrap 4-55	3006	Baldwin	1930	61527	Donated—Galesburg 12-62
3001	Baldwin	1930	61446	Donated—Ottumwa, Ia. 8-59	3007	Baldwin	1930	61528	Donated—Quincy, Ill. 6-61
3002	Baldwin	1930	61500	Rebuilt to 4000, 1937	3008	Baldwin	1930	61555	Reb. to 4003, 1938
3003	Baldwin	1930	61501	Donated—Burlington, Ia. 6-61	3009	Baldwin	1930	61556	Reb. to 4002, 1938
3004	Baldwin	1930	61525	Sold for scrap 4-55	3010	Baldwin	1930	61567	Sold for scrap 12-60
3005	Baldwin	1930	61526	Sold for scrap 4-55	3011	Baldwin	1930	61568	Reb. to 4004, 1938

3012 CB&Q 1935 Ex 5356-35 Built at West Burlington shops with
boiler furnished by Bald. Loco. Works. Sold for scrap 4-55

Class S-4-A, 4-6-4

No.		
4000	Rebuilt 1937 from No. 3002	Donated— LaCross, Wis. 8-63
4001	New engine, built W. Burlington 1938	Sold for scrap 10-60
4002	Rebuilt 1938 from No. 3009	Sold for scrap 11-60
4003	Rebuilt 1938 from No. 3008	Sold for scrap 11-60
4004	Rebuilt 1938 from No. 3011	Sold for scrap 5-55

Class D-2, 2-8-0

New CB&Q No. 1904	Orig.	No.	Builder	Date	
2980	CB&Q	397	Changed 1898 to		
	CB&Q	1397	Changed 3-01 to		
	B&MR	383	Aurora	1884	Rebuilt to G-4-C No. 1601, 1921
2981	B&MR	174	Bald. 8942	1888	Rebuilt to G-4-C No. 1602, 1921
2982	B&MR	176	Bald. 8951	1888	Rebuilt to G-4-C No. 1603, 1921
2983	B&MR	177	Bald. 8990	1888	Rebuilt to G-4-B No. 1647, 1918
2984	B&MR	178	Bald. 8991	1888	Rebuilt to G-4-B No. 1673
2985	B&MR	179	Bald. 8992	1888	Rebuilt to G-4-B No. 1676
2986	B&MR	180	Bald. 8993	1888	Rebuilt to G-4-B No. 1677
2987	B&MR	182	Bald. 8996	1888	Rebuilt to G-4-B No. 1674
2988	B&MR	183	Bald. 8998	1888	Rebuilt to G-4-C No. 1651, 1918
2989	B&MR	135	Bald. 9063	1888	Rebuilt to G-4-B No. 1671
2990	B&MR	187	Bald. 9067	1888	Retired as 2-8-0 12-22
2991	B&MR	188	Bald. 9066	1888	Rebuilt to G-4-B No. 1672
2992	B&MR	190	Bald. 9074	1888	Rebuilt to G-4-B No. 1668
2993	B&MR	198	Aurora	1888	Retired as 2-8-0 12-22
2994	B&MR	199	W. B. Shops	1888	Rebuilt to G-4-B No. 1670
2995	B&MR	200	W. B. Shops	1888	Rebuilt to G-4-B No. 1669
2996	B&MR	202	W. B. Shops	1888	Rebuilt to G-4-B No. 1667
2997	B&MR	194	Bald. 9640	1888	Rebuilt to G-4-B No. 1675
2998	B&MR	196	Bald. 9634	1888	Retired as 2-8-0 12-22

The engines for which no rebuilt date is shown were rebuilt prior to 1910. The retired dates for the rebuilt engines are given in the record of Class G-4 engines.

Class D-3, 2-8-0

New CB&Q No. 1904	Orig. No.		Builder	Date	No. Change 12-03		
3000	B&MR	335	Pitts. 1847	1898	B&MR	3300	Retired 9-28
3001	B&MR	334	Pitts. 1846	1898	B&MR	3301	Retired 11-28
3002	B&MR	336	Pitts. 1848	1898	B&MR	3302	Retired 8-28
3003	B&MR	333	Pitts. 1845	1898	B&MR	333	Retired 2-28

Class D-7, 2-8-0

New CB&Q No. 1904	Orig. No.		Builder	Date	Change 1903			
3030	I&StL	7	Bald. 22390	1903	9-03	B&MR	3450	Retired 11-28
3031	I&StL	8	Bald. 22408		11-03	B&MR	3451	Retired 11-28

Class D-4-A, 2-8-0

New CB&Q No. 1904	Orig. No.		Builder	Date	Shop No.	
3100	H&StJ	580	Schenectady	1903	26702	Retired 11-30
3101	H&StJ	581	Schenectady	1903	26703	Retired 6-33
3102	H&StJ	582	Schenectady	1903	26704	Retired 6-28
3102	H&StJ	583	Schenectady	1903	26705	Retired 11-30
3104	H&StJ	584	Schenectady	1903	26706	Retired 12-28

Class D-4-A, 2-8-0

New CB&Q No. 1904	Orig. No.		Builder	Date	Shop No.	
3105	H&StJ	585	Schenectady	1903	26707	Retired 12-28
3106	H&StJ	586	Schenectady	1903	26708	Retired 6-29
3107	H&StJ	587	Schenectady	1903	27734	Retired 12-31
3108	H&StJ	588	Schenectady	1903	27735	Retired 6-33
3109	H&StJ	589	Schenectady	1903	27736	Retired 11-32
3110	H&StJ	620	Schenectady	1903	26709	Retired 11-29
3111	H&StJ	659	Schenectady	1903	26710	Retired 1-33
3112	H&StJ	692	Schenectady	1903	26711	Retired 11-29
3113	H&StJ	790	Schenectady	1903	27737	Retired 11-29
3114	H&StJ	791	Schenectady	1903	27738	Retired 6-40
3115	H&StJ	792	Schenectady	1903	27739	Retired 12-31
3116	H&StJ	793	Schenectady	1903	27740	Retired 10-33
3117	H&StJ	862	Schenectady	1903	27741	Retired 11-33
3118	H&StJ	863	Schenectady	1903	27742	Retired 8-30
3119	H&StJ	864	Schenectady	1903	27743	Retired 10-46
3120	B&MR	3304	Schenectady	1903	26712	Retired 12-31
3121	B&MR	3305	Schenectady	1903	26713	Retired 11-32
3122	B&MR	3306	Schenectady	1903	26714	Retired 11-32
3123	B&MR	3307	Schenectady	1903	26715	Retired 1-33
3124	B&MR	3308	Schenectady	1903	26716	Retired 7-30
3125	B&MR	3309	Schenectady	1903	26717	Retired 11-32
3126	B&MR	3317	Schenectady	1903	26718	Retired 8-30
3127	B&MR	3318	Schenectady	1903	26719	Retired 1-33
3128	B&MR	3319	Schenectady	1903	26720	Retired 12-30
3129	B&MR	3320	Schenectady	1903	26721	Retired 9-31
3130	B&MR	3321	Schenectady	1903	26722	Retired 11-32
3131	B&MR	3322	Schenectady	1903	26723	Retired 11-30
3132	B&MR	3323	Schenectady	1903	26724	Retired 11-30
3133	B&MR	3324	Schenectady	1903	26725	Retired 11-32
3134	B&MR	3325	Schenectady	1903	26726	Retired 11-30
3135	B&MR	3334	Schenectady	1903	27694	Retired 12-30
3136	B&MR	3335	Schenectady	1903	27695	Retired 4-35
3137	B&MR	3336	Schenectady	1903	27696	Retired 8-30
3138	B&MR	3337	Schenectady	1903	27697	Retired 10-39
3139	B&MR	3338	Schenectady	1903	27698	Retired 4-28
3140	B&MR	3339	Schenectady	1903	27699	Retired 6-33
3141	B&MR	3340	Scnenectady	1903	27700	Retired 8-30
3142	B&MR	3341	Schenectady	1903	27701	Retired 6-33
3143	B&MR	3342	Schenectady	1903	27702	Retired 1-33
3144	B&MR	3343	Schenectady	1903	27703	Retired 6-33
3145	B&MR	3346	Schenectady	1903	27706	Retired 11-28
3146	B&MR	3347	Schenectady	1903	27707	Retired 12-31
3147	B&MR	3348	Schenectady	1903	27708	Retired 12-30
3148	B&MR	3349	Schenectady	1903	27709	Retired 6-29
3149	B&MR	3350	Schenectady	1903	27710	Retired 12-29
3150	B&MR	3351	Schenectady	1903	27711	Retired 11-28
3151	B&MR	3352	Schenectady	1903	27712	Retired 6-29
3152	B&MR	3353	Schenectady	1903	27713	Retired 11-30
3153	B&MR	3344	Schenectady	1903	27704	Retired 12-30
3154	B&MR	3345	Schenectady	1903	27705	Retired 11-32
3155	CB&Q	1900	Schenectady	1903	27714	Retired 12-30
3156	CB&Q	1901	Schenectady	1903	27715	Retired 12-29
3157	CB&Q	1902	Schenectady	1903	27716	Retired 11-29
3158	CB&Q	1903	Schenectady	1903	27717	Retired 11-32
3159	CB&Q	1904	Schenectady	1903	27718	Retired 8-30
3160	CB&Q	1905	Schenectady	1903	27719	Retired 11-32
3161	CB&Q	1906	Schenectady	1903	27720	Retired 11-32
3162	CB&Q	1907	Schenectady	1903	27721	Retired 11-29
3163	CB&Q	1908	Schenectady	1903	27722	Retired 6-29
3164	CB&Q	1909	Schenectady	1903	27723	Retired 7-30
3165	CB&Q	1910	Schenectady	1903	27724	Retired 2-33
3166	CB&Q	1911	Schenectady	1903	27725	Retired 11-30
3167	CB&Q	1912	Schenectady	1903	27726	Retired 1-33
3168	CB&Q	1913	Schenectady	1903	27727	Retired 11-30
3169	CB&Q	1914	Schenectady	1903	27728	Retired 11-32
3170	CB&Q	1915	Schenectady	1903	27729	Retired 5-40
3171	CB&Q	1916	Schenectady	1903	27730	Retired 7-29
3172	CB&Q	1917	Schenectady	1903	27731	Retired 3-30
3173	CB&Q	1918	Schenectady	1903	27732	Retired 11-30
3174	CB&Q	1919	Schenectady	1903	27733	Retired 11-29

Class D-4-B, 2-8-0

3175	H&StJ	693	Baldwin	1903	21899	Retired 11-32
3176	H&StJ	694	Baldwin	1903	21915	Retired 8-29
3177	H&StJ	695	Baldwin	1903	21943	Retired 11-29
3178	H&StJ	696	Baldwin	1903	21953	Retired 8-30
3179	H&StJ	697	Baldwin	1903	21960	Retired 3-29
3180	H&StJ	698	Baldwin	1903	21977	Retired 12-28
3181	H&StJ	699	Baldwin	1903	21985	Retired 1-33
3182	H&StJ	700	Baldwin	1903	22075	Retired 6-29
3183	H&StJ	860	Baldwin	1903	22076	Retired 11-30

No.		Shop No.	Builder	Date		Status
3184	H&StJ	861	Baldwin	1903	22214	Retired 12-29
3185	B&MR	3310	Baldwin	1903	21675	Retired 10-32
3186	B&MR	3311	Baldwin	1903	21676	Retired 11-32
3187	B&MR	3312	Baldwin	1903	21690	Retired 11-32
3188	B&MR	3313	Baldwin	1903	21695	Retired 11-40
3189	B&MR	3314	Baldwin	1903	21743	Retired 11-30
3190	B&MR	3315	Baldwin	1903	21744	Retired 12-30
3191	B&MR	3316	Baldwin	1903	21762	Retired 6-27
3192	B&MR	3326	Baldwin	1903	21765	Retired 12-29
3193	B&MR	3327	Baldwin	1903	21806	Retired 12-30
3194	B&MR	3328	Baldwin	1903	21802	Retired 9-28
3195	B&MR	3329	Baldwin	1930	21821	Retired 11-32
3196	B&MR	3330	Baldwin	1903	21849	Retired 8-31
3197	B&MR	3331	Baldwin	1903	21858	Retired 11-29
3198	B&MR	3332	Baldwin	1903	21869	Retired 8-30
3199	B&MR	3333	Baldwin	1903	21892	Retired 11-32

Engines in 500 series with H. & St. J. lettering were property of K. C. St. J. & C. B., in 700 series of St. L. K. & N. W., and in 800 series of C. B. & K. C. H. & St. J. No. 700 was probably the property of that road.

Class T-1-Comp., 2-6-6-2

No.	Builder	Date	Shop No.	
4000	Baldwin	1908	32722	Rebuilt to Class F-2 No. 555 8-27
4001	Baldwin	1908	32723	Retired 6-27
4002	Baldwin	1908	32724	Rebuilt to Class F-2 No. 553 7-27

These engines were built originally for the Great Northern R. R., the respective G. N. numbers being 1905, 1906 and 1907.

Class T-1-A-Comp., 2-6-6-2

4003	Baldwin	1909	33986	Rebuilt to Class F-2 No. 550 9-26
4004	Baldwin	1909	33987	Rebuilt to Class F-2 No. 556 12-27
4005	Baldwin	1909	34020	Rebuilt to Class F-2 No. 552 5-27
4006	Baldwin	1909	34021	Rebuilt to Class F-2 No. 551 3-27
4007	Baldwin	1909	34029	Rebuilt to Class F-2 No. 554 8-27

Class T-2-Comp., 2-6-6-2

4100	Baldwin	1910	34230	Retired 8-50	4105	Baldwin	1910	34269	Retired 8-51
4101	Baldwin	1910	34231	Retired 8-50	4106	Baldwin	1910	34297	Retired
4102	Baldwin	1910	34232	Retired 12-29	4107	Baldwin	1910	34298	Retired 7-53
4103	Baldwin	1910	34245	Retired 12-29	4108	Baldwin	1910	34299	Retired 7-53
4104	Baldwin	1910	34246	Retired 3-30	4109	Baldwin	1910	34300	Retired 12-31

Class T-3-Comp., 2-8-8-2

4200	Baldwin	1911	36775	Retired 8-34

Class O-1-A, 2-8-2

No.	Builder	Date	Shop No.	Sold for Scrap	No.	Builder	Date	Shop No.	Sold for Scrap
4940	Baldwin	1923	56572	5-55	4970	Baldwin	1923	56931	6-61
4941	Baldwin	1923	56573	4-54	4971	Baldwin	1923	56932	9-49
4942	Baldwin	1923	56574	12-57	4972	Baldwin	1923	56968	12-54
4943	Baldwin	1923	56575	6-43	4973	Baldwin	1923	56969	4-55
4944	Baldwin	1923	56576	4-54	4974	Baldwin	1923	56970	4-54
4945	Baldwin	1923	56704	5-55	4975	Baldwin	1923	56971	12-57
4946	Baldwin	1923	56705	4-54	4976	Baldwin	1923	56972	6-61
4947	Baldwin	1923	56706	6-61	4977	Baldwin	1923	56973	5-54
4948	Baldwin	1923	56707	12-52	4978	Baldwin	1923	56974	
4949	Baldwin	1923	56708	2-59	4979	Baldwin	1923	56975	12-54
4950	Baldwin	1923	56709	6-61	4980	Baldwin	1923	57073	10-60
4951	Baldwin	1923	56710	12-57	4981	Baldwin	1923	57074	5-55
4952	Baldwin	1923	56711	6-61	4982	Baldwin	1923	57075	4-54
4953	Baldwin	1923	56712	4-51	4983	Baldwin	1923	57076	6-61
4954	Baldwin	1923	56713	12-60	4984	Baldwin	1923	57077	4-54
4955	Baldwin	1923	56804	6-61	4985	Baldwin	1923	57096	5-54
4956	Baldwin	1923	56805	6-61	4986	Baldwin	1923	57105	6-61
4957	Baldwin	1923	56806	4-55	4987	Baldwin	1923	57106	4-54
4958	Baldwin	1923	56807	12-54	4988	Baldwin	1923	57107	12-57
4959	Baldwin	1923	56808	5-55	4989	Baldwin	1923	57108	4-55
4960	Baldwin	1923	56809		4990	Baldwin	1923	57109	9-55
4961	Baldwin	1923	56810	6-61	4991	Baldwin	1923	57110	6-61
4962	Baldwin	1923	56811	10-60	4992	Baldwin	1923	57111	7-60
4963	Baldwin	1923	56812		4993	Baldwin	1923	57112	6-61
4964	Baldwin	1923	56813	5-55	4994	Baldwin	1923	57113	
4965	Baldwin	1923	56814	4-54	4995	Baldwin	1923	57114	9-55
4966	Baldwin	1923	56815	6-61	4996	Baldwin	1923	57245	12-54
4967	Baldwin	1923	56816	6-61	4997	Baldwin	1923	57246	6-61
4968	Baldwin	1923	56817	4-55	4998	Baldwin	1923	57247	2-55
4969	Baldwin	1923	56818	5-55	4999	Baldwin	1923	57248	6-59

Class O-1, 2-8-2

5000	Baldwin	1910	35609	Retired	5005	Baldwin	1910	35614	Retired 5-47
5001	Baldwin	1910	35610	Retired 3-47	5006	Baldwin	1910	35615	Sold for scrap 4-51
5002	Baldwin	1910	35611	Retired 2-47	5007	Baldwin	1910	35616	Retired
5003	Baldwin	1910	35612	Retired 1-47	5008	Baldwin	1910	35685	Retired 9-27
5004	Baldwin	1910	35613	Retired 12-46	5009	Baldwin	1910	35686	Retired 10-46

Class O-1, 2-8-2

No.	Builder	Date	Shop No.	
5010	Baldwin	1910	35687	Retired 1-47
5011	Baldwin	1910	35688	Retired 1-47
5012	Baldwin	1910	35735	Retired 4-47
5013	Baldwin	1910	35736	Retired 6-42
5014	Baldwin	1910	35737	Retired 1-47
5015	Baldwin	1910	35738	Retired
5016	Baldwin	1910	35739	Retired 12-34
5017	Baldwin	1910	35740	Retired 9-34
5018	Baldwin	1910	35741	Retired
5019	Baldwin	1910	35742	Retired 8-47
5020	Baldwin	1910	35743	
Rebuilt to 0-8-0, Class F-3				Retired 10-39
5021	Baldwin	1910	35744	Retired 2-47
5022	Baldwin	1910	35745	Sold for scrap 4-51
5023	Baldwin	1910	35746	Sold for scrap 8-50
5024	Baldwin	1910	35747	Retired 4-47
5025	Baldwin	1910	35748	Retired 2-47
5026	Baldwin	1910	35749	Retired 11-46
5027	Baldwin	1910	35750	Retired 11-46
5028	Baldwin	1910	35751	Retired
5029	Baldwin	1910	35752	Retired 12-48
5030	Baldwin	1910	35874	Retired 2-47
5031	Baldwin	1910	35875	Retired 1-47
5032	Baldwin	1910	35876	Retired 12-46
5033	Baldwin	1910	35877	Retired 9-34
5034	Baldwin	1910	35878	Sold for scrap 5-47
5035	Baldwin	1910	35879	Sold for scrap 11-47
5036	Baldwin	1910	35880	Sold for scrap 2-51
5037	Baldwin	1910	35881	Retired 3-47
5038	Baldwin	1910	35882	Sold for scrap 5-47
5039	Baldwin	1910	35883	Sold for scrap 4-51
5040	Baldwin	1910	35884	Sold for scrap 4-47
5041	Baldwin	1910	35885	Dismantled 10-46
5042	Baldwin	1910	35886	Dismantled 2-47
5043	Baldwin	1910	35887	Dismantled 12-46
5044	Baldwin	1910	35888	Dismantled 1-47
5045	Baldwin	1910	35889	Sold for scrap 5-51
5046	Baldwin	1910	35890	Dismantled 1-47
5047	Baldwin	1910	35891	Dismantled 1-47
5048	Baldwin	1910	35892	Dismantled 12-46
5049	Baldwin	1910	35893	Sold for scrap 4-51
5050	Baldwin	1911	36998	Retired 4-47
5051	Baldwin	1911	36999	Retired 11-33
5052	Baldwin	1911	37000	Retired 1-47
5053	Baldwin	1911	37001	Retired 7-33
5054	Baldwin	1911	37002	Retired 1-47
5055	Baldwin	1911	37025	Sold for scrap 9-50
5056	Baldwin	1911	37026	Retired 2-47
5057	Baldwin	1911	37027	Retired 1-47
5058	Baldwin	1911	37028	Retired 1-47
5059	Baldwin	1911	37029	Sold for scrap 8-50

Class O-1-A, 2-8-2

No.	Builder	Date	Shop No.	
5060	Baldwin	1917	45359	4-54
5061	Baldwin	1917	45360	2-54
5062	Baldwin	1917	45363	2-54
5063	Baldwin	1917	45521	2-54
5064	Baldwin	1917	45522	10-53
5065	Baldwin	1917	45523	11-53
5066	Baldwin	1917	45621	3-54
5067	Baldwin	1917	45636	6-53
5068	Baldwin	1917	45664	5-54
5069	Baldwin	1917	45702	9-53
5070	Baldwin	1917	45703	7-53
5071	Baldwin	1917	45759	4-54
5072	Baldwin	1917	45760	4-55
5073	Baldwin	1917	45761	4-54
5074	Baldwin	1917	45792	6-53
5075	Baldwin	1918	48725	7-53
5076	Baldwin	1918	48726	7-53
5077	Baldwin	1918	48904	4-54
5078	Baldwin	1918	48949	10-53
5079	Baldwin	1918	48994	11-60
5080	Baldwin	1918	49072	4-54
5081	Baldwin	1918	49073	12-53
5082	Baldwin	1918	49228	11-60
5083	Baldwin	1918	49229	3-54
5084	Baldwin	1918	49301	11-60
5085	Baldwin	1918	49358	11-60
5086	Baldwin	1918	49409	2-54
5087	Baldwin	1918	49410	11-53
5088	Baldwin	1918	49543	10-53
5089	Baldwin	1918	49544	10-60
5090	Baldwin	1918	49640	6-61
5091	Baldwin	1918	49653	7-53
5092	Baldwin	1918	49654	4-55
5093	Baldwin	1918	50130	8-53
5094	Baldwin	1918	50362	6-53
5095	Baldwin	1918	50677	6-53
5096	Baldwin	1918	50787	12-57
5097	Baldwin	1918	50942	2-54
5098	Baldwin	1918	50988	
5099	Baldwin	1918	50989	3-54
5100	Baldwin	1920	54137	12-57
5101	Baldwin	1920	54170	5-54
5102	Baldwin	1920	54171	2-54
5103	Baldwin	1920	54172	7-53
5104	Baldwin	1920	54173	2-54
5105	Baldwin	1920	54174	12-53
5106	Baldwin	1920	54175	6-53
5107	Baldwin	1920	54290	7-52
5108	Baldwin	1920	54291	5-54
5109	Baldwin	1920	54292	8-53
5110	Baldwin	1920	54362	5-54
5111	Baldwin	1920	54363	11-53
5112	Baldwin	1920	54364	12-57
5113	Baldwin	1920	54365	3-54
5114	Baldwin	1920	54366	6-53
5115	Baldwin	1920	54367	4-54
5116	Baldwin	1922	55352	4-55
5117	Baldwin	1922	55400	5-54
5118	Baldwin	1922	55401	6-61
5119	Baldwin	1922	55402	11-60
5120	Baldwin	1922	55403	11-53
5121	Baldwin	1922	55404	10-60
5122	Baldwin	1922	55380	2-54
5123	Baldwin	1922	55381	6-53
5124	Baldwin	1922	55454	1-53
5125	Baldwin	1922	55455	5-54
5126	Baldwin	1922	55456	12-54
5127	Baldwin	1922	55457	9-55
5128	Baldwin	1922	55458	3-54
5129	Baldwin	1922	55459	11-60
5130	Baldwin	1922	55460	9-55
5131	Baldwin	1922	55461	4-54
5132	Baldwin	1922	55462	11-60
5133	Baldwin	1922	55497	1-54
5134	Baldwin	1922	55498	5-54
5135	Baldwin	1922	55499	3-54
5136	Baldwin	1922	55500	12-57
5137	Baldwin	1922	55501	3-54
5138	Baldwin	1922	55502	5-55
5139	Baldwin	1922	55503	12-57
5140	Baldwin	1922	55533	11-60
5141	Baldwin	1922	55534	4-54
5142	Baldwin	1922	55535	5-54
5143	Baldwin	1922	55536	12-57
5144	Baldwin	1922	55537	6-61
5145	Baldwin	1922	55538	10-53
5146	Baldwin	1922	55539	12-57
5147	Baldwin	1922	55540	5-55

Class O-2, 2-8-2

No.	Builder	Date	Shop No.		
5200	Baldwin	1912	38176	Rebuilt to 0-2-A, 3-28	6-51
5201	Baldwin	1912	38177	Retired 2-31	
5202	Baldwin	1912	38205	Retired 8-33	
5203	Baldwin	1912	38206	Rebuilt to 0-2-A, 12-25	5-51
5204	Baldwin	1912	38207	Rebuilt to 0-2-A, 8-25	12-51
5205	Baldwin	1912	38208	Retired 8-33	
5206	Baldwin	1912	38209	Rebuilt to 0-2-A, 2-25	5-39
5207	Baldwin	1912	38210	Rebuilt to 0-2-A, 5-29	8-52
5208	Baldwin	1912	38229	Retired 10-31	
5209	Baldwin	1912	38230	Rebuilt to 0-2-A, 8-28	1-52
5210	Baldwin	1912	38231	Retired 8-34	
5211	Baldwin	1912	38285	Retired 5-33	
5212	Baldwin	1912	38286	Retired 9-33	
5213	Baldwin	1912	38287	Retired 10-33	
5214	Baldwin	1912	38288	Retired 2-35	
5215	Baldwin	1912	38289	Rebuilt to 0-2-A, 1-28	12-51
5216	Baldwin	1912	38365	Retired 9-33	
5217	Baldwin	1912	38366	Retired 9-31	

No.	Builder	Date	Shop No.	Sold for Scrap
5218	Baldwin	1912	38367	Retired 9-33
5219	Baldwin	1912	38368	Dismantled 3-41
5220	Baldwin	1912	38369	Rebuilt to 0-2-A, 4-29 10-53
5221	Baldwin	1912	38370	Rebuilt to 0-2-A, 8-27 12-51
5222	Baldwin	1912	38387	Rebuilt to 0-2-A, 10-28 3-52
5223	Baldwin	1912	38388	Rebuilt to 0-2-A, 9-28 12-51
5224	Baldwin	1912	38389	Rebuilt to 0-2-A, 5-28 2-54
5225	Baldwin	1912	38330	Retired 10-33
5226	Baldwin	1912	38391	Retired 12-34
5227	Baldwin	1912	38392	Rebuilt to 0-2-A, 8-29 11-53
5228	Baldwin	1912	38428	Rebuilt to 0-2-A, 7-29 8-52
5229	Baldwin	1912	38429	Retired 12-30
5230	Baldwin	1912	38430	Rebuilt to 0-2-A, 3-26 3-52
5231	Baldwin	1912	38431	Rebuilt to 0-2-A, 12-28 6-51
5232	Baldwin	1912	38432	Rebuilt to 0-2-A, 9-29 10-53
5233	Baldwin	1912	38433	Rebuilt to 0-2-A, 3-28 3-54
5234	Baldwin	1912	38501	Rebuilt to 0-2-A, 7-28 12-51
5235	Baldwin	1912	38502	Retired 11-34
5236	Baldwin	1912	38503	Retired 4-31
5237	Baldwin	1912	38504	Rebuilt to 0-2-A, 7-30 Ret. 4-47
5238	Baldwin	1912	38505	Rebuilt to 0-2-A, 4-28 12-51
5239	Baldwin	1912	38506	Rebuilt to 0-2-A, 12-27 12-52
5240	Baldwin	1912	38507	Rebuilt to 0-2-A, 12-26 12-51
5241	Baldwin	1912	38508	Rebuilt to 0-2-A, 6-29 2-51
5242	Baldwin	1912	38509	Rebuilt to 0-2-A, 4-26 12-51
5243	Baldwin	1912	38510	Retired 2-35
5244	Baldwin	1912	38511	Retired 11-34
5245	Baldwin	1912	38512	Retired 8-35
5246	Baldwin	1912	38513	Retired 9-33
5247	Baldwin	1912	38514	Rebuilt to 0-2-A, 10-28 3-52
5248	Baldwin	1912	38515	Rebuilt to 0-2-A, 5-26 6-52
5249	Baldwin	1912	38516	Rebuilt to 0-2-A, 7-26 12-51
5250	Baldwin	1912	38768	Retired 5-33
5251	Baldwin	1912	38769	Rebuilt to 0-2-A, 8-28 12-51
5252	Baldwin	1912	38770	Rebuilt to 0-2-A, 11-29 8-52
5253	Baldwin	1912	38771	Rebuilt to 0-2-A, 5-26 3-52
5254	Baldwin	1912	38874	Rebuilt to 0-2-A, 6-27 12-51
5255	Baldwin	1912	38875	Retired 8-31
5256	Baldwin	1912	38876	Retired 4-47
5257	Baldwin	1912	38877	Retired 8-33
5258	Baldwin	1912	38878	Retired 3-35
5259	Baldwin	1912	38879	Rebuilt to 0-2-A, 10-29 12-51
5260	Baldwin	1912	38880	Retired 8-33
5261	Baldwin	1912	38881	Retired 10-39
5262	Baldwin	1912	38882	Rebuilt to 0-2-A, 6-28 9-53
5263	Baldwin	1912	38883	Rebuilt to 0-2-A, 1-28 12-51
5264	Baldwin	1912	38884	Rebuilt to 0-2-A, 2-27 5-51
5265	Baldwin	1912	38885	Rebuilt to 0-2-A, 10-30 12-51
5266	Baldwin	1912	38886	Retired 2-35
5267	Baldwin	1912	38887	Retired 4-36
5268	Baldwin	1912	38888	Retired 3-31
5269	Baldwin	1912	38889	Retired 10-33
5270	Baldwin	1912	38929	Rebuilt to 0-2-A, 11-26 12-51
5271	Baldwin	1912	38930	Retired 3-36
5272	Baldwin	1912	38931	Rebuilt to 0-2-A, 4-29 10-53
5273	Baldwin	1912	38932	Retired 6-33
5274	Baldwin	1912	38973	Retired 10-39
5275	Baldwin	1912	38974	Rebuilt to 0-2-A, 1-26 12-51
5276	Baldwin	1912	38975	Rebuilt to 0-2-A, 12-29 12-51
5277	Baldwin	1912	38976	Rebuilt to 0-2-A, 9-24 12-51
5278	Baldwin	1912	38977	Rebuilt to 0-2-A, 9-24 12-51
5279	Baldwin	1912	38978	Retired 12-35
5280	Baldwin	1912	38979	11-53
5281	Baldwin	1912	38980	Rebuilt to 0-2-A, 9-28 Ret. 10-3.
5282	Baldwin	1912	38981	12-51
5283	Baldwin	1912	38982	Rebuilt to 0-2-A, 11-26 Ret. 5-36
5284	Baldwin	1912	38983	8-51
5285	Baldwin	1912	39040	Rebuilt to 0-2-A, 1-31 3-52
5286	Baldwin	1912	39041	Rebuilt to 0-2-A, 7-25 3-52
5287	Baldwin	1912	39071	Rebuilt to 0-2-A, 8-29 Ret. 8-47
5288	Baldwin	1913	39072	10-53
5289	Baldwin	1913	39073	Rebuilt to 0-2-A, 7-26 7-33 Dismantled
5290	Baldwin	1913	39074	Retired 7-33 12-51
5291	Baldwin	1913	39075	Rebuilt to 0-2-A, 9-26 Ret. 10-46
5292	Baldwin	1913	39076	Rebuilt to 0-2-A, 3-26 4-34 Dismantled
5293	Baldwin	1913	39077	Retired 4-34 7-52
5294	Baldwin	1913	39078	Rebuilt to 0-2-A, 8-25 2-54
5295	Baldwin	1913	39079	Rebuilt to 0-2-A, 2-29 12-51
5296	Baldwin	1913	39080	Rebuilt to 0-2-A, 6-30 Ret. 9-39
5297	Baldwin	1913	39081	12-52
5298	Baldwin	1913	39082	Rebuilt to 0-2-A, 3-29 3-31 Dismantled
5299	Baldwin	1913	39083	Retired 9-39

Class O-3, 2-8-2

No.	Builder	Date	Shop No.	Sold for Scrap
5300	Baldwin	1915	42126	12-52
5301	Baldwin	1915	42127	2-51
5302	Baldwin	1915	42128	12-52
5303	Baldwin	1915	42129	4-51
5304	Baldwin	1915	42130	10-53
5305	Baldwin	1915	42131	7-52
5306	Baldwin	1915	42145	12-52
5307	Baldwin	1915	42146	2-51
5308	Baldwin	1915	42147	3-51
5309	Baldwin	1915	42148	1-51
5310	Baldwin	1915	42149	2-51
5311	Baldwin	1915	42162	1-51
5312	Baldwin	1915	42163	12-52
5313	Baldwin	1915	42164	2-51
5314	Baldwin	1915	42165	1-51
5315	Baldwin	1917	45361	10-56
5316	Baldwin	1917	45362	12-52
5317	Baldwin	1917	45525	12-52
5318	Baldwin	1917	45526	12-52
5319	Baldwin	1917	45527	4-54
5320	Baldwin	1917	45577	12-52
5321	Baldwin	1917	45578	12-52
5322	Baldwin	1917	45579	1-53
5323	Baldwin	1917	45630	12-52
5324	Baldwin	1917	45637	11-53 Dismantled
5325	Baldwin	1917	45665	9-55
5326	Baldwin	1917	45666	12-52
5327	Baldwin	1917	45667	12-52
5328	Baldwin	1917	45712	11-53
5329	Baldwin	1917	45713	7-53
5330	Baldwin	1917	45756	11-53
5331	Baldwin	1917	45762	4-54
5332	Baldwin	1917	45763	10-56
5333	Baldwin	1917	45764	12-57
5334	Baldwin	1917	45794	9-56
5335	Baldwin	1917	45795	12-57
5336	Baldwin	1917	45796	11-53
5337	Baldwin	1917	45831	6-53
5338	Baldwin	1917	45832	7-53
5339	Baldwin	1917	45833	12-53
5340	Baldwin	1919	51264	11-53
5341	Baldwin	1919	51275	4-54
5342	Baldwin	1919	51276	4-54
5343	Baldwin	1919	51347	7-53
5344	Baldwin	1919	51446	9-56
5345	Baldwin	1919	51480	9-55
5346	Baldwin	1919	51481	11-60
5347	Baldwin	1919	51519	11-53
5348	Baldwin	1919	51520	4-54
5349	Baldwin	1919	51521	11-54
5350	Baldwin	1919	51561	7-53
5351	Baldwin	1919	51562	11-60
5352	Baldwin	1919	51595	10-56
5353	Baldwin	1919	51631	4-54
5354	Baldwin	1919	51665	4-54
5355	Baldwin	1919	51709	10-56
5356	Baldwin	1919	51710	4-54
5357	Baldwin	1919	51742	11-60
5358	Baldwin	1919	51743	4-54
5359	Baldwin	1919	51760	4-54

Class O-4, 2-8-2

No.	Builder	Date	Shop No.	Sold for Scrap
5500	Baldwin	1919	51552	6-57
5501	Baldwin	1919	51553	5-60
5502	Baldwin	1919	51585	4-54
5503	Baldwin	1919	51586	5-60
5504	Baldwin	1919	51587	5-60
5505	Baldwin	1919	51588	5-60
5506	Baldwin	1919	51613	Sold to C&S
5507	Baldwin	1919	51614	Sold to C&S
5508	Baldwin	1919	51615	Sold to C&S
5509	Baldwin	1919	51616	Sold to C&S
5510	Baldwin	1919	51617	Sold for scrap 10-53
5511	Baldwin	1919	51618	4-54
5512	Baldwin	1919	51619	2-54
5513	Baldwin	1919	51620	Sold to C&S
5514	Baldwin	1919	51621	Sold for scrap 3-54

No. 5502 and No. 5514 leased to F.W.&D.
Class 0-4 built to United States Railroad Administration standards.

Class O-5, 4-8-4

No.	Builder	Date	Shop No.	Sold for Scrap
5600	Baldwin	1930	61443	5-60
5601	Baldwin	1930	61444	5-61
5602	Baldwin	1930	61496	6-60
5603	Baldwin	1930	61497	5-55
5604	Baldwin	1930	61498	6-60
5605	Baldwin	1930	61499	9-60
5606	Baldwin	1930	61522	5-60
5607	Baldwin	1930	61523	10-60

Class O-5-A, 4-8-4

No.	Builder	Date	Sold for Scrap
5608	W. Burlington	9-36	5-61
5609	W. Burlington	9-36	5-61
5610	W. Burlington	10-36	4-61
5611	W. Burlington	6-37	10-53
5612	W. Burlington	6-37	5-60
5613	W. Burlington	7-37	10-60
5614	W. Burlington	7-37	Donated— St. Joseph, Mo. 5-62
5615	W. Burlington	8-37	5-60
5616	W. Burlington	8-37	60
5617	W. Burlington	9-37	9-60
5618	W. Burlington	10-37	4-61
5619	W. Burlington	10-37	4-61
5620	W. Burlington	10-37	
5621	W. Burlington	7-38	4-60
5622	W. Burlington	8-38	5-60
5623	W. Burlington	8-38	9-60
5624	W. Burlington	9-38	5-60
5625	W. Burlington	10-38	3-54
5626	W. Burlington	4-40	11-60
5627	W. Burlington	4-40	11-60
5628	W. Burlington	5-40	9-60
5629	W. Burlington	6-40	Int.-Mt. Chap. NRHS Den. 9-63
5630	W. Burlington	6-40	9-60
5631	W. Burlington	7-40	Donated-Sheridan, Wyo. 2-62
5632	W. Burlington	8-40	
5633	W. Burlington	8-40	Donated-Douglas, Wyo. 5-62
5634	W. Burlington	9-40	5-61
5635	W. Burlington	10-40	4-60

No. 5625 had Franklin Steam Distribution System applied June, 1942.

Class M-1, 2-10-2

No.	Builder	Date	Shop No.	Sold for Scrap
6000	Baldwin	1912	37592	Retired 12-33
6001	Baldwin	1912	37593	8-50
6002	Baldwin	1912	37594	9-50
6003	Baldwin	1912	37599	Retired 12-33
6004	Baldwin	1912	37600	Retired 12-33

Class M-2, 2-10-2

No.	Builder	Date	Shop No.	Sold for Scrap
6100	Baldwin	1914	41453	12-51
6101	Baldwin	1914	41454	12-51
6102	Baldwin	1914	41455	8-52
6103	Baldwin	1914	41456	8-52
6104	Baldwin	1914	41457	8-52
6105	Baldwin	1914	41476	12-51
6106	Baldwin	1914	41477	12-51
6107	Baldwin	1914	41487	11-53

Class M-2-A, 2-10-2

No.	Builder	Date	Shop No.	Sold for Scrap
6108	Baldwin	1914	41488	12-52
6109	Baldwin	1914	41489	3-52

Class M-2, 2-10-2

No.	Builder	Date	Shop No.	Sold for Scrap
6110	Baldwin	1914	41737	12-51
6111	Baldwin	1914	41633	12-51
6112	Baldwin	1914	41634	12-51
6113	Baldwin	1914	41635	12-51
6114	Baldwin	1914	41636	12-51
6115	Baldwin	1914	41638	12-51
6116	Baldwin	1914	41639	12-51
6117	Baldwin	1914	41656	8-52
6118	Baldwin	1914	41657	12-51
6119	Baldwin	1914	41658	12-51
6120	Baldwin	1914	41659	12-51
6121	Baldwin	1914	41660	4-54
6122	Baldwin	1914	41661	7-52
6123	Baldwin	1914	41662	9-53
6124	Baldwin	1914	41684	Retired 9-35
6125	Baldwin	1914	41685	7-53

Class M-2-A, 2-10-2

No.	Builder	Date	Shop No.	Sold for Scrap
6126	Baldwin	1915	42087	12-54
6127	Baldwin	1915	42088	11-53
6128	Baldwin	1915	42089	2-54
6129	Baldwin	1915	42090	12-51
6130	Baldwin	1915	42091	6-53
6131	Baldwin	1915	42095	12-54
6132	Baldwin	1915	42096	5-54
6133	Baldwin	1915	42119	2-54
6134	Baldwin	1915	42120	6-53
6135	Baldwin	1915	42143	6-53
6136	Baldwin	1917	45581	6-53
6137	Baldwin	1917	45582	7-53
6138	Baldwin	1917	45622	10-53
6139	Baldwin	1917	45623	11-53
6140	Baldwin	1917	45646	12-51
6141	Baldwin	1917	45647	1-54
6142	Baldwin	1917	45661	11-53
6143	Baldwin	1917	45662	4-54
6144	Baldwin	1917	45711	Retired 10-47
6145	Baldwin	1917	45828	2-54
6146	Baldwin	1919	51604	12-53
6147	Baldwin	1919	51605	I2-54
6148	Baldwin	1919	51640	2-54
6149	Baldwin	1919	51641	5-54
6150	Baldwin	1919	51750	4-54
6151	Baldwin	1919	51751	1-53
6152	Baldwin	1919	51752	5-54
6153	Baldwin	1919	51753	4-54
6154	Baldwin	1919	51761	4-54
6155	Baldwin	1919	51762	4-54
6156	Baldwin	1920	54073	Leased to C&S 5-54
6157	Baldwin	1920	54074	Leased to C&S 2-54
6158	Baldwin	1920	54121	3-54
6159	Baldwin	1920	54122	2-54
6160	Baldwin	1921	54161	12-52
6161	Baldwin	1921	54162	3-54
6162	Baldwin	1921	54163	1-54
6163	Baldwin	1921	54164	12-54
6164	Baldwin	1921	54165	5-54
6165	Baldwin	1921	54166	4-54
6166	Baldwin	1921	54167	2-54
6167	Baldwin	1921	54168	5-54
6168	Baldwin	1921	54169	3-54
6169	Baldwin	1921	54360	5-54
6170	Baldwin	1921	54361	1-53

Class M-3, 2-10-2

No.	Builder	Date	Shop No.	Sold for scrap	No.	Builder	Date	Shop No.	Sold for Scrap
6300	Brooks	1919	59818	7-53	6305	Brooks	1919	59823	8-53
6301	Brooks	1919	59819	8-53	6306	Brooks	1919	59824	8-53
6302	Brooks	1919	59820	2-54	6307	Brooks	1919	59825	7-53
6303	Brooks	1919	59821	2-54	6308	Brooks	1919	59826	3-54
6304	Brooks	1919	59822	3-54	6309	Brooks	1919	59827	8-53

No. 6300 to No. 6309 leased to Colorado & Southern.
Class M-3 built to United States Railroad Administration standards.

Class M-4, 2-10-4

No.	Builder	Date	Shop No.	No.	Builder	Date	Shop No.
6310	Baldwin	1927	60210	6319	Baldwin	1927	60283
6311	Baldwin	1927	60211	6320	Baldwin	1927	60291
6312	Baldwin	1927	60252	6321	Baldwin	1927	60292
6313	Baldwin	1927	60253	6322	Baldwin	1929	60767
6314	Baldwin	1927	60254	6323	Baldwin	1929	60768
6315	Baldwin	1927	60255	6324	Baldwin	1929	60769
6316	Baldwin	1927	60262	6325	Baldwin	1929	60770
6317	Baldwin	1927	60281	6326	Baldwin	1929	60805
6318	Baldwin	1927	60282	6327	Baldwin	1929	60806

Class M-4 converted to M-4-A by application of 28x22 cylinders, roller bearings and cross counter-balance (main wheels only).

No.			No.			No.		
6310	1-37	Sold scrap 5-61	6316	11-39	4-61	6322	9-39	5-61
6311	2-40	11-60	6317	11-39	5-61	6323	6-35	4-61
6312	1-40	5-61	6318	12-39	5-61	6324	6-35	5-61
6313	8-39	10-60	6319	2-40	5-61	6325	9-35	5-61
6314	11-39	4-61	6320	7-39	5-61	6326	11-35	5-61
6315	10-39	4-61	6321	10-35	5-61	6327	11-34	5-61

Class B-1, 4-8-2

7000	Lima	1922	6248	9-53	7004	Lima	1922	6252	7-53
7001	Lima	1922	6249	7-53	7005	Lima	1922	6253	7-53
7002	Lima	1922	6250	11-53	7006	Lima	1922	6254	7-53
7003	Lima	1922	6251	6-53	7007	Lima	1922	6255	6-53

Class B-1-A, 4-8-2

7008	Baldwin	1925	58482	7-53	7015	Baldwin	1925	58514	11-53
7009	Baldwin	1925	58483	10-53	7016	Baldwin	1925	58515	10-53
7010	Baldwin	1925	58509	2-54	7017	Baldwin	1925	58602	11-53
7011	Baldwin	1925	58510	11-53	7018	Baldwin	1925	58603	5-55
7012	Baldwin	1925	58511	10-53	7019	Baldwin	1925	58604	5-55
7013	Baldwin	1925	58512	11-53	7020	Baldwin	1925	58605	5-55
7014	Baldwin	1925	58513	5-55					

Engine No. 1522, Class H-1 was built as a cross-compound by Rogers in 1892. The large low pressure cylinder on the right was later changed to simple. Renumbered to 1133 in 1904. Princeton, Illinois.

- Harry Boggs

Chicago, Burlington & Quincy Railroad Company

ASSIGNMENT OF LOCOMOTIVES AND MOTOR CARS, JUNE 1, 1935

CHICAGO DIVISION

*G 5 — 500 501 502 505 506 507 509

G 5 A — 510 511 512 514 515 516 517 518 519 520 521 522 523 524

*F 1 — 541 543 545 546 547 549

K 2 — 630 646 666

K 10 — 953 956

G 3 — 1425 1429 1494 *1531 1532 *1538 1544 1549 1566

G 6 — 1683 1685 1696 1697 1699

G 9 A — 1806 1813 1815 1822 1831 1848

*R 4 — 2026

*R 5 — 2071 a2094 2095 2098 2102 2106 a2107 a2118 2121 2152 2159 2169 2179 2197 2201 2202

*S 1 — 2801 2819 2847 2868

*S 1 A — =2812 =2816 X†2817 X2820 X†2821 =2822 X†2824 =†2835 X2833 X†2838 X2850 X2851 X2853 X2854 X†2858 X2860 X2861 X†2865

*S 2 — 2902 2918 2920 2936 2942

*S 2 A — =†2914 X†2921 =2924 X†2927 X2929 X2931 =2934 =2935 X2938 =2939 X†2946 X†2947 X2948

†▽=*S4 — 3000 3001 3002 3003 3004 3005 3006 3008 3009 3010 3011 3012

*O 1 — 5002 5005 5011 5042 5045 5047 5052

*O 1 A — X4942 X4943 X4944 X4945 X4946 X4947 X4948 X4950 X4951 =4952 X4953 X4956 X4957 X4958 X4959 X4960 X4961 X4962 X4963 X4964 X4965 X4966 X4967 X4968 X4969 =4970 =4971 =4973 =4974 =4975 =4976 =4977 =4978 =4979 =4980 =4981 =4982 =4983 =4986 =4988 =4994 o=4995 o=4996 o=4997 o=4998 o=4999 5065 %5067 %5093 =5116 =5119 X5129 =5132 5135 =5137 X5138 X5141 X5142 =5143 =5147

*O 2 — ƒ5245 5267 ƒ5271 ƒ5279 5283

*O 3 — 5309 ƒ X5324 ƒ5326

ƒ X*B1 A — 7015 7016 7017 7018 7019 7020

Diesel Electric — 9123

Total: 203

GALESBURG DIVISION

*G 5 — 503 504 508

F 2 — 550 551 552 553 554 555 556

G 10 — 561 569 581 582

K 2 — 659

K 4 — 706 718 721 723

K 10 — 957

*G 3 — 1520

G 4 A — 1650

G 8 — 1710 1714 1715 1722 1726 1769

G 9 — 1827 1828

G 9 A — 1808 1844

*R 5 — 2066 2165 2185

*P 5 — 2550 2567 2572

*P 6 — 2580 2583

*P 6 A — 2592 2596 2597

=*S 2 A — 2919

*O 1 A — X4954 X4955 =4984 =4985 =4987 =4989 =4990 =4991 =4992 =4993

*O 3 — ▽%5300 ƒ X5301 ƒ%5303 ƒ%5305 ▽5307 ▽ X5314 ▽5321 ▽5327 ƒ5332 ▽=5334 ▽=5336 ▽%5337

*M 1 — ƒ=6001 6002

▽X*M 2 — 6110

Gas Electric — 109

(70)

OTTUMWA DIVISION

K 1 — 617

K 2 — 633 637 642 644 647 651 656 657 660 664

K 4 — 700 703 705 711 712

G 3 — 1548

G 8 — 1713 1718 1720 1730 1732 1733 1739 1757

G 9 — 1823

G 9 A — 1805 1819 1826 1832 1839

*R 4 A — 2018

*R 5 — 2058 2103 2132 2138 2142

*R 5 A — 2062 2196 2215

*P 6 — 2582

*P 6 A — 2591

*S 1 A — X2815 =2839 =2844

*S 2 A — X2908 =2945

X*S 3 — 2950

X*S 3 A — 2951

*O 1 — 5024 5031 5038 5044

*O 1 A — 5123 5125

*O 3 — ƒ%5316 ▽%5317 ▽¶5318 ▽ X5319 ▽¶5320 ƒ%5322 ▽¶5325 aƒ%5328 ▽5329 ƒ%5330 ▽ X5331 ▽%5333 ▽=5338 ▽%5339 ƒ5340 ƒ¶5341 ƒ=5343 ƒ X5344 ƒ%5347 ƒ X5349 ƒ=5351 ƒ%5352 ƒ%5353 ƒ5354 ƒ5355 ƒ X5356 ƒ%5359

▽=†*O 5 — 5600 5602 5603

(85)

Total: 155

Beardstown Division

G 5 A — 513

*F 1 — 540 542 544 548

G 8 — 1729 1736

*R 4 — 1916

*R 5 — 2090 2111 2136

*F 3 — 5020

*O 1 — 5003 5006 5012 5014 5026 5032 5035 5037 5040 5043 5046 5049

*O 1 A — X4940 X4941 X4949 =4972 =5061 =5062 =5076 =5083 =5100 X5108 5118 X5120 =5122 5124 =5131 5133 X5140

ƒ X*O 3 — 5304

X*M 2 — ‡6101 ‡6102 ▽6107 ƒ6112 ‡6114 ▽6115 ‡6116 ‡6122 ƒ6123

ƒ*M 4 — =6310 =6311 =6312 =6313 =6314 =6315 X6316 X6317 X6318 X6319 X6320 X6322 X6326

C. & S.

=*E4 A — 800 801 803 804

Total: 68

HANNIBAL DIVISION

G 10 — 560 566 567 570 572 574

K 2 — 640 641 652 661 662

K 4 — 714

K 10 — 950 951 952 958 962

H 4 — 1220 1223 1224 1235 1240 1241 1257 1261 1262

G 3 — 1465 1486 1515 1522 *1545 *1557 *1563 *1573 *1574

G 6 — 1680 1684 1694

G 8 — 1711 1721 1727 1731 1735 1755

G 9 — 1817

G 9 A — 1825 1845

*R 4 — 1975

*R 5 — 2054 2085 2122 2158 2170 2192 2193 2198 2208

*R 5 A — 2052

*P 5 — 2552 2553 2555 2565 2569 2574

*P 6 — 2585

*P 6 A — 2595

*S 1 A — =2811 =†2813 =†2830 X2852

X*S 2 A — 2925 2937 2941 2944 2949

*S 3 — =o2952 X2958 =2959

X*S 3 A — 2962

*O 1 A — %5068 =5069 X5095 5101 5103 X5104 X5106 X5127 5128 =5145

*O 3 — ‡5306 ‡5308 ‡5313 ƒ X5315 ƒ5323 ƒ X5335

*M 2 A — ƒ X6108 ƒ X6109 ‡=6126 ▽ X6127 ƒ X6128 ‡ X6129 ƒ=6130 ƒ X6131 ƒ X6132 ‡ X6133 ▽ X6136 ƒ X6137 ▽ X6138 ƒ=6139 ƒ X6141 ƒ X6142 ▽ X6143 ƒ X6144 ƒ=6157

(114)

Q. O. & K. C. R. R.

*R 5 — 2050 2081 2125

*R 5 A — 2110 2191

(5)

Total: 119

ST. JOSEPH DIVISION

A 2 — 431

G 10 — 562 564 571 573 583 584 586 587 593 594

K 1 — 612 615

K 4 — 713 722

K 10 — 959

H 4 — 1255

G 6 — 1691

G 8 — 1712 1719 1728 1762

G 9 — 1842 1846

*R 4 — 1971

*R 4 A — 1949 1972

*R 5 — 2061 2117 2126 2153 2173 2199 2210

*R 5 A — 2057 2151

*P 5 — 2551 2554 2562

*P 6 — 2584

*P 6 A — 2593

X*S 1 A — 2800 2835 2855 2866 2867

*S 2 A — X2930 X2933 =2943

*O 1 — 5001 5004 5013 5021 5022 5025 5034 5048 5050 5054 5056

*O 2 A — ▽=5209 a▽=5222 ▽=5234 ƒ=5239 a▽=5247 ▽ X5249 ƒ X5259 ƒ=5278 ƒ=5284 ƒ=5295

*O 3 — ▽=5302 ƒ5310 ▽=5311 ƒ X5312

Gas-Elec. — 9111

Total: 75

OMAHA DIVISION

K 1 — 608 625

K 4 — 704 715 717

G 3 — *1528

G 8 — 1724 1725 1741 1742 1743 1744 1745 1747 1751 1752 1753 1754 1758 1761 1763 1765 1768

G 10 — 563 565 579 580 589 590

*R 4 — 1985

*R 5 — 2096 2145

*R5 A — 2149

*S 1 A — =2809 =2823 X2856

X*S 3 — 2953 2956 2963 2964 2967

D 4 A — 3119 *3138

*O 1 A — X5060 =5064 =5066 X5077 =5094 =5102 X5109 X5121 =5130

*O 3 — =ƒ5348

Diesel Electric — 9121

Total: 54

LINCOLN DIVISION

A 2 — 475

K 2 — 636 638 639 650 651

K 10 — 954 955 960 961 965 967

G 8 — 1716 1723 1734 1738 1746 1749 1756 1759 1766

G 10 — 575 576 577 585

*R 4 — 1928

R 5 — *2064 *2092 *2123

*R 5 A — 2053

*P 5 — ⊠2561 ⊠2568 2571

*S 1 A — X2827 X2837 X2864

*S 2 A — ⊠ X2916

⊠ X*S 3 — 2972

X*S 3 A — §2954

*O 1 — 5009 5041 5058

*O 1 A — X5071 =5085 X5088 =5096 =5098 =5105 X5107 X5110 X5111 X5112 X5114 5126 =5134 =5136 X5139 =5146

†⊠=▽*O5 — 5604 5605 5606 5607

ƒ*M 4 A — X6327

X⊠ƒ*B 1 — 7006

⊠Xƒ*B 1A — 7008 7012 7014

Diesel Electric — 9122

(68)

WYMORE DIVISION

K 1 — 627

K 2 — 632 634 649 653

K 4 — 701 710

H 4 — 1225 1227 1230 1233 1237 1254

G 3 — 1509 *1568 1576

G 8 — 1717 1764

*R 4 — a1910 1915 1956

*R 5 — 2075 2148

*P 5 — 2559 2563

*P 6 — 2581

*P 6 A — 2590 2594

*S 1 A — X2846

*S 2 A — =2903 X2907 X2923 X2928

X*S 3 — 2955 ⊠2957

*O 1 A — X5074 =5087 =5091 X5097 =5144

*O 2 A — =ƒ5254 =ƒ5280

ƒ*O 3 — X5342 =5345 =5346 =5350 X5357 X5358

Gas-Electric — 9120

Exhibition Engine — B&MR 35

(50)

Total: 118

McCOOK DIVISION

K 2 — 643

H 4 — 1228 1232 1242 1248

⊠G 6 — 1690

G 9 A — ⊠1812

□*R 4 — 1958 2016

*R 4 A — 1938

*R 5 — 2105

⊠*R 5 A — 2099

*P 5 — ⊠2558

*S 1 A — X2804 ⊠ X2826 ⊠=2832 ⊠ X2834 ⊠ X2849 ⊠=2862

*S 2 A — ⊠=2901 ⊠=2915

*S 3 — ⊠ X2960 ⊠ X2966 X2968 ⊠ X2969 ⊠ X2971

†*S 4 — =▽3007

*O 1 A — =5063 □=5070 ⊠ X5072 □ X5073 ⊠ X5075 X5078 ⊠ X5079 ⊠ X5080 ⊠ X5081 ⊠ X5082 □=5084 ⊠ X5086 □ X5089 ⊠ X5090 ⊠ X5092 ⊠ X5099 □ X5113 ⊠ X5115 ⊠=5117

⊠*O 2 A — =ƒ5237

▽=†*O 5 — ⊠5601

ƒ*M 4 A — X6324

⊠ X*B 1 — ƒ7005

⊠*B 1 A — Xƒ7009 Xƒ7010 =ƒ7011 Xƒ7013

(54)

STERLING DIVISION

§K 4 — 702 707 709 719

§K 10 — 966

G 8 — □1760

□R 4 — *1962

§*R 4 A — 1912 1937 1963 2005

§*R 5 — 2217

*O 2 A — §=5221 □ƒ=5276 □▽=5286

(15)

Denver

⊠G 6 — 1681 1686

G 8 — 1740

G 10 — □578 ⊠591 □592

*S 1 A — ⊠ X2857

⊠*S 2 A — =2922

*O 1 — □5010 □5023 □5027 5030 □5036 □5039 □5055 X5057 5059

(17)

Total: 86

ALLIANCE DIVISION

STERLING DIVISION

R 4 — □*1925 □*1930 □*1964

*R 4 A — §1948 □1957 ⊠1988 ⊠2027

*R 5 — §2077 □2084 §2204 §2211

*R 5 A — §2113 □2219

X*S 1 A — ⊠2806

*O 2 A — =§5207 X§5227 =§5228 X§5241

§*O 4 — X5500 X5504 X5507 X5509 =5512

(23)

LEASED

C & S

N. G. — 537

ƒ*O 2 A — =5200 =5206 =5215 =5252

ƒ*M 2 A — =6156

ƒ*M 3 — X6300 X6301 X6302 =6303 X6304 X6305 X6306 X6307 =6308 X6309

FW&DC

§*O 4 — X5502 =5514

B—RI

*R 5 A — §2189 §2222

Total: 20

ALLIANCE

§K 2 — 655 665

§G 3 — 1510 1553

§G 4 — 1668

§G 8 — 1737 1748 1750 1767

⊠*S 1 A — X2829 X2841 X2848 =2863

⊠*S 2 A — =2913

*S 3 — X§2961 X§2974

§D 4 A — 3170

§*T 2 — 4100 =4101 4105 =4106 =4107 4108

*O 1 — §5019

⊠*O 2 A — X▽5203 Xƒ5204 X▽5223 =ƒ5224 Xƒ5230 =ƒ5233 =ƒ5238 X▽5240 X▽5242 X▽5248 =ƒ5251 =ƒ5262 =ƒ5264 =ƒ5265 Xƒ5270 Xƒ5275 Xƒ5277 Xƒ5282 Xƒ5288 Xƒ5290 Xƒ5293

*M 2 A — ⊠ Xƒ6149 ⊠=ƒ6150 ⊠ Xƒ6151 ⊠ Xƒ6154 □ Xƒ6155 □ Xƒ6162 ⊠ Xƒ6164 ⊠=ƒ6166 ⊠ Xƒ6167

⊠*B 1 — Xƒ7000 Xƒ7002 Xƒ7004 Xƒ7007

C & S

§*C 3 — 330 331

*B 4 S — □530

(61)

Total: 84

CASPER DIVISION

§G 10 — 568 588

§K 10 — 968

§*R 4 — 1907 1942 1947 1955

§*R 4 A — 1924 2039

*R 5 — §2082

§*P 5 — 2564 2566

§*S 1 A — =2808 X2814 X2836 =2859

§*S 2 A — =2911 X2932

§D 4 A — 3114

*□D 4 B — 3188

*O 1 — X§5029

§*O 2 A — X5220 X5231 =5232 X5263 =5272 X5294 X5297

§*O 4 — X5501 =5503 =5505 =5506 X5508 =5510 =5511 X5513

(36)

SHERIDAN DIVISION

⊠G 6 — 1678 1679 1687 1688 1689

⊠*S 1 A — X2802

⊠*S 2 A — =2926

□*O 2 — ƒ5261

⊠*O 2 A — Xƒ5253 =ƒ5285 Xƒ5291

⊠*M 2 — Xƒ6105 Xƒ6125

⊠*M 2 A — Xƒ6134 Xƒ6135 =ƒ6140 =ƒ6145 Xƒ6146 =ƒ6147 Xƒ6148 Xƒ6152 Xƒ6153 Xƒ6158 Xƒ6159 =ƒ6160 =ƒ6161 Xƒ6163 Xƒ6165 =ƒ6168 =ƒ6169 =ƒ6170

⊠*B 1 — Xƒ7001 Xƒ7003

(33)

Total: 69

Stored Unserviceable

Lines West

□ƒ*O 2 — 5219 5256 5274 5281 5287 5296 5299

K 1 — 622

K 2 — 667

H 4 — 1236

R 5 — 2200

(11)

Lines East

A 2 — 417

G 3 — 1459

‡*M 2 — 6100 6103 6104 6106 X6111 6113 6117 6118 =6119 6120 6121 6124

ƒ X*M 4 — 6321 6323 6325

C. & S.

*C 3 H — 339

(18)

Total: 29

Total Locomotives Lines East 638

Total Locomotives Lines West 442

SHOP SWITCH ENGINES

Chicago	Galesburg	Ottumwa	Beardstown	Hannibal		St. Joseph	Omaha	Lincoln	Wymore	McCook	Sterling	Alliance (Sterling)	Alliance	Casper	Stored
300, 303	310	308, 312	302	301		307		305		306	304		311		Lines East 309

Total Shop Switch Engines Lines East 9

Total Shop Switch Engines Lines West 4

MOTOR CARS

Chicago		Galesburg	Ottumwa	Beardstown	Hannibal		St. Joseph	Omaha	Lincoln	Wymore	McCook	Sterling	Alliance (Sterling)	Alliance	Casper	Stored
9509 9565 9566 9772 9845 9846 9849	Zephyr 9901 9902	9450 9527 9528 9725 9726 9727 9767 9770 9811	9529 9733 9765 9769 9813 9837 9841 9850	9843	9530 9815 9816 9836 9844	9838 9839	9728 9731 9732 9814 9817	9729 9730	9568 9628 9812 9835 9840 Zephyr 9900	9847 9848	9734 9735 C & S 402		FW&DC 9842 C & S 9526 G. M. & N. 9525 9771		9571 9766 9768	Lines East 9505 9507
9		9	8	1	5	2	5	2	6	2	3		4		3	2

Total Motor Cars Lines East 41

Total Motor Cars Lines West 16

*SUPERHEATER §OIL BURNER ƒDUPLEX STOKER ▽DUPONT SIMPLEX STOKER ⊠L & B FRONT END =ELESCO FEED WATER HEATER
aAUTOMATIC TRAIN CONTROL %EXHAUST STEAM INJECTOR †BOOSTER XWORTHINGTON FEED WATER HEATER □LIGNITE COAL BURNER
‡STREET STOKER oNICHOLSON THERMIC SYPHON ¶ COFFIN FEED WATER HEATER

Chicago, Burlington & Quincy Railroad Company

ASSIGNMENT OF LOCOMOTIVES AND MOTOR CARS, FEBRUARY 1, 1952

LINES EAST									LINES WEST								
CHICAGO DIVISION			**GALESBURG DIVISION**			Beardstown Division	**HANNIBAL DIVISION**	St. Joseph Division	**LINCOLN DIVISION**			**McCOOK DIVISION**		**ALLIANCE DIVISION**		**CASPER DIVISION**	**LEASED**
AURORA DIVISION		La Crosse Division		Ottumwa Division	Creston Division		— / Brookfield Division		Omaha Division		Wymore Division		Denver	Sterling Division		Sheridan Division	

(The body of this table consists of dense columns of locomotive and motor car numbers and class designations distributed across the divisions listed above. The individual entries are not legibly reproducible.)

Summary totals (Lines East)

Steam		313
DE		127
GE		4
PMC		13
Shop Eng.		6
Exh. Eng.		1
Zep.		
Total Lines East		**564**

Summary totals (Lines West)

Steam		228
DE		72
GE		4
PMC		6
Shop Eng.		3
Total Lines West		**313**

Legend:

*SUPERHEATER ‖OIL BURNER ⌐STOKER †POPPET VALVES ⊠L & S FRONT END ▲RADIO §AUTOMATIC TRAIN CONTROL ⦿SECURITY CIRCULATORS

DE—DIESEL-ELECTRIC   GE—GAS-ELECTRIC   ⊠WORTHINGTON, ▬ELESCO, ‡WILSON—FEED WATER HEATERS   §—CAB SIGNALS

Locomotives of the Colorado & Southern
Narrow-Gauge Locomotives—1902[1]

C&S No.	Other Nos.	Builder	Date	Cylinders	Drivers	Engine Weight	Class Type
1[2]	UP 57	Mason	?[3]	14x16	38	38700	2-6-0
2[2]	UP 62	Brooks	?[3]	14x18	38	47400	2-6-0
3[2]	UP 63	Brooks	?	14x18	38	47400	2-6-0
4-5	UP 109-110	Cooke	1884	15x18	40	64000	2-6-0
6-10	UP 111-115	Cooke	1884	15x18	40	64700	2-6-0
11	UP 116	Cooke	1884	14x18	40	55299	2-6-0
12-13	UP 7-8	Cooke	1884	14x18	40	54000	2-6-0
14[2]	UP 3	Brooks	1882	15x18	38	46000	2-6-0
15-16[2]	UP 5-6	Brooks	1880	15x18	38	46000	2-6-0
17[2]	UP 161	Brooks	1882	15x18	38	52000	2-6-0
18-20[2]	UP 163-165	Brooks	1882	15x18	38	52000	2-6-0
21	UP 156	Brooks	1882	15x18	38	55000	2-6-0
22	UP 162	Brooks	1881	15x18	38	55000	2-6-0
30	UP 190	Baldwin	1880	15x18	37	53745	2-8-0
31[2]	UP 191	Baldwin	1880	15x18	37	53745	2-8-0
32[2]	UP ?	Baldwin	1880	15x18	37	53745	2-8-0
33-36[2]	UP 194-197	Baldwin	1880	15x18	37	53745	2-8-0
37-56	UP 198-217	Cooke	1883	15x18	37	54600	2-8-0
57-62	UP 260-265	Rhode Island	1886	16x18	37	61690	2-8-0
63-70	UP 266-273	Baldwin	1890	16x20	37	66000	2-8-0
71-73	UP 9-11	Baldwin	1897	15½x20	37	70500	2-8-0
74-75-76	DB&W 30-31-32	Brooks	1878	16x20	37	84730	2-8-0

[1]Built originally for the Denver, South Park & Pacific and the Colorado Central, later acquired and renumbered by Union Pacific.
[2]Sold prior to June 30th, 1903.
[3]Received in 1882, date of construction unknown.

1898-1958 Colorado & Southern Standard Gauge Locomotives

C&S Nos.	Other Numbers	Builder	Number	Date	Cyls.	Drivers	Engine Weight	Class	Type	Disposition
100	UP 395, CCJD 11, UP 32	Rogers	1472	1867	16x24	63	67100	C-2G	4-4-0	Out by 1903
101	UP 538, DT&FW 65, D&NO 5	Rogers	2874	1882	17x24	63	83100	C-2G	4-4-0	Sc. after 1918
102	UP 539, DT&FW 66, D &NO 6	Rogers	2875	1882	17x24	63	83100	C-2G	4-4-0	Out by 1903
103	UP 585	Schen.	1106	1878	17x24	61	75200	C-2G	4-4-0	Sold by 1902
104	UP 568, CC 5, UP 160	Taunton	462	1869	17x24	62	74500	C-2G	4-4-0	Out by 1903
105	UP 569, CC 6, UP 161	Taunton	463	1869	17x24	62	74500	C-2G	4-4-0	Out by 1903
106	UP 537, DT&FW 64, D&NO 4	Rogers	2873	1882	17x24	63	76000	C-2G	4-4-0	Sc. by 1902
107	UP 540, DT&FW 67, D&NO 7	Rogers	2876	1882	17x24	63	76000	C-2G	4-4-0	Sc. by 1903
108	UP 563, CCJD 8, UP 29	Rogers	1469	1867	17x24	63	77400	C-2G	4-4-0	Sc. by 1902
109	UP 564, CCJD 9, UP 30	Rogers	1470	1867	17x24	63	77400	C-2G	4-4-0	Sc. by 1903
110	UP 565, CCJD 10, UP 31	Rogers	1471	1867	17x24	63	77400	C-2G	4-4-0	Sc. by 6-1907
132	UP 521, DT&FW 111-4	Cooke	1856	1888	17x24	61	81000	C-2L	4-4-0	Out by 1904
133	UP 522, DT&FW 113-8	Cooke	1860	1888	17x24	61	81000	C-2L	4-4-0	Out by 1904
134	UP 523, DT&FW 118-13	Cooke	1865	1888	17x24	61	81000	C-2L	4-4-0	12-15-30
135	UP 524, DT&FW 120-15	Cooke	1867	1888	17x24	61	81000	C-2L	4-4-0	Out by 6-1907
136	UP 525, DT&FW 121-16	Cooke	1868	1888	17x24	61	81000	C-2L	4-4-0	Out by 1903
137	UP 526, DT&FW 122-17	Cooke	1869	1888	17x24	61	81000	C-2L	4-4-0	Out by 1903
138	UP 536, DT&FW 123-18	Cooke	1870	1888	17x24	61	81000	C-2L	4-4-0	Out by 1905
143	UP 630	Schen.	2792	1889	18x26	62	99000	C-2S	4-4-0	Sc. 1-5-25
144	UP 825 (Rebuilt 1892)	Hinkley		1867	18x26	69	102100	C-2F	4-4-0	Sc.
145	UP 830 (Rebuilt 1892)	Hinkley		1867	18x26	69	102100	C-2F	4-4-0	Sc.
200	C&S 502, UP 1117, DT&FW 125, C&T 27	Rh. Is.	1958	1888	17x24	51	82800	A-3B	0-6-0	Sc. 10-1-08
201	C&S 503, UP 1112	Baldwin	11395	1890	17x24	51	88000	A-3B	0-6-0	Sc.
202	C&S 504, UP 1113	Baldwin	11396	1890	17x24	51	88000	A-3B	0-6-0	Sc.
203	C&S 505, UP 1114	Baldwin	11402	1890	17x24	51	88000	A-3B	0-6-0	Sc.
204	C&S 506, UP 1115	Baldwin	11417	1890	17x24	51	88000	A-3B	0-6-0	Sc.
205	C&S 507, UP 1220, DT&FW 151, C&T 20	Rogers	3916	1888	18x24	51	94000	A-3C	0-6-0	Sc.
206	C&S 508, UP 1221, DT&FW 155, C&T 21	Rogers	3917	1888	18x24	51	94000	A-3C	0-6-0	Sc.
207	C&S 509, UP 1222, DT&FW 156, C&T 22	Rogers	3920	1888	18x24	51	94000	A-3C	0-6-0	Sc.
208	C&S 510, UP 1223, DT&FW 157, C&T 23	Rogers	3921	1888	18x24	51	94000	A-3C	0-6-0	Sc.
209	C&S 511, UP 1225, DT&FW 159, C&T 24	Rogers	3931	1888	18x24	51	94000	A-3C	0-6-0	Sc.
210	C&S 512, UP 1226, DT&FW 160, C&T 25	Rogers	3932	1888	18x24	51	96000	A-3C	0-6-0	Sc.
211	C&S 513, UP 1228, DT&FW 162, C&T 26	Rogers	3933	1888	18x24	51	94000	A-3C	0-6-0	Sc.
212	UP 1229, DT&FW 163	Cooke	1890	1888	18x24	51	113530	A-3D	0-6-0	Sc.
213	UP 1230, DT&FW 164	Cooke	1891	1888	18x24	51	113530	A-3D	0-6-0	Sold 10-29-26 Sc.
214	C&S 206, UP 1216, DT&G 69	Cooke	1886	1888	18x24	51	113530	A-3D	0-6-0	Sc.
215	C&S 208, UP 1218, DT&G 71	Cooke	1888	1888	18x24	51	113530	A-3D	0-6-0	Sc.
216	C&S 209, UP 1219, DT&G 72	Cooke	1889	1888	18x24	51	113530	A-3D	0-6-0	Sc.
220		Cooke	40238	1906	19x26	51	141920	A-3E	0-6-0	Sc. 1934
221		Cooke	40239	1906	19x26	51	141920	A-3E	0-6-0	Sc. 1934
222		Cooke	40240	1906	19x26	51	141920	A-3E	0-6-0	Sc. 1935

C&S Nos.	Other Numbers	Builder	Number	Date	Cyls.	Drivers	Engine Class Weight	Type	Disposition
223		Cooke	40241	1906	19x26	51	141920 A-3E	0-6-0	Sc. 11-20-46
224		Cooke	40242	1906	19x26	51	141920 A-3E	0-6-0	Sc. 8-19-46
225		Schen.	44317	1907	19x26	51	141920 A-3E1	0-6-0	Sc. 1935
226		Schen.	44318	1907	19x26	51	141920 A-3E1	0-6-0	Sc. 3-20-26
227		Schen.	44319	1907	19x26	51	141920 A-3E1	0-6-0	Sc. 10-25-47
228		Schen.	44320	1907	19x26	51	141920 A-3E1	0-6-0	Sc. 10-19-47
229		Schen.	44321	1907	19x26	51	141920 A-3E1	0-6-0	Sc. 1939
230		Schen.	44322	1907	19x26	51	141920 A-3E1	0-6-0	Sc. 1934
231		Schen.	44323	1907	19x26	51	141920 A-3E1	0-6-0	Sc. 10-17-46
232		Baldwin	35257	1910	19x26	51	151800 A-3E2	0-6-0	Sc. 6-9-43
233		Baldwin	35258	1910	19x26	51	151800 A-3E2	0-6-0	Sc. 3-10-47
234		Baldwin	25259	1910	19x26	51	151800 A-3E2	0-6-0	Sc. 2-27-47
235		Baldwin	35260	1910	19x26	51	151800 A-3E2	0-6-0	Sc. 8-31-46
236		Baldwin	35269	1910	19x26	51	151800 A-3E2	0-6-0	Sc. 8-27-48
250	C&S 214, UP 1362, DT&G 75	Rogers	4064	1888	17x24	56	105000 B-3H	2-6-0	Sc.
251	C&S 215, UP 1363, DT&G 76	Rogers	4065	1888	17x24	56	105000 B-3H	2-6-0	Sc. 9-1922
252	C&S 207, UP 1217, DT&G 70	Cooke	1887	1888	18x24	51	96200 B-3J	2-6-0	Sc. 5-1911
253	C&S 210, UP 1224, DT&FW 158-34	Cooke	1884	1888	18x24	51	96200 B-3J	2-6-0	Sc. 2-1914
254	C&S 211, UP 1227, DT&FW 161-36	Cooke	1885	1888	18x24	51	96200 B-3J	2-6-0	Sc.
300	UP 1037, DT&FW 150, C&T 1	Rogers	3812	1887	17x24	56	93400 C-3A	4-6-0	Out by 1907
301	UP 1038, DT&FW 152. C&T 2	Rogers	3830	1887	17x24	56	93400 C-3A	4-6-0	Out by 1903
302	UP 1039, DT&FW 153, C&T 5	Rogers	3868	1887	17x24	56	93400 C-3A	4-6-0	Sc.
303	UP 1040, DT&FW 154, C&T 6	Rogers	3870	1887	17x24	56	93400 C-3A	4-6-0	Sc.
304	UP 913, CC 92, UP 92	Baldwin	1716	1868	18x24	56	86300 C-3B	4-6-0	Out by 1903
305	UP 958, CC 12, UP 236	Taunton	777	1881	18x24	56	86350 C-3B	4-6-0	Sc.
306	UP 959, CC 13, UP 237	Taunton	778	1881	18x24	56	86350 C-3B	4-6-0	Sc.
307	UP 961, CC 15, UP 251	Taunton	797	1881	18x24	56	86350 C-3B	4-6-0	Sold 1902
308	UP 912, CC 91, UP 91	Baldwin	1715	1868	18x24	56	86300 C-3B	4-6-0	Sc. 1902
309	UP 1408	Rh. Is.	2455	1890	19x24	62	135000 C-3E	4-6-0	Sc. 10-1936
310	UP 1411	Rh. Is.	2458	1890	19x24	62	135000 C-3E	4-6-0	Sc. 8-1928
311	UP 1413	Rh. Is.	2460	1890	19x24	62	135000 C-3E	4-6-0	Sc. 1926
312	UP 1406	Rh. Is.	2453	1890	19x24	62	135000 C-3E	4-6-0	Sold 1938
313	UP 1409	Rh. Is.	2456	1890	19x24	62	135000 C-3E	4-6-0	Sc. 1926
314	UP 1412	Rh. Is.	2459	1890	19x24	62	135000 C-3E	4-6-0	Sc. 9-29-23
315	UP 1405	Rh. Is.	2452	1890	19x24	62	135000 C-3E	4-6-0	Sc. 1927
316	UP 1407	Rh. Is.	2454	1890	19x24	62	135000 C-3E	4-6-0	Sold 1924
317	UP 1410	Rh. Is.	2457	1890	19x24	62	135000 C-3E	4-6-0	Sc. 1926
318	UP 1414	Rh. Is.	2461	1890	19x24	62	135000 C-3E	4-6-0	Sc. 1927
319	UP 1415	Rh. Is.	2462	1890	19x24	62	135000 C-3E	4-6-0	Sc. 1926
320		Rh. Is.	3208	1900	20x26	63	135000 C-3G	4-6-0	Sc. 1925
321		Rh. Is.	3209	1900	20x26	63	135000 C-3G	4-6-0	Sc. 1926
322		Rh. Is.	3210	1900	20x26	63	135000 C-3G	4-6-0	Sc. 1925
323		Schen.	25226	1902	20x28	67	169500 C-3H	4-6-0	Sc. 1935
324		Schen.	27314	1903	20x28	67	186380 C-3H	4-6-0	Sc. 1936
325		Schen.	27315	1903	20x28	67	186380 C-3H	4-6-0	Sc. 1936
326		Schen.	27316	1903	20x28	67	186380 C-3H	4-6-0	Sc. 1936
327		Brooks	40235	1906	20x28	67	187450 C-3H	4-6-0	Sc. 6-2-45
328		Brooks	40236	1906	20x28	67	187450 C-3H	4-6-0	Sc. 1939
329		Brooks	40237	1906	20x28	67	187450 C-3H	4-6-0	Sc. 1942
330		Baldwin	31153	1907	20x28	67	187450 C-3H1	4-6-0	Sc. 9-7-50
331		Baldwin	31195	1907	20x28	67	187450 C-3H1	4-6-0	Sc.
350		Baldwin	35771	1911	25x28	69	243300 F-3A	4-6-2	Sc. 9-7-50
351		Baldwin	35772	1911	25x28	69	243300 F-3A	4-6-2	Sc. 7-31-47
352		Baldwin	35795	1911	25x28	69	243300 F-3A	4-6-2	Sc. 6-14-47
353		Baldwin	35796	1911	25x28	69	243300 F-3A	4-6-2	Sc. 6-15-51
354		Baldwin	35797	1911	25x28	69	243300 F-3A	4-6-2	Sc. 1938
370	CB&Q 2970	Baldwin	48731	1918	27x28	74	276400 F-3B	4-6-2	Sc. 10-30-53
371	CB&Q 2973	Baldwin	49071	1918	27x28	74	276400 F-3B	4-6-2	Sc. 10-20-53
372	CB&Q 2965	Baldwin	48261	1918	27x28	74	276400 F-3B	4-6-2	Sold for Scrap 11-60
373		Baldwin	55569	1922	27x28	69	301070 F-3C	4-6-2	Sc. 4-18-55
374		Baldwin	55570	1922	27x28	69	301070 F-3C	4-6-2	Sold for Scrap 10-60
375		Baldwin	55571	1922	27x28	69	301070 F-3C	4-6-2	Sc. 9-1953
400	UP 1364, DT&G 73	Pittsbg.	1008	1888	18x24	51	107000 B-4H	2-8-0	Sc.
401	UP 1365, DT&G 74	Pittsbg.	1009	1888	18x24	51	107000 B-4H	2-8-0	Sold
402	UP 1312, DT&FW 200	Baldwin	10361	1889	20x24	51	124400 B-4H	2-8-0	Sold to T&BV No. 8
403	UP 1313, DT&FW 201	Baldwin	10360	1889	20x24	51	124400 B-4H	2-8-0	Sold to T&BV No. 9
404	UP 1314, DT&FW 202	Baldwin	10365	1889	20x24	51	124400 B-4H	2-8-0	Sold to T&BV No. 10
405	UP 1315, DT&FW 203	Baldwin	19363	1889	20x24	51	124400 B-4H	2-8-0	Sold to T&BV No. 11
406	UP 1316, DT&FW 204	Baldwin	10364	1889	20x24	51	124400 B-4H	2-8-0	Sold to T&BV No. 12
407	UP 1317, DT&FW 205	Baldwin	10431	1890	20x24	51	124400 B-4H	2-8-0	Sold to T&BV No. 13
408	UP 1318, DT&FW 206	Baldwin	10433	1890	20x24	51	124400 B-4H	2-8-0	Sold to T&BV No. 14
409	UP 1319, DT&FW 207	Baldwin	10434	1890	20x24	51	124400 B-4H	2-8-0	Sold to T&BV No. 15
410	UP 1320, DT&FW 208	Baldwin	10435	1890	20x24	51	124400 B-4H	2-8-0	Sold to T&BV No. 16
411	UP 1321, DT&FW 209	Baldwin	10436	1890	20x24	51	124400 B-4H	2-8-0	Sold to T&BV No. 17
412	UP 1322, DT&FW 210	Rh. Is.	2318	1890	20x24	51	124400 B-4H	2-8-0	Sold to T&BV No. 18
413	UP 1323, DT&FW 211-120	Rh. Is.	2340	1890	20x24	51	124400 B-4H	2-8-0	Sold to T&BV No. 19
414	UP 1324, DT&FW 212	Rh. Is.	2342	1890	20x24	51	124400 B-4H	2-8-0	Sold to T&BV No. 20
415	UP 1325, DT&FW 213	Rh. Is.	2343	1890	20x24	51	124400 B-4H	2-8-0	Sold to T&BV No. 21
416	UP 1326, DT&FW 214	Rh. Is.	2344	1890	20x24	51	124400 B-4H	2-8-0	Sold to T&BV No. 22
417	UP 1327, DT&FW 215	Rh. Is.	2345	1890	20x24	51	124400 B-4H	2-8-0	Sold to T&BV No. 23
418	UP 1328, DT&FW 216-122	Rh. Is.	2341	1890	20x24	51	124400 B-4H	2-8-0	Sold to T&BV No. 24
419	UPD&G 100	Baldwin	15139	1897	20x24	51	138300 B-4H	2-8-0	Sold to T&BV No. 25

C&S Nos.	Other Numbers	Builder	Number	Date	Cyls.	Drivers	Engine Class Weight	Type	Disposition
420	UPD&G 101	Baldwin	15140	1897	20x24	51	138300 B-4H	2-8-0	Sold to T&BV No. 26
421	UPD&G 102	Baldwin	15141	1897	20x24	51	138300 B-4H	2-8-0	Sold to T&BV No. 27
422	UPD&G 103	Baldwin	15608	1897	20x24	51	126700 B-4M	2-8-0	Sc. 1929
423	UPD&G 104	Baldwin	15609	1897	19x26	51	126700 B-4M	2-8-0	Sc. 1927
424	UPD&G 105	Baldwin	15610	1897	20x28	51	126700 B-4M	2-8-0	Sc. 1927
425	UPD&G 106	Baldwin	15611	1897	20x28	51	126700 B-4M	2-8-0	Sc. 1928
426	UPD&G 107	Baldwin	15612	1897	20x26	51	126700 B-4M	2-8-0	Sc. 1929
427	UPD&G	Baldwin	17178	1899	20x26	51	126700 B-4M	2-8-0	Sc. 1929
428		Baldwin	17653	1900	20x26	51	142800 B-4M	2-8-0	Sc. 1935
429	C&S 450	Cooke	2510	1900	19x26	51	144700 B-4M	2-8-0	Sc. 1931
451		Rh. Is.	3203	1900	21x28	57	163360 B-4P	2-8-0	Sc. 1931
452		Rh. Is.	3204	1900	21x28	57	163360 B-4P	2-8-0	Sc. 1934
453		Rh. Is.	3205	1900	21x28	57	163360 B-4P	2-8-0	Sc. 1931
454		Rh. Is.	3206	1900	21x28	57	163360 B-4P	2-8-0	Sc. 1932
455	UP 1361, DT&FW 19	Rh. Is.	3207	1900	21x28	57	163360 B-4P	2-8-0	12-29-47
501	UP 1361, DT&FW 19	Cooke	1875	1888	17x24	49	60100	0-4-0	Sc.
520		Rh. Is.	27302	1903	22½x32½	57	206100 B-4S	2-8-0	Sc. 1939
521		Rh. Is.	27303	1903	22½x32	57	206100 B-4S	2-8-0	Sc. 4-3-48
522		Rh. Is.	27304	1903	22½x32	57	206100 B-4S	2-8-0	Sc. 2-28-52
523		Rh. Is.	27305	1903	22½x32	57	206100 B-4S	2-8-0	Sc. 9-12-47
524		Rh. Is.	27306	1903	22½x32	57	206100 B-4S	2-8-0	Sc. 1940
525		Rh. Is.	27307	1903	22½x32	57	206100 B-4S	2-8-0	Sc. 1939
526		Rh. Is.	27308	1903	22½x32	57	206100 B-4S	2-8-0	Sc. 1940
527		Rh. Is.	27309	1903	22½x32	57	206100 B-4S	2-8-0	Sc. 1954
528		Rh. Is.	27310	1903	22½x32	57	206100 B-4S	2-8-0	Sc. 8-16-54
529		Rh. Is.	27311	1903	22½x32	57	206100 B-4S	2-8-0	Sc. 4-14-48
530		Rh. Is.	27312	1903	22½x32	57	206100 B-4S	2-8-0	Sc. 9-6-56
531		Rh. Is.	27313	1903	22½x32	57	206100 B-4S	2-8-0	Sc. 5-1955
600	C&S 460	Rh. Is.	3301	1901	22x28	57	194180 B-4R	2-8-0	Sc. 1928
601	C&S 461	Rh. Is.	3302	1901	22x28	57	194180 B-4R	2-8-0	Sc. 1928
602	C&S 462	Rh. Is.	3303	1901	22x28	57	194180 B-4R	2-8-0	Sc. 2-61
603	C&S 463	Rh. Is.	3304	1901	22x28	57	194180 B-4R	2-8-0	Sc. 1926
604	C&S 464	Rh. Is.	3305	1901	22x28	57	194180 B-4R	2-8-0	Sold G & E
605	C&S 465	Rh. Is.	3306	1901	22x28	57	194180 B-4R	2-8-0	Sold for scrap 12-60
606	C&S 466	Rh. Is.	3307	1901	22x28	57	194180 B-4R	2-8-0	Sc. 1929
607	C&S 467	Rh. Is.	3308	1901	22x28	57	194180 B-4R	2-8-0	Sc. 1934
608	C&S 468	Rh. Is.	3309	1901	22x28	57	194180 B-4R	2-8-0	Sold for scrap 12-60
609	C&S 469	Rh. Is.	3310	1901	22x28	57	194180 B-4R	2-8-0	Sc. 1933
610	C&S 470	Richmd.	25853	1902	22x28	57	191701 B-4R	2-8-0	Sc. 9-6-56
611	C&S 471	Richmd.	25854	1902	22x28	57	191701 B-4R	2-8-0	Sc. 1939
612	C&S 472	Richmd.	25855	1902	22x28	57	191701 B-4R	2-8-0	Sc. -55
613	C&S 473	Richmd.	25856	1902	22x28	57	191701 B-4R	2-8-0	Sc. 1927
614	C&S 474	Richmd.	25857	1902	22x28	57	191701 B-4R	2-8-0	Sc. 1927
615	C&S 475	Richmd.	25858	1902	22x28	57	191701 B-4R	2-8-0	Sc. 1929
616	C&S 476	Richmd.	25859	1902	22x28	57	191701 B-4R	2-8-0	Sc. 6-15-51
617	C&S 477	Richmd.	25860	1902	22x28	57	191701 B-4R	2-8-0	Sc. 1929
618	C&S 478	Richmd.	25861	1902	22x28	57	191701 B-4R	2-8-0	Sc. 1940
619	C&S 479	Richmd.	25862	1902	22x28	57	191701 B-4R	2-8-0	Sc. 9-6-56
620	C&S 480	Richmd.	25863	1902	22x28	57	191701 B-4R	2-8-0	Sc. 4-61
621	C&S 481	Richmd.	25864	1902	22x28	57	191701 B-4R	2-8-0	Sc. 1930
622	C&S 482	Richmd.	25865	1902	22x28	57	191701 B-4R	2-8-0	Sc. 1940
623	C&S 483	Richmd.	25866	1902	22x28	57	191701 B-4R	2-8-0	Sc. 1927
624	C&S 484	Richmd.	25867	1902	22x28	57	191701 B-4R	2-8-0	Sc. 1924
625		Brooks	40252	1906	22x28	57	191701 B-4R	2-8-0	Sc. 1927
626		Brooks	40253	1906	22x28	57	191701 B-4R	2-8-0	Sc. 1927
627		Brooks	40254	1906	22x28	57	191701 B-4R	2-8-0	Sc. 1936
628		Brooks	40255	1906	22x28	57	191701 B-4R	2-8-0	Sc. 1934
629		Brooks	40256	1906	22x28	57	191701 B-4R	2-8-0	Sold for scrap 12-60
630		Brooks	40257	1906	22x26	57	191701 B-4R	2-8-0	Sc. 1934
631		Brooks	40258	1906	22x28	57	191701 B-4R	2-8-0	Sold for scrap 12-60
632		Brooks	40259	1906	22x28	57	191701 B-4R	2-8-0	Sold for scrap 12-60
633		Brooks	40260	1906	22x28	57	191701 B-4R	2-8-0	Sc. 4-18-55
634		Brooks	49261	1906	22x28	57	191701 B-4R	2-8-0	Sold for scrap 12-60
635		Brooks	40262	1906	22x28	57	191701 B-4R	2-8-0	Sc. 1935
636		Brooks	40263	1906	22x28	57	191701 B-4R	2-8-0	Sc. 1927
637		Brooks	40264	1906	22x28	57	191701 B-4R	2-8-0	Sc. 1936
638		Brooks	40265	1906	22x28	57	191701 B-4R	2-8-0	
639		Brooks	40266	1906	22x28	57	191701 B-4R	2-8-0	Sc. 1927
640		Brooks	40267	1906	22x28	57	191701 B-4R	2-8-0	Sc. 9-6-56
641		Brooks	40268	1906	22x28	57	191701 B-4R	2-8-0	**Leadville**
642		Brooks	40269	1906	22x28	57	191701 B-4R	2-8-0	Sc. 1927
643		Brooks	40270	1906	22x28	57	191701 B-4R	2-8-0	Sc. 1927
644		Baldwin	30996	1907	22x28	57	194650 B-4R1	2-8-0	Sold for scrap 12-60
645		Baldwin	31017	1907	22x28	57	194650 B-4R1	2-8-0	Sc. 1941
646		Baldwin	31018	1907	22x28	57	194650 B-4R1	2-8-0	Sold for scrap 4-59
647		Baldwin	31066	1907	22x28	57	194650 B-4R1	2-8-0	Sold for scrap 12-60
648		Baldwin	31067	1907	22x28	57	194650 B-4R1	2-8-0	Sold for scrap 12-60
649		Baldwin	31166	1907	22x28	57	194650 B-4R1	2-8-0	Sc. 1934
700		Baldwin	31272	1907	21x28	57	181950 B-4Q1	2-8-0	Sc. 1927
701		Baldwin	31273	1907	21x28	57	181950 B-4Q1	2-8-0	Sc. 1927
702		Baldwin	31289	1907	21x28	57	181950 B-4Q1	2-8-0	Sc. 1928
703		Baldwin	31290	1907	21x28	57	181950 B-4Q1	2-8-0	Sc. 1927
704		Baldwin	31291	1907	21x28	57	181950 B-4Q1	2-8-0	Sc. 1932
705		Baldwin	31330	1907	21x28	57	181950 B-4Q1	2-8-0	Sc. 1929

706		Baldwin	31331	1907	21x28	57	181950	B-4Q1	2-8-0 Sc. 1931
707		Baldwin	31358	1907	21x28	57	181950	B-4Q1	2-8-0 Sc. 1928
708		Baldwin	31385	1907	21x28	57	181950	B-4Q1	2-8-0 Sc. 1930
800		Baldwin	35894	1911	26½x30	57	283340	E-4A	2-8-2 Sold Sc. 4-59
801		Baldwin	35895	1911	26½x30	57	283340	E-4A	2-8-2 Sc. 9-25-56
802		Baldwin	35896	1911	26½x30	57	283340	E-4A	2-8-2 Sold Sc. 4-59
803		Baldwin	35897	1911	26½x30	57	283340	E-4A	2-8-2 Sold Sc. 4-59
804		Baldwin	35898	1911	26¼x30	57	283340	E-4A	2-8-2 Sc. 11-18-53
804	CB&Q 5500 (USRA)	Baldwin	51552	1919	27x32	63	320950	0-4	2-8-2 Sold Sc. 12-60
805	CB&Q 5506 (USRA)	Baldwin	51613	1919	27x32	63	320950	0-4	2-8-2 Sold Sc. 12-60
806	CB&Q 5507 (USRA)	Baldwin	51614	1919	27x32	63	320950	0-4	2-8-2 Sold Sc. 12-60
807	CB&Q 5508 (USRA)	Baldwin	51615	1919	27x32	63	320950	0-4	2-8-2 Sold Sc. 12-60
808	CB&Q 5509 (USRA)	Baldwin	51616	1919	27x32	63	320950	0-4	2-8-2 Sold Sc. 12-60
809	CB&Q 5513 (USRA)	Baldwin	51620	1919	27x32	63	320950	0-4	2-8-2 Sold Sc. 12-60
900		Baldwin	42082	1915	30x32	60	376245	E-5A	2-10-2 Sold Sc. 4-59
901		Baldwin	42083	1915	30x32	60	376245	E-5A	2-10-2 Sc. 9-25-56
902		Baldwin	42084	1915	30x32	60	376245	E-5A	2-10-2 Sc. 6-61
903		Baldwin	42085	1915	30x32	60	376245	E-5A	2-10-2 Sold Sc. 4-59
904		Baldwin	42086	1915	30x32	60	376245	E-5A	2-10-2 Sold Sc. 12-60
905	(USRA)	Baldwin	51983	1919	30x32	63	387284	E-5B	2-10-2 Sc. 4-1955
906	(USRA)	Baldwin	52002	1919	30x32	63	387284	E-5B	2-10-2 Sc. 3-9-54
907	(USRA)	Baldwin	52003	1919	30x32	63	387284	E-5B	2-10-2 Sc. 4-18-55
908	(USRA)	Baldwin	52004	1919	30x32	63	387284	E-5B	2-10-2 Sc. 3-17-54
909	(USRA)	Baldwin	52005	1919	30x32	63	387284	E-5B	2-10-2 Sold Sc. 12-60
910		Baldwin	55574	1922	30x32	60	404070	E-5C	2-10-2 Sc. 4-18-54
911		Baldwin	55575	1922	30x32	60	404070	E-5C	2-10-2 Sc. 9-25-56
912		Baldwin	55623	1922	30x32	60	404070	E-5C	2-10-2 Sc. 9-25-56
913		Baldwin	55624	1922	30x32	60	400810	E-5C	2-10-2 Sc. 9-25-56
914		Baldwin	55625	1922	30x32	60	405710	E-5C	2-10-2 Sold Sc. 12-60

Where a previous number is shown, it is the number the engine bore prior to the final renumbering of 1906.
Engs. 520-531 were originally Tandem Compound, with cylinders 16X28&32 and weighed 178000, were rebuilt in the 1920's.
Engs. 804-809 purchased in 1957. No. 804 duplicated. Eng. 5509 never renumbered C&S 808, but was delivered and never used.
Union Pacific original numbers if below 300, 1885 renumbering if above 300.

NOTES & ABBREVIATIONS FOR ROSTER
C&S—Colorado & Southern Ry.
C&T—Colorado & Texas Ry. Const. Co.
CB&Q—Chicago, Burlington & Quincy
CC—Colorado Central
CCJD—Colo. Central Julesburg Distr.
D&NO—Denver & New Orleans
DT&FW—Denver, Texas & Ft. Worth
DT&G—Denver, Texas & Gulf
T&BV—Trinity & Brazos Valley
UP—Union Pacific
UPD&G—Union Pacific, Denver & Gulf

Locomotives of the Fort Worth & Denver

Number	Builder	Date	Type	Cylinders	Drivers	Boiler Pressure	Weight	Tractive Effort
1-2	Schenectady	1881	4-4-0	17x24	60			
3	Danforth & Cooks	1881	4-4-0	17x24	57		42,200	
6-8	Danforth & Cooke	1881	4-4-0	17x24	57		42,200	
9-10	Cooke	1885	4-4-0	17x24	54		48,650	
11-12	Cooke	1886	4-4-0	17x24	60			
13-16	Schenectady	1886	4-4-0	17x24	63		48,450	
17-20	Cooke	1887	4-4-0	17x24	60		48,650	
21-22	Schenectady	1886	2-6-0	18x24	52		78,500	
23-24	Schenectady	1887	2-6-0	18x24	52		78,500	
25-26	Cooke	1888	4-4-0	17x24	60		48,650	
27-30	Rhode Island	1888	4-4-0	17x24	62		52,000	
31	Cooke	1888	0-4-0	16x24	48			
32-33	Cooke	1888	2-6-0	18x24	52		78,600	
34	Schenectady	1889	4-4-0	18x26	62		62,000	
35	Rome	1888	4-4-0	18x26	62		59,600	
36-37	Schenectady	1889	4-4-0	18x26	62		62,000	
38	Schenectady	1890	4-4-0	18x24	62		62,000	
39-40	Brooks	1889	4-4-0	18x26	62		62,000	
50-51	Schenectady	1906	0-6-0	20x26	51		145,000	
60-62	Richmond	1907	0-6-0	19x26	51		138,450	
63-67	Richmond	1908	0-6-0	19x26	51		138,450	
101-105	Rhode Island	1900	4-6-0	20x26	63		118,000	
106-107	Schenectady	1902	4-6-0	18x26	67		135,000	
108-109	Schenectady	1903	4-6-0	18x26	67		135,000	
110-111	Schenectady	1903	4-6-0	18x26	67		98,000	
150-155	Brooks	1906	4-6-0	20x28	67		138,500	
156-157	Richmand	1907	4-6-0	21x28	69		146,500	
201	Rhode Island	1903	2-8-0	20x28	57		142,000	
202	Rhode Island	1903	2-8-0	20x28	50	200	158,875	
203-204	Rhode Island	1903	2-8-0	20x28	57		142,000	
205	Rhode Island	1903	2-8-0	20x28	50	200	158,875	
206-211	Rhode Island	1903	2-8-0	20x28	57		142,000	
250-252	Rogers	1906	2-8-0	20x28	57		157,000	
253-262	Richmond	1907	2-8-0	20x28	57		161,300	
263-265	Richmond	1908	2-8-0	20x28	57		161,300	
301	Brooks	1906	2-8-0	22x28	57		173,051	
302	Brooks	1906	2-8-0	22x28	50	200	200,854	40,418
303	Brooks	1906	2-8-0	22x28	57		173,051	
304	Brooks	1906	2-8-0	22x28	50	200	200,854	40,418

305-309	Brooks	1906	2-8-0	22x28	57		173,051	
310-311	Richmond	1908	2-8-0	22x28	57		173,051	
312	Richmond	1908	2-8-0	22x28	50	200	202,204	40,418
313	Richmond	1908	2-8-0	22x28	57		173,051	
314	Richmond	1908	2-8-0	22x28	50	200	202,204	40,418
401-410	Baldwin	1915	2-8-2	27x30	56	200	274,000	58,092
451-452	Baldwin	1919	2-8-2	27x32	56	200	319,500	62,949
454-455	Baldwin	1919	2-8-2	27x32	56	200	319,500	62,949
456-460	Baldwin	1920	2-8-2	28x32	56	200	320,000	66,640
461-463	Baldwin	1922	2-8-2	28x32	56	200	327,775	66,640
464-465	Baldwin	1922	2-8-2	28x32	56	200	334,445	66,640
501	Baldwin	1911	4-6-2	25x28	62	200	236,875	43,110
552	Alco	1920	4-6-2	27x28	66	200	296,775	46,890
554	Alco	1920	4-6-2	27x28	66	200	296,775	46,890
501	Baldwin	1910	4-6-2	25x28	69	160	197,000	34,500
502-505	Baldwin	1911	4-6-2	25x28	69	160	197,000	34,500
551-555	Baldwin	1920	4-6-2	27x28	74	180	283,000	42,200
556-557	Baldwin	1922	4-6-2	27x28	74	200	284,200	42,200

Weight on drivers is given for all locomotives except Nos. 106-109, 202, 302, 312, 314, and 401-554, for which engine weight is given.

The above roster, compiled from Colorado & Southern annual reports, builders' records, and Fort Worth & Denver motive power records, is unfortunately incomplete. It is virtually certain, for instance, that engines numbered 4 and 5 were built by Danforth & Cooke along with the others in 1881, though no records remain.

Section 5

MISCELLANEOUS PHOTOGRAPHS

A view of the engine terminal at Casper, Wyo. No. 5272, Class O-2-B is shown moving on to the turntable in Sept., 1937.
—B. G. Corbin Collection

The Burlington & Missouri River Railroad's "Lt. Gen. Grant" locomotive was an early switch engine built by the New Jersey Locomotive Works in 1866. This engine was renumbered to CB&Q No. 244 in 1875. —Burlington Route.

Class E-1, No. 1382, on an early day work-train. Princeton, Ill. in 1899.

—B. G. Corbin Collection.

Air failure and a leaky throttle caused No. 5349 to burry her nose in the Council Bluffs turntable pit on Nov. 22, 1954.   —Co. Bluffs Nonpareil.

A mishap on the

Edwards River east

of New Boston, Ill.

in March, 1909.

—R. R. Wallin

Collection

Engine No. 59 was backing up light on grade-filling work at New Market, Iowa in 1912 when it derailed and landed upright.

—B. G. Corbin Collection.

The result of 4-4-0 engine No. 305 hitting a cow while backing up at Milford, Nebr. in Oct., 1907.

—B. G. Corbin Collection.

All that was left of the boiler of Pacific No. 2818 when it exploded on trian No. 8
coming into the Omaha station on July 19, 1933.   —Bostwick Studio.

The devastated chassis of No. 2818.

The result of a collision between a switcher and a 2-6-2 Prairie in the Denver yards in 1910.

—B. G. Corbin Collection.

High water at Omaha. The Missouri River played havoc with rail operations in 1943. Amphibious engine No. 1753 splashes her way through the yards.

—B. G. Corbin Collection.

An accident at Stanton, Iowa in 1921. A west-bound Class S-3 Pacific on Train No. 1 plowed into the wreckage of two east-bound freights which had scattered cars over the tracks. The entire incident had occurred so quickly that No. 1 was unable to be flagged down.
—B. G. Corbin Collection.

Engine No. 141, Class A-1, brings its train to a station stop at New Market, Iowa in 1905. This was on the Humeston & Shenandoah Railroad built in 1885, later taken over by the Keokuk & Western and then the CB&Q. The road was torn up in 1945.

— B. G. Corbin Collection

Many of the S-1A and S-2A Pacifics spent their last days in surburban train service between Aurora and Chicago, Ill. No. 2850 heads a westbound train through La Grange, Ill. on a warm August day in 1949. Those 8 early-vintage, open-platform coaches have vanished from the railroad scene along with the veteran 4-6-2.
— Jim Scribbins

Mikado No. 4999 arrives in Centralia, Illinois with a train load of coal from the mines near Herrin Junction on November 22, 1957.

— Ray Burhmaster

Westbound local freight pulled by a Class O1-A, No. 4976 has power to spare for its five cars as it rolls across the prairie near Atlanta, Nebraska on July 3, 1953.
— Ray Burhmaster

Coffin feedwater equipped Mikado No. 5318 moves a freight upgrade through Red Oak, Iowa, July 26, 1942.

— B. G. Corbin

Under the broken clouds on a late afternoon day in April, 1945, engine No. 6325 rolls a freight under the signals through Hastings, Iowa.　— Wm. Phillips

Hudson No. 3000 rounds a curve with 13 cars of train No. 48, The Blackhawk (Minneapolis to Chicago), at Rochelle, Ill. in August 1947. The graceful 4-6-4 types were among the finest mechanisms created by man, especially the class S-4 engines on the Burlington.

— Jim Scribbins

Mountain type passenger engine No. 7015 was built by Baldwin in 1925. Several of this type engine were equipped with a box-pok main wheel center and roller bearings on the driver axles.

— Burlington Photo

A powerful 4-8-4, No. 5634, eases westbound tonnage away from the N. Y. C. connection at Zearing, Ill. in November 1956. The box on the boiler between the stack and sand dome is the train control unit. Mars lights were used during the last 10 years of steam operation.

— John Pickett

Westbound tonnage was moving through Western Springs, Illinois in the early dawn on September 20, 1956. The train was pulled by throughbred No. 5634 built at West Burlington in September 1940.

— Ray Burhmaster

No. 6315, the last 2-10-4 to run on the Burlington was a double-header trip with the 5632, asked for by the rail fans. The Q agreed to put the massive engine on at Clyde and run it one way to Galesburg. All went well until the movie run at Zearing where the 6315 broke down and was then pushed to Galesburg by the 5632. Photographed near Zearing, Illinois, September 6, 1959.

— Ray Burhmaster

The rustic quiet of the hills was shattered by the roar of No. 5632's exhaust while heading a train of rail fans. The fireman made sure that plenty of smoke would please the fans on this photo run. — R. R. Pictures

Assuming her usual role of late, No. 5632 polishes the iron at Bristol, Ill. on a fan trip. Curious spectator has gotten out of his car to get a better look at the sleek 4-8-4.

— Burlington Photo

—316—

Watch those cinders in your eye! No. 4960 with fans in open gondola (and loaded hopper?) pulls out of the Aurora, Ill. station. Footboards and sloping tender sides were applied to many of the class O-1A engines for yard service.

— Burlington Photo

On a cold and snowy April 1, 1962, The Illini Railroad Club ran a doubleheader fan trip from Chicago to Savanna via Mendota and Denrock with the 4960 and 5632 and returning directly via Aurora with the 5632 alone. Here about three in the afternoon the pair gets orders (4960 in lead) handed up at the tower at the east end of the Savanna yard.

— Jim Boyd

The last two active steam engines on the Burlington, No. 4960 and 5632, team up to give the rail fans a thrill on a recent winter fan trip. How long before the hiss of steam and the mournful cry of the whistle will be still forever?

— Railroad Pictures

End of the line—No. 5028 is being dismantled at Eola, Ill. in 1934.   —Robert Graham

The Burlington Zephyrs started a new diesel age in railroading, but that story begins where this book ends. The Pioneer Zephyr (after a car had been added) at Council Bluffs, Iowa in July, 1935.   —Bostwick Studio